Emma Curtis Hopkins

BIBLE INTERPRETATIONS

LESSONS ONE TO SEVENTY FIVE

(1891-1892)

®2017 McAllister Editions. (McAllistereditions@gmail.com). This book is a product of its time, and it does not necessarily reflect the same views on race, gender, sexuality, ethnicity, and interpersonal relations as it would if it was written today.

CONTENTS

BOOK ONE. .... ¡ERROR! MARCADOR NO DEFINIDO.
BIBLE INTERPRETATIONS .... ¡ERROR! MARCADOR NO DEFINIDO.
   LESSONS ONE TO SEVENTY FIVE. .. ¡Error! Marcador no definido.
   INTRODUCTION 4
   BIBLE LESSON I. ALL IS DIVINE ORDER 10
   BIBLE LESSON II. JESUS CHRIST AND NICODEMUS 14
   BIBLE LESSON III. CHRIST AT SAMARIA 19
   BIBLE LESSON IV. SELF-CONDEMNATION 24
   BIBLE LESSON V. FEEDING THE STARVING 27
   BIBLE LESSON VI. THE BREAD OF LIFE 31
   BIBLE LESSON VII. THE CHIEF THOUGHT 35
   BIBLE LESSON VIII. CONTINUE THE WORK 38
   BIBLE LESSON IX. INHERITANCE OF SIN 43
   BIBLE LESSON X. THE REAL KINGDOM 48
   BIBLE LESSON XI. IN RETROSPECTION 52
   BIBLE LESSON XII. John 11:1. MARY AND MARTHA 56
   BIBLE LESSON XIII. John 12:20. GLORY OF CHRIST 61
   BIBLE LESSON XIV. John 13:1. GOOD IN SACRIFICE 66
   BIBLE LESSON XV. John 14:1. POWER OF THE MIND 70
   BIBLE LESSON XVI. John 15:1. VINES AND BRANCHES 75
   BIBLE LESSON XVII. John 16:2. YOUR IDEA OF GOD 80
   BIBLE LESSON XVIII. John 17:1. MAGIC OF HIS NAME 85
   BIBLE LESSON XIX. John 18:1. JESUS AND JUDAS 90
   BIBLE LESSON XX. John 19: 1. SOURGE OF TONGUES 97
   BIBLE LESSON XXI. John 19: 17. SIMPLICITY OF FAITH 102
   BIBLE LESSON XXII. John 20:1. CHRIST IS ALL IN ALL 107
   BIBLE LESSON XXIII. John 21:1. RISEN WITH CHRIST 112
   BIBLE LESSON XXIV. Review. THE SPIRIT IS ABLE 118
   BIBLE LESSON XXV. Isaiah 11:1. A GOLDEN PROMISE 123
   BIBLE LESSON XXVI. Isaiah 26:2. THE TWELVE GATES 129
   BIBLE LESSON XXVII. Isaiah 28:1. WHO ARE DRUNKARDS 134
   BIBLE LESSON XXVIII. Isaiah 37:1. AWAKE THOU THAT SLEEPEST 139
   BIBLE LESSON XXIX. Isaiah 53:1. THE HEALING LIGHT 145
   BIBLE LESSON XXX. Isaiah 55:1. TRUE IDEAL OF GOD 151
   BIBLE LESSON XXXI. Jeremiah 1:6. HEAVEN AROUND US 157
   BIBLE LESSON XXXII. Jeremiah 35. BUT ONE SUBSTANCE 162
   BIBLE LESSON XXXIII. Jeremiah 32. JUSTICE OF JEHOVAH 167
   BIBLE LESSON XXXIV. Jeremiah 39. GOD AND MAN ARE ONE 173
   BIBLE LESSON XXXV. Ezekiel 4:9. SPIRITUAL IDEAS 177
   Bible Lesson XXXVII. Isaiah 40:1-10. All Flesh is Grass 181
   Bible Lesson XXXVIII. Psalm 1:1-6. Realm of Thought 186

Bible Lesson XXXIX. Psalm 2:1-12. The Power of Faith 192
Bible Lesson XL. Psalm 19:1-14. Let the Spirit Work 196
Bible Lesson XLI. Psalm 23:1-6. Christ is Dominion.....................199
Bible Lesson XLII. Psalm 51:1-13. External or Mystic.................205
Bible Lesson XLIII. Psalm 84:1-12. Truth Makes Free 209
Bible Lesson XLIV. Psalm 103:1-22. False Ideas of God 214
Bible Lesson XLV. Daniel 1:8-21. But Men Must Work 219
Bible Lesson XLVI. Daniel 2:36-49. Artificial Helps....................223
Bible Lesson XLVII. Daniel 3:13–25. Dwelling in Perfect Life 228
Bible Lesson XLVIII. Daniel 6:16-28. Which Streak Shall Rule.....233
Bible Lesson XLIX. Review. See Things As They Are.....................240
Bible Lesson L. Psalms 72:1-19. Value Of Early Beliefs...............247
Bible Lesson LI. Acts 1:1-12. The Measure of a Master..............252
Bible Lesson LII. Acts 2:1-12. Chief Ideas Rule People 258
Bible Lesson LIII. Acts 2:37-47. New Ideas about Healing 265
Bible Lesson LIV. Acts 3:1-16. Heaven, A State of Mind 272
Bible Lesson LV. Acts 4:1-18. About Mesmeric Powers...............276
Bible Lesson LVI. Acts 4:19-31. Points in the Mosaic Law 283
Bible Lesson LVII. Acts 5:1-11. Napoleon's Ambition 289
Bible Lesson LVIII. Acts 5:25-41. A River Within the Heart 295
Bible Lesson LIX. Acts 7:54–60. Acts 8:1-4. The Answering of Prayer
....300
Bible Lesson LX. Acts 8:5-25. Word Spoken By The Mind 305
Bible Lesson LXI. Acts 8:26-40. Just What It Teaches Us 310
Bible Lesson LXII. Review. The Healing Principle 315
Bible Lesson LXIII. I Cor. 11:23-34. The Science of Christ 321
Bible Lesson LXIV. Acts 9:1-31. On The Healing of Saul..............327
Bible Lesson LXV. Acts 9:32-43. The Power of the Mind Explained 333
Bible Lesson LXVI. Acts 10:1-20. Faith in Good to Come 338
Bible Lesson LXVII. Acts 10:30-48. Emerson's Great Task 342
Bible Lesson LXVIII. Acts 11:19-30. The Teaching of Freedom 346
Bible Lesson LXIX. Acts 12:1-17. Seek And Ye Shall Find 350
Bible Lesson LXX. Acts 13:1-13. The Ministry of the Holy Mother 354
Bible Lesson LXXI. Acts 13:26-43. The Power of Lofty Ideas 359
Bible Lesson LXXII. Acts 13:44-52. Acts 14:1-7. Sure Recipe For Old Age
....363
Bible Lesson LXXIII. Acts 14:8-22. The Healing Principle 367
Bible Lesson LXXIV. Acts 15:12-29. Washington's Vision 371
Bible Lesson LXXV. Review of the Twelve Lessons. (LXIII through LXXIV)
....377

These Bible Interpretations were given during the early nineties at the Christian Science Theological Seminary at Chicago, Illinois. This Seminary was independent of the First Church of Christ Scientist in Boston, Mass.

INTRODUCTION

From time to time there have been men and women of a character and work unquestionably marking them as sent of Him to announce His will and purpose to the children of men. When such have come among mankind they have not needed the great churches back of them, nor the recognition of the learned and powerful among men to support their claims as ministers of the Gospel of the Good.

It has always been accorded by the wise that the baptism of the Holy Spirit, or the quickening influence of the principle of divine Intelligence is the test of the called to teach the words and will of the Supreme of the universe. Those so called have not needed to quote authorities or precedents for their actions or teachings. They have all spoken as having authority, and not as the scribes or recorders of other men's teachings. They have all come like messengers of goodness and freedom to men at just the time when the recognized teachers of the world were quoting authorities to hold their doctrines in repute among a dissatisfied and restless people.

When the ancient prophets of the Lord came to teach Truth to the wondering multitudes they found the great lawgivers and teachers holding their own by showing how closely they were keeping to the laws of dead Shemaiah and Abtalion, and because they had no authority in themselves through the quickening Spirit's influence they must quote Shemaiah and Abtalion, and with passionate zeal discourse upon the terrible importance of the kind and quality of wood best for altars, or the moral deadliness of the use of blood, or the imperativeness of circumcision on the eighth day.

But the sent of the invisible God said; "Thus saieth the Lord," and the people feared, and repented of their sins at their voices.

When the divinely appointed Jesus came He found the learned Rabbis quoting Hillel and Shammai, and daring not at all to claim wisdom from the Most High Intelligence.

And they were amazed at His doctrine because He taught as vested with authority. Like all the inspired who had preceded Him He proved Himself God-sent by doing God-like works. The suns which had daily set upon crowds of sick and miserable people arose at morning time to overlook joyous multitudes, healed by the divine minister of the Gospel of health. The wicked turned from the error of their ways. The mad and despairing smiled and were at peace. The poor were helped and fed. He did not have to say: "Thus heard I of Hillel or Rabbi Meir or Rabbi Joseph," but only, "The words that I speak unto you it is not I that speak, but the Father that dwelleth in me. He doeth the works."

His example has been the inspiration and direction of millions since His time, and when the devoted hearts the world has known have been moved by the best within them to teach mankind of the goodness of the Supreme of the world they have pointed to the unacknowledged Jesus and walked bravely along lonely and untrod ways, teaching and helping the ignorant and unfortunate, regardless of whether the great and proud esteemed them, or the learned recognized their greatness.

There have been such lonely workers in our own time. They have all heard the voice of the Spirit and felt the impulse of goodness stirring them to go forth to help the world. They have looked over the religions and sciences of the intellectually great which have held sway in the hearts of the people, and have noted that under their ages of dominion there have been abuses and unjust dealings which the religions and sciences have proved powerless to abolish or bring into disrepute.

Their hearts, being moved in compassion, have strengthened their judgments till they cry with one voice against the old disputations, and with one voice declare for a new and a true, wherein the poor may be taught and befriended, women walk fearless and glad, and children be safe and free. Every fibre and thread of their being, every instant of their time is absolutely dedicated to the prophesied new dispensation of the Holy Spirit with its Ministry of healing from every ill known to the old times.

They are called Christian scientists* because they have set in order the teachings of the one who was called The Christ, and because they can do the works which are the outcome of His teachings understood. (*The term "Christian science" as used in these lessons stands for the scientific teaching of Jesus Christ as understood by Emma Curtis Hopkins).

In all particulars they are a repetition upon a new plane of His experience in giving to the world His doctrine of salvation from fleshly bondages. In all particulars they are a repetition of the experiences of those who followed Him and believed in His doctrines one thousand nine hundred years ago. They preach the powerlessness of evil and the unreality of the material universe. They declaim against the necessity for evil in any form of sin, sickness or death. They declare the Omnipresence of God, the Good, and deny the presence or working power of any other principle but the Good. They demonstrate that the denial of evil as a reality or working principle puts evil into the nothingness from whence it sprang, by putting all forms of evil completely out of and away from the life experiences, when they deal with principles of Goodness, the only reality. They are proving daily what was the teachings of Christ and His immediate followers by new interpretations of His words and imitation of His works. They insist that the right interpretations of His words have never been given to the people by the great intellects who have taken them in charge to expound and explain.

They urge that the misinterpretations of His teachings are accountable for all the pain and suffering and wickedness believed in by all mankind since His beautiful lifetime, when the multitude rejoiced in health and peace wherever He walked among them, teaching a doctrine whereby men could know blessedness, and not pain forevermore.

They do not ask those preachers who have wrested His wonderful words from their true meanings to give sanction to their right interpretations nor beg of them to recognize them as a ministry of the old interpretations, whose inefficiency they scorn. They set boldly forth with His true teachings, as sure of their calling to the work as Peter of old, who preached salvation to the Gentiles because it had been spiritually revealed to him that true salvation was for Gentiles as surely as for Jews, or as boldly and bravely as Paul, the Roman Citizen, who had all his travels and works mapped plainly out for him by that Holy Spirit, whose mark, being set in the forehead, none may dispute its authority.

These people are the apostles of a new dispensation. They usher in the dawn of a new time when evil shall be known no more among men, because Christ the Truth has come again in the way of His perfect doctrine revealed anew to the waiting world. They have for their rallying cry, "Not by might, nor by strength but by My Spirit saith the Lord," which was a watchword of the inspired prophets of old. They lay hold with a mighty faith upon the God of the ancient Hebrews as the only God able to save from evil beliefs. They are fulfilling that prophecy literally which reads, that in the last days of the world of belief in evil, "Men of all languages shall lay hold of the skirts of Him that is a Jew, saying: we will go with you, for we have heard that God is with you."

They teach of Him as a very present help in every time of trouble, even to the saving from fiery furnaces, lions' teeth and angry kings, as unto Daniel and the holy men of Israel, who, believing in His own presence, did not put off the day of salvation from sin, sickness and death to a heavenly future, but showed that all things of evil are unreality now to them that speak the truth. They bring up the testimony of the devout and good in their highest moments of inspiration through all time to corroborate their conclusions.

Not the testimony of the good when disputing their own words, nor the words of the powerful and proud who know not inspiration, but the best and truest words the best hearts have ever spoken, and they are bound by all that is best within them to square their lives by them and base their hopes upon them. Certain of the faithful have formed themselves into a body with the sole purpose of urging these principles upon an unbelieving and skeptical world. They are so young in their own doctrines and so hard beset by the questionings and criticisms of the churches and schools that they have not been coherent or unanimous upon certain points of doctrine, and in forming this body have subjected themselves to each other's severest tests, that there may be from henceforth no dissensions or differences, and that what is according to Christian science may be very clearly defined in their minds.

In thus reviewing their relations to true Christian doctrines and practice they have repeated the experience of the early apostles of its first perfect preaching, and in today's proceedings we see the concluding ceremonies of the examining council of Jerusalem in the year of the first Christian dispensation.

Paul, Peter and Barnabas have preached the full salvation their Lord and Master Jesus Christ had taught them. But some of the converts have opposed the absolutely radical stand taken by Peter and Paul in their free and kindly fellowship with all believers in the Christ doctrine, whether of the Gentile or Jewish world, and their criticisms have been so decided that it has become necessary to know what does and what does not constitute sound doctrine, and who are not to be sustained in their common endeavors to convert the world to Truth. "The liberty wherewith Christ hath made us free" was their decision, and the yoke of the former belief in evil bondage was to be known no more among them. Then they shook hands like loving brethren, and went forth to minister to the world and to martyrdom.

We of the new dispensation have decided in like manner of the true children of the science, we free from all the evil beliefs of the old forms of faith, in whatever guise they may present themselves, whether as Satan of the recognized evangelical church or mesmerism of the later church, and we hereby ask all Christian science workers the world over to give us the right hand of fellowship on the doctrine of freedom from all evil and fearlessness of every evil thing; or thought. We ask the old church to take notice of our ministry that it is apostolic in principle and practice, and we ask it to bid us God speed on our healing mission to a world neglected in full spiritual ministrations. We ask the world, which is to be our church, to turn and listen to our preaching, for it is the quickening message from the Supreme of the universe announcing the second coming long expected, when every mountain of trouble shall be removed, every hill of difficulty obliterated. Pride cannot hold its own where the spiritually taught are speaking, and learning cannot defeat the wisdom of the children of Divine science. Listen, for we will speak of excellent things, and the opening of our lips shall be right things. As we thus set forth upon this ministry, with the deliberate intention of converting the world to Christian science, we ought to tell somewhat of our relations to those ministrations held in reverence by other ministers of Christian doctrine. The ordinance of the Lord's Supper, baptism, marriage, and what other observances come in the way of the faithful minister's calling. In these matters we shall heed Paul's injunction literally for the present. "Let us give ourselves to the ministry of the Word," as if our only mission were to be that ministry which the Word itself, faithfully uttered, can carry. The ordinance of the Lord's Supper has no meaning to thousands of those who partake of the bread and wine which symbolizes the flesh and blood of Christ. But to the trained in Christian science, flesh and blood themselves are only symbolic of the thought and word of the Christ, and if we partake of the word and thought, till we have let the same mind be in us that was in Christ Jesus, our Lord, we have really fulfilled the ordinance of the Lord's Supper. To this interpretation we shall adhere, and the external forms will in no way be used by us, although their use by the external church is in no way deprecated or depreciated by us. The various forms of baptism used to symbolize the cleansing blood of the Christ have a deeper meaning than the red blood of the bleeding Savior to us. Baptism means the cleansing word of denial of all evil, spoken by the Christ, used, refusing to believe in the fatherhood of any other being but God, the Spirit manifest, refusing to see the evil of the world as reality, judging not according to appearance, but judging the righteous judgment of those translated out of such false beliefs into the white light of truth spoken.

The changeless word of truth shall be our ministry of baptism.

Marriage is to the Christian scientist the most sacred of all the symbols of Christian doctrine, symbolizing the Father-Mother principle of the Godhead complete in its beauty and wonder when the Oneship of Trinity is perfectly understood. We know that the motherhood of the race symbolizes the Holy Spirit or motherhood of the Trinity and that, while unchaste thoughts or unjust dealings are tolerated or believed in, the presence and office of the Holy Spirit will hardly be known on earth. When men and women, with right and true conceptions of the divine significance of marriage and the home shall be found, the Christian science ministry will be divinely appointed to speak the words that pronounce the marriage benediction. But the present ministry is not called upon for such office, and will give itself wholly to the words that purify the heart and life to be worthy of true marriage.

Now from this presence we send you forth to the world that waits for the healing benediction of the Spirit with which you have been baptized. You have been tried and not found wanting. You have been called and been answered by that fullness of power by which the devout in all ages have prayed. You can heal the sick by the word of your speaking. You can cheer the fainting. When hearts are cast down you shall say, "There is lifting up." You are the revival of the full ministry of the times of old. The Lord himself shall guide you continually, and you shall want for no good thing. Be not afraid of the speech of people, nor seek for the world's favor. Speak the word boldly that is given you to utter. For this is the faith of the fathers, The faith the apostles delivered.

Delivered in Chicago, 1891.

BIBLE LESSON I. ALL IS DIVINE ORDER

No place where Jesus preached, or day upon which He wrought a miracle, but what has divine significance. Nothing is by accident.

All is divine order. "Cana of Galilee." Cana is the closing of the circuit, or circle of Galilee. Here the boy attains His majority and publicly celebrates His own marriage to the ministry of the Holy Spirit.

The circuit is closed on the third day—the day of fulfillment—the marriage day. At Cana He is joined unto Spirit forever. The complete surrender of the soul to the way and will of the Holy Spirit is fitly symbolized by the happy marriage of His young friends on Wednesday. The beautiful virgin to her beloved, Jesus to God. "Thy Maker is Thine husband."

Jesus never wrought any miracle till He thus publicly closed His recognition of Church and State and domestic authority over His speech and actions, and with only His mother for a witness solemnly pledged Himself to recognize as supreme the Inner Voice and the outer call of the Divine Spirit.

Two things He thus makes clear to the students of His teachings, viz; that He never condemned the institution of marriage, and that no unvarying success in miracle working may be looked for till there is complete surrender of the heart and hand and judgment to divine will.

Therefore, no matter how many mental demonstrations one may make he does not indicate utter surrender to the spirit of God, except he from thenceforth show his dominion over all external conditions by bringing forth order out of what seems chaos, health out of what seems sickness, life out of what seems death, peace out of seeming discord. "Miracle" working is the sign of being absolutely united to Spirit.

"If I do not the works of the Father, believe me not."

How beautifully Jesus Christ sanctions true marriage. There is no scornful reproval— no insinuation against it. He spoke of the obligation of one man and one woman to be true and faithful to each other for ever and ever. He stamps His image on honorable marriage. He is the only speaker of ancient times, in the Bible or out of it, who speaks so plainly that there is no mistaking His meanings— "They twain," and twain means two. Paul's words can easily be construed to mean another way. John the Revelator never carries the intimation of reverence for marriage in spite of his using it for a figure.

David's ideas are repulsive. But Jesus Christ—no wanton wandering from the plighted troth—no infidelity to the vows spoken to bind us to be faithful forever can we find excuse or sanction for in His teachings.

He or she untrue to the marriage pledge cannot expect the power of the Holy Ghost to work miracles through him. It was at this pledging time that Jesus wrought His first miracle.

The Spirit bore witness with Him that He was ONE with it. This marriage "in Cana" was the outward picture of the primal union or marriage of Jesus Christ with Spirit.

Madame Guyon sought to be married to God. She succeeded in catching glimpses of this union several times, but she accused God as sending so much evil upon those united unto Him that her words made a cloud of darkness perpetually between herself and that "Maker who is thine husband." There is wine and mirth and friendly joy in marriage with God—Spirit. "Wine" is a word signifying reviving, refreshing joy. They who know Jesus Christ indeed, drink refreshing, reviving, invigorating words. The refreshing, reviving, invigorating words Jesus made the wine of, wine praises of the goodness and tenderness and bounty of God.

How perfectly He demonstrated that He was actually in love with Spirit by immediately doing the works of God! After this celebration of His own eternal Oneness with God, He could restore a palsied hand to vigor in an instant. He could call the living to come forth out of coffins and graves. He could make bread and fish self-increasing. He could coin gold on the instant for meeting all current expenses. He did not believe in owing even the proud government of Caesar anything. "Render unto Caesar the things that are Caesar's."

Unless we can do all the works that He did we have not closed in with the old ways at Cana and started the circuit of Galilee in Spirit. "The same works that I do shall ye do."

The "works" He did we realize were all accomplished by His knowing that when one came to Him drooping in body it was the outward picture of a drooping hope. When one came in consumption it was the outward picture of a hope departing or consuming. He could see that a word would quicken the hope—would restore the hope.

Looking into the mind realm where the thoughts were dwelling, a meek little woman, who understood Jesus, saw that a young man's hope was failing. What hope was it that was failing? The hope that he might be a success among men. The people said his nerves and muscles were failing. She saw his hopes drooping. She understood, because she understood

Jesus Christ well, that there is no hope ever stirs within one of us but that God hath for us the actual fulfillment of that hope.

So she told him by silent ministry akin to the invisible marriage ceremony of Jesus Christ, that truly God would fulfill his expectations. Then aloud she said: "You will be successful, child." This was the "Wine" he was waiting to drink. It was the Word of God. "Thy words were found, and I did eat them and Thy word was unto me the joy and rejoicing of my heart." So he was well from that hour.

This is the power of prophecy. "Prophecy is mine and sound judgment." They can tell of good to come who have united with the Spirit that is Divine Goodness all bounty without lack or failure. Whoever believes in weakness has not yet come into Cana. For Jesus Christ teaches that the truly joined to Spirit are filled with Omnipotence: "All power is given unto Me in heaven and earth."

Whosoever believes in sickness is not united unto Spirit, for Jesus Christ was explicit and definite, "heal the sick." Do not leave people in their sickness. Do not accuse God of sending sickness.

"As I live, saith the Lord, I know my thoughts and I think towards you thoughts of peace and not of evil, to bring you an expected end."

The end we all expect is good unto ourselves. We deeply and profoundly love prosperity and peace and health. These we have a right to and nothing else.

"Woman, what have I to do with thee?"

"Gracious lady! Keeper of my past; now I am listening for the voice of the Spirit. She does not yet bid me act."

So He broke away from the ways of Galilee's former hastenings, and without doing anything, did all things speedily. With the power of Spirit hastening through us there seems to the world delay, but all the world's armies of power and learning could not overtake our ministry if we are truly joined to God. *Festina Lente*.

All who obey the voice of Sophia (the Spirit) heed not the ways of the guests at the marriage, yet they do satisfy their hearts fair hopes. Then even the great ones at the former marriage obeyed Him. So it is always promised to the spiritually minded that they shall have "Kings come bending" and all the earth shall be theirs.

Notice that a woman, a "Gracious lady" recognized that He was great in Spirit. Kadijah recognized Mahomet. So "Woman" shall always know when the voice of the Spirit is speaking. And she shall tell the world what is true of Jesus Christ; also what is true of you and me.

"Six water-pots of stone." Here is our lesson for today put so plainly that he who runs may read. When Jesus Christ demonstrated the power of Spirit He always took the materials at hand such as they were; He did not take any loaves and fishes except such as they had on hand to look up and praise God with and feed the multitudes.

He took Lazarus just as He found him. He took the "Six stone water-pots" and water they had at hand. Nothing else. This signifies that you are to take your rough circumstances, your bodily conditions, your human affairs, just as they are and holding them in your mind give thanks and bless the providing Jehovah that within them is the wine of peace and success and health. This giving thanks and praising God the down-bending Spirit for the wine of joy and goodness, surely contained within your circumstances the stone water-pots of your affairs just as they are, is the silent transmuting potency of Jesus the Christ.

A man who takes his last copper pennies and looking up to heaven gives thanks, is doing that action which is the key turning into re-enforcements of Jehovah laid up for him from the foundation of the world. The copper pennies are all he needs to work with. The stone jars are your own affairs. They are just what is given you to manage with to show how powerful the Spirit is in dealing with you for your increasement.

Archimedes said give him standing place and he would move the world. But Goethe was more like Jesus Christ by saying, "Make good your own standing place, and move the world."

Jesus Christ said He would lay down His body and take it up. Moses took his own rod and made it a serpent; his own hand and made it leprous with a thought; his own hand and healed it with a thought.

The queen was surprised that they had such dirty rags in a rich paper mill. But soon the manufacturers sent her some shining white paper made from those same rags. So by this lesson you may learn that you do not need one single thing to do with more than you already have if you know the law of praise and thanksgiving. At a faith-cure meeting a man kept praising God that he was so well, while a great tumor or some other kind of swelling was plain to be seen by his neighbors. This was his "stone water-pot." But he praised God publicly that he was so well for a whole fortnight. Long before the fortnight was up he was well, so that even his neighbors could see it so.

Take the home as you find it, child, and turn it into a home indeed by praising God that there is a Spirit of Goodness working with you and through you and by you and for you to make all things well.

Take your business as it is, child, and praise Divine Love that there is a strong, wise way out of your dilemma. Take your professional hopes, your children, your work— nothing can be more common than stone waterpots—and set them right by praising the Spirit. Praise is the "wine" of daily experience. The praise of Divine Love—the Motherhood of God is the plenteous wine of Cana of Galilee. *Chicago, July 19, 1891.*

BIBLE LESSON II. JESUS CHRIST AND NICODEMUS

There is always, amid the formal sectarianism of the most formal and sectarian body of people, one who is "A man of the Pharisees named Nicodemus." That is, by reason of his being called upon to teach and being in some way a leader among his colleagues, he has found himself unconsciously concluding that there are finer meanings and deeper intentions in religious precepts than he has been taught.

Mind always puts out tendrils and lays hold on new meanings if it is not willfully set to a prejudice. The mind that makes God its theme will sooner or later meditate much on Jesus Christ, unless it is the mind of one determined to gratify bodily passions. Jesus Christ draws the mind that thinks on God as a magnet draws a steel filing. "No man cometh unto Me save the Father that is in Me draw him." We are drawn to those who have a quality akin to something within ourselves. So Nicodemus was drawn to Jesus.

There is some great idea that your mind has been meditating upon, some principle not definitely understood by you, but which it is possible for you to understand perfectly. You ought to get acquainted with that idea. You notice, don't you, that in all the pauses of the business or conversations of the day the vague but great idea comes up? So Nicodemus had for days been looking towards the idea of the power of faith as the prophets of the past had demonstrated it, and as the young man traveling about the country was demonstrating His principles. How did it happen that Elijah raised to life the Zarephath child, was fed by ravens, had such prophetic powers? How did Elisha raise the boy to life, heal the waters, cure leprosy? Was it not by the presence and working of the same God that he, Nicodemus, worshiped? Why should not this God work miracles now as in the old days? Surely God had never departed as the health of His people, the strength of their life, and the answerer of their prayers, yet nothing was done as in days past. Why not?

Maybe the young Jesus was right. He would go and see. He. had been a moralist, Nicodemus had, and taken pride in his morality. So he came to

Jesus. High moral conduct, coupled with thoughts of God, is liable to strike the white heat of goodness as Christ quality.

Jesus Christ preached His most stupendous doctrines to audiences of one and two. He taught over and over again not to despise the smallest circumstance or opportunity. "The situation that hath not its duty, its ideal, was never yet occupied by man." James Holmes found at Castle Bar an audience of three to hear him where he had been publicly announced to preach. Instead of shutting his mouth he opened it and preached so earnestly that one of the three, a young man, was converted, and was afterwards called the "Tongue of Fire", because he was so fervent in Spirit.

Jesus Christ waived the personal praise. He never received it from anybody who revealed His Being among them as another man with just a few points of ability, perhaps, above the usual Rabbi. Praise of His teachings He received. Praise principle, not person. Do right because it is right, and not through fear of somebody or love of somebody. So He drove straight to the need of Nicodemus, "Except a man be born again, he cannot see the Kingdom of God." "Nicodemus, except a man look into the Spirit only, utterly refusing to call any man of flesh, or any earthly circumstances, his environment as help or hindrance, he cannot set his home life, his health, his affairs, or his neighbor's health and affairs into harmony."

How coarsely Nicodemus answered Him. The mathematician responded to the entranced musician concerning the marvelous music, "Yes, it is wonderful to see the violinist move his elbow so many times in a minute." So "The natural man receiveth not the things of the Spirit, for they are foolishness unto him, and he cannot know them, because they are spiritually discerned."

But Jesus Christ understood the law of mind. He knew how to hold the concentrated attention of His hearer till he should understand that "Never the Spirit was born, the Spirit shall cease to be never; end and beginning are dreams." He knew that it must be by the recognition that all power whatsoever is of the Spirit and not of intellect or physical force. "Except a man be born of water and of the Spirit." The Rosetta Stone to all miracle-working is that lesson on the increasement of loaves and fishes. The Rosetta Stone to this birth of water and Spirit is the statement, "If any man will come after Me, let him deny himself."

Now, He never taught that we should deny the good in ourselves; certainly He meant that we should deny the evil. He told His hearers that it was His words of which He was speaking and the power of His words, so we know that the baptism of water of which He spoke to Nicodemus was the use of the washing words of denial, whereby the mind that has thought things not true is cleansed of its errors, as a body is cleansed by water.

There was certain errors or mistakes called profitless and nothingness and uselessness by Him, serving to hide the power of the Spirit. To deny these errors is to call them by name and reject them. This is the water baptism this great metaphysician meant. Now Naaman's seven washings in Jordan were typical of the seven denials every mind must make to be cleansed of error. By looking them over we know exactly what errors to reject and what to eschew.

The first washing we do must be the rejection of the belief in another power operating in the universe besides omnipresent, omnipotent, omniscient Goodness. There is no power of evil. This denial is the washing away of evil imaginations, so that we do not any more believe in the possibility of any cruelty or greed or crime coming nigh us forever-more. According to the law of mind action, we find that it sets the world free from evil also.

The second washing we must do is the speaking of the positive Word of rejecting the belief in another substance than Spirit. If God is omnipresent Spirit, then indeed Spirit is the only substance present anywhere; so the rejection of the supposition of the reality of matter is a necessary process. Matter has no reality, or, there is no matter. This Word of denial has the effect of cleansing us from as much experience of the hindrance or burden of matter as the law of the Word brings, spoken as an experiment or in faith. You certainly do find the hard tumor, the stiffened joint, or the heavy indebtedness grow less. This second washing is very, very efficient in making hard ways easy and heavy burdens light, exactly as the personified Word of truth promised that it should.

The third washing Word (remember that Jesus Christ was always teaching words and thoughts and states of mind by material terms) is the denial of our false notion that there is any life, substance or intelligence in matter, for if there is no matter surely God is the only life, Spirit the only substance, Omniscience the only intelligence.

An enchanting freedom comes with the third washing enjoined by Jesus Christ. The mind throws off the ugly nightmare of its third delusion by boldly announcing that there is no life, substance, or intelligence in matter. The heart rises with quickened hope. The friendship and beauty and goodness of living we see. The mind is clear to understand what is reasonable and right. Knowledge of Truth is freedom. Gautama Buddha and Jesus Christ both said so and proved it.

Take the fourth washing Word boldly. Naaman hesitated and was petulant. We will press boldly forward for the mark of the high calling of Regeneration, which is the subject of this lesson. By this time you see that Regeneration means giving your spirit perfect freedom. The fourth Word of self-denial states that as matter is not a reality its sensations are fallacious. There are no sensations in matter. This Word will cause pain to falter and fail; will cause sensual appetites to fall away. We have no taste, sight, or hearing but for Spirit. "Taste and see that the Lord is good." "Feel after Him."

The fifth washing is a severe one for some of us to take, but there is no escaping the metaphysical meanings of Jesus Christ. Sin, sickness, and death are delusions. This does not make a stealing or a slaying good, but announces that they are delusions, without power to hurt or hinder. The temptation to falsehood, the inclination to transgression, are unreal. To know this sets us free from them. Sickness and death are a myth.

Can Spirit be diseased or die? Since God is Spirit, the only Substance, the speaking of this washing Word of denial is the sure setting free from sin, sickness, and death.

These five cleansing waters are suitable and essential for all the world. There are two special ones applying to each man, woman, and child, besides the five for all the world. You can easily find out what two you ought to make for yourself.

There was once a woman who loved money so much that she saw everybody through her thought of money. If she looked at you she thought first of how much you were worth, or how much she could make out of you. You see by her looking at everybody and everything through money eyes, she got blind— quite blind. Money is blinding. If she wanted to see clearly she should deny herself of looking through money. It would be well for her to say much, "There is no money in Spirit."

A child's toothache will depart if you say, "There is no pain in Spirit." Your burden of poverty will clear off if you say, "There is no poverty in Spirit."

There are many who look at their acquaintances and friends and all circumstances, through jealous ideas of some sort. They unconsciously or consciously wonder how much of their own rights, or position, or possessions, the other will get away from them. So they have lost one or more of their faculties, for jealousy is cruel and lops off from us our fondest hopes. Such should deny themselves of looking and judging through jealousy. Let them say, "There is no jealousy in Spirit."

Notice that this lesson reads that we must be cleansed by water and clothed by Spirit. Jesus gave the idea that we should take the house, swept and garnished, and fill it with good "Spirits." "Spirits" are words, as "My Words are Spirit."

There are seven Words of affirmation that are the hot glory of God over and through all who make them. Ye came forth from God. "No man upon earth is your father." Thus these Words are the shining forth of your own nature with which you were endowed from the great Forever without beginning of years or end of days.

None of the miracle-working power Nicodemus wished to be master of is ours till we have boldly announced the spiritual nature and office we are endowed with.

This is the first affirmation of Spirit: Life, Truth, Love, is God. Then we recognize all Life as God and all Truth and all Love as God. We hail and welcome and praise all the living Beauty, all the living Strength, all the living Kindness; we recognize, knowing that it is God. This recognition of Good is the shining forth of our own Goodness. Once it was thought that we were able and capable if we recognized vanity or deceitfulness in a neighbor, but now we know that since vanity and deceitfulness are nothingness and profitless that it is a waste of time on the insubstantial. That which we see of Good is our own thinking or our own shining forth of our own Spirit.

We learned by last Sunday's lesson that everything has the potentiality of Good ready to increase itself by our praise and blessing.

The second Word of Spirit is: "I am the idea of God, and in God I live and move and have my being." As God is omnipresent, we move safely and boldly on. This "Spirit" or Word of the I AM makes us bold and joyous. All is joyous in Spirit.

The third is: "I am Spirit, I am Mind; I shed abroad Wisdom, Strength, Holiness." Such a fire baptism as this Word radiates or reflects from us over the world to make people wiser, stronger, holier where we are, is only brought to pass by this affirmation, or "Yea, yea," of Christ.

The fourth baptism from above is our announcement that God the Spirit works through us to will and to do all things well. This is our Word from above, or birth from Spirit, that makes us efficient in healing and helping all with whom we come in contact. The old ways of depreciating our words and our works are done away with. We now rejoice in our efficiency, since we know it as God the Good doing all things.

There is the fifth Word from above that secures our immunity from sin, sickness, and death, and that makes all the people secure when we come near them. Like the fifth denial the fifth affirmation takes strong rising "To do the will to prove the doctrine."

I am governed by the law of God, and cannot sin, nor suffer for sin, nor fear sin, sickness, or death. As Spirit we cannot swerve from our orbit any more than a star in its course. To swerve and falter would be sin, but Spirit cannot sin for God is Spirit. "He'll surely guide our steps aright." There is the safe walking of all who speak these Words through all the thorny ways of delusion.

Then the two "Other Spirits" or Words of affirmation which belong to each of you, you must find out for yourselves. Notice that Paul says that in his greatest weakness is his strength. So you can see that if you have believed yourself inefficient or ignorant you must let the Spirit of Truth drop down over you with the bold affirmation: "I am strong and efficient. I praise the Spirit that now works with me and through me and by me and for me to do all my work faithfully and well. I am wise with the Wisdom of Spirit." This is the full potency of the treatment Jesus gave Nicodemus. "Marvel not." Only the carnal intellect marvels, wonders, asks questions. Spirit knows.

So Nicodemus rallied his faith. He had entered the presence of Jesus with hope. Hope is only the left hand; faith is the right hand. "Hope thou in God". Have faith in the Good. Your faith will show forth; your works of good faith will be good when you have learned how to be born of water and of Spirit according to this meaning of Jesus. **July 26, 1891.**

BIBLE LESSON III. CHRIST AT SAMARIA

The reason for keeping the Bible records, is because they describe the religious experiences of every mind under each class of circumstance recorded. Every mind has its religious aspiration, which is its perfume, as every flower has its perfume.

Political history teaches ethics, fixing the mind on the results of injustice, justice, oppression, liberty, as carried on by civil authorities.

Material history teaches what can be done with materiality. The silver cup lost by a workman in a jar of acid, precipitated by Faraday, re-made by the silversmith, satisfies us that we need not be utterly bereft of silver cups, though they seem utterly gone. The Bible records use no meaningless or unnecessary terms.

Jesus Christ means Word of Truth, or Child of God. The religious aspirations of each mind is its Jesus Christ idea—its Word of absolute truth. The mind is a kingdom or realm of thoughts. The most powerful, the oldest, the noblest, is its highest Word of Truth, or Jesus Christ. "Come and reign over us, Ancient of Days."

Thus the walk of Jesus Christ through this realm of carnal or earthly experiences is at each step of His going a living teaching of what to do under all the kinds of experiences we each have, in order to show forth Jesus Christ, or "Let the same Mind be in us that was in Christ Jesus."

Here is the lesson of what to do when we have been trying to be good and true for a long period, and as nothing seems to come out of it we are tired and discouraged.

We have been told positively by the spiritually-minded of every age that.

But though we have striven faithfully we are the most burdened and unfortunate of anybody we know.

Jesus Christ took up all our experiences on purpose, and in the midst of every one of them He spoke those Words which we must speak under like circumstances. Here He took up the weariness and discouragement of our good motive when it sees no fruits in prosperity. He "sat thus on the well."

Do you remember the lesson He gave of what to say when you have had nothing to eat for a long time from any cause whatever? Do you remember what Words He told us to speak when physical anguish and the desertion of friends have broken our hearts?

Well, in the same fashion He tells us what to do when exhausted, discouraged, disheartened with the struggle to succeed. He sat thus on the well in Samaria. Samaria means watch post, or posted notice. Perhaps there is nothing that will mark itself on your face or give your whole character away to your acquaintances like what you choose to do when a turning point or crisis of thinking is reached by your mind.

There comes a time when the young man who has thought worldly thoughts steadily, suddenly carries on his face the sure sign that he is a man of the world.

There comes a time when the blooming matron is called an old lady. This point just reached is Samaria. If the man or the woman can realize just the instant of weariness of the whole way of thinking and living and sit deliberately down and make the right resolve, a noble look will steal over the face of the young man and a new beauty will illumine the woman's.

Once a woman caught the gleam of this rest on the wall of Samaria all in a flash and that which we are now carefully repeating was told to her from on high. So she sent out this word to all who would hear it: When you are disheartened and heart-sore with the journey of your best efforts through this strange world, sit down and rest for the prayers you have prayed and the true Words you have said to be unto you a well of Living

Water whose best draught you are about to drink, as Jesus announced the most refreshing doctrine He had ever put forth from the well of Samaria upon which He rested. When you have done the best you could, seemingly all to no purpose, put on your best clothes and sit down to wait for the heavenly guest who is to pass over your threshold that day.

This is the time when you are to "Rest in the Lord and He shall bring it to pass." So a poor, tired, little mother with her hungry children clinging to her knees, deserted of her husband, friends insisting that if she had done differently things would have been different, while she was doing her very best, obeyed this message and rested to wait for the heavenly Good that must come to her that day. And the Good came. This is a working principle to go by. In the science of mind or metaphysics as taught by Jesus Christ we are taught all those Words of Truth which are Everlasting Arms underneath, or the well of Living Water upon which we may rely for each part of our journey.

For instance, suppose that you have been told that God, the Divine Principle of Goodness, is your sure Health, and, according to the law of prayer, or affirmation of Truth, you have daily and hourly spoken the words, "God is Health: no sickness or disease can get any hold on this Health, which is God." Yet sickness and disease do seem to have a hold upon your health, and you are disheartened, do not force yourself to speak the words then. Rest, wait. The True Health Thought is bending over you. Soon it will descend. This is the moment of fruition. Far in the Oriental past they taught that the flower of Truth blooms in the Silence after the storm and stress of effort. This is the time when, if you speak or work or struggle, you must start the work over again.

An innocent man condemned to be hanged says faithfully: "I am innocent. I trust in my innocence to defend me. Innocence is a wall of defense. Innocence is God. You cannot hang me, I defy you." Yet he stands on the scaffold. There he stops for pure weariness the long night watches spent in this prayer of innocence. They cannot hang him. The words of Truth are sure. He does not look to the people to defend him. People always fail us. He does not look to the law books to show his cause just, for the law books are double-minded, but he trusts Omnipotent Principle.

So if the event has hung long and heavily over your home and you have faithfully declared God would loose the clutch of the trouble, you must cease from prayer at Samaria and "Trust in the Lord, for He shall bring it to pass." The Lord is the Law of the Good made manifest.

The fact that Jesus spoke to the woman of low origin in Samaria; the low, shows that the most trivial circumstance of daily transaction is to be dealt with exactly as the most momentous.

If in making a garment, it does not come out right after your hardest efforts, rest, wait. Now you will do it perfectly. When looking for a situation, if you become tired or disheartened, rest, wait, no matter what the contingencies may be. Weary discouragement is the "Hail to Thee" of Samaria reached. Here is an offer better than you imagined. "I that speak unto thee am He."

You who have been battling for your life with noble words such as the Science teaches concerning the impossibility of the clutch of death upon the life that is yours omnipotent, give up at Samaria and see how quickly the Living Water will now spring up within you. As Jesus Christ walked among the lowly so let this Principle guide you through every vicissitude, great or small.

The woman pointed to the mountain Gerizim in plain sight, where the very same lesson was taught by Abraham's giving up the tension as to his offering all that he had to the Lord, trusting utterly.

All the ages have had their ministers of this Law of Life, that there is a sure Helper near every man, woman, and child, who will bring everything to pass for us when we give up the expectation of getting help from any other source.

"I will lift up mine eyes unto the hills from whence cometh my help. My help cometh from the Lord, Which made heaven and earth." Give up the tension. The eagle ceases from flapping his wings, and yet on and up it soars with folded pinions, resting in the Law.

The mountain unto which we look is the memory of the highest thought we have ever thought, or the highest Word that now comes into our mind. Jesus Christ said that this was the worship in Truth and in Spirit.

Whatever is true of Spirit is true. In Spirit all is good. Thus when we speak of evil we are not speaking Truth, for only that which is true of Spirit is true at all. This is the only worship of God that is acceptable. "I am God and there is none beside." God is Spirit. Thou art my all. There is no higher Truth we can speak than, THOU art my all.

Whoever rests securest in this statement is manifesting Jesus Christ most. To him we go for help as we go to a spring for water instead of going to a sand bank.

The quality of your faith makes the quality of your ministry. If you believe in God as your support do not stop short of the highest faith of Jesus Christ, who made the fish precipitate the gold within his being to pay the civil tax with. Faith is he alembic wherein the right Word is crystallized that makes you master over every situation. Neither in this place nor that place, neither for one alone but for all.

If you trust in the goodness of the Divine Law working for you and believe that all thing are made ready for you, you cannot but be a well of trust, a mountain of good faith to which the doubting and hungry come and dip in their cups for your ministry.

Stand boldly by your faith. "I that speak unto thee am He." The-saving-from-poverty thought is the confidence in God as your only supply. There have been people who prayed till they arose from praying and found money on the table or in their purse to help them with. Then they were ashamed to hold on to the words of acknowledgment that God had indeed shown forth through them exactly as in Jesus Christ.

Did He not say, "Where I Am, there ye may be also?" Why should we not be in the Spirit of Truth enough to believe that "All things are possible with God?"

How many who read that wonderful little blue magazine were ready to believe that the Spirit had helped those people as recorded in it?

Why even those who realized the manifesting power of the Word of faith were hiding the copy which told of miraculous answers to prayers.

If one believes in the bounty of God, keep close to him for you may dip your empty cup into his full waters of supply and by a metaphysical process catch the Prosperous Mind. If one believes in God as his unfailing Health, keep close to him for that metaphysical process which is like the outer air cleansing the air of a room when the window is opened, so may you catch Health from his Spirit of Health.

Good, all Good is yours by divine right. How well your deep heart knows this. It is your Jesus Christ thought. Hold fast to it. "I Am He—thy Savior from poverty, misfortune, pain, trouble—I Am Messiah." Come boldly up to that high thought in your mind. Trust it.

Your highest thought is that one which if it reign over you, will make you glad, strong, vigorous, healthy, prosperous. It is your Savior—Messiah. Not to come, but here already. Look for help from this Truth.

August 2nd, 1891.

BIBLE LESSON IV. SELF-CONDEMNATION

All is Mind and Mind's ideas. Every idea unfurls itself from your mind, as the pattern within a roll of cloth unrolls and exposes itself. Every thought we think first exposes itself in our own body, and then in our circumstances and environments.

The mind is a garden-bed where the thoughts spring up. We are the husbandmen keeping the garden—each one our own garden. Another cannot sow a seed in our garden unless we please. And there is no hiding what thoughts we have chosen to think when the pattern of them unrolls itself and shows our body and acquaintances. If once we let an angry thought arise in the mind we may be sure that there will be a bad state of our blood, and that somebody will get very angry with us, and also that some angry acting circumstances will surround us. The pattern of our thought which we let spring up within us does not show forth, sometimes, for months or even years.

You see the first statement of this lesson is, "My Father worketh hitherto, and I work." This is the Law of mind, to think and show forth. So we think and show forth our thoughts as our Origin, Mind, does. If we once thought an unjust thought we must not be surprised if the physical affliction we suffer seems very unjust when we have tried to be so good. Then there is the man or the woman who uses us so unjustly. Then the circumstances and environments.

This lesson for today takes up our thought of self-condemnation which we once indulged in, and shows us how to speak words and think thoughts which will utterly undo the results of our self-condemnation. Jesus Christ voluntarily took upon Himself all our experiences after they have fruited in the worst possible consequences, and made it very plain for us to know exactly what to do. Sometimes we condemn ourselves for having done exactly what we ought to have done, as if, for instance, it were against the rules of the house where we were stopping to feed beggars, but we had not only fed one, but taken her in and washed and dressed her because we saw that she was a good, worthy woman. There in Jerusalem it was against the law of the city to heal a man in public on the Sabbath as Jesus had healed the paralytic man at the pool of Bethesda.

If you will read this (John 5. 17:20) you will find out what to do and say when your motive was all right, but things have all turned out wrong because you condemned yourself, and now people are blaming you terribly. You are to let the motive be its own justification. A good motive is the power of God working in you to will and to do of its own good pleasure. Just lean hard on the motive itself and declare as Jesus Christ did, "God moveth and I must act."

The Bethesda lesson which introduces this, is quite important. A man had been paralyzed in body thirty-eight years to show that once he thought a wrong thought. Bethesda means Healing Mercy. Nobody ever had even a whole garden bed of sickening thoughts but what he vaguely or definitely thought of mercy at the same time.

Many people have put their thoughts of healing mercy together and caused an angel (which means pure thought, manifest or unmanifest) to come and stir their conscious minds to a quickening faith in actual healing. They saw their thought manifest as a lovely being stirring the pool, and into this they dipped their sick. But this man had thought a thought which had now externalized in even his environments being paralyzed. Do you see by this how it is that so many people are not cured of their diseases even by the combined healing thoughts of their acquaintances? Do you not see that it takes the presence of Jesus Christ face to face with all the power of the Jesus Christ word to heal certain kinds of troubles?

Now, no matter what the garden of your mind, where the thoughts spring up, may be full of, just know this, that you are given power to pull up and burn whatever thoughts you have thought, and if you will close the soil of your mind tightly around one word, not allowing another single word to grow up there till the full ministry of this new word is accomplished, you will find that everything in your experience will be different.

According to this lesson the word we must speak is Jesus Christ. Every word carries its own quality of power with us and through us and by us and for us when we speak it. Notice that no other word of Healing Mercy availed this man at the pool except Jesus Christ. "In Him is all the fullness of the Godhead bodily." The Egyptians, Persians, Greeks and Romans all used to heal by names. They wrought many miracles by giving all their mind to the holding of one name to the exclusion of every other name. But there was always a point where their names stopped its potency. The name always carried the idea of its ministry or the ministry of the man who bore it. As his ministry was limited and imperfect his name suggested limitation. Once, "In the beginning the Word was God," but by thinking of God as a Being sending pain and trouble a veil has come over the name to us, and since the unlimited perfect ministry of Jesus Christ we have to speak that name with our whole heart till all the perfect work which His name conveys is manifested in us. "There is none other name given under heaven whereby we can be saved." So there are certain ones among you who will never be healed, never helped out of your troubles, till you have spoken the name,

Jesus Christ, with your whole mind as intent upon it as it is possible for it to be. The names David, John, Moses, anybody else but Jesus, carries a panorama of limitation, failure, sin.

The faith-cure people have wrought many miracles in the name of Jesus, but it is noticeable how afraid they are of draughts, night airs, accidents, other religious beliefs, etc. So there is not perfect ministry by them. The Christian scientists have wrought many miracles by the name of Christ, carefully explained as Truth, but there have been divisions, strifes, intolerance among them and thus there has been something lacking. So now this lesson explains, that is the verses before the seventeenth do, that it must be by the whole name that we are to be wholly saved.

When the officers asked of Peter and John in whose name they healed the man born lame, they answered: "In the name of Jesus Christ." Do not stop to explain the word. Make haste to clear your mind of its old errors, exactly as the Bible lesson No. 2 declares, and proceed to hold the full word Jesus Christ till the full ministry is done in you and you have clear access to the Father. This makes you equal with Jesus Christ in the power of the Spirit, as He promised: "Where I Am there ye may be also." "Ask in my name."

Jesus Christ on this occasion, while showing us what to do when we seem to have broken some man-made law, taught us that as He troubled the old Jewish Sabbath right near the place where the angel troubled the waters, so we may put all actions prompted by high motives onto the responsibility of The Father or The Spirit which is the good motive itself and need not explain ourselves.

Only "What He seeth the Father do." The Father is Love. Only what Love bids us do can we do if we have a good motive. Good Motive is God. God is Love. "Sheweth Him all things." We are shown exactly what to do under all circumstances and in all places. The son of God is the perfect motive to do good." The Son quickeneth whom He will." The perfect word in the mind will quicken those who seem dead. We shall see the whole name Jesus Christ quicken the dullest and stupidest people to thinking so harmoniously that the red blood will flow swiftly, the hard joints will limber, and the eyes will flash with light. This name spoken will teach us to raise the quickening life and beauty of our friends into plain sight.

"He that believeth shall not come into condemnation." This text is the main point for self-treatment when all things point to our having made some seemingly very false moves which nobody approves. We must deny self-condemnation and the condemnation of others. "There is no condemnation." Do not forget to say, "I am not under self-condemnation. I am not under the law of condemnation." Your mind will clear itself, and you can speak the word "Jesus Christ" unto swift power.

"The resurrection of life and the resurrection of damnation," said Jesus. He meant that you would see the life, of the True Word demonstrated and the death or disappearance of the false word. The idea of condemnation of good motives for any actions, the idea of persecution for the Jesus Christ healing, will be demonstrated as pure nothingness. "My judgment is just." Why is the Jesus Christ judgment just? Because no earthly ambition is consulted. The Jesus Christ word makes you no time-server. You are on the side of Omnipotence when you are in the right. Lean hard on the right and say, as Jesus did: "All power is given unto Me because My judgment is just." When Abraham Lincoln was asked if he was sure God was on his side, he answered: "I am not so much concerned to know whether God is on my side as whether I am on God's side."

"Be strong, and of a good courage; fear not nor be afraid of them; for the Lord thy God, He it is that doth go with thee; He will not fail thee, nor forsake thee." **August 9th, 1891.**

BIBLE LESSON V. FEEDING THE STARVING

This lesson is about Jesus Christ's going across the Sea of Galilee, up into a mountain and sitting down to the working out of a problem of human life.

The going across the sea, instead of around it is a hint of the metaphysical Law of taking the straight line as the shortest distance between two points.

By this lesson I know that there is no need of waiting for summer and winter, seed time and harvest to feed people. Also, Jesus Christ settled the question for all time as to the duty of the spiritual or Christian teacher in the matter of feeding the multitudes as well as healing and comforting them.

You may be sure that there is a short cut or direct route to all accomplishments. French and music should be learned at once without long years of drill. Success is your immediate right without years of painstaking effort. Are you not one with the Origin of all power and all knowledge? Does that substance or divine region of you have to learn anything? No. Let the Divine of you reign and like Jesus Christ you enter at once upon your inheritance.

Simply because you have heretofore gone around and not across the sea of your life, need not count against your acceptance of the divine guidance now with you and for you and in you. Jesus of Nazareth settled the question once what to do when falsely condemned; of what to do when deserted by your friends and in humiliation; of what to do when there is a death in your family, of what to do with sickness, of what to do when you yourself are buried in a tomb past all hope. Today He settles the question of feeding starving, people.

This vital spark of divinity you now represent might be fanned by you into a living, quickening fire of bright genius if you would let it have its way. Genius always does things in a new, unexpected way. Napoleon conquered armies, not by the usual arts of war or military tactics, but in his own way. Abe Lincoln won victories and ran the government to a new tune. Jesus Christ took this time to set aside the circuit of summer and winter and seed time and harvest and make bread at once. He explained the *modus operandi* of quick accomplishments.

Elijah once kept a widow's cruse full at Zarephath. Elisha replenished one at Gilgal and fed one hundred men with twenty loaves of bread, but neither of them explained the process. Jesus here explains it.

First, "He went up into a mountain and sat down." This means that He went into an exalted state of mind. There is no power of healing in a depressed state of mind.

There is no quickening of the exhausted by a sorrowful or anxious state of mind. In order to work your best, metaphysically, you must be in an exalted state of mind. Now, there are two ways of getting into an exalted state of mind. There is the short and direct way of Jesus, and there is the longer but just as sure way of Job.

The short, direct way of Jesus Christ is the one now used by the Christian scientists. It is by denial and affirmation, as explained three or four weeks ago. You remember that He denied the reality of material things by saying, "The flesh profiteth nothing." He denied the power of evil by saying, "It is a lie from the beginning." He affirmed "All power is given unto Me," and "I and the Father are one." His manner of speaking has a very exalting effect upon the mind, and to rest in that state of exaltation is the sure healing of your sick mother and the sure bringing to pass of success. Exaltation is a magnet for all good things of the universe to hasten to you. Depression and anxiety are a magnet for trouble to fly to you.

But you are saying, "How can I be other than depressed and anxious when my father has failed in business, my brother is a drunkard, and my mother is paralyzed?" Then you must take Job's way of getting into an exalted state of mind. Job reasoned with the Almighty. He told the

Almighty face to face that His own hands having fashioned him he could not be wicked and that he would maintain his righteous cause before Him.

This reasoning out your own case with that divine Presence that folds you so close is a mighty help to your state of mind, and never was known to fail anybody. The poorest and most unhappy can plead their cause with this Presence. An old colored woman reasoned her's out this way, "Dear Lord Jesus, if I was you, so great and powerful and happy, I'd help you ef you'se a pore ole cull'd mammy and had lost yore nice little picaninny, as I have. Sho' you can't be not so good as me ef I was you, dear Lord Jesus." And the Lord Jesus took hold of the old mammy's hand and led her through the bogs and the morasses and the forests and the white men to her picaninny.

The great account made of "sparrows" fills our hearts with gladness. A man who had to feed the soldiers in a camp, was ordered to give them half slices at a time when they had been extra worked and were extra hungry. He reasoned with the divine Goodness as a man talketh with his brother, that according to the righteous law of supply and demand these men should have double rations instead of half ones. Then he ordered his under officer to double the thickness of the slices, and before he got through distributing the first lot a wagon load of provisions drove into camp.

Be sure to be very definite in stating your case. Do not let your emotion consume your words. Be on hand to mumble out something besides intense emotion of grief, or anger, or fear. The "Word" is very essential. "Without the Word was nothing made." "If a man eat of the Word I give him, though he were dead, yet shall he live again." Then when your mind gets into an exalted state, trust God. "Whom have I in heaven but Thee, and there is none upon earth that I desire beside Thee." This is the confidence of mind which Jesus emphasized by sitting down in the mountain. Now, in this calm state of confidence you may take deliberate account of your assets and liabilities.

The same is true in cases of illness and domestic sorrow, as in this case of penury or seeming failure of supplies in running your home or affairs of any kind. So if we understand this case, we understand all cases. You take account of liabilities and necessities. That is your Philip thought. Notice how Philip said that there were five thousand people and it would take thirty-four dollars worth of bread to feed them. Andrew told the assets, "Five barley loaves and two fishes." Without noticing the hopeless calculations of Philip or the tiny comfort of Andrew, Jesus Christ bade the five thousand to "sit down on the grass" just exactly as if there were plenty on hand.

So you, when your faith hath come into its word, "All my trust on Thee is staid; all my health from Thee I bring," do you go right on with your affairs and works just exactly as if your bounty was visible. This is not the time to economize and withhold. This is the time to use right up to the last of the assets, right on to the heels of the last penny, as the two widows poured freely forth what seemed the last of the meal and the oil.

Every stroke you make towards penuriousness and retrenchment of fair expenses will cost you double. This is the time when you look up and give thanks for your assets, give loving thanks for five loaves and two fishes to do a five-thousand dollar business with.

Jesus Christ did not roam around despising the meeting of people on their own ground of wants, but He found out their wants and wills and met them there. Who cares about flying round a throne on wings with our children and mothers after death, when a good home and ability to make it happy here is what the heart craves? Jesus Christ helped people here to see that there is in themselves all power to get out of every condition undesirable, and beyond that the ability to do great works in proof of Sonship and Oneness with the One who created them. Nothing is too small or too simple to reason with Jesus Christ about. Jesus Christ is God manifest. To reason with Him is to become more and more merged in Him.

By this time you have caught the secret of reasoning with Jesus Christ, or the Almighty. You cannot help seeing that if we become like those we converse with we should soon become so lost in the knowledge of the Character of Jesus Christ that His very miracle-working power would be ours. You have now caught the Principle, have you not, that if you describe God you become exactly as great as you describe God to be, as fast as you realize what you are talking? A man once had a habit of lying with his face down praising God for knowing him altogether. After a time he got so wise that he could tell all the past and present and future of all the people he met.

So if you praise God as Supreme giving—Supreme bounty, you may hand out and hand out and hand out, for back of you is infinite supply. "There is that scattereth and yet increaseth, and there is that withholdeth more that is meet and tendeth to poverty."

This teaches that God is unto us according to our faith; therefore dreadfully economical people do not have much faith if they carry their careful saving unto hoarding up lest they come to want. If they hoard for giving farther after all the present bounty has filled their neighbors they will increase it and increase it till they have to call to the streets of foreign cities to get people enough to partake of their bountiful stores.

Wonderful words are those with which you describe the Almighty. They react on you so wonderfully. They are alive. There is no wonder that so many people have said, "There is no God only the one you imagine, because you get exactly what you imagine God to be giving."

Then again, it was a very good expression of one man to say, "An honest God is the noblest work of man," because if you describe God as revengeful you soon get revengeful; if you describe God as love and justice you soon become just and loving. If you describe God as niggardly and apt to send afflictions you soon get stingy and full of sorrows.

This lesson enjoins strict reasoning, strict truth—right description of God. **August 16,** *1891.*

BIBLE LESSON VI. THE BREAD OF LIFE

It is one of the first teachings of metaphysics that all environments, circumstances, conditions, all the people who come near us, and everything else, existed first as ideas in our own mind and now appear in plain sight to be known and read plainly.

The science of metaphysics which Jesus Christ taught deals with the meta, beyond, and physics, that is beyond, out of the range of, the physical. The mental is the metaphysical.

This being true, he is our greatest teacher who can tell us how to think such thoughts as shall keep us from making failures, sorrow's, blind people, deaf people inferior people, hard circumstances to surround us. He is our greatest teacher who can tell us how to make harmonious circumstances, success in our undertakings, perfect people to surround us. He is our greatest teacher who can tell us how to redeem our life from those failures, hardships, poor people our former thoughts have fruited into.

He will be our divinely good friend who shall teach us to think such thoughts as shall cause us to sit down in due season under the vine and fig tree of our exactly right ideas.

Jesus Christ is this teacher and this friend. There was no circumstance and no condition which we have walled ourselves into that He did not take upon Himself and teach us how to redeem ourselves from the consequences of our erring thoughts. Redemption was the story Jesus Christ taught. And redemption is the theme of all these lessons, where He is making an object lesson of Himself for our benefit.

He taught us to say, "How I am glorified," when physical anguish and desertion of friends come upon us for believing in the power of evil and the reality of matter.

Have you learned the lesson so well that you also have redeemed yourself from physical anguish and have chosen unto yourself many loving friends when you seem to have none? No? Then you need not be surprised if anguish still gets a hold on you and you still feel lonely. Words are ideas. True words are alive and good.

So if you are in the deeps of sorrow you speak living words that can bear your mind out on their wings into a paradise of peace. True words are angels.

Once a woman believed that Jesus Christ meant it as a signal to her of what to say for her feet, which had a habit of paining excruciatingly. So she said: "Father, how Thou hast glorified me." And she felt as if she were actually being borne upon wings of delight, so free and at peace her feet hastened to be.

He taught us what to say when we have come to our last dollar and have no visible means of support. He taught us what to say when we are condemned by our family and neighbors for having acted according to our highest light. He here condescends to our low estate where we have brought around us a tribe of sycophants, or people who think of us as simply a provider, and feeder and caretaker for them.

He here shows us what state of mind we must have been in to have caused such a state of affairs. He shows that it has been because of our mixed beliefs, as first we have believed in the necessity for hard work to accomplish that which we wished to accomplish; and secondly, we have been ambitious for fame of some kind, some earthly honor or emolument; thirdly, we have believed that we ought to carry out our own will at whatever cost somewhere or sometime along our journey over this planet.

The people who followed Jesus this time went for the food, not for His doctrine at all. He takes us at the point where we realize that people want to use us, not to honor us by being near us. You have all had this experience more or less, and it always stands for the coming to outward expression of your self-will, ambition, and belief in the great results of hard work.

The Christian scientist often has this state of affairs, and is grieved by it. He or she has the definite instruction of what to do with the thoughts to be "raised up" at the last extremity of such a situation. Perhaps it might all be summed up in that general statement of Truth which the scientist makes when learning the lessons of mental responsibility. "There is no life, substance, or intelligence in matter;" but this direction is much more explicit than that, and tells you to deny that there is any necessity in your lot for hard labor, deny that you ever hoped great things from earthly honors, and deny emphatically that you were ever self-willed.

When the Christian scientist suddenly discovers that her patient is not her friend and does not believe in the science, though he has said he was and did, but was only making believe in order to get his arms cured, failing which for a time he repudiates the whole doctrine and his obligations of every kind to her, she is grieved and astonished, often discouraged.

Now nobody has any more religion than just as much as he can command in time of trial. This religion of Jesus teaches you exactly what to do and say to redeem yourself from grief, disappointment, failure. Also that if you deal exactly right with your own mind, the people around you will spring right up into right conditions. Even the patient who shows that he or she just looked upon you as a useful penwiper or doormat for them and so were not promptly cured, he will be cured if you understand this lesson. Jesus Christ did not despise healing the people, feeding them, furnishing money or anything else for them. He did not look down upon any humble ministry, but He knew that to look at money for its own sake, or food for its own sake, or healing for its own sake, is a belief in the value of earthly things which must be denied. There must be no belief in the necessity for hard labor in anybody's lot. Rest remaineth for the people of God as to manual labor for meat, bread, house, health.

The seeking of God first through faithfully speaking right words will bring anybody into such spiritual power that "all these things are added" without effort. Ambition to merit reward by works is discountenanced by Jesus Christ. Nobody is saved by works. Salvation by works was the early teaching of Christian science as set forth by William S. Adams fifty years ago in his book on Christian science. John Knox was told that his good works would save him. He fought all night against the belief that they would. He came into the understanding that faith in Jesus Christ, or believing the Word of Christ, which is Truth, was salvation.

Here Jesus Christ urges every man, woman, and child to believe in the heart what is true, and this believing, or right faith, will feed, clothe, support them. This one must do by words that are right, very vigorously uttered, when he has been brought up to believe that his bread and butter for himself and family are dependent upon his hard efforts. It is a bad idea to get its hold in any mind. Ben Franklin had that belief so hard that he ran it into a saving up and hoarding state of mind that nearly warped the happiness out of the lot of nearly all the farmers' children of New England.

It is a very unspiritual idea, and must be boldly handled, torn up by the roots, out of mind.

Say positively: "I do not believe in hard work as necessary for myself or anybody else to live comfortably in God's universe." This saving by works will make a man or woman who has struggled hard, feel that he or she has earned some rights to extra blessings in heaven. It will cause a certain class of mind to think that outward actions will satisfy all the demands of God on the soul, as Admiral Nelson, who broke his wife's heart, but did so much service to his country, felt sure he had earned the right to an extra good place in heaven.

The Lord looketh on the heart! Nothing is worth working for except a right state of mind. All the greatest, good men and women the world has ever known have found out a great principle of life in the knowledge that we are not walking over this planet for the purpose of making for ourselves a great name, gathering to ourselves riches, honors, friends, but to do the will of God in that estate whereunto we are called.

The preacher must come to where he knows it is not to convert men to Christ, not to make the world better, not to be great in the cause of God, but to do the will of God, willingly. The will of God often pushes the great man or the great woman into the quick fruits of his mistaken thoughts, so that he is in mean and small circumstances, out of which he must extricate himself by speaking the same simple truths the washwoman and hod-carrier must speak. He will find himself in great extremities, or "at the last day," as Jesus here in this lesson expresses it. But if he do the will of God, or meekly speak the right words he will be "raised up."

The righteous man often has a belief in hard labor, is ambitious to be great, is self-willed, so he has great things depending upon his efforts, has people depending upon him who ought to be doing for themselves, and is harassed by the failures of his plans or their delay in coming out right till he is brought to great extremities. He must take the denial of Jesus, "I came not to do mine own will. I do not care for earthly honors. I am no time server."

Then when he has said in all sincerity, "I am doing the will of God," this denial and affirmation will cause his plans to be "raised up." They will be wonderfully successful. He himself will be honored. He will be "raised up" in joy and delight. Notice that the "raised up" is, first, for the works or plans, and second, for the man. All things were taught by this man of God, Jesus Christ. He is our highest idea of man as a Son of God. If you understand Him, you will be redeemed from evil and will redeem your world from evil.

August 23, *1891*.

BIBLE LESSON VII. THE CHIEF THOUGHT

"When Christ Cometh." These people were expecting a Messiah or Christ. That which they were expecting as a body of people, each one of us is always expecting.

Look carefully into your own mind, examine your kingdom of thoughts, and you will see that there is always a region of you which is intensely looking for deliverance from your environments. This is your Jewry. Now your Christ or deliverer is standing right in yourself, telling you the exact way out this minute.

Job said: "Is not my help in me?" Within me is one thought, that if I heed it will lift me out of every situation and circumstance which the Roman yoke on the Jews typified, So with you. What is true of you is true of every sentient thing. Now the Christ thought in you; which will save you, you do not let have its way with you. Why don't you? Each mind is a kingdom of thoughts. We have all power over the kingdom of our own thoughts. We may let a Pharisaic thought or a chief priest thought shut off the beautiful one within us which always says "I Am thy Savior."

Hush all your realm of thoughts for a moment and let that one which says "I am Christ" speak. You can. actually work miracles if you let that thought have full sway over your other thoughts. These lessons of Jesus Christ among the Jews and Gentiles represent your Jesus Christ thought within yourself. Each thought says "I am" You let that one have reign over you which you please. "I am envy," says one thought; "I am bigotry," says another; "I am success," says another; "I am your Savior from all evil," says the greatest One within your realm.

This greatest thought is your oldest thought. It was with you in the beginning, is with you now, and ever shall be with you, world without end. It is the "Ancient of Days." "Come and reign over us, Ancient of Days."

Notice this, if you please, that your pious thought, representing the traditions of the past as to the severity of God, is quick to take and bind your Jesus Christ thought, Your Pharisaic thought, representing your past teachings as to your inferiority before God, always chokes down the generous, Sabbath-breaking Christ thought.

Now Jesus Christ, or the power of Truth, is in you all. This power of Truth you cannot kill, but you may hide it if you please for a while. "Yet a little while am I with you," it says just as quickly as your piety and bigotry are roused. For the power of God is never manifested where pious bigotry is allowed rule.

When this knowledge of the ways of thoughts in the mind became known to some very brave thinkers they voluntarily let all their thoughts keep perfect silence while the Jesus Christ thought spoke in them, saying: "I Am the Messiah. I Am Jesus Christ." They all reported wonderful experiences. It seemed to them as if their whole being was God being. There was nothing but God "above them all and through them all and in them all." Jesus Christ is God. This is not person, but Principle. Jesus Christ is the voice, the power of God. These people all became strong through and through. They became well and sound through and through. Their judgment became strong and healthy. They are sure that if you will not let your old prejudices blind you, but will let your highest thought have freedom, you will rise like a bird out of the snare of the fowler, free in God.

Listen to that highest idea within your realm of ideas. Here is its message: "If any man thirst, let him come unto Me, and drink." You know you are thirsty for something. If your friends love you, you still are thirsty. If you have money you still are thirsty. If you have fame you still are thirsty. If you are learned in books you still are thirsty. You will always be thirsty for something till you let your highest idea reign over you.

It says: "I am your lover, your friend, your counselor, your satisfaction." There is no other way of receiving Jesus Christ except this one. It is the principle that is never absent from the mind of any man or woman or child. No matter what you have done or thought, if you will let your thoughts all hold still for this one to rise in its majesty, you are good and great and wise and healthy that moment. The satisfaction of living is yours when forth from you flows the living water of your highest idea only. This is not the doctrine of salvation by works. It is not the doctrine of salvation by faith in anybody or anything.

It is salvation by the "let there be" of Moses and Jesus of Nazareth. It was by keeping silent for God to be the whole of Him that Jesus was enabled to say so boldly, "I and the Father are one. He that hath seen Me hath seen the Father." Spinoza was so lost in finding the power of God over and through and in him so wonderfully, that he was called the God-intoxicated man.

Many people have been afraid to let their Jesus Christ thought be their only thought. It seemed suddenly to them as if they themselves were all Jesus Christ, all God, nothing else of them. Why they could possibly be afraid to have their mind occupied by one perfect idea is a mystery. To hold back from speaking this idea in the mind, or rather letting the idea speak itself, is to put off the power of the Holy Ghost (according to this lesson.)

The Holy Ghost is the quickening power of God. The Holy Ghost has not come while you are sick, while you are poor, while you are lame, while you are unhappy. And you cannot have the Holy Ghost till you have been silent enough for the Jesus Christ idea that is within your realm of ideas to speak its words within you very definitely.

Do not be afraid of being Jesus Christ. Do not be afraid of any experience that comes with letting this wonderful idea speak within you. Do not let your thoughts rise up with all kinds of babblings like they did in the Nazareth Man's time. They said: "Shall Christ come out of Galilee?"

You may comfort yourself by knowing that the high doctrine of "Let these be" says: "Let the same mind be in you that was in Christ Jesus our Lord." Your mind is not too low a place for your best thoughts to reign over your poor ones in. The poor ones are completely redeemed when they lie still as death for that ever-present one to say: "I Am thy Messiah. I Am thy Savior, thy Friend, thy Counselor, thy mighty Judgment, thy Power and Majesty forever."

Here the Jews refused the Messiah because they feared that Galilee was not good enough for Him to come out of. You are exactly that when you think you are not good enough to have a thought anywhere within you which is the Savior, the Righteous.

Some men have not let this thought in their mind be Jesus Christ because that word seemed to them to be a man with a religious system to urge and not a principle, so they have let this supreme thought within them say: "I am God, and I reign over thee." Now, in the beginning that was indeed the Word, but by accusing God of so many dealings He could not possibly be guilty of, we have all drawn a veil over our faces, and the Deep crying unto Deep within us saying, "I am God," does not bring the power of God so quickly as by letting the idea Jesus Christ be spoken till the veil is rent. At the same time there is no difference in the meaning of the words. The principle idea within your mind is the God idea. You are expected to work miracles. Every one of you who takes this mode of dealing with the mind will find yourselves converted to uprightness, rejoiced with new powers, filled with health. There is nothing out of the power of one who lets all his mind rest for one thought only to speak. You have the power to call back those who are called dead. You have the power to turn copper into gold. There are strange powers lying dormant, as it were, within you, which, keeping all your thoughts still for one thought to rise in its glory, would quicken. This is the "mystery of Godliness." It is spoken of as the Lion of David, because only victorious people are supposed to have the powers of God with them. But everybody is a victory over the world by this process.

There is nothing to do, nothing to believe, only "Let be what is; let speak what is true."

Of course you have heard that Truth is Omnipotence. I assure you that it is. Let speak within you that secret, silent word, while all your other thoughts lie low. "Behold, I have put My Name upon thee." Even while you thirst for the child to be well, the home to be harmonious, the environments not to cramp you so, behold in your midst, that is in your realm of thoughts, stands the Christ.

So now you see how the Kingdom of Heaven is within you. Many people are letting this thought in the midst of them speak till there is great meekness and lowliness of heart where before was pride and arrogance. They do not care for name and fame and rule where before they were ambitious. For you know that Jesus Christ is not ambitious. Your highest thought is meek and lowly of heart.

Let the night watches find you still while your highest "I *am*" speaks. All that you dream of as desirable is in that redeeming word. So many people catching this knowledge of the metaphysical instructions given by Jesus Christ for our example are the hastening on of that time of which the prophet spoke, "Many saviors shall come up from Jerusalem." Jerusalem means peace. So from the peace of letting thoughts He still for the Christ one to say, "I Am thy Redeemer," saviors are springing up all over the earth. "They shall all be taught of God" is the prophecy. This God-thought that waits within you, being led to say, "I *am*" will teach you all things and remind you of that country from whence you came forth and unto which you return.

You have a wonderful kingdom of thoughts. Which one reigns now?

August *30*, *1891*.

BIBLE LESSON VIII. CONTINUE THE WORK

"If ye continue in My Word," said Jesus Christ, "then are ye my disciples." This discourse of Jesus before the Jews in the court of the Temple at Jerusalem, is all about the Power of the Word.

If anyone is unaware of the potency of the idea he is holding in mind to strike out over his daily affairs and into his bodily conditions then he is not yet acquainted with Christian doctrine.

Take the idea that you are at this moment holding. What is it? The strongest idea one set of people hold is that if something does not turn up within a certain time only a miracle can save them from something or other that is threatening. This is an idea that makes the atmosphere strained and attenuated and gives the children nervous cramps, and the rest of the family neuralgia.

Take that idea and change it into this one: "I have a right to the best, and I will trust to my rights to bring me out right."

As your child has a right to your love and to your protection, and trusts his right, so have you a right to protection in this universe into which you are born.

Trust bravely. Trust like a child and a potentate. Socrates said that a state of grief or anxiety would attract sickness, waste of property, and death. Grief is a word held in the mind. A word is an idea.

"For the lightest word thou shalt give account." The words of Jesus Christ, He promised, would lead into comfort, joy, peace, power. Alike attracts like. You hold a strong, loving thought on purpose; hold it tenaciously; directly, strong loving successes will crown your efforts. This is metaphysics. This is a psychologic study left out in the school books, but is, indeed, the metaphysics of Jesus Christ.

Here He shows what will be the effect of speaking His words, which are all true. Ye shall be free. "The Truth shall make you free."

The Truth He told is so stupendous that many a noble preacher has refused to speak it. Take this word He told you to speak, for instance, "I and the Father are one." People think mostly that He meant only Jesus of Nazareth was one with God. Not at all. He meant that you and I are one with the Father. "Where I Am there ye may be also."

You are looking for freedom of some sort. The fact that you are searching for freedom is evidence that you do not know Truth. "The Truth makes free," remember.

The Russian peasant cowered and shrank like a frightened spaniel while he believed that the shadows in the field were filled with vampires, but when he knew that there was no such thing as a vampire in the shadow he stood up and walked free. The Truth made him free. When you know that a draught of air has no neuralgia or rheumatism in it for you, you will not shrink and cower like a spaniel when a damp draught strikes you. "The truth shall make you free."

"But," you say, "the damp draught does give me neuralgia." No. That idea of yours about the failure of your business, or the injustice of your neighbor, or the envious thought against another, brought the neuralgia. "Oh," but you say, "my little innocent child has the neuralgia from damp air." No, it has not; it was your idea that folded it around like a magnet to draw trouble unto its little self. "Envy is the rottenness of the bones," says the Scripture.

To believe in the claims of weather, inheritance, climate, etc., is to be in bondage. There is a way of getting free from the effects of false words in good science. You take each word as it comes into your mind and mix it and mold it and rectify it by right words till you would never know it to be the word you set out with.

Each word of Truth is a setting-free principle. The Scriptures are true. See how senile decrepitude is getting the bondage over your eyesight. Do you know that instead of losing your sight as the years go on you ought to increase in sight? Can you imagine what idea made you put on glasses? It was something along the line of your human experience which you said about the "Lord having dealt very bitterly by you," or making your lot hard, or your burden heavy.

This compels you to take up that thought which, though it lies unconscious in your realm is there just the same, and needs rectifying. Say to the old past, bitter cry, I see that God is good to me, God is good to me." Mold and mold that old-time word till it rises within you a joyous certainty that God is indeed good to you. Then your eyesight will return to you.

Suppose that your hearing is feeble. That shows that you have had many gods or idols. Some things have been very, very dear to you, or very, very powerful over you. "Hear, O Israel, the Lord our God is One." Take your dearest treasure or your greatest fear and say, "There is only One God—One." Soon your hearing will be restored. In this lesson Jesus Christ speaks of continuing in His Word. His Word. By this He intimates what deaf and blind often do, begin good words and drop speaking them soon. "Repetition is the mother of wisdom." If you keep speaking the right word, which is the word that fits your particular case, you will get great light on the principle involved by the word. This is explained by the speed with which a child understands the principle of the multiplication table, if he speaks it much.

There are reasons why sight and hearing must be mentioned in this connection, it seems; notice how He speaks of what He sees with His father and what they see and do with their father. Sight and hearing are entirely dependent upon our own ideas of God. Wrong ideas of God are now causing the whole human race to show out deafness and blindness as never before. Even the children are getting blind and deaf. "The earth waxeth old as a garment." Those of us who changed radically our ideas of God began to have very acute hearing and wonderful clearness of vision far superior to the eyesight and hearing of our childhood. Then there began to be quickened another visual and another auditory power besides the regular.

"Awake, O earth!" "Arise, shine, for thy light is come." "Awake! arise!" "Rise from the dead, and Christ shall give thee light."

There are some new ideas going about the decrepit eye that everybody carried in his head; not an embryonic or crude eye, but an aged eye; aged as our other two eyes are getting to be in the race head. The true doctrine renews the strength of the aged; try the true doctrine. The true doctrine renews the vigor and vitality of those who are stepping over the lines into weakness; try the true doctrine. The new doctrine quickens that other seeing and hearing faculty within the already young and vigorous till they can see that other dimension in space which Jesus Christ saw so plainly.

There are said to be people who can untie knots which the most skillful cannot loosen, because by an unexplainable faculty they can do it. They use without knowing it, the fourth dimension in space. This quickened seeing faculty enables one to sit down and scan his own universe and set it into such order as he wishes it. You know, do you not, that any tangle in your affairs is the sign of incomplete knowledge? The true knowledge would untie the knot. There is one little link, one little point which would set everything right in a moment. So lovely and practical is the teaching of Jesus Christ that you cannot possibly miss knowing exactly what to do under all circumstances if you follow His directions. Do not be too proud to sit meekly down at His feet and learn about the fourth dimension in space. Learn the quickening words of our Father which He told us. He calls the word of Truth "the Son." He urges us all to get free by the Son, or the word continually spoken. He was aware that if your hearing and sight are quickened by "the Son" or "the Word" there will be no going back. Mechanical appliances and material compounds are sure to lose their powers. So do the words of the strong human will or the mesmeric touch; but "if the Son make you free, ye are free indeed." He brings up Abraham to show that mere belief in physical descent is no healing or setting-free principle.

It must be the quickening word of "the Son" in them, just as it was in Abraham, by which they shall be free. Unless they had that they were only children of the devil, or error, and would have the senile ear and eye, and tangle in affairs forever. Abraham was quickened by trusting in God supremely as the Only Spirit. Abraham called every dream and every vision he had "a word of the Lord," till he got so ho was complete master over all things. "While people were wondering halting, doubting, Abraham was trusting God.

These Jews knew nothing of such faith, and were therefore nowhere near being children of Faith. Just know that every single affair lies clearly soluble by a right word in the mind. Walk close to God with the words, "I and the Father are One. I tell you the Truth." Notice that the golden text of this lesson is the gist of it all. "As many as received Him, to them gave He power to become the sons of God." To receive Christ is to become the Christ through and through. The Christ is the Son of God. The Son of God has all power, has all knowledge. As you are well aware that you are children of God already, you know that this "becoming" simply means that you show forth your powers.

There is nothing will pay you like the continual repetition of the words of Jesus Christ. You will soon be quickened through and through. There is the very power of God within you folded as a rosebud folds its petals and sepals and perfumes. His words will cause you to show forth your powers. What do you claim that you are? A little feeble child? Then you are drooping round with very limited powers. Do you claim to be a poor worm of the dust? Then you are prematurely old. Do you claim to be inferior in your nature to Jesus Christ? Then you are still wondering when the world will grow to love each other and do right by each other. Are you claiming that environments make you? Then you are an idolater, and subject to contagious and increasing liabilities to disease.

Why don't you spring forth the potentiality of that nature with which you were vested before the days of Abraham? In other words, why don't you say: "I and the Father are One," "All power is given unto me," "I arise from my dream of error, I know my royal descent and my universal privileges, by my noblest word let mo be judged."

This will cause you to make the atonement manifest. This will manifest your unity with the Christ. Unity with the Christ is marriage with the Holy Spirit. Union with the Holy Spirit is atonement. I will speak to you about the atonement next time.

Meanwhile, quicken your powers—resurrect them into the sight of all the world by understanding this lesson as treating of your absolute freedom and absolute power in Spirit, and your nothingness and powerlessness as materiality.

Defy death. Defy pain. Defy weakness. Quicken--quicken into satisfactory living by true word. **September 6, 1891.**

BIBLE LESSON IX. INHERITANCE OF SIN

This lesson of Christ and the blind man includes the whole Christian doctrine of salvation. It takes in the Christian teachings of all the Christians before the time of Jesus and since His time. Christ means truth, so all truth speaking is Christian teaching. Here in this lesson is the whole scheme of salvation by works, faith, and atonement. The pious Dervish and the modern churchman are trying to get into heaven by appeasing their deity with "works." But there is nothing heavenly about the lot or looks of either of these types of workers for salvation. It is only one side of the triangle of religious law. Incompleteness is always unsatisfactory.

The trial at salvation from evil, by the practice of the mind called faith is also unsatisfactory as heretofore demonstrated. It is only another side of the triangle and is not complete doctrine. Jesus Christ preached "works", as, "If I do not the works of the Father believe Me not." "Have faith in God." "Have the faith of God." But He lived and demonstrated atonement or the unity of His mind with the mind that is God. "I and the Father are One."

The effects of the practice of faith are remarkable, almost attracting one to study to have faith. There are two kinds of faith practiced, active and passive. An earnest young man gave all his fortune to the support of the poor, believing that his unseen God would provide for him. He charged nothing for arduous labors, verily believing in a sure sustenance, which, with all that belongs to human necessities, was actually provided always after intense assurances before his unseen God of his unshakable faith. A woman who had no faith but had been told what wonder might be wrought through faith sat down and deliberately determined to learn it. She sat down in the midst of her poverty and loneliness with her little children about her and practiced *leaning*. She seemed shiftless to her neighbors, but it was astonishing what "luck'" that woman always had. Something good was always "turning up." Her children were all talented, beautiful, prosperous.

Yet there was something lacking. Incompleteness is unsatisfactory. Neither the man or woman type pleased their neighbors by its demonstration well enough to practice it. Faith is a state of mind dependent on the will. Works may be quite external. Faith is mental. Atonement is the understanding and experience of the actual Oneness of the Spirit that is God; of the mind of man with the Mind that is God.

This lesson teaches the whole doctrine of salvation according to Jesus Christ, as to his own duty and experience and the effect of such doctrine *in toto* upon all who receive it. He took a man "born blind" and healed him. Such blindness was considered incurable then as now by material methods.

His disciples ask Him, "Who hath sinned, this man or his parents?" What made them put the man before his parents in the matter of responsibility for that blindness? Why that was the much-talked-of doctrine of reincarnation, whereby a man was not considered new at the time of birth in the flesh, but old from having lived some previous existence and who now deliberately chose certain people for his parents to demonstrate prolonged existence by an experience with earth life.

Jesus Christ promptly denied the whole theory, "Neither hath this man sinned." Whatever of eternal life the man as a sinless spiritual being might have realized, mortal ways were desired and the reincarnation of sin rejected.

In Christian science we always recognize humanity as spiritual and deny the claim of sin in the individual and his ancestors just as Jesus Christ did. We do not believe in an inheritance of sin. "Neither hath this man sinned, nor his parents." We believe in an inheritance from God alone. "Hath not His hand fashioned me?" "Thou knowest that I am not wicked." "Call no man upon earth your Father."

As it makes a mighty difference to our health what we believe, of course you can see that it is much better to believe that God is our Father than that any other being could hand us down an inheritance. It was a common belief in those days, as now, that we have what we have of disease and pain as a consequence of sin.

But Jesus Christ, who told us to be sure and keep His words and be in a state of mind exactly like His, said, "Of all that Thou hast given Me, I have lost none save the son of perdition." "Son" means idea, speaking metaphysically, and since "the flesh profiteth nothing" we will not speak any other way. So "son of perdition" means idea of sin and its history. I drop no idea except the idea of sin; that I reject; for in a universe created by the Good, occupied by the Good, and tolerating only the Good, there is no reality in sin, so there is no place for sin.

It will cause an appearance of blindness and deafness to hold the idea that there is any reality in evil of any kind. It is a limitation of powers and faculties. "I set before you an open door." There is universal freedom with ideas of universal Good.

To keep the mind fixed to a prejudice has a limited effect upon some function of the body. This lesson is about dropping limitations and receiving light. Our missionaries to foreign lands ought to take their mind from looking at the natives through the idea that they are all to be damned if they don't know the history of the man Jesus of Nazareth. That idea has hidden the sight of their eyes and their children's eyes. They do not destroy the sight, but they hide it by an idea.

Milton hid his eyesight by thinking the false idea that there was a Satan in Paradise. We hide our vision by trying to put limitations on our fellow men.

We see a man who says things of God in a laughing, hilarious fashion and we immediately think he ought to be hushed up, but how do we know but that he is a demonstration of the text, "The Lord laugheth in the heavens?" Man can do only one thing for his neighbor—give him his freedom. To throw around you an atmosphere of freedom will make men good—rather, give them a chance to show forth their inherent goodness.

Keep hold of this idea of the righteousness of freedom and you will find other faculties of sight and hearing opening up. I do not mean intuition; I mean a present sight as definite as your sight of that bookmark and the page you wish to place it in. You have the hidden faculty of seeing what that missing link is, which, if you will look at it, will set your affairs right in an instant, cure the imbecile man at once, make a healthy artist of your consumptive daughter, and all such practical things. All these powers are natural, inherent, waiting to break forth as the morning. Only one door closes against them. That door is a false notion. Drop the false notion and the faculty is free in an instant, whether it is a hunch back, a short leg, or a congenital blindness. The saying, "I believe in universal freedom" will start you on the right road.

The peculiarity of the blind man at the temple gate was his obedient spirit. There were throngs of blind men at those gates, but Jesus Christ saw that one who was willing to be the laughing stock of a city street by running through it with two clots of mud on his face in obedience to the command of the only mind that carried any possible hope in its tones.

Obedience was his characteristic. They had told him that some of God's children must be beggars and he believed it. They told him he was blind, and he believed it. But he sprang like a bird from the snare of her fowlers when a loving heart said, "I deny these statements."

As an idea that gets possession has such remarkable effects, you had better be careful to get the idea of unlimited Good. You had better be meek enough to obey this law even though it be broached to you by a Christian scientist. Obedience to principle in spite of the comments of your neighbors will do as marvelous things for you as for this blind man.

Martin Luther was of an obedient mind and so was chosen to be the reformer instead of the far abler Melanchthon. Melanchthon was more careful of "an intelligent public opinion." Saul of Tarsus was obedient to the highest ideal he realized and so was chosen to convert the gentiles and preach the Holy Spirit. Remember that the "intelligent public" is never a friend to the seeker for Truth till after it has "throughst him out," as the Jews did this blind man, and his cause has worked like leaven to gain the respect and love of the bold and fearless.

Jesus here speaks of the necessity for works, or the significance they bear to the power of a man's doctrine. Such cases as this must not be going around, he said, "I must work the works of the Good." All healing by your doctrine is evidence of the spiritual power thereof. "While it is day," He said. He meant that span of duties laid in the pathway of all who are walking over this planet. Each one of us meets just such a set of affairs as we are perfectly capable of setting into right relations. We must not refuse any one of these duties. Do our highest best by every one of them, with no slighting of any task. Nothing is impossible. "As thy day is, so shall thy strength be." If you will take notice the greatest foe your mind has in its realm is the belief in limitation. It is sometimes called doubt. Jesus Christ said He would do His faithwork, or show what an idea in faith would work, and then let their night-ways or doubt-ways deal with the world for a while.

It has been these night-ways or doubt-reign since the crucifixion, but now the morning of understanding breaks. Health springs forth speedily. Our joy no man taketh from us. Christ has come again. We will not believe that there is any power in an evil idea. We do not believe that God intended or permits blindness, pain, poverty. These things are but the false teachings of men who have insisted, as Beecher did, that "suffering is a part of the divine idea." We hurl this lie from our mind, and lo, here is a new strength. Here is the ability to throw away our spectacles. They were only our externalization into works of our belief in suffering as part of God's plan.

Jesus Christ made clay and anointed the eyes. He took this same old curative preparation and made it work to show how it was the difference in His state of mind from theirs. They had used it many times on this same man while they believed in the law of sin and death as part of God's plan. He knew better, and His state of mind took the same stuff and had a different effect. Everything you touch will be successful when you drop your "son of perdition," or idea of the badness of God.

"Go wash," just as this blind man did; that is, deny or reject your old notions, "in the pool of Siloam," in the waters of pure Goodness.

You are by nature the lily of Siloam. If you speak these words you will prove it: "I drop my belief in the law of sin."

Then when the blind man saw, they "put him out." Of course, "in the world ye shall have tribulation." Put you are not expected to mix with the world. You are to triumph over every one of its beliefs by rejecting them, no matter if the greatest orators give them credence. "I am the light of the world." Any man who tells Truth is a light. Any man who announces a principle is a light.

You must announce five things with great vehemence. These they are:

God is the unending, changeless life of the universe.

God is the undeniable, unchanging health of the universe. God is the unfailing, irresistible strength of the universe.

God is the unfailing, ever present support of the universe. God is the immovable defense of the universe.

These principles have not been announced till now. They have always been hidden by the words, "death, disease, weakness, poverty, danger."

A word is a great thing. "For the lightest word there is account." Keep these last words out of your vocabulary in simple mercy. Wash clean in the holy Siloam of these words:

"I do not believe in an inheritance of sin.

I do not believe in the race experience of sin.

I do not believe in the contagion of sin.

I do not believe in myself as a sinner.

I believe I am a child of God."

"How sweet the lily grows." Now, you can deny blindness in the same washing words, can't you? Try it. No matter who taught you of an inheritance of failing vision, say, "I deny it." Do you remember the prophecy John made, that the "old dragon" should be destroyed in the last days by the testimony of the saints? The old dragon is the belief in sin. You are one of the saints to stand before the throne and shout your testimony. "I testify that I know that God is all, and in Him is no darkness of sin." After the testimony the man was received into union with Christ by thinking the same thoughts Christ thought. Think Plato's thoughts and get one cold mind with him. Think Aristotle and get away from home and honor with him. Think Jesus Christ and step into your Father's house. "Let the same mind be in you that was in Christ Jesus." How? Why, by thinking His thoughts. He made no mistakes.

Leave Fenelon, a Kempis, and Guyon out of your ideals. They believed in the atonement by suffering. They were mistaken. There is no suffering whatsoever connected with marriage with the Spirit. Atonement is uniting or marriage. Be united to God only, the Holy Spirit. "Thy maker is thine husband." "I have set My Name upon thee." "I have espoused thee." "The Spirit and the bride say, come." Fold yourself round with the glory of Truth till you do not see any evil in all your universe, for you have given that testimony which has destroyed it, or rather has caused the eternal day of God to break over. See, the dark corners of earth wait your testimony.

Then thou shalt have no need of the sun, neither of the moon, to give light unto thee, for "The Lord shall be thy everlasting light, and the days of thy mourning are ended." Testimony will break down the middle walls of partition and be an open sesame into this fair kingdom that lies around us. People have hidden God's kingdom by accusations against Him.

We make it visible by refusing to believe in those accusations. We take the words of Truth and are at one mind with God. "I and the Father are One." **September 13, *1891*.**

BIBLE LESSON X. THE REAL KINGDOM

"He that entereth not by the door into the sheepfold—the same is a thief and a robber."

The "sheepfold" is the kingdom of heaven. The kingdom of heaven is not a place, though the place where we are may seem heavenly. The real kingdom of heaven is the right state of mind.

The right state of mind is where there is perfect health, perfect judgment, and perfect prosperity. These are all secured by right reasoning. The most exalted or freest reasoning gives the most exalted state of mind. If anybody stops short in his reasoning he stops short in his health and judgment; also in his prosperity.

The only way to get into heaven or a perfect state of mind is to reason to the highest ultimates your mind can conceive without regarding whether it would be considered *reductio ad absurdum* by the old-fashioned doctrines or not.

As everybody is trying to get into the "sheepfold" here mentioned, let us consider "the door", or the doctrine taught by Jesus Christ so consistently that He called Himself "the Door."

We may readily conceive of ourselves as so one with our doctrine, that we are it, if we have thought and taught and demonstrated it as Jesus Christ did His doctrine.

"The sheep" are your thoughts. The calling of your thoughts "sheep" is very appropriate, because thoughts are docile and obedient like sheep. You yourself are the keeper of your thoughts and lead them where you will.

Every obedient little idea has faithfully pictured that pink glow on your cheek, or that happy light in your eye.

The thoughts referred to here are your thoughts of God particularly and what those thoughts do at all times.

There is one thought you have which you have always held strongly and definitely or indifferently and indefinitely; it is the thought: "God is my friend."

If you started this thought long ago and held it warmly and confidently, you are a good friend to everybody and you now number among your comrades one warm, strong, efficient, unchangeable, loving friend. There is another thought which is of the obedient character of the sheep here meant. It is the idea that "God is omnipotent." This idea, held in confidence, has made you strong in yourself. The most obedient thoughts you have are your thoughts of God. Jesus when speaking of sheep refers entirely to ideas of God. It is ideas of God which if you shepherd well, will get you into that state of mind called heaven, when you have health, judgment, prosperity. Jesus Christ was sure that His doctrine was the door, and everybody else's the climbing in some other way. They had all before Him proved themselves thieves and robbers. Why? They had robbed men and women of health, judgment, and prosperity. Ninety years before Him there had ridden through the streets of Rome, Pompey, proclaimed conqueror of the whole world. Nine hundred cities, 1000 castles, sacked; long lines of manacled captives, with heads hung low and speechless tongues, sightless eyes, broken hearts.

There was splendid triumph for Pompey and the nations shouted his greatness. But Jesus Christ said that was not the doctrine that would make heaven manifest on the earth. His doctrine was the only "door." His doctrine would bind up the brokenhearted, loose the dumb tongues, unstop deaf ears, open blind eyes, lift up the cast down heads. Not only that, but all over the universe you might look for captivity where His doctrine had been preached (or His door opened) and you would not find captivity itself for He had "led captivity captive."

Whoever has any bondage to anything whatsoever, believes more in Pompey's doctrine than in Jesus Christ's. For Pompey believed in bondage, but Jesus Christ believed in freedom. Jesus Christ was sure He had the only doctrine that would set absolutely free. A locksmith is sure he has the only combination that will open the safe. If another man has the same combination he can get in; otherwise not. Jesus Christ knew His doctrine to be the only door into safety.

A mother had a baby that she loved so much she was like a barnacle to its little life. She felt ownership, clinging fondness for it. So the baby boy began to dwindle and pine away. Hungry love always drives its object away.

If you long after and hunger for and eat with fondness in your affections the object of your affections will take every means to keep out of your way. So this little boy was getting away in self-defense. No treatment helped the puny child till the mother said over and over in her heart: "You are God's child, you are God's child."

She kept this up till she loosed the tentacles of her mind off his life, and he sprang forth as free and robust and hardy as a boy could be. This was the door or teaching of Jesus. "One is your Father, even God."

Is not that teaching theft and robbery which takes away sight, hearing, hopes?

Jesus Christ had nothing to say against Pompey as a child of God, but his expecting to enter into heaven by his beliefs was folly. Jesus explained that the porter at the door of heaven is the Holy Spirit. The true doctrine will bring you face to face with the Holy Spirit who will lead you into greater and greater knowledge. The Holy Ghost will teach you all things—guide you into all truth. Just as soon as you take the doctrine of Jesus—actually take it—there is a fall of sweet, loving power over all thought. Once you spoke carelessly, "I believe in God as my friend," but now you speak it in delightful assurance that "whatsoever things ye ask for ye shall have." Every friend who comes to you, you know very well that they are the coming to you of your words about God. All truth about God brings good friends, good success.

Jesus Christ praises Himself as His doctrine, and praises His doctrine as Himself. He lives in blissful ignorance that there is any idea that His doctrine and Himself are not God. When you praise yourself you begin to know yourself. Try it. Praise yourself silently at first, for you have not at first shown that your words are true by your works. Say, "I am wise. I am bold. I am good. I am able to do everything perfectly." You will soon show forth to all the world that you are indeed all this. Then you will have a beautiful effect upon the people. But, indeed—

Now try once speaking some of Jesus Christ's doctrine. He set before you an open door which no man can shut (or no prejudice or fear of anybody keep you from getting the benefit of). Let all your thoughts lie still as the pool of Bethesda for a little while. Now, if your mind is quite placid stir it with this beautiful text: "I am the resurrection and the life, he that believeth in Me though he were dead yet shall he live again."

He had unbounded confidence in Himself. You must have unbounded confidence in yourself. Your Father is the same one that Jesus Christ had. Your substance is exactly like His substance. Your powers are exactly like His. You have the same privilege to ignore your birth in the flesh that He had. You can demonstrate over hardship, pain, trouble, as well as He if you have His combination, or doctrine, or "door." When you have got His teachings truly, you will not follow after strange doctrines.

When you once have said "I do not believe in the power of evil to come nigh my life" and somebody tells you your house and children are burned, you will boldly say: "I do not believe it."

Your calamities will turn out not calamities at all. The stronger you hold onto your words the nobler your blessings. After once saying: "Spirit is the only substance," nobody can make you believe that a whole tide of spirits exists.

After saying: "God is good: God is all," you would not credit the story of anybody who should say that in a vision he had a picture of hell. There would not be in your mind the slightest credence of the accuracy of that little girl's vision of Jesus Christ taking her by the hand to show her the sight of many people in hell. It would not be consistent with your knowledge of His saying that children's true thoughts always behold the good only.

He said He came with a teaching that would give life more and more abundantly. A woman's beloved husband lay dying (according to other men's opinions.) She knew that according to Jesus Christ he had a right to more abundant life. So she leaned hard on some words of Jesus Christ. These were: "God is Love." She said them over and over and the air became vivified with Love. The man revived and lives, strong in God.

A man who felt himself ignorant got down on his face on the mountain side night after night, saying to the folding presence of God: "Thou knowest all things." He repeated the words often. Repetition of truth is the quickening. After some days he became very wise. There was an extraordinary judgment and intelligence about the man. Whoever comes nearest to the principle of speech announced by Jesus Christ is really most successful in life. Life—such life as His words give is miraculous. His words are pure reasoning. Be careful not to stop short on your reasonings along His lines, for that is to stop short in health intelligence, prosperity.

Right reasoning leads you on to the topless heights of the hills of God, from whence cometh our help. The most exalted reasoning concerning yourself as that substance and manifestation of God is the most exalted reward. Where have you stopped in your reasoning? There where you have stopped is where old age begins to seize you, pain lays hold, sickness settles. You have a right to rise to the hills of glory on the wings of the words of Jesus. Speak these words of His: "I am the root and the offspring of David, and the bright and morning star."

See how hereby you announce yourself one with God in the beginning, now His manifestation by your word, and the shining glory of His goodness in the sight of all mankind. "Heaven and earth shall pass away, but My words shall not pass away." September 20, 1891.

BIBLE LESSON XI. IN RETROSPECTION

Today we are requested to make a definite review of the lessons of the last quarter, remind the Christian believer of his duty as a missionary of his doctrine, and speak for practical temperance in the conduct and speech of the human race.

As one gets newer and newer ideas of a landscape by looking at it intently, so to look at a Bible text steadily, thinking it over carefully, we come to newer and newer revelations of its meanings.

So a review of the lessons of the last quarter will give us new spiritual insights.

Two ways of teaching the practice of divine principle have been in vogue; first, the statement of the whole doctrine in one short sentence, as in St. John, I., and then the particularization of that doctrine in living application, as in the statements following the first of John. The second method is the statement of particular cases and the explanation thereof according to universal principles, as a teacher might tell his pupil to take in, item by item, the views of his landscape and report the whole in the order of his survey.

The method of John concerning the meaning of Jesus and His principle is to say that "In the beginning the Word was with God and the Word was God."

God is the eternal Mind. Without Him was not anything made that was made.

The thought of a mind is its word. As the Word that filled the Mind of God was God, of course the Word was equal in presence, power, and knowledge with Its Thinker, Whose Mind it absolutely occupied.

And John taught that this Word made all that was made.

Looking over the universe and seeing the earthquake swallowing its thousands, the tidal waves drowning cities, with the countless other manifestations of what does not coincide with this affirmation of John and Jesus and Moses—that all that the Word made was good—we find that an explanation of what they did indeed mean it necessary.

Nobody can make us call earthquakes and pestilences good. "Woe unto them that call evil good."

Those who call calamity good always try to get away from it.

The martyrs who did not try to get away from persecution had their minds so filled with the name Jesus Christ that they did not notice what was going on around them. They did not explain that it was the absorption of their own mind with the name that gave them no room or space in mind for any other idea, that kept them from pain, but so it was.

One whose mind is absolutely occupied by an idea has no room for a thought of pain. Now the Word that occupies the mind of God is God. And the creation of that Word is all good.

Paul says there is a veil over the eyes of those who read the Scriptures about God. This is because people have accused God of creating both good and evil.

"As I live, saith the Lord, I know the thoughts that I think towards you; thoughts of peace and not of evil." The word satan held in mind steadily would make all things dark and horrible and ugly toward us. We would finally conclude with Schopenhauer that God, the ruling force of the universe, is gigantic evil evolving into good. It would not make it true but would make everything hopelessly uncomfortable for us.

On the contrary, the word God held in mind will fill all things with glory and a noble ecstasy for us.

People have held in mind the words Holy Ghost, and the words Holy Spirit, till their mind was so renewed that their bodies were rejuvenated.

People have urged holding the mind to the words "praise God," because so many men and women with tangled business affairs have straightened them out so satisfactorily by looking them straight in the face and saying, "Praise God."

"With God all things are possible." The word God is the password into the kingdom of joy and gladness. God is Spirit. The word Spirit is the passport into substantial satisfaction. Not the word "spirits;" there are no spirits. There is one Spirit only— God.

John secondly bore record of Jesus Christ as the living demonstration of one who had held the word God in mind. He showed the way out of all the circumstances and conditions into which mankind has complicated itself by believing that God made evil as well as Good.

There is no failure of knowing exactly what to do when the mind is set free and made true and joyous by the true thought of God.

The Texas Compass plant always points truly north and south when it is not burdened with dust. Our judgment is perfectly true when one theme only occupies it.

John tells, thirdly, that what no one could ever accomplish by practicing any external science, or even by faith in the good presence of God, could be brought to pass instantly after the experience of the atonement—or at-oneness of the mind of man with the Mind that is God through thinking of God.

Jesus Christ took the six stone water-pots, representing the six ugly situations of the human lot, and filled them with rich wine to symbolize how the homeliest lot can be made joyously satisfactory by our being united to God in mind.

Jesus then explained to Nicodemus that the showing forth of the mind after it is sure of its oneness with God is so beautiful that it is like being born again.

The process of systematic thinking to cleanse and quicken the mind is called in the science of mind denial and affirmation. We deny the reality of the principle of evil, and affirm the good only as a principle of action.

John tells how Jesus taught His lesson of rest after labor by walking the long journey towards Jacob's well and resting thereon. Almost everyone has some goal toward which his efforts are made. If he has done his best and the end seems as far from attainment as at first he must give it up—rest.

The time of discouragement and weariness and what seems failed hope is the time to give up and rest. Look for the sudden bloom of your hopes when you are willing to give up your hopes.

The best and the highest powers and words spring forth after letting go with the mind. After His rest He announced Himself as the Messiah. He called Himself the Well of Living Water. All who speak truthfully of their spiritual nature are found to radiate a peculiar refreshment and healing.

Take one who boldly announces himself as a believer in the unfailing bounty of God and you will find yourself suddenly devising wise ways and means for the management of your affairs while you are in his society. Take one who believes in God as his unfailing health and you will find in his society great impetus toward health. Take the one who announces that be believes in God as his unerring judgment and your own judgment will be nobler in his presence.

"I will tell you, Socrates, a thing incredible, yet nevertheless true, I made a great proficiency when I associated with you, when I was in the same house, though not in the same room."

The next lesson was for the instructing of us all out of the habit of self-condemnation. Self-condemnation leads to condemnation by other people who find fault with us.

We must take the good word into our mind that, "There is no condemnation."

Seventhly, John taught how Jesus fed multitudes with small visible resources simply by giving thanks and praising the Spirit of God for the law of the self-increasing potency of every substance. Take the few pennies or the small revenues you are possessed of and do likewise and you will surely see the increase.

Then John laid plainly before us that we must not believe in the necessity for hard work in order to live joyously. Also that we must give down our will into the Divine will by saying, "I came not to do mine own will," or else we would run our necks headstrong into great obligations and responsibilities.

He showed in the tenth that what we see in others is the sight of some word in our own mind, and our eyesight depends upon how we see people, whether spiritually born or carnally born.

Here also we discover the fact of the other seeing faculty once owned by the human race which now we are quickening again.

In the eleventh we are told to deny reincarnation and the heredity of sin.

Twelfthly he proves by the results of the teachings of Jesus we may see that His doctrine is the only door into satisfactory living.

The lesson on missionary work shows that no matter if the Red Sea of difficulty seems to lie in our path, we are to preach the gospel we know to be true.

The temperance lesson opened up to us the joyous information that no man ever wanted strong drink. He wants only strong words. When those are given the rum appetite is gone. Temperance means good judgment. Even children love good judgment. They naturally have it. But if somebody tells a child that he does not know what he is about, or fears all the time that he will do something wrong, his sweet, true judgment is hidden, and he goes seeking among tobaccos and cards for his hidden faculty. Whoever would set him free must praise the hidden judgment till it springs forth a glorious goodness; not for anything describe the poor judgment with which the Divine is covered.

A child that is told of "spirits" loses judgment or rather has it hidden. There is only one Spirit. "Do not I fill heaven and earth?" To tell a drinker of ardent spirits there is but one Spirit, even though you tell him silently will "satisfy his soul in thought," while "describing his evil case" will be your accusing.

You remember that John the Revelator saw four angels (accusing words) given power to hurt the earth.

But other angels sealed the servants of the Living God in their foreheads to keep them from the four accusations.

The four accusations against God's people are that: First, they are liars; second, they are unsound; third, that they have wicked propensities, and, fourth, that they are made of a dying substance called mortality, if the beautiful temperance women would spend their generous energies speaking to and of the living goodness of the soul that the accusers have hidden, the goodness of mankind would break forth as the morning.

"I, Jesus, have sent mine angel to testify that this is true."
September 27th, 1891.

BIBLE LESSON XII. John 11:1. MARY AND MARTHA

"Martha" represents the preachers and active workers in religious bodies since ever there was any teaching in the world concerning the Being and office of God. These have ever asserted that God is Omnipresence and without flaw or imperfection of any kind, absolutely good.

At the same time they have been telling of many grievous things happening, as earthquakes, death, loss, which could not possibly have transpired if God's mercy had been shown forth, or if God had not been the "absence of the good" then and there. Such discrepancies of statements as that God, the absolute Good, is Omnipresence and "the absence of good" have necessitated "Martha's" placing Deity on a throne somewhere in the far spaces, as a Being with uncertain moods, who might and might not reward and punish, according to petitions.

The truth is that God is Principle. The principle of goodness. Goodness is best. To do the best you can is to serve the best, and the best as a principle will reward you. "His reward is in His hand." Just as surely as you do the best you can the best will come to you. This is the principle of righteousness. To trust the sure action of this principle will demonstrate the sight of the best speedily. Not to trust its intelligent action retards the sight of the best.

And the best you could imagine, and "greater" will come to you by trusting that, no matter what you accomplish, your motive being good, the best is sure to come to you. This is Principle.

It is either worth while to trust to the righteousness of your motive to bring you out right, or it is not worth while. The sooner you make up your mind whether you will trust to the motive to bring to pass, or to the method of action, the better for your peace of mind. This is the chief tenet of Christian science doctrine- not the method, but the motive. The good motive is the Christ presence - Christ principle - never absent, always working. To do the very best you can is sure to bring you out right; an unfailing, unalterable law.

Suppose that you have had some noble idea of what was right to do under certain circumstances, as, for instance, that by some special attention, you could bring forth the genius so near to the surface of the loud woman or the coarse man? You must give them your kind support and friendly counsel. You know this to be right. But some of the people you love best withdraw their acquaintance and friendship on account of your new comrades. You must trust that the simple being in the right will be your satisfactory demonstration. The best will come of it, because you did your best. Trust it and the demonstration thereof will be speedy.

It is a question of what is right, and you must trust it to act.

When Martha's brother was sick they did the best they could, and that best was the Christ's presence. If they trusted it they would have seen it work whether Jesus was present or not. Lazarus would have got well. It was not to trust that Lazarus would get will, nor to any method of hot or cold applications, drugs or poultices, but to trust their motive which prompted every action. The successful healers often do very poorly according to the world's ideas of methods. They succeed because they do trust to their ideas of right.

The difference between a small trader and a merchant prince is that the small trader looks anxiously to his pints and quarts and wonders how they will act with him next, while the merchant prince knows of the wheat crops of the world, who owns the ships, and what winds are blowing, to determine the prices in advance. That you are in the right must sustain you. That your highest ideal of what is right must be carried out by you - must be your principle of action.

This was the doctrine of Jesus Christ: "Have Faith in God." God is Good. Good is right. Right is best. A lively confidence in the success of the doctrine of doing your best will be like the confidence of Jesus Christ. If a man should set out that he could feed all the world's hungry children he could do it if he loved the idea enough to persevere in practicing it. People might call him a fanatic or an idealist, and prophesy that he would break his neck on his ideals, but back of him would be the infinite bounty of the right idea.

Two women were conversing about giving forth freely their highest ideas to the people. One said she thought it a conservation of energy to keep your original ideas to yourself. Original ideas were not plentiful. People did things over and over, and great ideas would soon give out if you gave them forth freely. The other said that she felt like a clear pane of glass through which bright ideas went freely till she tried to hoard them, then she felt like a pane that had gathered dust.

The first one not only did not bless the people, but got into a confused and timid state of mind with a sick body. The second one grew clearer and clearer and blessed and cheered and delighted the lowest as well as the

highest, besides having a body as healthy as her mind. Both knew that it is right to believe in the bounty of God as unfailing. One trusted the principle, the other did not.

Mahomet was asked to put away Kadijah for a younger and fairer woman. "No! By Allah! She made me," he said.

Napoleon was asked to put away Josephine. "The star is mine, Napoleon," she reminded him. He yielded to the temptation, however, and from that hour his decline began. The days find his name slipping from the praise of men, while the years increase the millions who honor Mahomet. There is such a for the principle of right and failing it!

"Even now," said Martha. The church always says that if only some one had been on hand to trust the God principle. Why did not the church herself have the faith? It is a working principle. Why not exercise it? Jesus tarried away, hoping they would realize that the truth of God is never absent as a livesaving certainty. They had heard Him tell that they must speak true words as intensely as they feared or grieved. Fear and grief are intense feelings to which the world sets fearful and grievous words. Thus the fruits are grievous. No matter how much grieved you are, never say, "I am grieved." The grief is a fertile soil for such words, and grievous things come up quickly to you if you speak such appropriate words. Say, instead, "In my idea of good there is no grief." A wonderful change of mind will take place which will be a forerunner of good tidings.

Martha assured Jesus that she expected Lazarus to rise at the "last day." Why at the last day? Why not now? "Now is the accepted time" with the Good. A hospital patient was told to wait till after death for her cure by pious physicians, but one who believed that Lazarus ought to be raised today cured her this side the tomb, and she rejoices to know that there is a difference between a great idea believed in and doubted.

"I am the Resurrection," said Jesus. Anybody who believes in the life and goodness of the principle he advocates will demonstrate it. He will be so at one with the principle he advocates that he will not know the difference between himself and it. Jesus advocated the power of a right confidence to change the particles of our bodies into a transcendent substance incapable evermore of seeming to die.

"Believest thou this?" Martha told Him that the expected Messiah would do this. This idea of a Messiah had got mixed with the sight of the Roman conquerors. They wanted someone who would trample on the living necks of their enemies till they were dead. But this Messiah who had come in answer to the prayers of the saints had refused to take away life. "I came that you might have life ... more abundantly." I did not come for your honors, your social distinctions, your favors; I came to tell you how to trust God for your bread and home and health.

Then "Mary" came out and wept and spoke exactly as "Martha" had. "Mary" represents the modest laymen who always do exactly as the preachers and bold workers tell them to do, but who have a better trust than their leaders. It is their very simplicity of faith that leads them to do as they are told, but when they hear a principle they love it and verily wish "Martha" would let them act out their deepest convictions.

Then Jesus "groaned." He was indignant. He was to what extremity bondage to doubt of the good would lead. He spake within Himself some bold, good words to match the intense feeling. When your environments grieve or anger you, do not let your thoughts run down their gloomy track, but rise with the clear utterance of the conviction that has never been whispered by you. This is it: "there is good for me and I ought to have it." The bird says this and flies hither and yon, and the stones look up and around for the good they know is theirs by right. The galley slave believes this and the prince reels through the banquet halls to find it. Just as soon as the idea has utterance, that which is for you

Will rise the hills and swim the sea

To fall, fair sunshine, full on thee.

The stenographer at her keys and the sewing girls at her dull task must speak forth this long-chained conviction, speak it boldest when the hours are blackest. The streetcar man and the cash boy - kings are they all, and into their inheritance they begin to come with the utterance of the confidence of their hearts: "There is good for me and I ought to have it." There is infinite fullness of good for you, child.

Roll away the stone of belief in future good. Say, "Now." Don't be afraid to speak intensely; "I do not believe there is any power in the universe can keep me away from my good."

"Martha" objects to hopes being raised and says that if the child you pray for should live he might grow up a drunkard, or that prosperity might spoil him.

Jews believed that an angel dropped a bit of gall on the people whom death had covered. Death is nothing but the fruit of doubt. This is the preaching of resignation to disappointed hopes. Don't you be resigned to evil of any kind. Throw it out of your faith. Refuse traditions. Refuse to hear anybody who says the worst is good.

There are beautiful ways for God to work. Do not believe that a railway accident has harmed your family though all the papers say so. Get their rooms and table ready. Roll away the stone. Give thanks that you have faith in the action of the good and do not believe in mixing your ideas of good with any kind of evil. Then call to them to come home. The low lands will answer, "Coming" and the uplands will cry, "We come." For omnipotent love hears the prayer of faith. "By faith the dead are raised." Faith is only confidence in the action of a principle as sure as mathematics.

You believe that water will run downhill. Well, "Let the Lord be thy confidence. He will not suffer thy feet to be taken." Loose Lazarus from his grave clothes when he is risen. Loose the maimed bodies of your loved ones from the murmurs that they are not returned home as sound as they went away. Loose your partial cure which came in answer to prayer from

your complaining that it is not all restored.
Praise God for what has come so far forth.
Hold fast what thou hast,
Then they will soon be "every whit whole."
The morn swings incense silver gray.
The night is past!
No priest, no church can bar its way,
The night is past.
The spirit and the bride say come. Come
boldly up and drink, thirsty heart.

October 4th, 1891

BIBLE LESSON XIII. John 12:20. GLORY OF CHRIST

Last Sunday you ought to have read "There is good for me and I ought to have it" in that line which said, "This is good," etc. The sewing girl at her task and the cash boy running at orders of another human being must not say, "This is good," for that is the old teaching of resignation to What we do not like. The white stone of revealing is, "There is good for me and I ought to have it." Keep this omnipresent, omnipotent truth going in your mind and you will be a magnet for success and joy.

"Also you must read "grief is a fertile soil" instead of "futile evil," for if you put a strong truth into your feeling of grief the union of the word and the feeling will make a fertile soil for a great good to grow up in. For Grief is the call for a bold statement of faith in the good.

This lesson tells you what to do when, having espoused a great principle or determined to cast yourself upon your righteous motive to take you safely through, you find yourself persecuted and lightly esteemed by the people among whom you have east your lot, and are invited by another class of people who recognize your greatness and your goodness to come and be identified with them.

The Jewish church was the chosen field of Jesus. It held Him as a bright, headstrong young fellow who, though a carpenter, might have done well and been considered of some account if He had not got into such strange notions.

The Greeks Who came to Him at this time came as representatives of the worship of externals carried to the highest ultimates.

Many thoughtful Greeks had felt that there was something radically Wrong about the worship of beings with the appetites and passions and frailties of mankind, even though such beings did inspire the genius of a Phidias; so they had turned to the Jewish worship of the God of Abraham, Isaac, and Jacob.

The Jehovah of Abraham was the provider. There should be no lack when this God was trusted. The Jehovah of Isaac Was the defender. There should no ill befall when this God was trusted. The Jehovah of Jacob was the principle of righteousness. There should be no failure Where this God was trusted. Jehovah-jireh. Jehovah-nissi. Jehovah-tsid kenu. One Lord and His Name One.

To cast yourself on the Good as your Provider would be sure bounty. To cast yourself on the Good as your Defense would be sure protection. To cast yourself on the Good as your Rewarder would make every good action and word its own justification.

This principle seemed, indeed, a more reasonable lawgiver than Olympian Jose, with his ivory limbs, gold draperies and eyes of jewels, or Minerva with her immortal beauty. A principle with unvarying laws was greater than an unreliable god of the clouds. This was the way the Greeks felt.

To be a Daniel with the understanding of this Being of power was more worthy than to be a Phidias. For Phidias had no safety from lions' jaws and angry kings, while Daniel was safe as a babe in its cradle though such terrors folded him.

One step towards independent thinking always compels the next step and makes it easy. It is such a joy to find yourself thinking, as is reasonable to yourself instead of as somebody has told you. A Universalist who was snubbed by the Methodists, Baptists, Congregationists a few years ago, is sure to take every new thought and look it straight in the face.

So the proselyted or converted Greek Went to see Jesus, the young Jew who was faring so savagely at the hands of the high churchmen. They were interested in His extraordinary claims, making Himself equal with God, and telling even the common fishermen that they were as great as Himself. They were attracted by the reasonableness of the doctrine that one may be so one With truth that he calls himself Truth - may be so in love with Goodness that he is lost in the omnipresence, omnipotence, omniscience of Goodness.

They recognized the teaching as exactly adapted to fascinate the philosophical Greeks, as an ethical culture with spiritual potentialities. So they formally invited Him to be a recognized teacher of spiritual ethics.

Philip and Andrew presented their claims as a formal committee. Philip was the one who told Jesus that there were 5,000 people and that 200 penny-worth of bread would not feed them. Andrew was the one who counted up that five barley loaves and two fishes were all they had on hand.

So Philip, true to his character, told what a noble way of living his Master was worthy of; how highly His genius and talents would be appreciated; What wonderful libraries, handsome estates, and dignities would be His if I-I would go among the Gentiles. Why He might be even more highly regarded than Apollonius of Tyana-the companion of Princes.

Andrew reminded Him that there were so many teachers of high repute among the Jews that even though He (Jesus) might have a doctrine greater and truer than them all, yet He would stand no chance in His lifetime of being anything among them; said they had been treated dreadfully and had made only a very few converts. It would serve the Jews right to leave them. But Jesus knew He was the answer to the prayers of the pious prophets and noble mothers of Israel, whose hearts had been true to the true God in the midst of temptations.

They had been the only ones to hold on to the Being of love and goodness unchangeable. The promise had been that ten men out of all nations should lay hold of the skirts of the Jews, for they had always had God with them. He knew this promise and knew His doctrine as its fulfillment.

He called it His glory to stand there in His lot until the end of the days. He recognized the treatment of the Jews as the greatest proclamation possible to call attention to His teachings. Nothing tempted Him from the sight of this law whereby all nations should be beckoned on. He hastened the coming crucifixion by saying, "The hour is now come."

He knew the law of the hastening power of those words which state that a thing is already come to pass when it is not yet seen. An epileptic man cured himself in a few minutes, forever, by ecstasy: "Praise God I am healed!" when he had not any intimation of being healed, but had this law of saying that it is finished before you see it so.

Jesus did exactly the same way on the cross. Before it was apparently finished He said, "It is finished." He never saw the transactions going on with their eyes for a moment. It was all success and glory to Him. The Christian scientist who is true to his affirmation that the good is working with him and through him and by him and for him, does not see or hear anything but good, while the rest see evil. He will not let his idea of good get any mixture of evil.

Why the international committee chose as the title of this lesson "Death" when it is all about Glory is a wonder. Jesus Himself was prophesying glorification, but they say He was prophesying death. God cannot be anything but glorified. Remember this. He here tells them by this mention of the grain of corn that unless We put our living truth right down boldly into the hard, ugly experiences of everyday life and let that truth defy and deny and push away the material seernings to show its omnipotence, we shall be forced to go out of this world Without demonstrating What great power over environments we have. He explained that the world around us must show back to us our highest ideals, but unless We boldly proclaim the truth it will not. We must announce a principle of action and live it out. Hating the temporary notions offered by emoluments and dignities we are most prosperous by loving our principle.

If you were asked to rent your corner block to a rum seller for three times the rent a Methodist or Baptist bookseller Would offer you, you would not look at the first offer though you had not enough to pay the taxes and needed the money apparently. Shall you sell the land to the man when you know it will ruin him because it has depreciated and he does not know it? Can you trust the principle of righteousness to bring you out right? Shall you overcharge the man who does not know prices? One way is keeping your life; the other is hiding it. Earthly life or Ways count for nothing. Principle is everything.

"Shall I yield to these offers?" Jesus asked. "Never! I came to show men how to live the principle of righteousness - not by donating large gifts to orphan's homes, nor by building charity institutions, though these are Well enough, but by honorably and justly dealing with the fathers of those children."

"It is not by sheltering My physical body nor by protecting My name that I can show a man how to stand steadfast to his highest ideals, but by demonstrating the power of the spirit of man over every sort and kind of circumstance. I could have saved myself from every indignity to which I have been subject. I know the law of my ownership of all the earth. Forty days in the wilderness I studied this question for the nations; for the beggar, the prince, the priest, I know but one law."

Here he felt the principle of righteousness so strong within Him that it was the voice of God. A11 good men and women from Moses down through Gautarna and the saints have heard a living Voice speak when they have been stirred to the foundations of their being. This Voice proclaimed that It had always and would forever honor Itself when proclaimed. You do not need to fight for a great Truth. You have only to proclaim it. You need not fight evil. Speak Truth and evil falters and fails. Evil is a lie. Truth kills lies by its own quality. Evil fought is like the rock that resists the iron wedges driven by sledges, but yields to the wet Wooden wedge as it swells Within its bosom.

Sharper than steel is the sword of the Spirit,
Swifter than arrows the word of the Truth is,
Stronger than anger is love and subdueth.

Some thought this Voice was an angel. Others said it thundered. When you live up to your highest conception of right some will say you are a good person, but deluded. Others will say you do everything to show off your personality and get to yourself praise of mankind. He told them that the judgment of the world was now going to be that He was crucified; that His body was stolen and His doctrine was a failure because it would not demonstrate His own safety.

But He knew that whenever this deed was mentioned men would ask Wherefore He was lifted up, and then when it was explained that it was because He had preached the power of God the Good Spirit and the powerlessness of evil in every form that these men Would say He was right and they again would lift up the cross in their Way as He in His. The down beam of the cross is the saying, "There is no power in evil." The cross beam is," "The Good is all power." This shall be preached until every knee shall bow and every tongue confess the glory of Truth.

He told them to believe in Truth while it was among them. Whoever preaches the right of way of Truth and Goodness, he is right. Listen to him. Whoever says man and God are ONE, hear him, for mind is as great as it has courage to declare itself, and demonstrates its greatness to the extent it can lose itself in its declarations.

Do not believe in persecutions or death or failure. They are not your portion. You have a light within that enables you to know when a preacher is in the right. Walk according to the highest you know and your light will increase. The temperance Women, who, in their zeal for the rights of the home, got those pictures of diseased stomachs into the schools to show the effects of alcohol, have seen the strongest light of judgment shine which says that as a musician would have only perfect tones before his pupils so the teacher of life should describe only noble lives else our children will get like what they have heard described.

"Vice seen too oft, familiar with her face,

We first endure, then pity, then embrace."

The good is life described as unchanging, unending goodness. The eyesight and hearing will not fail when life is described.

Health teachings stimulate health. When this law of Truth is the light of the mind, the cities shall not need the sun, for God is the light. The material sun but symbolizes the light which the principle of righteousness makes within us. Our idea of good is our LIGHT. October 11th, 1891

BIBLE LESSON XIV. John 13:1. GOOD IN SACRIFICE

When one proposes to make sacrifice of himself in any way he must be sure to ask himself the question, "What good am I doing by this action?" For unless there is some actual good to be attained or achieved by doing menial or servile tasks it is the misuse of talent to put it to doing what others are better adapted to doing. Talent along any line should exercise itself to its highest expansion along that line and not intrude itself upon the domain of another without righteous cause.

Out of the action of Jesus Christ in washing the feet of His companions, a religious ceremony of Washing feet has come to pass among a certain sect. But if He meant by His action simply to teach a state of mind and not a ceremonial to be observed, we had better understand the mental lesson rather than the best method of washing our neighbor's feet.

Some people think that if we keep up the ordinance of the "Lord's Supper" we ought to keep up the ceremonial of washing feet. Some think that if we believe in the literal bodily healings of Jesus we ought to believe in the fastings He practiced as duties incumbent.

In any case if we have made up our mind that this Teacher was exactly right in everything He did, we ought to find out how much indeed of the letter of His life it is our duty and privilege to perform. If He meant that it is possible to get into a state of mind which will be a healing potency to others; and into a state of mind Where though of royal heritage we are willing to do the most servile services for our neighbors; and into a state of mind where spiritual ecstasy is wisdom and takes the place of eating; and that these states of mind are the desideratum of life, why we are one and all eager to attain unto them.

They intimate powers and immunities which are the summum bonum of human hopes. Was it the fasting, was it the eating, was it the washing, which He was teaching? Or was it mental status?

He said Himself that the flesh (or material performance] counted as nothing. ("Profiteth nothing") I.e., that it is sure to be right if the animus is right. There has been a great criticism of the idea that the motive is the justification of the action, as much as to say that a man with a very good motive might be loose in his conduct. No. That is exactly what he could not be. Right motive makes right action.

The right motive is the conviction in the heart that right is right. And this conviction of right has never been secured till it demonstrates right actions. "Conviction is not, properly speaking, conviction till it develops itself into action." One says that this law of righteous motive will not work in daily affairs. Would the righteous choose to have a set of china fired without breaking, keep the china pieces from breaking if there were air bubbles under the glazing?

Most certainly. You would become so intuitive by the idea steadily held that you must do everything well which you attempt to do, that you would discover a process of firing imperfect china safely and another process of perfecting imperfect china.

There is a law of right in itself which conducts to right actions. It is metaphysical to think only of the right itself. It is the highest schoolmaster.

Joshua did not know the first thing about that law of a body resounding when its keynote is struck. But Joshua was so sure he was in the right that he thought out a quick way to sound the keynote to the walls of Jericho till they tumbled down.

The missionaries on the desolate island were so sure of being in the right and were so confident in the power of goodness of their God that they flung the American flag to the breeze when the natives were about to slay them. This reminded the natives what a nation backed the missionaries. They never thought of the flag till they had prayed to God. Joshua never thought of the rams' horns till he prayed to the same God.

This God unto whom they prayed for such assistance will help us in the simplest maters. Nothing is too low or ignoble for God to be the worker. "Who sweeps a room as to his God makes all the act divine."

Joseph Cook said that Lionel Beale was wishing somebody would get back into the secret of natural law and upset what seems to have so much power against. The secret is understanding of God. The feet symbolize understanding. We must keep our understanding clear and speak such words as will wash or clear the understanding of our neighbors.

There are certain words which the mind can use that have the effect of clarifying it. The judgment can be trained to be exactly reliable by these thoughts. Jesus Christ taught the ideas that act so powerfully with the judgment.

Judas Iscariot had had an idea put into his mind that dulled or hid his judgment. This idea was that a sum of money in hand is more worthwhile than a steadfast kindness of heart.

The principle of evil is the devil sometimes, and sometimes it is many small devils. Then again, it is the vicious temper or the false idea. The whole claim might just as well be met by us now and faced up with the question, How much profit is there in it? How much power? How much satisfaction?

Jesus Christ called the whole claim nothing. "A lie," He said. There is nothing to the Whole of it.

The high church dignitaries were greatly afraid that the young man who made such stupendous affirmation of Himself and the fishermen would upset everything. And so He Would. They would soon find out that there was a greater among them, and no lesser. They would soon find out that there were no Romans, and no Jews, no high priests and no lepers.

All these were a lie of belief in a partial God. There is in reality no such being. A menial task like washing the feet is no lower than the blowing of Gabriel's trumpet. "There is one Lord (Law) and His name One."

Jesus preached this boldly and lived it just as boldly. He ate with publicans and sinners. He touched the lepers. He blessed sick women. He washed men's feet. Having proclaimed the principle that all are one He must act it out.

He told the commonest kind of mixed audiences to have the faith of God. How could they have the faith of God? In order to have a faith equal to God's faith they must certainly have the courage to omnipresence, omnipotence, omniscience.

Somewhere there was a teaching then, dropping around into whatever soil would receive it, to the effect that the mind is as great as it has courage to and demonstrates its greatness to the extent it has confidence in its affirmations.

Knowing this truth, you see, Jesus could not ask them to any less of themselves than He knew they had a right to. He was not perceiving their flesh. He was not examining their intellect. He was recognizing their divinity.

Napoleon Walked over the French generals by affirming his power to do so and handled them like chessmen because he had the self-conviction he could do it. How high have you affirmed of yourself. How much courage in affirmation have you sprung to?

You have the teachings of Jesus to the effect that there is no substance to you except Spirit. And Spirit is God. Whatever you give voice to you may be sure you will expand to its stature. Would you not like to forget all things except your omnipotence, omniscience, omnipresence? Then do forget all things in the affirmations of your spirit.

Now there is a law of the effect of a truth told which makes it seem as if you had to face up evil appearances after you have spoken very highly of yourself with your mind. Grief, anger, disappointment, failure appear just like these natural consequences of Jesus and Judas and the high priests meeting with such different affirmations. You must make a firm soil of character by a declaration of faith, after which the most servile duties will be ennobled by your doing them.

In the midst of your anger, or grief or disappointment utter this idea intensely, "I do believe that my God is now working with me, through me and by me and for me to make me omnipresent, omnipotent, omniscient."

Directly your mind will take a new base. The experience will be exactly like the precipitating of camphor when water is dropped into the alcohol holding it in solution. Your mind now fixes its faith. After your faith is grounded your words will bring to pass wonderfully.

You remember Jesus Christ did not say, according to your denials, or according to you affirmations, but according to your faith.

Here at this point of the knowledge of His greatness, the faith in His greatness, He was as meek as a slave of the Orient, faithful as a mother to her baby; He Washed their feet. The greater the sweep of His affirmation, the lower His condescension of love.

You often see that in great and able men there is less ostentation than in those pretending to be great and not believing in their greatness. Von Moltke attended a peasant baby like a good brother while its sister who had it in charge went to see the king and the great General pass by. When she was disappointed at not seeing Von Moltke in the crowd he invited her to the hotel, where he appeared in full uniform.

A small would not have done it unless he had believed in his own greatness of spirit. Then if the small officer had so believed in greatness of spirit he would soon be taking the honors of Moltke. It is such a glorious knowledge to enter into: that we are as great as we have courage to expand into (or of ourselves) and can demonstrate as much greatness as we believe in.

He who taught us of our inheritance of power, our kingly heirship, taught us meekness and docility. Fidelity to any task is the exhibition of God. The understanding of Peter needed washing or clarifying. His pledge to the ministry was already being well carried out (hands) so Jesus did not Wash his hands and head. Once he recognized the Messiah he had not to recognize Him over again, but only to understand His teachings.

Here are the cleansing waters for your understanding: "In my good there is no mixture of evil. On my spirit there is no burden. There is no absence of life, substance, or intelligence." There is nothing to hate. "There is no sin, sickness, death in my idea of good."

Now you may make the highest affirmation your courage will spring to. You are already it. Have faith in yourself. Do the loyal service of true greatness. Right in that lot where you are called to serve is the chance to exercise your talent. What lies nearest at hand, do bravely. An artist may be sending the glory of living pictures into the imagination of some bedbound child while she tends the baking in her country home.

No genius is lost to the world because its fame is not yet emblazoned. The high preparation time is thinking your highest while doing lowest tasks. Tasks which require no thought give time for the noblest thoughts. See how the doctrine of this Servant of men comes quickening our hopes today. As great as you have courage to mentally proclaim yourself and sure to demonstrate as well as your faith in your greatness, decides! Therefore have faith in God. Have the faith of God. There is no se1f — sacrifice. "I am myself now and I know myself. My highest idea: I am it!"

So is every heart that knows the right, And choosing it, rejoices That what it thinks is true. "Itself is that." October 18th, 1891

BIBLE LESSON XV. John 14:1. POWER OF THE MIND

Jesus Christ said to His people when He was about to go away out of their sight and they were deeply troubled about it, "Let not your heart be troubled. . . . I go to prepare a place for you. . . . The Comforter Whom the Father will send in My Name shall teach you all things."

His command at this particular time to these disturbed hearts is evidence of His knowledge of the supreme power of mind over the most intense feelings. He evidently did not believe in letting the passions master mankind, even thought the recognized leaders of thought were teaching the world at that time that since the passions are masters of mankind and not mankind of the passions there is no way of ridding ourselves of the passions but by annihilation.

Look at the man torn by jealousy: who is the master, himself or jealousy? Look at him under the wind of anger; who is master, the man or anger? To live thinking this is not life, therefore let us be rid of life. But Jesus of Nazareth paid no attention to sophistries. He knew that every man is as great as he has courage to declare himself and will demonstrate as much greatness as he has confidence in his affirmations. "I am myself now that I know myself. My highest ideal — I am it! So is every heart that knows the right, and choosing it, rejoices that What it thinks is true — itself is that."

He had already taught them of their equality with Himself, and here again He reiterates that He and His Father are in them and that if He goes out of their sight and mind as a man of flesh and blood they will be so thrown upon their own indwelling spirit that they Will better realize their power and greatness. He did not believe in greater and lesser. He believed in universal equality through universal recognition of the truth concerning the impartial God indwelling everywhere.

There is nothing more heart — breaking than separation from those you love best. There is nothing more despair-filling and frenz — stirring than to see the failure of all your cherished plans, your earthly hopes and ambitions, with abundant evidence that even your religious aspirations will never be realized, and nothing of your teaching will demonstrate what you have proclaimed. This was the state of mind of those men the Master was talking to.

Those Jews who had given up their old form of faith for the one He taught, and had publicly espoused Him and His cause, were now told that He was to be crucified as a malefactor in the utmost disgrace. They were told that He would leave them to the companionship of a being or principle of action which they had never seen, viz., the Holy Ghost. Their hopes had been raised to the highest pitch of enthusiasm that their Messiah would conquer the Romans and set Israel free. They hoped for the noblest prosperity of His teachings. His triumph would be their triumph. They wanted to see the old church converted to their Teacher's doctrine of the unreality of material things and the reality of Spirit. They hoped to see their Master's announcement that the devil is a lie from the beginning prevail — not so much because it was true, but to triumph over the rest.

They were sure in some mysterious way that all things seen and touched are but symbols of What is real, and as their chosen leader was making great demonstrations in explanation of how the wonderful healings were performed by the miracle workers of all ages, they wanted to see Him succeed.

He made God seem so real to them, so near, so mighty to save, so substantial, yet evidently they loved the man Jesus better than they did the God He preached. There had been a great many strong minds teaching that ideas are the only real things, but at present Jesus was more comforting than an idea of one.

Their love for Him was intense. Their reverence for Him was unbounded. Their confidence in His power was stupendous. So their disappointment at the way things were turning out had troubled their hearts with anguish. It was the opportunity of Jesus to give them to best lesson is self-treatment that He had ever given. It is very good to know how to treat ourselves so as to be in no need of a physician. It is better to understand self-cure than to rely upon the best doctor in creation. The effect of disappointment and grief is disease, Waste of property and finally death. Socrates had taught this law long before Jesus Christ. So right here was the chance to handle the cause of poverty and disease before it had resulted in anything — while it was raging.

Political disappointments, social humiliation, religious despair: He told them not to let these feelings have any place in their being. He said He had their highest good at heart, and unless He went away they would never step forward into their rightful place at all. They must know that it was totally unscientific to lean upon any man, woman, or child for strength, power or advancement. He personified all their thought of leaning — all their inclination to depend upon something or somebody, and not until they put Him out of their mind as a personal being would their mind spring forward into its rightful place.

They had stood back and let Him in person, not principle, fill all their mind, till He was their support, their teacher, their defender, and the principle He taught was lost sight of. They literally must step forward in their own estimation as Spirit. They were in substance self-increasing and self-supporting, self-defending and self-rewarding. "My mind to me a kingdom is."

It is better to love principle than persons. If we love principle best we find ourselves growing in strength, or, rather, showing forth that strength which we always had. We find ourselves showing forth better and better judgment. We find ourselves more and more the personifications of fearlessness. If we love persons best we find ourselves swayed more or less, swerved more or less from our highest judgments.

Such is the effect of dependence upon people for our happiness, or support, that, even while we are not with them, the thoughts they are thinking cause our fears and tremblings, our elations, and depressions, which seem so unaccountable. There is no dependence to be placed upon one who is good because his love for or his fear of his companions make him so. When a stronger love or a stronger fear stirs him he will go its way. Your child kept from tobacco simply because he is afraid of you or loves you is not safe. There is a Way of teaching that will make the love of right in the heart, and all the tobacco stores and saloons in a great city would be no temptation.

It is better to learn this teaching than to deal with people. There is a Way of thinking in the secrecy of your own room that will cause the shadows of temptation to fall away as nothingness. The Word of this principle is omnipotent. Temptations flee. Appetites fall. Anger is forgotten. It is the

Word of Truth concerning the Spirit of mankind; the responsive, noble Spirit, indwelling everywhere.

"If I make my bed in hell (send my word down to the worst seeming of evil) Thou, God, art there."

Sharper than steel is the sword of the Spirit. Swifter than arrows the word of the Truth is. Stronger than anger is love and subdueth.

This does not mean that you are not to love your friends and your family. By no means. But it does mean that your love is a sentimental feeling, not capable of withstanding the pressure of some temptation peculiarly powerful over you, till you are grounded into principle first.

"Principle is God. Seek first the kingdom of God and all these things (friends unfailing, goods abiding) will be added." To Jesus, religious supremacy, political victory, social honors, counted for nothing except they were the outshowing of a true principle proclaimed and lived. He knew that a church that is held together and owns its memberships by reason of the personal influence of a man is on a shaky foundation. A government that trusts its name and honor to one whose name and honor are not synonyms of a mighty principle is laying a foundation of quicksand.

God is awake — alive. There is no social prestige, attainable worth noticing if it is secured by your personal magnetism, your natural possessions, your education, if you do not stand to your companions as the exponent of some worthy cause which is the principle you live.

When a great preacher is careless about his many obligations, or keeping his engagements, and is a respecter of persons, there is a screw loose in the future prospects of the church. They saw in Jesus the man their ambitions fulfilled. They must see in the principle He preached the glory of the world.

"Ah, but," you say, "you would not have us entrust a ship in a storm to a man simply because he was good when the captain who is recognized as a bad man understands ailing? You would not trust the government to a good man when the bad man is the better statesman?" The ship is not safe if the captain is not upright, and the government will court downfall from its deliberate choice of an immoral statesman. What do you think of that time when the fair ship on smooth waters Was sailing so peacefully under its notedly good captain, and a lover of God suddenly came to him in the night and urged him to steer the ship straight north? The captain laughed at him but upon his appearing three times during the night with the same entreaty, finally did turn the ship, and was saved from the iceberg floating down from the north, preparing the meet the ship at right angles.

What do you think of the ship in the hurricane with her greatly trusted captain and trained crew utterly hopeless, when the man who dwelt in the midst of the principle of righteousness said, "Turn this Way," and at once they were swung into that center of peace which is the heart of the cyclone, the hurricane, the simoon, the whirling suns?

This principle of goodness trusted, regardless of external fitness, is the government which shall "reign from sea to sea and from the river to the uttermost parts of the earth."

"Of its kingdom there shall be no end." Under its reign no mother will die, no child meet with accident. Love and trust this principle and all things that you can ask, better than you can imagine, will

Rise from the deeps,

Sail over the seas And down from the stars

Haste, the nations to please.

Jesus had taught these people this law of trust in the right: trust in the good itself. But no, they crowded their human relations, Himself included, into their heart so tightly that they were even then losing sight of the principles I-Ie announced. They quarreled as to who should be the greatest in the kingdom of heaven — greatest in the Spirit! They forbade children, women, beggars, to get near their majestic leader. But He said all were equal in God. He spoke of the sure goodness of children. He called the despised Women daughters of God. I-Ie asked the beggars tenderly What service He could render them, touching the lepers as though they were princes.

He trusted to the principle He proclaimed to hold its own. He preached eternal life and trusted the principle itself to take Him safely through. He trusted to goodness itself to feed and house and clothe Him, and laid Himself so hard to the Winds of His teaching that it did feed, clothe, house Him.

Hero Worship is not good. It is that for which the heroes stand that we Worship, then our love for them is healthy. He knew that the noble thoughts and trust in God of ages of goodness bloomed in Him. Did not the poetic feelings and unconscious observations of the past of Anglo-Saxon human experiences find expression in Shakespeare? So Jesus Christ was the bloom into manifest life of the confidence of all who had lived before Him, that goodness is safer to trust than human skill. E1isha's confidence in his God as able to do mighty works had turned away from the gates of Samaria the armed besiegers, when the King and his lords had failed. Worldly policy had starved the people, but trust in God put fine wheat and sweet barley into their fingers.

Where did the wars and the famines and the pestilences (Worldly policies carried out) spring from? But Jesus was the fruit of trust in God. His teachings would save from all evil. To watch flesh or material processes is deteriorating. To say that Spirit is the only substance, we do not believe in any law but the Spirit, is increasing in health, increasing in judgment, increasing in prosperity. Shall We not hear this Man teach that even to look at Himself as a Man is to forget principle, and either get to hating or loving without judgment?

Dante was looked at as a person trying to put his fame up, and they ignored his principle and exiled him; Socrates likewise; Columbus the same; also Bruno, Galileo. Cleopatra was personally adored, and her people were slain at her whim, smiling at her with love. But principle studied, loved, obeyed, puts us into our right mind — the place prepared for us. There is room enough in omnipresence for us to spread the Wings of our love over all the earth. There is power enough in omnipotence for our spirit to conquer the elements. Principle studied increases us to be one with it. So Christ comes again as doctrine, principle, spirit, and makes His abode in us as God, and then there is no taking away of our joy.

There is no oneness with Christ until we understand His teachings. The love of the personal Man is not what He taught. He took that away for the principle of righteousness to be first in our mind. He lives and reigns as an eternal teaching concerning the dominion of goodness. There is nothing to expect from human statesmanship, religious supremacies, social elevations. All things to expect from putting all these things out of mind to understand the principle of righteousness, as to its power, its efficiency, its swift — coming to conquer. This comforts. And the Comforter is the Holy Ghost. October 25th, 1891

BIBLE LESSON XVI. John 15:1. VINES AND BRANCHES

It is the nature of vines to put forth branches. It is the nature of mind to put forth thoughts. Every thought of the mind bears fruit after its kind. The mind of Jesus Christ thought only pure thoughts, so all His Works were perfect. Every thought the mind thinks personifies in some circumstance, or thing, or human being before our eyes. No two people see the circumstance, or object, or person exactly the same. Each mind sees its own belief about the matter. When we all believe the truth we shall all see everything exactly as it is. John, James, Matthew, Philip, Peter, etc., all stood for true ideas in the mind of Jesus.

John represented His tenderness. James personified His strong word that He so often spoke to others. Matthew stood for His benevolent thought; he never failed to speak when a case could be best reached by being benevolent toward it instead of strong, or tender, or argumentative. "Find out men's wants and will and meet them there."

Philip was His swift Word. Some of our thoughts go instantaneously where We are thinking. See how quickly Philip ran towards the eunuch in the chariot of the Queen of Ethiopia and converted him in no time. Peter stood for the idea that people want substantial help like bread and meat and health and shelter, rather than promises of comfort in a future paradise. All these ideas are good ones and Jesus Christ said that was because His mind was so true. "I am the true vine." "My Father is the husbandman." My good judgment keeps me from thinking anything but truth. Husbandman always means good judgment. There is only one side of the question when good judgment handles your vine (that is, your mind and its thoughts).

There is no power given to evil at all. All thoughts of feebleness or weakness or inefficiency are lopped off and burned up. You have nothing to do with them. Did you ever have a good, kind feeling towards anybody, and when you saw them sick or crying you pitifully wished you could do something for them, but felt powerless to do what they needed? If you had understood this lesson well you would not have felt powerless, you would have known that your kindly feeling towards them contained within itself the ability to draw from the very forces of the universe all the help they needed to them.

That kindly feeling put into a definite Word whether silent or audible should be pruned of the useless twig of helpless feeling. Euripides said, "One right thought is Worth a hundred right hands." So it is. The thought that backs the action is What wins.

Abraham Lincoln spent a Whole night putting forth his loving kindness of heart over the universe to bring help to what he considered a righteous cause. And the principle of loving kindness in the universe stirred as waters stir when we throw a stone into them, and the loving kindness in every heart was stirred, aware or unaware of what moved it to respond, "we're coming!"

The captain of the Monitor hastened, he knew not why, the unpromising boat stirred as though it were alive, and the crews fired the airs to victory. He would not take no for an answer. He would not receive any other action from the universe but loving kindness. Loving kindness in the heart put forth into the airs of loving kindness will Wake the echoes again and again till everything that can help your neighbor comes hurrying to help him. There is plenty to help him with. Get it. You get it if your refuse to feel helpless. Does not the vine that is pruned draw rich sustenance? Mind is all. It will turn the hands and train the voice and trim the actions to success. A man on a desert island cast away with the rest of the crew of a ship took the thought, "Living Water," into his mind instead of describing how thirsty he was. It was very hot and they were dying of thirst, but while the rest were putting the forces of their minds into describing their thirst, their heat, their misery, he put the whole force of his mind into the Words, "Living Water, Living Water!"

These words caused his hands to seize a spade or shovel, and these words caused him to begin to dig, while his companions' words caused them to lie down in despair on the hot sand.

They derided him, but he did not notice. The words of his mind mastered everything so did theirs. But you see his words were very different from theirs, even under the same circumstances. "By thy words thou art justified." Michelangelo never noticed how rough or how hard the marble was — he Was thinking of the image. This man struck the Living Water and it was so deep that they had to help him out or he would have been drowned they said.

You must trust the loving kindness of your heart. Can you not say, "Loving Kindness, in you is sufficient help!"

You do not remember you have no money, no influence, that people have thought you too sympathetic; all you think of is the omnipotence of loving kindness. This is a possible state of mind. When a child or companion seems to get into Wrong ways Why do you droop and cry when you know that there really is a little struggling hope in your heart that he will do better some time?

That very hope is the salvation of the loved one. Refuse every thought but your hope. Let all the force of your mind rally to trust your hope. Hope, even so little a streak of it, is better than ten thousand men at work to help you. Hope is the best beloved messenger of God. She was never yet killed. Men and women have shut down on her, tried to smother her, hid her deep in their bosoms, but, immortal defender that she is, she was never quenched yet.

Trust your hope. Never mind who tells you the particulars of downfall or disaster — trust your hope. It is a branch from the deathless soul that dwells in you as the true vine or true creation of God.

"I trust Thee, Hope!" Run all your energy into your confidence in your hope to lead you to success. "But it would have to be a miracle," you say, "to bring this state of affairs out to my satisfaction, for the situation is irretrievable, according to human judgment."

Who cares anything for human judgment? It is God's judgment that tells a Michelangelo there is a goddess, or a David, or an angel in the rough marble, and tells a man on the island that there is Living Water Where none was ever found before! There is not time or energy to be spent in crying. Lean hard to the Winds of your hope. Your highest aspiration is that which you are intended to fulfill, and if you have heretofore let any environments or circumstances sap your confidence in your aspirations, it is time you pruned your ideas.

Here Jesus Christ assures them that let His Words abide in them, they may ask what they will and it will be done. The student of astronomy would know more about the stars after an hour of trust in his hope to know, than after years of patient investigation of the heavens. Once an astronomer searching the skies in vain and figuring in vain, told one who knew nothing about stars his dilemma. The other was a firm truster in the law that "the Spirit will teach you all things." He responded quickly, an answer which the astronomer proved to be accurate.

Miracles are your birthright. That is what your hope tells you and your hope is correct.

You shall see every man, Woman and child saved if your goodness of heart will receive all your living forces. Here is a book Written by a man who scans material stars and reckons on the letter of prophecy, and he says that we are on the verge of destruction as an unbelieving race. We live in the last week of history. The "Holy Spirit grieved beyond all endurance" is about the leave us to face incarnate evil.

Now What does the husbandman of your mind — its good judgment, say of a Holy Spirit that gives up the fight so easily as that, when the prize to be won is the redemption of a race whose only crime is that they have listened to a teaching just like his, viz, that they must smother hope?

No. The sorrowful planet shall sing for joy and "the gates of hell shall not prevail against" the Truth. The worst of mankind is as entitled to the best of the universe as the best of us, for the worst of them have not refused to trust their hope (the one branch that puts forth from the soul again and again, even to the last breath of consciousness) any more than the best of us. "Herein is my Father glorified that ye bear much fruit." Not any little scrimpling achievements, but the safety of a globe is your mission. Did you ever trust a friend that what he told you of truth was true?

Listen. What hope tells you of truth is true. Trust her and you trust God. For she is the truth of God. Faith in her will quicken and quicken faith till the universe only shall be large enough to contain your faith.

Do you look longingly for mankind to be just — for goodness to prevail? That longing is the stir of the goodness in your heart. Trust that stir. She is hope unfurling her White wings. Assure her that you trust her. I trust thee, Hope! Come, goodness, come! "The nations shall learn war no more." "The wicked cease." Hope has been rewarded with all she ever asked of mankind, namely confidence in her. Over there in the business mart whither your trembling footsteps go tomorrow, fearing there may be disaster Waiting, stirs one little hope that a miracle may be wrought to save you? Tell that little hope you love it. Tell it you trust it. It speaks to the Principle of Bounty — God omnipotent, omniscient!" Hope has been more faithful to God than any messenger to man. Give her your trust, and she will Work any miracle you ask. "Ye shall ask what you will." "Have hope towards God."

"It shall be done unto you."

Bright drink the angels

From her glory,

Though none have scanned

Her glorious way!

Bright speak the words of

Her living story,

And over our star

Dawns her endless day!

"Henceforth I call you not servants but friends . . . for all things that I have heard from the Father I have told you." Now Jesus Christ is in them when they know all the words that He knows and they speak all that He speaks and they trust their words as He trusts.

The Comforter is that power that comes into your consciousness with the name Jesus Christ. That name is the saving Truth. You had better speak it until the same mind fills and thrills you that thrilled the only One who ever demonstrated supreme mastery over all kinds of claims of evil. "In My Name the devils tremble. In my Name the power of the Holy Spirit reigns triumphant. In My Name immortal life. In My Name goodness. I am the true vine. The way I begin to reign in you is when you trust your highest aspirations, your only hope, and prune boldly the tremblings of apprehension, of short — sightedness of prophecies of evil. Nothing shall prevail against Me," says Jesus Christ, in man the hope of glory.

November 1st, 1891

BIBLE LESSON XVII. John 16:2. YOUR IDEA OF GOD

The swift summary of text for our notice is Jesus Christ's prophecy: "Whosoever killeth you will think that he doeth God service, because they have not known the Father nor Me. It is expedient for you that I go away; for if I go not away the Comforter will not come. He will reprove the world and guide you into all truth.

When one is speaking of nature or the nature of man he either means the carnal nature, with its blind force, Whose operations bring earthquakes and cyclones, bloodshed and bondages, or he means that deep sense of righteousness implanted in every creature which John called "the Light that lighteth every man."

Two people speaking of the nature of man will greatly differ, and one will grossly misunderstand the other simply because the other is speaking from the standpoint of the spiritual nature while he is making conclusions from physical experiences.

One says it is the nature of man to think thoughts whose outcome will be corporations and Whose intentions shall be to make your daily bread impossible and your meat a thing of memory.

They insist that it is nature's exercise of itself in men which make them unjust toward women. It is natural, they tell us, to connive against the weaker when the stronger is pitted against it. Man is but following out his inherent nature when he makes sex distinctions, and laughs in his sleeve at the deserted wife, the hungry bird, the drowning baby, for does not nature's sun shine and her rivers run smiling on, indifferent to the welfare of men or angels?

Sweet and low the west winds blow,

Careless sing as they careless know,

How hearts were broken long ago.

Nature connives against the helpless, against Women, against minorities. "Therefore," says the English Lionel Beale, what is wanted is something to upset natural law."

It is well he puts into conscious expression the unconscious Wish of the World. It is the stir of the bird's wing for the air it was made to fly in, for truly they who would choose to see every creature on the planet glad and protected and powerful, stand ready to put their hand on the main spring of sorrow and say "Broken!" and their fingers to the clock of time of pain and say "Stop!" so soon as they shall know this law, so plainly taught in this lesson by Jesus. "He shall reprove the World and send the Comforter."

Another says, "There is no such nature to stop. The only nature there is that is real is the principle of righteousness stirring within all men and all creatures. The savages know what it is right to do. The hordes in the slums of London choose that the brave young men and the good young girl in the play shall come off victorious when trickery is pitted against them, else they will hiss the play." "This is nature," says one whose face is set that way till he sees nothing else. Pythagoras called it the salt of men in all ages. Plutarch called it the unerring guide; Socrates called it the Divine sign; John said it lighted every man that ever came into the world.

So One Man, determined to let this nature speak its own way with all its might, through Him, said in triumph, "All power is given unto Me in heaven and in earth." Then the rest seized upon Him because He, being a man like themselves, made Himself God. He carefully taught them the mortal shall not say, I am God. Only the immortal shall speak of its Godhood. But, looking at the flesh as the truth of themselves, they fought against the speech of the Spirit. The flesh warreth against the Spirit to this day when you two are speaking together. One of you insists that God does not send the cyclone and earthquake, the famine and the survival of the stronger. The other says; "He must, because He made all things, and surely we see that these things exist."

One of you says, "There is but one side of this question, viz., the God side." The other says, "There is the side of the law which sends evil as good." These disciples of Jesus were here being prepared to speak only from the standpoint of the Spirit of Good, when in after time men assail them with the claim of the power of evil. They could not speak entirely from that standpoint while a Man with infinite powers to protect and feed them stood near them, upon Whom they might lean.

He showed how by speaking and thinking entirely from the standpoint of the principle of right He could increase loaves and fishes and gold at their call. He did what the whole body of Jews did not dare to do with the moneychangers who, having got hold of all the Hebrew coins, made the people pay heavy premiums for half-shekel pieces. He put them out bodily and made them respect Him as a force He could demonstrate when He pleased. His disciples forgot the principle He announced in their admiration of its feats. So He Went away to throw them on their own understanding of Truth. They were beset by those who verily thought they were doing their God service by opposing them.

And truly if it was the God they believed in who ruled the world, they were right pleasing unto Him, for the god of the external world as described by those who see it, is glad when a Lisbon lies low and a Johnstown swims in tears.

But the true God is mercy, tenderness, and loving kindness. This is the God of Jesus Christ.

God is love. His mercy brightens
All the path in which we rove.
Bliss He wakes, and woe He lightens,
God is wisdom, God is love.

In Jonah's time "every man prayed unto his God." It makes all the difference in the creation to your powers and experiences what God you believe in and what you believe your God does.

Elijah had supposed God sent the cyclone and earthquake and famine, but being a sincere man his heart was in ashes of despair, just as every heart is that is mistaken in its suppositions about God; so he became silent, and found that the still small Voice counseling mercy and tenderness and freedom was the true God. Thus he had not been true to the true God in slaying the prophets of Baal at the brook Kishon.

Thus supposition about God, and not God indeed, had stirred to earthquakes and hot Winds of terror. The Roman governors and proconsuls afterward hunted the Christians to please their imaginary God, viz., the sender of calamities. They tied them to wild beasts and set them for bonfires in Nero's gardens. But, —

Speak, Victory! Who are life's victors?

Unroll thy long annals and say!

Are they those whom the world called the victors, Who won the success of a day?

The Spartans who fell at Thermopylae's tryst,

Or the Persians and Xerxes?

The martyrs or Nero?

Pilate or Christ?

I am my own idea of God. Nothing can be plainer than that 1 am my own idea of God, and you are your own idea of God.

The man who chases from the prize fight to the gambling hall believes in a God who chases him around seeing every evil thing he does and getting a punishment ready While he himself has things just as he pleases regardless of the feelings of others. Those who believe nearest in the true

God are safest. Those whose idea of God is absolutely true are absolutely safe.

What God do you believe in? What is your idea of God? John Knox had been thinking What a mighty fortress is our God when he found himself rising from his place at the table. A bullet came crashing through the window, but he was safe. Mungo Park thought of his God as his unfailing provider. But he forgot to think so at one time and was utterly destitute in the wilds of Africa. A little cheery tuft of live moss reminded him of its happy trust of his own God and as soon as he took hold of the true God again he was amply provided with all things. "Do you think" asked a pious believer in the God who sends earthquakes and famines, "that you can make an impression on 4,000,000 Chinese?" "No," said the Doctor, "but my God can." This God was different from the God of Louis XIV, for he compelled the Huguenots at the point of the bayonet by fire to destroy 700 churches because they did not worship as he did.

Richard Boyle, Earl of Cork, rose from the lowest position to the highest rank by taking for his motto, "God's good providence is my inheritance." A child living with a mother who had an idea that God sends poverty and want took it into his mind that God would hear every time they scraped the bottom of the meal barrel. And the child's idea fed them.

I am my own idea of God. It was a step ahead for the child to have an idea of God that He would not let them actually starve, but it is a greater step to have the true idea, viz., that God never lets His children have any bottom to their barrels of plenty. If the idea of Good is the mainspring of human experience, you have the power to upset the apparent order of things.

If your idea of God swings the clock to the time of pain and poverty you may stop it when you please. Jesus Christ told you to keep that affirmation of His till you should strike down the idea of God that throttles the nations.

"All power is given unto Me."

Jesus Christ had the true idea of God. God is Love. John said: "If a man love God he will love his brother also." Whatever your idea of God is what you will treat your family With. A mother who had an idea that God sends sickness for some good purpose blew the simoon of this notion against her little girl and she had typhoid fever. Then she besought that God of hers to remove the fever that her own idea was plowing like a hot Wind over the child. All to no purpose. Because she had an idea that God sometimes does and sometimes does not do as you want Him to. By and by she went into a room alone and took off her thought from the little girl and put up her thought entirely to the true God that His good will might be done and that she should see that good will.

Then the child got Well at once. The true God always wills well. Never anything else. Look out there at the mainspring of your world what you are doing! Do not let it be said of you as of Nero and that mother, "because they have not known the Father nor me."

Physicians sit in judgment on a man. They believe in nature's laws of waste and decay and death. "According to thy faith be it unto thee." So they blow their cold idea over the man. Yet when they should look away from him they would say that one with the true idea of God could restore him to health. While they are looking away he breathes better. Why do they not spend all their time and all their energies studying that law of the true idea of God that can always heal as Jesus healed? That idea that fills the mind touches other minds. Keeley the motor man has thought of force, We are told, till he can start a whole swing of machinery to working which the best mechanic cannot stir till Keeley touches him on the shoulder.

When the true idea of God fills the mind you shall touch shoulder to shoulder with all the universe of mankind till health and joy and peace reign supreme.

You must Withdraw your ideas of mankind being subject to natural laws of fire and frost, death and sickness. The true idea of God gives you the true idea of mankind. They shall feel your touch on the mainspring of the universe. If the child of his generation can stir the machinery of the factories by his idea of force you shall stir the nations by your idea of God.

Jesus Christ promised all things to them that should hold His Name in mind. His Name should forever stand for the true idea of God. The Comforter should come in His Name. The world should be reproved. Those who have held His Name in mind till it has gone away as man and has come in as the principle of righteousness, have seen those they meet change from foolish-appearing to Wise; from unsteady to reliable. "Whose findeth Me findeth life." "In Me shall all the nations of the earth be blessed." When we strike at the false idea of God and let the true idea live we are letting Jesus Christ live as He meant in us: not as flesh but as Truth. "And Christ lives on in His strength and glory. He lives and loves with a love divine. By the light of His Name I read life's story. And the key to the world is mine."

November 8th, 1891

BIBLE LESSON XVIII. John 17:1. MAGIC OF HIS NAME

Jesus teaches all about prayer in this lesson. He discloses His mission to the world, the mission of His disciples and your mission also.

Here He sets apart certain ones to devote all their time, energy, money, mind, life, to preaching the truth concerning the true God. Henceforth they should not be known among men as lawyers and physicians or fishermen, but as preachers of the peculiar doctrine of Jesus Christ.

Here, you observe for the first time, He calls the Name in which all the miracles of the future are to be wrought--Jesus Christ.

He had told them of the magic power of His Name. In it was contained the power of the Holy Ghost to comfort, heal, rejoice, prosper. By thinking His Name they were to be imbued with power from on high, and illuminated with great spiritual understanding.

It was customary in old times for miracles to be wrought by speaking certain names. They spoke these names inaudibly. They would not tell the name they used in some cases because the careless use of the name would not accomplish anything. Each name stood for certain powers and limitations of powers. It represented much. The Egyptians used Serapis, Osiris, Isis. The Indians used Buddha. The Persians used Ormuzd. Brainerd, the missionary to our American Indians, could not tempt them by the name Jesus Christ, because they had names that were miracle Working.

Constantine noticed that the names used by the heathen worked destruction more than life. He tested one of his magicians on a fierce bull. When the magician whispered one name into its ear the animal fell dead. The same name Whispered into the dead ear would not raise the beast to life. But a Christian, who had supreme faith in the name Jesus Christ, raised the animal to life instantly with that Name.

All those old practices which we have so long regarded as Worthless superstitions we are now finding out to be hints of the Way to our own demonstrations of power and goodness. He had told them to put out of their horizon their father, mother, husband, wife, children, that His Name might start the wheels of their mind and life over again. Did you ever try holding His Name in mind to the exclusion of all other names till its high significance as salvation from all evil came thrilling and quickening you with delight?

No? Then how can you judge as to whether He Was mistaken when telling the world that all its prayers should be granted in His Name?

You would like to heal all the sickness of the world, ease all its misery, rejoice all its hearts. You have tried many ways. Have your tried that Name till its significance as the demonstration of God through you Worked miracles? If you are eager to help the world — so eager that you would do anything, as you have so often said — try Writing this Name in every blood-drop and on every string of your heart.

He said you would be found preaching the good word without any mixture of evil (The idea of evil is the son of perdition. He taught that every son or word of His mind would demonstrate except the word of perishing, or devil word, the lie — from-the-beginning Word. The errors should not count.) You are to heal, stop vicious tempers, raise all who seem to be dead to life again. Then if you faithfully work at these things with His Name in mind you need not take any thought about what to eat, drink, wear, nor as to whom you shall marry nor what you shall lay up for old age. The four works will make the living on the square which will then draw around you the perfect circle of a beautiful and satisfied life.

And if you can demonstrate satisfactory living, you can teach others how to demonstrate. You must not only be sanctified yourself, but all the world must be as glad as yourself. "He lifted up His eyes." This is stated not carelessly. The Way the mind thinks will teach the Way the eyes turn. Take the man who is always meditating on high themes for his own sake, and he will look down. The man who thinks with his head down is apt to conclude to do things to advantage himself Whether others are advantaged or not. The man who looks straight ahead is one who gets on fairly well with the World and generally gets to feeling that he can hold his own with the world. He often gets philanthropic and wide-hearted. The man whose thoughts are on God as all, has an upward look of eyes that, Without being conspicuous, you catch while you converse with him. The man who brings all his help from above and acknowledges it, does not believe anything is impossible. The man who looks out straight towards the horizons, believes in great obstacles and names what he must meet. The man who looks down believes in submission to the existing order of things and feels that he must yield to the worst with as good a face as he can make up.

The Chinese teach certain kinds of people to sit in a circle and practice steadily looking up to a clear stone, that will drop down, sometimes, answers to their needs. A colored washerwoman had got the idea into her mind that "de good Lawd was a showerin' blessin's on" her from His seat in heaven.

A nice pious Woman told her with the corners of her sad mouth downcast like her eyes, that it seemed dreadful to her to see so much levity and lightness where there was so much likelihood of misery to come any day. "Supposing you are taken sick with rheumatism and can't Work; or supposing your employer dies?" she was arguing.

"Stop!" said the washerwornan, "I neber suppose De 'Lawd is my Shepherd 'n I shall not want.' And, Honey, it is yo'r supposin' as is makin' yo' so rnis'able."

Jesus Christ had just been looking around on them all. "I call you not servants, but friends." Then He took them as one with Him to the Holy High Place, where all His thoughts dwelt in exalted ecstasy and called down the healing glory of the God within Him.

All who have tried mental healing have found that an exalted state of mind or an ecstatic state of mind Where the glory of God is seen and realized as very near and real, is a sure healing state. Then it is found that it is very direct communion with this down-falling glory to praise and bless and glorify It. To thank It. To give all credit to It. Cromwell asked the House of Commons to give God the Whole glory of his victory at Naseby. Jesus Christ was praising God for the crucifixion, as to its outcome. He did not see the crucifixion: He saw the time when we should know Him as principle demonstrated, not as a man of flesh and blood. Whoever undertakes to be spiritually minded or to look straight to God for all things, will always come out successful.

The business man seeing God will find that when very bit of news brought to him is bad, every deal he makes slips up, his collectors run away with rents, etc., that at the end he has had more income than if all these had come out right when he was not seeing God nigh within the exalted place of his mind. Nor height nor depth nor any other creature can keep you from demonstrating success when you glorify God for His Being. Of course God is not in the ether of the sky. God is in His kingdom Within your mind. The eyes just signal or symbolize your way of thinking

Chrysostom was threatened with exile if he preached God in Christ Jesus.

"Thou canst not exile me. The world is my Father's house."
"I will slay thee."
"Thou canst not. God is my life."
"I will take away thy possessions."
"Thou canst not. They are in God."
"I will take away thy friends."
"Thou canst not. God is my friend."

A missionary in Russia was once Waited on by a court official to tell him that his Imperial Sovereign would not consent to his preaching Christ Jesus in that kingdom. The missionary said, "My Imperial Sovereign does not ask anybody's consent to send His good word through His own Kingdom."

There is nothing can Withstand your power of influence when you give God the glory of your life, your health, your possessions. Queen Mary feared John Knox more than she did an army of ten thousand soldiers. All good is from God. "I drew them with the bands of love, and they knew not that I healed them." Let us praise God who dwelleth in the high place of our own mind. Praise God for healing us before We see the healing. "I healed them and they knew it not."

Your bodily organs love to be praised. A thousand little mouths are stretching open Within you, hungry for praising. You must praise your heart for its sweet happy beating. Do you not know that its substance is God? Praise your liver for its lovely life and Wholesome working. Its action is God. "I drew thee with the bands of love, yet thou knowest not My healing." Even the stones will sing if you praise them. Many an inactive organ within you needs the oil of your praising to set it into happy action.

This is what Jesus Christ teaches me. Why, what a simple lesson it is! Praise! This is where you become like Jesus Christ, then your principle of action will win. Rest and Freedom are names of Jesus Christ.

A sperm Whaler believed in the Sabbath as God's rest for his men. He, as captain, refused to have his men work on the Rest Day. The mate threatened to have him dismissed. "God will be justified," he said. Then an awful hurricane came up, and down the mate got in terror, but the captain smiled and drew into a port where they never thought of such a thing as a cargo, but they got a full cargo in one third the time.

How can we help loving God? All my trust on Thee is staid.

All my help from Thee I bring,

Cover my defenseless head

With the shadow of Thy wing.

Spurgeon called $43,000 per year to his orphanage by asking God. That is the greatest honor you can pay the true God — the "one God above you and through you and in you all" give Him the glory for everything.

And the gates of hell are nothing against your fortress where God, the true God, is praised as the sender of all your blessings.

Another man saw the sweet freedom Jesus Christ had by having God so reign in Him, and he opened his art collection and hired a band for the villagers to come to his house Sunday evenings. The pious ones were horror stricken, but somehow, he remembered how Jesus Christ told the man to carry his bed home one time when even to wear heavy shoes was against the sabbatical law of carrying burdens and also bruised corn when even to walk in grass was prohibited. He saw that freedom was a name of God, not bondage to notions. So when a gale of financial stress struck his business what did those villagers do but rise like one man to help him out.

You see there is a principle of goodness that is better than regulations of man. Recreation is rest. Freedom is rest. God is rest. The true God makes you kind, merciful, trustful. This is life eternal to your hope, to your joy, to your friendships, to your loving. There is nothing to hate. You forgive everybody and everything. You give for the ugly pain a loving word: "I forgive you." To the sharp circumstance: "I forgive you." You have a reservoir of healing oil that you pour over the affairs of your daily lot, in "I forgive everybody and everything." Nothing to hate. Did you suppose there was any merit in your hating tobacco and rum?

Tell them that you forgive them. They will lose their stings. The sting of them is your hate. You have the power to take up any deadly thing and it shall not hurt you. Cannot God touch God and be undefiled? All is God. Hate nothing. The attraction of everything is God. Now that you know this, you will not be hurt by any of these things any more, will you? "The Truth shall make you free."

Today Jesus Christ prays for some in particular. Dear hearts, now and then you must be very, very definite in telling Whom you would have especially blessed and naming your particular request. Jesus Christ did this. God is not above helping you out of the tiniest little troubles. The buttercup is as softly painted as the tulip. Your blessing — name it at the foot of the throne Within the Holy Place of your mind.

"It shall be done unto you." And God shall wipe away your tears, and heal your heart. Today you may tell what you would like best for your beloved in your home.

I pray for these today,

My heart folds these today,

Speed busy world today,

For these I pray today.

November 15th, 1891

BIBLE LESSON XIX. John 18:1. JESUS AND JUDAS

Here there are two central characters figuring out the chief idea of human life. Jesus and Judas standing for the praise of prosperity. Prosperity or satisfaction is the chief aim of every creature that lives. Judas stands for the idea of getting prosperity by worldly methods, unspiritual, prosaic. He praises success. His very name means praise of success.

"Get money," he says, "honestly if you can, but get money." Jesus stands for the idea of prosperity by spiritual law, confidence in God, idealistic methods.

"There is but one way given under heaven," He says. His very Name means praise of success in understanding of the principle of goodness. There comes a time in the experience of every mind, every organized body, and the planet also when the two ideas are face to face, and here you see the demeanor of each and the merits of each with the prophesy of each standing boldly out on the canvas of human life.

Caiaphas means depression of spirits, or pessimism. Annas means the common lot of humanity as seen daily. Malchus means the outward action of Caiaphas and Annas, or how they act when given reign. Anarchy, nihilism, communism are the soldiers of the pessimism that steals over the mind of a man or planet when it has been conferring with Judas as to how to be successful in life.

As Jesus faced Judas, so the two plans of the planet are met today in face-to — face issue. God is my prosperity, or gold (the symbol of God) is my prosperity. Which? "My mind to me a kingdom is." When I settle the question for myself, I am either mastered by Jesus or Judas.

The planet has its nations, its tribes and peoples, which are its thoughts. Today it is called to settle the question of how it shall secure its highest good, or its prosperity.

There is a spiritual sphere enfolding and penetrating and permeating the planet. Above all and through all and in all is Spirit, lying close and filling full, as substance to shadow.

Every now and then somebody breaks out of the shadow and speaks from the sight of the substance. Sir Thomas Browne said, "The severe learning of the schools shall not take from me the idea that everything upon the earth is but the shadow of some substance lying nigh it."

Milton said, "What if the earth be but the shadow of heaven and things thereon each like to other more than on earth they seem?"

Balthazar the Egyptian is made to say, "There is a kingdom on the earth, though it is not of it; a kingdom wider than the bounds of the earth, though they were rolled together as finest gold and spread by the beating of hammers; its existence is a fact, as our hearts are facts, and we journey through this kingdom from birth to death without seeing it, nor shall any man see it until he hath known his own soul."

It is told by those who have shaken off the slumber of the shadow enough to speak plainly, that to look into this kingdom is to be free from all the bondages of earthly Ways.

They tell us that we may not seem to our neighbors and friends to be different in form or color or speech from themselves, yet that we may have the light of that Kingdom in our eyes and the knowledge of that Kingdom in our heart so truly that the promise of the Bible may be fulfilled in us, "When thou passest through the Waters I will be with thee, and through the rivers they shall not overflow."

"When thou passest through the fires they shall not burn thee, neither shall the flame kindle upon thee." "At destruction and famine thou shalt laugh." "Ye shall know the truth and the truth shall make you free."

Those who examine the shadows carefully, viz., the material universe, dispute the possibility of such things. They tell us we must not get too ideal in the face of facts. Their eyes are fixed steadily upon the seeming processes, and their hearts are heavy because the long night of sorrow, treachery, and dying promises no quick dawning, if indeed there ever is to be any change in nature's performances.

Among these there is always some John of the Apocalypse promising that in a far-off future there surely will be "no death, neither sorrow nor crying; neither shall there be any more pain, for the former things have passed away." But the sight of the shadows causes Schopenhauer to declare that there is no God, only a "gigantic evil evolving into good." He sees the sight of evil stretch so far ahead that there is only hopelessness in his heart.

What is the matter with Schopenhauer and his followers? They have conferred with Judas. They lived and longed for prosperity. They had a right to prosperity. But they should have conferred with Jesus.

Jesus said, "Seek first the Kingdom of God, and all these things (riches, and honors, and health, and love, and gladness) shall be added unto you."

Judas had told them that while they are in the world they must look to the World's way and meet it in its own fashion if they would be successful.

After conferring with Judas, hear the verdict of the boldest and most intrepid magazine of our age representing the summing up of the conclusions of centuries: "Europe is cankered and honeycombed with pessimism"

(Caiaphas was high priest that same year.)

"It needs no very long stay in Europe to detect a strange drooping of spirit."

"Neither Pope nor church, peace societies nor alliances can check its course."

"Schopenhauer and Von Hartman, with their black pessimism, lead the continent."

"Nothing in fiction or music is believed in by the world now," they add, *"except pessimism."*

Optimistic teachings are not listened to.

"Wagner, St. Beauve, Carlyle, Matthew Arnold, Scherer, Tolstoy and Ruskin are under the evangel of bafflement and despair." Metaphysics has caught the echo and assures us of a great unconscious movement of evil besides the apparent.

If you give Ruskin his sleep and his food and his shelter and his police defenses of the best, you cannot secure him from having his brain pummeled so that it will show how the invisible action of mind upon mind in deadly apposition can manage his destiny.

If the father is unjustly severe in his thought against his child it will have brain fever or diphtheria. "We wrestle not against flesh and blood, but against principalities, against powers against the rulers of darkness, says the metaphysician, who has conferred with Judas. "Be not afraid, I have overcome the world." "Your joy no man taketh from you." "Thou couldst have no power at all except I gave it thee." "All power is given unto Me." "I am in heaven." "Where I am there ye may be also." This is the conclusion of those who refuse to confer with Judas as to the best means of being successful, that even the earth and the fullness thereof are seen to be their own birthright.

All the forces of bafflement meet Jesus the teacher of spiritual law today. They feel angered against ideality and optimism.

And Jesus says, "Whom seek ye?" The drill sergeant answers, "The Nazarene." That is, "that ignis fatuous promise of God that has claimed to be something but is nothing." "I Am He!" The "He" is not in the Greek, and all those who stood by understood Jesus to speak from the highest Son of Man or Son of God — the God-man standpoint — I Am God "I Am;" to them all was the name of Jehovah.

Some have contended that Jesus did not speak of Himself directly as God. They give away their ignorance of Greek by so saying. Here He meant to show man's idea to be God's idea, when man proclaimed his highest.

Their idea of man was limited to their study of the shadow side. "Our days upon the earth are as the shadow that declineth;" we are "worms of the dust," was their doctrine. The common lot is sorrow.

His idea of man was of one with dominion over all things, death and starvation included: master and king and lord through spirit instead of subject and slave and cringing subject through believing in the power of matter over man.

When He said "I Am," the soldiers and officers immediately went backward and fell on their faces. The pessimist always falls back when the Christ faith looks him in the eye. In supreme moments many a man and woman has felt the God power rise and swell and burst forth. Eliza can take her baby across impossible icefloats. The Red Sea divides. All these things become possible. "Is anything too hard for Me?" A good man in a lonely mountain pass was assailed by lawless ruffians. As they came forward the glory of a Supreme Power sprang forth from him. It spoke through him. It was Him. "You cannot! I am God!" They fell back aghast. But then, as in this case they sprang forward again. "We will kill you for saying that!" But as he looked at them, they fled.

"Because thou being a man maketh thyself God."

At each stop of your Way "keep My words" and you will step out free from all these experiences I am taking. When pessimism, hardships, violence, threaten you, announce your spiritual nature at its highest. I AM! Jesus is very sure of victory for the spiritually taught.

"Let them go." He tasted all this hour which tempts your own mind and the mind of the planet. He knew His power through the Word. If We keep His words we will step into freedom.

No other teacher ever gave us a sure recipe for safety in time of danger, or for health in place of sickness. Plato said the world needed a teacher who should show man how to be master instead of subject. He had carefully noted that Socrates did not help him to master his environments and destiny.

Here you and I are shown that within the self is one thought, that if it be given utterance poverty and sorrow and failure will be no more.

Why should We let other thoughts come up and argue with us to prove our powerlessness when that one announced would prove our power? What an affirmation is demanded of man when Annas and Caiaphas and Malchus, incited by Judas, face him!

Hold your own! Hold on to the great Word! All the thoughts of the mind must join forces with the bold affirmation Jesus teaches.

All things you would see brought to pass wait the rise and swell and glory of the God within. Therefore, come boldly up and be steadfast. All matter quails. The earth is clean dissolved. Prospero shows that he had his thoughts under control, so that he could calm or enrage the seas at his will; but he knows not Jesus Christ. All to him is but the "baseless fabric of a dream" — easily dissolved. He was right, but he had nothing better to turn to. You have. Speak boldly.

Boldness hath genius, power and magic in it.

What you can do, or dream you can, begin it.

Let the old ways be dissolved like a breath when you speak from the true power you already possess. The true keeper of the words of Jesus Christ is the true Christian.

As a Christian you must expect miracles. If you do not believe in miracles take off the name Christian.

"Either change your name or honor it," said Alexander to a soldier named for him who had acted ignobly.

Ask much of the principle you serve. Ask richly. "He remembers that I am a king and should give like a king. Honor his claim," said a king of one who had asked so great a gift that the treasurer was afraid.

You must expect to open prison doors, feed the nations, raise the dead.

The King you serve is Jesus Christ in you, conqueror over all things. The Emperor Theodosius liberated his prisoners and cried out, "Would God I could open the graves and set those captives free."

Place no limitation on yourself," says the spirit of this lesson. Notice that Jesus Christ stood still at the place of His capture and set His people free. He stood still where He was and quelled the solders. He stood still where He was and healed the ear of Malchus. He stood still preaching when the officers could not take Him. He hung still on the cross and saved the thief.

Right here is the spot where you are called to live and Work — here is your place to demonstrate dominion.

"Away, says the fiend. Rouse up a brave mind, says the fiend and run." "No, my honest friend Launcelot Gobbo, being an honest man's son, budge not!" "Budge, says the fiend." "The fiend gives me more friendly counsel. I will run, fiend. My heels are at your commandment. I will run."

This is the plausible reasoning of those thoughts that would argue that you could do better in some other field than the one where you are.

What saith Scripture? "Stand thou in thy lot till the end of the days." Till What belongs to you to do there is finished.

Breathe California spices,

Roll blue Pacific waves,

Here open the paradises,

Here close for us the graves.

Felix of Nola, being hotly pursued, fell into a cave near at hand, and the spiders wove a web across it and the dews fell on it and on went his pursuers.

Right there Where you are, set the people free. Why should a thought within you depress you or discourage you? Are you not master within your own realm?

When depression at the sight or feeling of your own hard lot or that of theirs seizes you, announce your Jehovahship. Then you can handle your own thoughts.

Would you like to tell the law to stop making it possible for one man to own $150,000,000, while his next — door neighbor can hardly feed his children?

You can set that right in the world if you can site it right in your own mind first. The ideal of equal rights and equal opportunities is a Christian one. And Christ shall reign from sea to sea, and from the river to the uttermost parts of the earth.

You are the result of your own arguments, but you need not be the result of anybody e1se's arguments.

Though all around thee courage fail,

Do thou be strong.

Though all around thee doubt prevail,

In faith move on!

"Put up thy sword," said Jesus. And He healed the anarchist. They tell us that in Europe there is nothing heard of but "smokeless powder, small-bore rifles, heavy iron-clads, swift cruisers, torpedo boats, and dynamite guns." France and Germany have 6,000,000 soldiers armed to the teeth.

If any Christian Peter thinks to meet anarchy and nihilism with the World's weapons he is as foolhardy as Peter. "The weapons of our warfare are not carnal but mighty through God to the pulling down of strongholds." "Put up thy sword."

You need not describe the cancer spots of city life, nor scold the ministers for not going down into their midst and knowing what is going on.

Your own thoughts of powerlessness are all your accusations amount to. If you believe they can be cured you are the one who can cure them. Did God invest any minister of the gospel with more power or more opportunities than He invested you With? No! God is no such God.

You have no right to expect anybody to do what you are not already doing, and cannot teach them how to do. I Can! and I Am! is your affirmation. You do not need the city government, police force, nor public sentiment on your side; all you need is the agreement of your own thoughts.

"Shuffle off the mortal coil" of your own thoughts.

Give all thoughts the lie except that one which says, "I can stream like a flood of glory down into the dark places with my limitless omnipotent love, and I can feed and warm and love them. And I can go like an angel of goodness to the hearts of the banqueters and tell them how the God of them - the Christ in them — loves to give of their substance of their love, their wisdom. So I will tell them till I see the rich and the poor meet at one common table of knowledge of their own birthright of all things.

Did you suppose God is less God in the high gambler than in Jesus? No. But Jesus announced it boldly. If you do not declare your goodness and power and divinity, how shall you measure whether the gambler is worse or better than you? All he has done is to let his thoughts not divine, parley with the highest ideal just as you have.

He has listened to the Judas idea that he must practice the World ways to be successful. Have you ever parleyed in that way? Over the turbid waters of Cedron walked Jesus into the garden of peaceful thought.

Stop not to argue with the worldly wise, or the ways of the shadow. Look over them all into the peace country that is all around you.

The parched earth traveler shall be glad when he hears this doctrine that when he lets this I AM speak, his vain thoughts must fall back, and his bread and his milk and his honey shall never more fail.

The pale mother may feel the reviving airs of the hilltops of heaven blow across her brow with refreshment. She shall set her tired feet into the beautiful country where there shall be no more pain, neither sorrow nor crying, when she knows that Within her own soul is the key to glad living here and now by speaking the words that are true.

Therefore, let the high thought be born in whomsoever these teachings are received.

In the beauty of the lilies Christ is born across the sea,

With a glory in His bosom that transfigures you and me.

November 22nd, 1891

BIBLE LESSON XX. John 19: 1. SOURGE OF TONGUES

"Pilate took Jesus and scourged Him." But Jesus said never a word. We do not speak when the scourge of tongues is upon our character, our work, our motives.

We do not think anything when the scourge of adversity is upon our undertakings. We do not think or speak when sharp pains scourge our bodies. We answer never a word when one who has wronged us sorely tries by adroit accusings to make us speak some retaliatory words to engage us in quarrel. We give the "soft answer that turneth away wrath" when one has come to feel that he has just cause for anger against us. Thus is the summary of this lesson. According to the Gospel of Jesus Christ, all evil is a lie from the beginning — pure delusion. But the loving kindness of the Gospel is such that we may know exactly what to do under every circumstance and condition of human experience to rise out of suffering which seems real.

According to the Gospel, suffering of any kind was not made for the children of God; and We are the children of God.

Jesus told us that if the cup of sorrow should be pressed to our lips we must refuse it, saying: "I will not drink it. I refuse it." He tasted it once for the purpose of telling us we need not drink it. He showed us we need not drink it. He showed how the refusing to feel sorrowful at a sorrowful state of affairs would set the affairs straight.

This is the Gospel. Under the law and the prophets we have cause and effect, physical and metaphysical.

Under the law we have the cold to chill our bodies into consumption and the failing mental state to show a wrong thought once held.

Under the Gospel, "None of these things move me."

At each point of human experience touch your lot with the Gospel and be free from cause and effect.

The oldest teaching known to the race is that all things we see and feel and hear and taste were wrought and built by some thoughts we used to hold.

We have now riches or poverty, health or sickness, sorrow or gladness, friends or foes, according as out thoughts have formulated. Edwin Arnold gives us this as the teaching of Buddhism:

Thought in the mind has made us.

What we are by thought was wrought and built.

If a man's mind hath evil thoughts,

Pain comes to him as comes the wheel the ox behind.

Once they taught in ancient books that We are surrounded by a cosmic ether or matter principle which receives every thought we think and every Word we say and brings it forth as the soil brings up the seeds.

Some thoughts are slow to come to fruit, just as some seeds are slow. The apple seed is longer than corn; the corn longer than the pea.

Every affirmation is a prayer. An affirmation is a positive statement that something is. Every affirmation carries the tacit asking for something and also carries the tacit expectation that it will be so proved. A certain quick-tempered feeling, for instance, is the tacit asking for someth8ing bad to happen. We speak impulsively the affirmation, "You are a hateful thing." We, of course, expect something to result from our speaking: either the pain or the despair of somebody.

Then We forget our word, but afterwards we are lame or some member of our family is disabled. "For the lightest word thou shalt give account in the day of judgment." Judgment is when the Words have come forth in solid pictures.

There is a physical mode in trying to set things that are consequences right. The oculist, the artist, and the surgeon are as busy as can be rectifying consequences. Our popular magazines often have page after page of descriptions of successful management of consequences by surgeons, artists, oculists.

But the metaphysician or moralist says so long as the causes remain, the consequences will follow as "comes the wheel the ox behind." If a strong prejudice caused cataract the cataract will stay till the prejudice is gone; it will form and reform, says the moralist. If Napoleon III shoots causelessly at Maximilian in Mexico, Napoleon's son must be shot causelessly in the jungles of Africa.

For every shriek of the drowning slave thrown overboard to lighten the slave ships in the storms, a Harvard boy, a Yale youth or a farmer's son must fall on the battlefield of the Republic in the civil War that sets them free.

From Genesis to Revelation "Eye for eye and tooth for tooth" for everybody and everything out of Christ. The cheating of the ear-conductor out of your fare, though you argue that the corporation is rich and you are poor, will put you behind sixty and an hundred fold more than the fare.

Confidence in the God of right will add to you sixty and an hundred fold. "He that leadeth into captivity shall be led into captivity, and he that killeth with the sword, shall be killed with the sword," whether it be sword and bondage of tongue or steel.

To annul this We follow Christ Jesus. We cannot make believe follow His ways, either. Making believe brings failure and loss. "The hypocrite's hope shall perish." Here is a beautiful lesson in Christ of how to act under the stings of the tongue of the law, when we are in some bodily torture or mental pain, or hurting circumstance. Keep still. There is a breathing finer than the nostrils and the lungs and the airs experience. There is a pulse beat more irresistible, and a heartbeat for ever steady, which it is impossible to watch with the muscles relaxed and the mind intent. When the little widows of India were asked how they endured the scourgings of their lot one of them explained that they had learned that they had a finer life within them which would live and bear it, if they would be still enough. Shall we not see the Christ in the innocent victims? Is not the Christ able? ls not Christ in us? This is the finer life that can make scourgings nothing if we relapse into it.

Within the alchemy of mind is the peaceful Spirit. Within the chemist's fire is the crystal ice. Within the sun, a center of peace. Within the cyclone, stillness. Within mind, God. "My peace I give unto you." That finer life within us all knows no suffering; knows no death never heard of any of them. We all have the same faculty given us of watching the subtle, sweet life when the pains and torments of our past thoughts come to their fruitage, and thereby not feeling the pains.

We may call it the faculty of wrapping the mantle of our own thoughts around us, as we are taught in science to do on the Sabbath.

Indeed, the teachings of Jesus are the twelve simple lessons of Christian science put into practical living. The silent life of us is the triumphant power of us. It will speak and live so perfectly for us, We get into the way of letting it, that we see and hear and know only that life, and to us it is no longer silent.

In these days of noise and hurry we must not lose sight of that fine victorious life ever coursing through us, willing to do a11 things for us.

In a newspaper we were all told lately that everything nowadays has to be loudly heralded. "To depend upon merit is obsolete and chimerical. The only winning card is assurance." But Jesus Christ's teachings were for all time and for every situation. He taught a sure rule for success. Success means good health, good judgment and prosperity. All other ways except His way have failed. Let us try His way.

The letter fails and systems fall,
And every symbol wanes;

The Spirit overbrooding all,
Eternal love remains.

Try for your health the silent way, the supremely still way. A few years ago a number of invalids, scourged, beaten things they were, had an idea come to them all over the world simultaneously, as an idea of a patent car — coupler would strike ten thousand minds just ready for it simultaneously. They determined to lie still — still — still, and see what would become of them. They all got well. How many have stopped their vain searchings and hard studying to suddenly find themselves thoroughly enlightened on the subject that had them. "Be still and know that I Am God." You can get best financial and professional success by relying upon the still principle.

Serene, I fold my hands and wait,
Nor care for wind or tide or sea.
I rave no more 'gainst time or fate,
For lo! My own shall come to me.

Some people will not turn to the silence of the fine life within them till they are driven by the winds of sore failure of every other plan. There is a wind flower in South America which will not show its sweet bloom unless the rough winds blow, but we need not wait for calamity to blow wore winds, or the scourging of pain. We may sing the Benedictus from a silence not enforced like Zachariah's. We need not wait for the law to imprison us before we write a great book like Bunyan. Here We are taught to cease from fretting at sore trials for they simply mean that old ways of thinking and old material conditions are being struck off.

We have got into set ways of thinking, supposing feeling. When we have believed in the necessity for summer and winter, seed time and harvest, we have come to believe in toil — hard toil. If we believe in hard toil we believe in unavailing toil this always brings death or famine to the individual and to the planet. Death of peace, hope, substance, happiness, friends - death of something.

"As comes the wheel the ox behind."

Pilate, whose name shows that he stands for a hand of the law and the prophets, finds no real fault in us. He is simply an instrument of the people with some hint of a soul. He lays all the blame of the scourging onto somebody else. His wife Warns him.

Whoever acts the Pilate will be Warned in advance.

Before you speak harshly to your boy for some supposed offense, stop. You had a warning not to do it by a feeling the other day that something bad was going to happen to him. You are the thing that is going to happen to him. The child must not be scourged by your tongue or our ships, for Pilate acted out always has a fearful end.

"Take ye Him," said Pilate. Now be no coward. If it was right for Pilate to scourge Jesus it was right for him to finish the punishment. The Adam type never likes to be responsible. The Christ always is. Bold, intrepid people have more admiration from us than shrinking, shirking ones.

Cortez wins our admiration, though his boldness was engaged to ignoble uses. We see how he was a hand of the law, not afraid to destroy those Aztecs in a religious frenzy as those Aztecs had boldly destroyed twenty thousand noble youths every year in cruel religious frenzy. Cleopatra was intrepid, fearless to the last breath.

"We have a law," shouted the populace, "whereby He ought to die." This law was Lev. 24:16, which put their neighbors to death for blasphemy. But who should judge what is blasphemous?

Luther haughtily refused to shake the hand of the gentle Zwingli because he thought the kindly heart had blasphemed God. But is haughtiness honor of god? Is not mercy and tolerance more Godlike? How can the Presbyterians, Episcopalians, Catholics, etc. know whether they or the Briggs, Newtons, Brooks, McGynns, etc., are more nearly Godlike, save by the mercy, gentleness, love, forgetfulness of opinions they show? Who is more likely to be honoring the Maker of all things, he who calls himself a worm of the dust, a helpless child, or He who rises and says, "All power is given unto Me in heaven and in earth, for I and my Father are One?"

The Pilate nature is in great doubt when he gets between the two factions, one calling himself a helpless infant and the other God in His Greatness. "Whence?" But Jesus answers nothing, for Pilate is determined not to hear the Jesus idea. He is mortally afraid of the people. Do no explain yourself to one who is afraid the people are not ready to be told of their omnipotence and omniscience. Your silent presence is all they can bear.

Whatever you know of your power and wisdom will treat them. They will catch the idea from your atmosphere. If you said yesterday to anything, "I hate it," or "I hate you," somebody coming near to you today will feel a little hate of you come suddenly into his mind. You cannot think a thought but somebody will catch it, and if your mind is absolutely absorbed with any theme everybody will catch it.

So you see how the disease germs will spread by thinking of disease germs. You see how a doctor may actually drop down into your house the idea of that last case he attended and you will be another just like it on his list pretty soon.

To study nosology, classification of disease, astrology, causes of disease, symptomatology, symptoms of disease is not nearly as healthy a state of mind to carry around as the absorption with the idea, "The Spirit maketh you every whit whole." Now Pilate gets angry. What at? Why, because he has done Jesus a great wrong, and His patience under it makes Pilate hate Him.

Rosina Vokes in one of her plays says, "I have done him a great Wrong and I hate him for it? The audience laughs knowingly when she repeats the little truism of the Pilate type.

Here is where Jesus speaks. Pilate begins to feel it was cruel of Jesus to get him into such a predicament. "Pilate," He says tenderly, "you would not have done it if you had acted out your own best judgment." There is no real power in being wrong even with members on your side. Power is in being in the right. He shows him how his foolishness came from Judas, the luster. Weakness had its rise in lust of some kind. So, whoever is cowardly or Weak or faltering of courage of mind or body needs the whole six treatments of science.

Pilate refused the divinity side and gave over to the material side of the question. All those who parleyed with Judas ended violently. They had to, because they kept under the law of cause and effect, as "he that killeth shall be killed."

Judas, Pilate, Herod, Caiaphas, Annas, where are they? How ended the? Jesus and His doctrine were they crucified, killed? To the Christ that never was crucified, to the Christ that never was entombed, to the Christ that never had to rise, being already risen, to the triumphant Christ, high over principalities and powers and nations, be joined. Ye are of like Substance. The fine, still life within you, watch it: it is Christ Within you, victorious over all, never knowing defeat of health, or wisdom, or wealth.

November 29th, 1891

BIBLE LESSON XXI. John 19: 17. SIMPLICITY OF FAITH

"He, bearing His cross, went forth into a place called the place of a skull." The history of Jesus Christ is the history of one Who, knowing that He owns great possessions, takes upon Himself the estate of the lowliest people, not to give to them as if they were objects of His charity, but to teach them how to have as much as He has.

He is the history of one who takes upon Himself all kinds of sicknesses to teach sick people how to get well.

He is the history of one who takes the deepest grief upon Himself to teach us how to rise out of it. He is the history of one who teaches how to get very wise and successful While being ignorant and unfortunate. In other words, He bore the cross of the world.

If He, being rich, had given large provisions to the poor, He would have been a failure. If He, being powerful, had simply healed a few and lifted up a few and enlightened a few, He would have been as great a failure as those powerful people who condescended in the time of the cholera in Naples. A very rich man rode among the poor people in his carriage carrying broths and medicines, but they were so enraged at him, that they mobbed him, broke his carriage in pieces, tore the harness off his horses, and nearly held a riot in the city. King Humbert went among them, dressed just like one of them, helped them nurse their sick and bury their dead, and they never touched him, though they knew that he was richer than the other man.

This was because he did not flaunt the difference of his position in their faces. Now, if King Humbert had told them that they might as well have sixty and an hundred fold more possessions than they had, and explained it to them how they might be as powerful and well fed as himself, it would have been something like what Jesus Christ did.

He bore your very experiences and told you the exact Way out of them. He was offered money and houses and castles and kingdoms if He would take the world way of getting them. He was shown how able a financier He was by nature; how able a ruler He would make; how noble He would appear as a prince, and if He would deal the world's way He could even the Caesars.

He saw that He had magical healing powers; that He could perform all the mighty tricks of legerdemain Solomon had excelled in. It had been considered that Solomon was wonderful, because he could pierce a delicate pearl, string intricately perforated diamonds, and answer peculiar conundrums. All this was so simple and easy for the young Jesus.

But he said, "I will not get my greatness that way. I will get wise in the knowledge of Spirit, I will get all my powers from God in straight communion with God, and not till I can explain how God as the Father is impartially good to all the children of men will I take any of the goods of earth."

"I believe in God as able and willing to do all things that mankind can ask or even think. I do not believe in there being any poor people or old people or unhappy people. I believe God is good to all or that He is not good at all. I do not believe in ignorance. I do not believe in failure. I do not believe in dishonesty. These things are not necessary. There is a noble, satisfactory way of living. That way I will demonstrate in such fashion that not one creature can be too ignoble to imitate."

And he did. The seemingly heavy human affairs that despite the goodness of God He bore and said, "Be not afraid; I have overcome." "The flesh profiteth nothing." "The devil is a lie from the beginning." "Keep My Words." "My words are Life." "My words tell the power of Spirit. Seek first the knowledge of God and all these things shall be added unto you that you desire."

He said God was in Him. He said God was and is in all. He said that this God in each of us is able and willing to help us in wonderful ways. Nothing is too hard for Him. He explained that nothing is too commonplace for us to lay before this God and get aid.

He said that He Himself was the bodily demonstration of God. But He laid great stress upon the fact that just talking and thinking as He did (being absolutely right] would put Him and His powers forth from each of us.

A very poor woman not very long ago felt that she heard the voice of Jesus Christ speaking within her mind saying, "I am Jesus Christ." She said, "Yes, I know, but I do need help so much! Won't you please help me pay my rent?" The voice within her mind never said "Yes." She listened to her own mind and so gently and lovingly the same Words came, "I am Jesus Christ!"

If she had let this voice speak aloud through her lips her neighbors would have said she was blasphemous. But she did not. She said again, "Yes, dear Jesus Christ, I know you are the highest thought of my mind- able to do all things, won't you please help me pay my rent?"

And again all she could get was the affirmation stronger and fuller from the deeps of her own mind. And immediately after that she had help on her way. "Ye shall ask What ye will in My Name."

According to Jesus Christ you do not have to ask any man or Woman or corporation to help you; Jesus Christ will attend to it. Not the historic Man of Galilee but the omnipotent Jesus Christ quality of your own mind.

Jesus Christ is the demonstration of good. Just to listen to the one thought that Whispers within you is your demonstration.

It is not right for you to be poor. It is not right for you to be sick. It is not right for you to fail. It is not right for you to be unhappy. Why will you be when Jesus Christ says, "I am within you able to do all things. Nothing is too hard for Me. Do not look afar unto Me, but let My Name be spoke within you, and love Me and believe in Me."

You can do everything when Christ Jesus is your chief word. By and by the world will not seem heavy to you. You will not be Atlas with the World on his shoulders, but Jesus with the world under His feet. Your whole business in life is to "learn of Me," or to learn how to let the Jesus Christ thought within you reign supreme. This thought that is named Jesus Christ is the noblest thought within your mind. Let it keep saying "I am Jesus Christ." Tennyson kept repeating his own name till he felt as if he was as big as the planet. Some mystics kept repeating certain syllables, but Jesus Christ said, "Repeat My Name." Then you will not feel as if you were the planet but as if the world were under your feet. You will not become senseless, like the mystics who repeat senseless syllables, by speaking My Name, but will come into your inheritance of health, wisdom, and success.

The place of a skull was where they crucified Him. You intellect is supposed to be located within your skull. This intellect is a great enemy to Jesus Christ, "The natural man receiveth not the things of the Spirit." One has to walk right over the Words and teachings of the intellect just as Jesus did. There is a higher faculty than the intellect within you. It is Spirit. Intellect is more powerful than muscle. It is more successful than muscle. Intellect is as unreliable, however, as muscle. The powerful intellect will tell us that We must not give to the worthy poor because if We heed to every cry of pain we would soon be as poor as the poorest. Spirit says, feed every one with a portion of your bounty and you will have all the more. Intellect says, I must put my money into institutions that will praise my name and cut down my employees afterward.

Spirit says, I must put every creature into the Way of earning its own living. If it cannot do the way of the world, so much the more cause for my protective care and Wise instruction. I must not do my aims to be seen of men. Honor among this generation counts for nothing. The future will read my motive as clear as a book.

The intellect is proud over muscle. Spirit is proud over nobody and nothing, but far transcends all the powers of all the creatures. Intellect has its place in the skull. Jesus Christ has no place. Fills all place — unbounded, limitless, infinite.

Algazali, a pious Arabian, said he was completely astonished when he found how the senses deceived him, and his judgment had to be all corrected by his intellect. He noticed how the stars are reported to be small as money pieces by sensation, but corrected by intellect are called suns and worlds. He was sure of everything and everybody being different to the judgment from What the senses state. Then be began to doubt the reports of his intellect.

He said he was satisfied enough with his senses until intellect denied their testimony. Then he grew dissatisfied with intellect and wondered if there were not some higher faculty still that could correct it. Jesus here explains that He will teach us a higher than the greatest intellect.

Pilate, the representative of the world that acts according to its feelings, jestingly and willfully calls the spiritual teaching the ruling intention of Judaism.

The coward does the way of the world. He says the spiritual world is chimerical; says it claims to do everything, but so far as he sees does nothing.

Religious teachers try to explain that indeed they do not believe in spirit as their provider and healer and teacher. "We do the same ways you do; We try the tricks of all trades just like you; We believe in business ways and We employ doctors to examine our pulse and prescribe for our livers just like you; we study books as hard as ever we can to learn about God's laws with earthquakes and cyclones. Indeed, please, great worldly mind, don't think for a moment that We are so foolish as to believe in spirit." "Write not, King of the Jews."

But the world always will insist that it is the very nature of religion to teach a better way than material performances to be successful and happy.

There Was no anguish you can go through with of mind or body any greater than this great Jesus Christ took upon Himself to show you the Words to speak to set you free.

Here He shows that if you feel anguish of mind or body you may be sure something good is coming to you. You can hasten its coming by saying, "It is finished." If you have been very sick and you let that thought Within you speak, saying "I am Jesus Christ" and then you ask that thought to make you well, you will very likely have a very strange feeling of mind and body which no word will express better than anguish.

This feeling shows that a great good is to be born in you. Anguish gives us birth. You are to say, "It is finished. Jesus Christ took this cup and said I need not drink it. He said I might refuse it. So I refuse to be in anguish. I declare that what was meant for me is here now, according to Jesus Christ. I am perfectly well now."

Keep on speaking these words. You do not have to be put through any pain or sorrow or humiliation at all. But if you have got into these straits there is a quick Way out.

Jesus Christ in you, the hope of glory, is your freedom. There is nobody so free as the one who lets this name be spoken within his mind. He finds that if he does not choose to go into the slums of the city to work he can help the people While sitting in his own room. He finds that if he does not choose to go into the slums he has a right to do so. He is under nobody's orders and nobody's criticisms weigh with him. He is not afraid of "the terror by night, nor the arrow that by day." Criticism calumny, censure, praise, they are all one to him.

"It is finished," He says. Jesus Christ in you speaking tells you that all evil is finished. It is ended. These things shall not be upon the earth. You can speak this Name within your mind till the kingdom of heaven is open to your sight. In you the Gentiles will trust. As it is written "In My Name shall the Gentiles trust." That is, if you keep letting the Divine thought whisper within you, "I am Jesus Christ," even the people who do not believe in spiritual laws as transcending intellectual methods will trust you, will lean on you.

Jesus received the vinegar. But you need not receive the vinegar of having to take favors from the hands of those who have wronged you. He said to declare it as finished and to hold His Name steadfastly in mind would keep you free from all the pains and sorrows and shames of human experience. "I am victor over these things, in your mind first and then in your body and world."

There is salvation in none other name, but in My Name the vinegar and the gall and the wormwood of human experience are nothing. I promise you immunity from everything, if before you have got into trouble you will speak My Name. But if you have never been taught the power of My Name and are now in great anguish, say that you refuse the cup of trouble, and declare that "I in you am even now able to save you from poverty, debt, disgrace, desolation, sickness;" say, "It is finished." At the eleventh hour "call upon Me and I will hear." "Keep My Word and live." "I cannot be crucified; I cannot be entombed. Nothing is too hard for me." "Now is the accepted time. Now is the day of salvation." December 6th, 1891

BIBLE LESSON XXII. John 20:1. CHRIST IS ALL IN ALL

All over Christendom, when people use the expression which is the subject of this lesson, they mean to have us know that a principle supposed to have been dropped out of favor long ago is now come to the front as a power.

The idea which the dominant church supposed had been slain with Galileo is now risen smiling and calm as the orbit itself: "Christ is risen."

Did you reject is as absurdity when you first heard it spoken that visible material objects have, indeed, no reality as matter, but that as spirit is omnipresent their only substance is spirit, and therefore there is no matter?

But now you begin to understand it, do you not? This is Christ risen again in you, the hope of glory. Your hope begins to be quickened, does it not? You have an indefinable expectation of something good coming to you from seeing the point, do you not? This expectation will not fail you. Truth never fails to bring something good to the one who recognizes her. Christ is Truth. Did you feel exceeding indignation when the metaphysicians not only insisted upon the unreality of matter, but also declared that all evil performances are only a delusion of the mind?

If you put the idea away and refused positively to entertain it, or consider it at all, then you rolled the stone of unbelief against the place where you hid the idea in your mind.

But the mind is very mysteriously retentive where a truth is concerned. Some day you will find that that idea is as clear as crystal to you. It rises smiling and loving and living as ever. There is not a truth you have ever heard spoken but What it is now milling within you and preparing to appear to you again. This is the nature of Truth. Then there are more intense statements of Truth than that evil is a delusion and matter is non est.

Mary Magdalene represents one who has cast out the seven false ideas of the human mind, and taken the seven right ones to replace them. You remember she had seven devils cast out by Jesus Christ. As Jesus Christ was strictly scientific in His mode of dealing with people, you can see He must have given her the seven noble affirmations of Truth to satisfy her mind With. Naaman washed seven items in Jordan to typify the seven cleansing words of mental law. The man mentioned by Jesus put out the seven devils or spirits or errors from his house or mind and neglected to receive the seven good words that belonged to him. It is to be expected that you will have put out these seven notions, viz., that there is any evil mixed with the omnipresent good in this universe where we dwell, and second that there is any matter or material thing in this universe.

You have learned that, strictly speaking, there is no absence of life, spirit, or intelligence. That there is nothing to hate, and that there is no reality in sin, sickness or death. You have also declared that there is no burden on your spirit or in your life, and have gladly put out of your mind the foolish idea that anything or anybody could get away from you anything that belongs to you. At first, very likely, these denials of what seems were rather hard for you to make, because all your past teachings and experiences belied them. But it is not at all a question of what We have been taught to believe, but a question of What is true.

Some people have been taught that they must live and think in a certain way or after they are dead they will be changed into bats and owls; but even if they believe it profoundly it will not be true. There are certain ways of believing which will make you nobly intelligent, perfectly healthy, and always successful. You are entirely dependent upon how much Truth you believe. The more Truth you believe the more successful you are. Failure along any line is sure evidence that you believe something that is not true very determinedly. If you have been failing in your undertakings you had better say very positively within yourself, "I hold no prejudice against anybody or anything in all the world." Such a message sent out of your mind will be sure to put the notion out of your mind which keeps you unsuccessful.

Only Truth is successful. If you answer me back that some liars are quite prosperous, I will point you to some great truth they do believe profoundly. Successful people generally laugh at certain notions you are hugging. All notions are prejudices against somebody or something.

All the regular denials of science have intenser exclamations of themselves. It was when Mary Magdalene had had the first statements of science, and had begun to speak them with deeper realization of them, that she is chronicled to have been found at the empty tomb, and to have spoken face to face with Jesus Christ.

For even the highest scientists there are still greater illuminations. Even the seven denials of science have harder statements of themselves. These harder statements operate with the advanced metaphysicians exactly the same as the first ones operate with those people who have believed in evil as a reality, in matter as having laws, and in sickness, misfortune and death as necessary adjuncts to existence.

The more metaphysical science you are acquainted with the more mastery you have over human conditions. Simple acquaintance therewith, however, is not high safety. Loving fellowship with them is the safety I am speaking of.

Often the highly scientific metaphysicians withdraw in horror from their colleagues when those colleagues make the denials of science over again according to their deeper meanings.

They cry as Mary: "They have taken away my Lord, and I know not where they have laid Him." If they stand by, however, they will see the truth come face to face with a newer glory. It is not a good plan to run away and cut yourself off from your colleagues simply because they have spoken high science, just as it is not good for you to refuse the simple statements of science and roll a stone of unbelief against the door of the place in your mind where the statements are lying.

There is a noble principle involved in standing by and seeing the angels who have power to roll away unbelief. Angels are perfect thoughts — pure thoughts. They are the head and foot, the alpha and omega, of good. Your mind had better take them now in one Name, spoken while the joy of truth is not in you.

The joy of truth in you is when you realize that it was the true words you spoke that brought you this noble prosperity, and can see how exactly it will be so with you always. The angels are the words themselves, spoken faithfully because you have nowhere and nothing else to turn to but what you can say.

It is a pretty lonely time, seemingly, when you have nobody and nothing to turn to but your own prayers. But if you keep on speaking your faithful words you will find how they will turn you right around face to face with answered prayer.

Just one word is praying — or rather it is two words in one. This is the Name. Speak it. Jesus Christ. The words are alive. They will turn you into the right place, into the very arms of help.

A woman had been speaking this Name with all her might because so many things had happened which had desolated her mind and heart and life. Suddenly she stopped. Every one of the events changed in her judgment and before the day was out they had actually turned around so that they were better than she had even imagined.

Her home was saved. Her child was spared. Her undertaking was successful beyond description. Tolstoy says that it was actually taught by Jesus of Nazareth that in this life we shall have an hundred fold more prosperity than the world's people if we hold to Jesus Christ, but he mournfully looks at the poverty-stricken, feeble Christians and asks, "Do we?" If all those who have been prejudiced against prosperity, feeling it to be a snare of the devil, will turn right straight to What Jesus Christ taught, they will begin to make the denials of science and the affirmations of science, and instead of feeling their helplessness and inferiority and ignorance they will realize that their natural right is the dominion over the world, the flesh and the devil, which Jesus Christ had. To be owner of great possessions, to be wise in disposing of them; to be strong and buoyantly glad every minute, with the rich ability to teach all the rest of the world how to be so too, is the right of the Christian.

But if he be prejudiced against these things or prejudices his own fortune against them by trying to persuade people to love poverty and hug disease, he will never demonstrate his birthright. When you have once been brought to see how nobly rich the King's ministry is in reality you will hear your own name spoken. Ah! The name that is in your forehead, which is your keynote.

That name of yours is always with you. It is your secret recognition of the presence and office of Jesus Christ. You know Jesus Christ in your own way. You are not expected to know how Jesus Christ Works with your neighbor to make him successful but you may know just exactly how Jesus Christ works with you to make you a transcendent delight.

When Jesus Christ said to Mary here, "Touch Me not," He meant to teach us that even when we are most rejoiced with what we have received we have not even then known the height and the depth, the length and the breadth of the riches of Jesus Christ.

We must keep on naming the Name. We must not stop naming the Name to watch phenomena of any kind. To watch any phenomena as it looks to be is touching Jesus with human notions. Keep on naming the Name even if again for a season you do not see any sign of Jesus Christ in your lot but have only the memory of answered prayers.

Tell over what prayers you have had answered. Tell over and over What great things you have had done for you. Jesus Christ is coming to abide with those who understand. The coming of Jesus Christ simply means understanding Truth. The abiding of Jesus Christ simply means the constant understanding of Truth.

Constant understanding of Truth has compelled those new statements of the metaphysics of life which are now demonstrating the freedom from all experience of pain, sickness, misfortune of those who make them. Suddenly the mind is illuminated to realize that there never was any such God as even the churches have described when most eloquently picturing Him forth. Suddenly it has been found that Jesus Christ is no such character as they tell us and had no such mission as they explain. Suddenly the whole fact looms up that mistaken teachings concerning God and Jesus Christ have built our prisons, waged our wars, pitted labor and capital against each other and given one home luxuries while the other starved.

Suddenly it is clear that the ministers in their pulpits, the moralists on their platforms, the Tolstoys in their books, must stop their teachings and ask Jesus Christ what is true, regardless of what they have been taught was true, for Jesus Christ preached as life, health, strength, support defense, just as the Name means, is risen never to go down behind the stone of unbelief in the hearts of those who have cried "Rabboni!"

December 13th, 1891

BIBLE LESSON XXIII. John 21:1. RISEN WITH CHRIST

"If ye then be risen with Christ, seek those things which are above," is the golden text of this lesson.

To be risen with Christ is to suddenly discover that you know a great truth about your own life as related to the God life. The instant we know such a truth we are changed in our bodies and in our minds.

There are statements of truth, glory beyond glory, and so there is no realization of what is true that has not a still higher realization in itself for us. Whenever Jesus Christ was with His disciples on the sea of Galilee or Tiberias, you will notice how they are always closing out an old dispensation and beginning a new one, as in this case.

We all have our closing out of our old ways of thinking about Christ, as the church at large is always having its close of dispensations. There is a time when we must live on a higher plane from What we have hitherto been living on, or we shall deteriorate in every way. We are risen with Christ when We realize that there is a higher plane to think and live on than that we have been thinking and living on. We shall demonstrate new powers if we commence to live there the moment we see how it is. We are never where we do not come to such places. The Christian scientists have taken the highest statements concerning Christ that were ever taken, but they also find their times when they must rise to still higher statements of the same Christ. To refuse these risings with Christ is to deteriorate--to stop our prosperity.

A whole body of people may stop its prosperity along some line by not rising with Christ when somebody tempts them, or their pride or conservatism tempts them to take a lower view of life from what they see (dimly in the early morning, as the disciples of Jesus on Galilee) might be taken. Here the seven affirmations or two words embodied took the higher statements concerning Jesus Christ, viz., that He is not above doing the commonest favor for those who rise to accept His teachings.

Everything in this lesson has its exquisitely spiritual significance. It shows also how it is a sign of the acceptance of Christ from a higher plane when We can be fed and clothed and prospered by Him without feeling that it is demeaning Him any more than those people did who let Him help them at the time of this lesson.

Jesus Christ was Jesus of Nazareth, so full of understanding that there was nothing to Him, in Him, or of Him, except Christ or Truth. Whoever will be filled to overflowing with Truth, as Jesus was, will do as wonderfully as He, and be as much Christ as He.

"Where I am, there ye may be also."

He never told people to do anything but what He Himself could do and did do. He said, "Preach the gospel," and then preached so entrancingly that the very soldiers forgot to arrest Him, even when they might be executed for such neglect. Ambition, that subtlest and strongest passion of man, was forgotten under the spell of His voice. "Man, proud man, dres't in a little brief authority"--glad to "play such fantastic tricks before High Heaven as make the angels weep," was tamed at the very moment when it was his chance to show his authority.

He told them to heal the sick and palsied hands, and leprous scales shone forth as wholesome flesh. "Multitudes came unto Him and He healed them every one" as easily as you would set a chair into its right place in your parlor or hang a picture straight on your walls.

He said, "Cast out demons," and took Mary Magdalene and cast seven out of her, leaving her one of the noblest characters of history — last at His cross, most efficient at His embalming, weeping at His burial, first at His rising. The sin of the woman in adultery was erased. The man's heinous offenses Were made nothing. The demoniac boy was set free.

He said, "Raise the dead," and the daughter of Jairus, the widow's son, Lazarus and others came forth at His call to show that homes were never made to be decimated by death and we may unite all our families again if we will follow His teachings, rising to the acceptance of every new truth we hear which puts us farther away from the teeth of material laws and earthly experiences.

Last of all, He raised Himself, to show that we may never be so dead in any way, but that the Truth He told us will give us strength to rise full of quickened life as the solid dough rises with the quickening leaven.

He said that if We had His words in our mind, though we were dead yet should We live again. He said that if we should have His Words already quickened within us we should never die — never even see death. Every single one of His works has been accomplished by some one or more of His disciples, except the self-raising. Not one has come forth into our sight after having been buried, and not one has proved his ability to live on and on indefinitely right here among us.

We must take into consideration how all truth has been received when spoken, to appreciate Why no Christian has demonstrated protracted appearance among us. All of them had but newly come up out of the Egypt of materiality, and the smell of the smoke of the old ways was upon their garments while they were trying to tell how spiritual thoughts were capable of helping them out of all evil. Now and then they drooped and faded and fell from the reception their doctrine met. At the least sign of failure their neighbors and their families sneered. So they gladly, as Paul said, "preferred death rather than life," with such scorn at every step. Young in spiritual life is every Christian scientist. At their failures do not sneer.

It is better to have tried. and failed

Than never to have tried at all.

We are the Work of Providence,

And more the battle's loss may profit those who lose

Than victory advantage those who win.

Here Jesus comes forth smiling and loving and healing as ever. For the third time He comes in substantial presence with substantial help. Christ is substance. Christ is substantial help. Believe this. You may have your shoes provided by Christ if you will rise to believe it. When a woman tells me she feels the power of the Spirit so strongly that the very cyclone stops when she speaks, I believe her and rejoice that she is risen into Christ of Truth. Why is she afraid to tell you this? When a woman or man tells me that she or he has received some financial assistance direct from God without a bit of intervention from human beings, Why does my heart burn with delight as if I had conversed with one who had lately come from Jesus Christ on the banks of Galilee, While they would tremble at your peculiar smile or turning aside?

I suppose it is because I believe in the substantial, everyday friendship of Jesus Christ, and do not care at all about the harps and crowns and feathers of a faraway heaven.

Christ dwelleth not afar,

The King of some remoter star,

to the disciple who has been fed and warmed under the shadow of the tender hills of Galilee.

Notice that He appeared to seven. Those seven are all named except two. You will often notice that two have no names when the risen Christ is near. Those of you who read the twelve lessons of Christian science will remember that there are five affirmations every mind on the planet ought to make, and then that each human being has two affirmations that belong to himself alone.

On the way to Emaus (or to the knowledge that "they shall prosper that love God") two nameless disciples had Jesus with them. You will get Jesus Christ to warm your life with delight when you discover your own two.

Please do not disapprove of your neighbor's two if he tells you them as very different from yours. You remember that to be a critic was formerly considered to be very smart, but that old dispensation has closed with the knowledge that criticism makes heart disease and sharp twinges of rheumatism. You have risen with Christ if you stop criticizing when you know the law.

Suppose your neighbor feels the God — power speaking so forcefully through him, that like Jeremiah, he says, "l am God and I make my world," all the time meaning the Spirit of himself and not the mortal at all. Will you let him use these two affirmations, even if your neighbor says he has not business with them, for his affirmations are, "I am Spirit and all my world is Spirit?"

These two affirmations not printed in the books have helped many. Try them: 1. "I am the friend of everybody and everything." 2. "I forgive everybody and everything." You will find you are a reservoir of kindness that can warm the whole world. You can make everything lovely and blessed where you walk. You are bursting, overflowing with forgiving balms. You can pour oils over the troubled thoughts of the world. There is no limit to the conserved good Within you that begins to demonstrate very soon after you start these two affirmations.

Here is a lesson of how sure Jesus Christ is to come to those who have just about got discouraged after trying very hard to believe that He is their helper and not seeing Him. Peter and Nathaniel and five others, finding they were objects of derision since their truth had met with What seemed ignominious defeat, made up their minds they would go back to their old business of fishing.

Often the very most spiritually-minded minister of God gets to feeling that maybe he has mistaken his calling because, in spite of his higher efforts, he has failed, and so concludes to go back to his old business. Here Jesus Christ gives him every bit of success that comes to him. At first he will toil unavailingly. Then when he has got discouraged in this also, and feels that it is a mystery whatever he was born for anyway, or Why he is here, he makes a little lucky turn.

This is the Jesus Christ within him that has just got ready to act. This lucky turn is the casting of his net on the right side. Remember that there is not a single situation in which you can be placed that has not one little turn for you to make with it to make you absolutely successful.

This is the fourth dimension in space — or the Jesus Christ of you. All success shows the action of Jesus Christ. No matter on What plane you achieve success you are successful by the rising of the Jesus Christ within you.

Simon Peter drew in the net for them full to overflowing and yet the net did not break. Once before they had drawn in such a large netful that the net had broken. And this lake is the very place where Jesus found them on the very material plane of catching fish for their living in the first place. You see they were at the end of the material dispensation when Jesus called them first, and promised they should be fishers of men. And they were told by the second haul of fish, where their nets broke, that the first church that should come by their preaching should last a certain period, and should catch a very motley crowd and class of people, so that it would seem as if the Christian Church must break up and end by reason of such people as it would enroll upon its lists.

Under sanction of the church roll, men in high office might grind down the faces of the poor, and without censure prove unfaithful to the home. Under this dispensation men should believe in two powers good and evil. They should believe in two beings — God and devil. They should believe in two personal characters, interceding and interfering with man--Jesus and Satan. Men should have their eyes so blinded as to which personality was dealing with them that they could not tell Whether their actions were dangerous or safe, their thoughts powerful or weak. Just at the close of this dispensation they would not be able to turn to anybody or anything for help in health or happiness till they had cast their net on the right side--till they had done one little turn to help themselves.

Let me illustrate. In the streetcar the other day I saw a capitalist belonging to a church of the old dispensation shut the door crossly in the face of a little street-singer. Now that little face looking up was Jesus Christ. Some day that church member cannot recover the money he will lose till he has made his peace With Jesus Christ by doing something for the sake of that child. To do this would be casting his net for success in health and everything else, though it were at the eleventh hour.

Once a man told a good little Christian woman that if she would cure his boy he would give her a thousand dollars, but though the boy was cured he never paid anything to the laborer whose labor he had employed. He has lost $10,000. He will never recover the amount until he makes good his promise. Swedenborg saw that health comes to a time when the moral law must be observed in the heart and extend way into the actions or the body must lie down in a grave to begin the work over again. The old dispensation is closing when this law is heard of. Then for those who have received that and come to an end of it, or lived it, there is the constant knowledge of only good--only God--only Jesus Christ, so that they have nothing to do but sit down and take the bread and fish Jesus Christ provides without questioning — just knowing "It is the Lord."

Sometimes people say of those who are determined to face the material world and the church of the old dispensation with the statement that there is but one Principle, one Presence, that if they should have pain or sickness or death or poverty in their home then they would find a principle of evil pretty real.

No. If they have these things they show that they believe now that evil is real and God owns a devil. "According to thy faith be it unto thee." They are under the old dispensation. This is the dispensation of supposition. The new dispensation supposes nothing. It knows in whom it believes, and its net never breaks. Its friends stand true to each other forever. Its families trust each other with a reason for the trust that is in them.

"Aunt Nancy you should be laying up some money for a rainy day," says a member of the old dispensation to the member of the new. "Suppose your employer should die, suppose you should have rheumatism; suppose" -

"Stop!" says the colored believer in the new dispensation. "I neber s'pose nuffin'. De Lawd is my Shepherd, 'an I shall not want. And honey, it's all yo' sposin' as is makin' yo' so mis'able."

They shall hunger no more, neither thirst any more, under the last dispensation of the church where Jesus Christ is the daily provider acknowledged. "There shall be no more pain" when you have stepped out from under the yoke of the belief in sin and death into the freedom of the gospel that these things are all the results of supposing things that never could be true.

"The inhabitants shall not say, 'I am sick,' anymore," in all the earth where men hear the voice of Jesus on the shore at the close of their old ways of living, and make right restitution for the past and receive the gospel as it is in Truth.

You who are in trouble, failure, sickness, the old dispensation cries, Halt! The new dispensation says, "Come, eat with Me." God is Good omnipresent, Love omnipotent, Spirit omniscient. There is only God. Thus there is only Good. There is only Love. There is only Spirit. Do you believe there is any opposite of God in the field of omnipresence? Careful now. "According to thy faith be it unto thee."

Do you not feel the circuit of the old faith closing and hear the voice of the new calling? Be risen with Truth! "In that day there shall be one Lord and His name One." "Do not I fill heaven and earth?" "Is there any beside me? Nay, I know not any." December 20th, 1891

BIBLE LESSON XXIV. Review. THE SPIRIT IS ABLE

Six points are suggested to be considered by this lesson: temperance, the history of Jesus Christ as to His birth, His preparation for His ministry, His teaching as a whole and the particular doctrine of salvation from evil by the atonement. Also the effect of His teaching upon the race Which, when truly one with His doctrine shall be in itself "The Risen Christ."

To consider all these points in detail is to fill the mind with a vivid picture of the character of Jesus Christ. To have in the mind a vivid picture of the character of Jesus Christ is to have the same mind in us that was in Him to as great extent as we realize and love that character.

It is a well-known law to metaphysical students that the mind is sure to become like the mind it associates With, whether by reading its writings or face-to-face conversations. To think much about a person or his or her characteristics is to become like him or her. A young girl thought so much about a relative who was demented that, although she prayed vehemently not to get demented she became exactly like the relative whose character she thought upon so much.

If you think profoundly with Plato by reading his books and his life you cannot help getting polished and coldly scholarly like him with the same helpless feeling about the mastery over human experiences which he had. "We look for one," he said. What for? Why to show power over nature instead of subjection to nature like the race at large.

Suppose you looked upon the ways of Theotymus of whom St. Ambrose tells, you would certainly get willful enough to damage yourself for the sake of carrying out a sensual purpose.

"Vale lumen amicum," he said, when he found that his willfulness was destroying his eyesight. "Farewell sweet light."

If you read the book of a prejudiced mind or one that cannot keep its body Well you are likely to copy the very thought that makes the bodily ailment, and soon your prejudices will be exactly like that one and your foot will be lame or your head shaking with the same palsied tremble of the one whose book you read.

Any thought is communicable. Do you know the thought that made your eyesight fail? Well, when you get hold of what it was and will drop it, your eyesight will be splendid.

Jesus Christ taught the gospel of healing by keeping His doctrines and character so much in mind that other thoughts would have to fall off, and with their fall your health should "spring forth speedily."

The study of His life and ministry is the lifting of Him up in the mind. We are under orders from the Captain of our salvation to lift Him up in our minds till He draws all men unto Him. His words and character being held in mind will make us wise, strong, bold, efficient, full of health and healing love- He promised that anybody having Him supremely in mind should draw all men unto confidence in spirit — unto love of God — unto goodness of life.

This has been proved true in more Ways than one. For instance, it is true of your own thoughts. If you lift Jesus Christ up, and make it your particular word, holding it steadfastly, whether it seems a reasonable thing to do or not, all the rest of your thoughts will turn towards it as flowers turn to the sun, and the drooping thought that makes you so drooping in the morning will become invigorated so that you will spring up with new life each morning.

This is the best way to effect temperance among your own thoughts and among the race of people in the world, for what an army of people could not do to put steady officers into our high seats this one name could do easily.

"Is anything too hard for Me?"

"Nay, I know not any."

By holding His name in mind and by studying the character in earnest, you will find yourself going back to Mosaic science where the proposition is made that God made everything good. Then you will see there is no power in grape juice fermented or unfermented, in tobacco plants green or dry, to do any hurt. You will see that all the sting they have is our false thoughts regarding them. That as soon as we Withdraw our accusations from the things we have found growing or have manufactured from them, that they will prove their generic harmlessness.

This is the review of the year's temperance lessons. Our review is the summing up of the testimony of ideal science, which is the voluntary withdrawal on our part of the four accusations hurled by error against mankind, and caught up by the beasts of the field, the fowls of the air, and the plants of the earth.

If ever you have agreed with either of these accusations, withdraw them today and lift up the theme of this lesson. John the Revelator saw that the four angels or four thoughts of error were: first, that the children of God have lustful passions and sensual appetites; second, that they are liars; third, that they are sinners; fourth, that they are foolish and ignorant.

There is one angel who stops them from hurting the people or the things of the earth. That angel is a perfect idea. Lift it up and earth is redeemed from all the stings of accusations. If you have believed any of these four evil thoughts against mankind, Withdraw your accusings and refuse to believe the angels of accusing or the thoughts that are false. This is good judgment. Good judgment is temperance.

No other temperance lessons will count in demonstration.

"Jesus was born in Bethlehem of Judea in the time of Herod."

This you may take home to your own minds where your thoughts spring up. On the map of your mind there is a colony of thoughts all of the Judean quality. There is born among that herd of ideas one little thought that it is really possible to perform healing and supporting and defending by a law not material. The little sweet idea comes to you that you need not fear that any harm will come to your children or to yourself for God will take care of you. This is Jesus born in Bethlehem of Judea.

The next thought you have is the Herod one that there is no knowing what strange idiosyncrasies such a notion might lead you into. Maybe you would lose your social position or your business if this notion were allowed to grow to its full stature with you for a notion is so apt to make people peculiar; so you determine to out off such a notion. You cannot quite destroy it however. It is never utterly smothered in any breast, but you do relegate it to Nazareth or to the lowest place, as that only the fakirs and dervishes and mediums are miracle Workers. No respectable persons do such things.

Now, miracle-working is the noblest idea you can believe in.

It is Jesus Christ. To give that idea its chance to grow within your mind would make you Wise Without books, strong without muscle, efficient without effort. "No ill should come nigh thy dwelling." Your every action would bring benefit and blessing.

You could take the common clay and make it heal blindness just as Jesus did. You remember how those other men had tried clay on the eyes of that blind man, and the clay would not work, but it worked loving healing as soon as He used it.

It is all according to the mind that uses a remedy as to Whether it heals or not.

The physicians have found that more depends upon the mind with which they administer doses than upon the doses. Some physicians in a certain city wondered why one of their number never lost any cases, no matter how sick they were. One of them who was highly learned in drugs Went to the successful one and asked him to prescribe exactly for his cases the very same as he would for his own, which he did, and every case died, just as usual.

The mind that you hold while you cook your food or while you write your editorials heals or slays, according to what you believe. The unsuccessful physician held some idea antagonistic to Jesus. Herod ruled in his thoughts. It is healthy to believe in miracles.

Jesus, it is said, was 30 years old when He began to preach and Work spiritual doctrines. So also was John. This shows that you ought to let the belief in spiritual doctrine get complete sway over your mind. One man Worked 60 years to get to where he could actually feel the spirit of God present with him. The Spirit is able, ready, willing to do all things that we can ask or think of, but unless we give it complete sway we show the scars of conflict with opposition to Spirit. He taught patience by this waiting. "Patience, my heart, in loving; patience, my heart, to Wait."

His whole ministry was the assurance that He might have the Kingdom of heaven right here and now. He taught the necessity for getting into the standing place of the mind, and beginning over again with a true idea of God. Everything depends upon our idea of God.

The prison houses will open when We start over the World strongly the right idea of God. The Russian starvelings will be fed if we start the true idea of God to fold the planet in. The dwarfs and old people will be straightened out with bright joyousness when the breath of our true word fans their hopeless foreheads. We made the dwarfs and the starvelings. They are our personified thoughts — our embodied false ideas of God.

You say, "I never thought of a dwarf till I saw one." Oh, no, you did not need to imagine a dwarf to make one. All you had to do was to think there are high and low, rich and poor in the universe which you have admitted God made. This will create a dwarf if you only believed it for a minute. You have only to believe that you must Work and struggle to lay up for old age and feebleness, after you have once said that "the Lord will provide," to have a host of old and feeble people hanging around you.

Jesus went into the wilderness and fasted forty days to refute every false belief of the race. Fasting is simply the mortal rejection of false notions. You must learn to think for yourself quite independently of what people believe or tell you or write in books as the result of experience or observation. Unless it is good it is a lie from the beginning. Hypnotists say that as long as they can make a man think that if they tell him he is blind or lame, whether he is or not, he will act so until he rouses to think for himself, and then he is well enough.

All that we see and experience is the result of thoughts, the result of beliefs. Unless what we see is joyously good it is the product of a false idea. Fast from ideas for a while. Begin anew. This was what Jesus meant by His fast. He taught the atonement as the redemption of the world. Atonement means at-one-ment, or at-one-mind. To be exactly of the same mind as Jesus Christ you see we have to think exactly as He did. To partake of the atonement is to find that the earthquakes could not close over us, the fires could not burn us, the water could not drown us.

These things have power over one who has not partaken of the atonement. No man passeth over this land (or over this kind of experience) and comes out alive. Only the Spirit can come up smiling and hold and unhurt when the natural forces get to working. Tottin sees that the planet is in her last throes.

"Abstract good and abstract evil are about to close in for a final conflict," he says. Once in a While all old false ideas come gathering around you and you say you have a terrible amount of sorrow and trouble. Now, if you will close you mind from thinking of your troubles and think entirely of Jesus Christ you will be lifted right up and taken over the hard place. No flesh can live where the beliefs in evil have headed. They all die unless they close their minds to the thoughts of What is going on and think of the Captain of their salvation, Jesus Christ, the righteous. When Jesus Christ was here embodied there was only Himself believing in the omnipotence of the good.

Now there are hundreds and thousands who will stand forth and sing the absoluteness of the good. Whosoever believeth and hath not doubted in his heart that God as Good is omnipresent, as Love is omnipotent, as Spirit is omniscient, is passed from death unto life.

As the risen Christ, or risen into this faith through the gospel, we are to preach good news to all nations, beginning at Jerusalem or beginning at ourselves. We cannot do great things with the world till we have got down into the starting place of our own thoughts and got true.

Thou must be true thyself; If thou the truth would teach.

Jonathan Edwards found out a great truth when he found that the Whole purpose of God with him was to have him one with Himself. The works would be sure to follow one who had made his peace with God.

"Acquaint now thyself with Me and be at peace." "They that understand (God) among the people shall be wise and do exploits."

December 27th, 1891

BIBLE LESSON XXV. Isaiah 11:1. A GOLDEN PROMISE

"And there shall come forth a rod out of the stem of Jesse, and a branch shall grow out of his roots."

Isaiah, a Hebrew prophet, writing about the time of the founding of Rome (753 B.C.), is here foretelling the coming to the world some time in the future from his own period, of a man who should know all things without instruction from any other man and do all things without any example to incite him

There are two Ways of prophesying coming events. One is by scientific information reckoned from unvarying data according to unvarying law, and the other is from the spirit of revelation when the mind opens a closed gate and discloses scenes and events about to take place or already transpired.

The prophet of revelation saw the darkness of the day on which Jesus was crucified ages before "there was darkness from the sixth unto the ninth hour."

The Chaldean astronomer calculated the eclipse of the sun for the exact date, and the astronomer at Greenwich today will agree with him that on the hills of Galilee and over the doomed walls of Jerusalem's proud temples the sun was forbidden to shine on the day of the crucifixion.

The Revelator always sees the mental or metaphysical cause for the transaction while the scientist is regulating his telescope and figuring solis stationes. History notes both with impartial pen pictures.

In Isaiah we find prophecies of a Messiah to come. When He should have come people would be different. In astronomy we read of new planetary relations necessarily affecting physical nature.

Jewish revelators were not the only ones who were expecting a great Master and Teacher and Savior to come. Egypt and India were looking for one who should understand the mystery of life and handle death and misery with the fingers of an artist skillfully transforming smeary pigments into living landscapes.

The question of ages had been then as now, "Who am I, whither am I bound and what is my mission?"

The highest philosophy of India had concluded that to "get rid of life, to get rid of living," was the only way to mastery over human conditions — unless one should come to teach them better. They said, "The passions are evil. The passions are masters of mankind, not mankind of the passions. Thus evil is master. To live knowing that old age, disease, decrepitude, death, await us, is not life that is worthwhile. Let us get rid of life — rid of the necessity for living."

So they stilled their sensations by their will and buried themselves in the sand, or lay like logs under the sal trees till the birds of the air nested on their faces and taught their young to fly from their still foreheads. Yet it availed them nothing.

The Egyptians had concluded that the "I Am" of the universe is as present in man as the gods, but only the dead must have the book telling man that he is "I AM THAT I AM," for the truth at its highest is dangerous for the masses; only He that should come could live knowing truth and how to save from the evils of nature."

"Why do I feel powerful, yet the signs of my power are wanting?" they cried.

"Why should the earthquake, the tidal Wave, hunger, separation, injustice, triumph of wrong over right, foil me?"

They had no answer.

They out their flesh and went naked, cold, hungry, despised and rejected, hoping to propitiate Deity, win worthiness of mastery — yet still no satisfaction.

They had a strange habit of blindfolding themselves and turning around and around to shut off their knowledge of Where they might be, and while all their comrades waited eagerly questioning for the right Way to mastery over nature, the blindfolded gave answers.

It is blessed to know that they got truth after truth in their eager searching, but mastery should be given only to him who should live the life knowing the law, obedient to law, transcending the law.

The constant mention of the true God had given the Jews of old a truer conception of Deity than any other people of the earth held, and this germ of truth should never die from among them, their prophets declared, for even in the last days of the World ten men should be found "laying hold of the skirts of him that is a Jew, saying, 'We will go with you, for we have heard that you have the true God."

Out of the twelve tribes of Israel there was only one left as a kingdom in Isaiah's time. That was Judah, and she was fast approaching the most ignominious humiliation. She was about to be known no more as a kingdom, but only as an outcast memory of greatness.

The twelve tribes of Israel signify the twelve divisions of the mind. They all have some spiritual word or feeling, but the tribes Israel and Judah, hold out the longest when the pressure of the material claims is great. Ten parts of the mind are easily led Captive to Babylon, or the claim that "we shall all die when our time comes, suffer old age, poverty, sorrow, and none can stay us," if nature so orders.

This is not true, and two parts of the mind resent it — Israel, the spiritual feeling, and Judah, the spiritual word; but Israel the feeling, and Judah the word are not united and the feeling is lost or hidden while the Word keeps on speaking.

"The kingdom of Judah shall go down," said Isaiah. The martial greatness of David is a long past memory, the gorgeous victories of Solomon are ages departed. The follies of David and the adulteries of Solomon have wiped out the chances for worldly honors for the religious kingdom for evermore, and not until the religion of truth shall be based to its lowest point with no sign of any possibility of rising, shall the simple father of kings, Jesse, the Bethlemite, send forth from the humiliated stern or stock of his descendants, Jesus.

Isaiah knows that Where the true God is named there will be always a possibility of beginning anew, like the oaks of Palestine which will bud and branch at the smell of water as long as there is a stump remaining.

Assyria, the intellect, and Egypt, the senses, may be cut down like the fir and the pine and the cedar never to flourish against spirit anymore, but though the word of truth be hushed up and shamed down, like the oak trees of Bushan up it will spring when a Mary of Bethlehem is dedicated to Jehovah.

More than seven hundred years after Isaiah promised this rod from the stern of Jesse, Jesus came fulfilling all the prophecies, "The spirit of the Lord (the law), the spirit of wisdom, of understanding, the spirit of counsel, of might, the spirit of knowledge and of the fear of the Lord," did indeed rest upon Him.

These seven "spirits" or seven words of affirmation found by scientific reasoning were all with Him from the beginning and He needed not to be taught of them.

Isaiah makes three movements of this prophecy. First, the description of the man; second His teachings; and thirdly, the effect of His teachings when at the last the ensign or banner of God should be raised and unto it as a doctrine flashing from west to east, the gentiles or whole world should come, and "its rest should be glorious," for "they shall not hurt nor destroy in all My holy mountain."

He should know how to raise the dead, heal the sick, cast out sins, give good everywhere by His word.

The very wisest who had lived before Moses and Abraham had found out that there is a vital spark glowing within every living creature.

While this vital spark is burning through the system, life and health shine as an alabaster vase might shine with an oriental candle flaming within it. When the system gets covered with the dust of earthiness or the ways of the flesh, intellect, the vital spark, does not illuminate it, and the body Wraps itself around with death.

They said, those magi of old, that the vital spark of life was not in any human being's power to restore when once it ceased to burn.

They noticed that a man might keep his physical body healthy and alive by eating and drinking and by satisfactory honors and ample possessions, up to a certain point, but beyond that point, unless he knew how to feed the vital spark so that it would spring anew within him, his end had surely come, and none could restore him.

They did not know what would rekindle or feed the vital spark of heavenly flame. They saw that though you might eat the finest flesh and drink the choicest Wines, though you might have the loveliest home, and princes and potentates might flatter and fawn at your feet, this vital spark would turn away unfed, and would not glow to fan your body into life or health unless it had been fed with its own kind of food. And nobody knew what its food should be.

Jesus, who could rekindle the vital spark in the most dead of all appearances, said, "The flesh profiteth nothing; the words that I speak unto you, they are spirit and they are life."

He knew that the master in Israel had no rekindling quality unless he knew His Words. For the vital spark which has power to keep us alive and well forevermore, will only feed on words; and, moreover, will only glow and flame when the words of Jesus are spoken. Hence there is no life outside of Christ Jesus. "My words are life to them that find them and health to all their flesh."

There is a science of the Christ, or an orderly and systematic finding of the vital spark so that it shall glow and shine brighter and brighter, as there is a science of the stars and their movements. This science was prophesied by Isaiah as to be perfectly demonstrated by the Man who should be born in Bethlehem from the humbled stem of Jesse.

Isaiah felt as a revelator what We now know as a science, that a mind that has a Word of the Christ quality whether as courage or judgment or knowledge of law, will spring forth at the least sign of hope as the stumps of the Palestine oaks will branch at the smell of Water.

The coral animals that build the islands can only live in the aerated foam formed by breasting the angry billows. So some natures will only rise to breach spiritual food and demonstrate spiritual vitality when the heavy Waters of sorrow, defeat, ignominy, beat them back.

King Bruce of Scotland felt his noble courage faltering when pursued by enemies and distrusted by friends. At the sight of a persevering little spider defeated again and again in its attempt to rise to a certain height on its tiny thread, but finally at the tenth effort succeeding, Bruce sprang to his feet. "Shall a Bruce have less courage than a spider?" he cried, and he put forth the rod of his courage to victory.

"Build on resolve and not upon regret."

Whoever faces the deepest feeling that stirs him when failure seems to have him down will find that there is a conviction within his own soul that he has a right to success. This is the vital spark ready to flame if you feed it with Words.

"Thy word was a lamp unto my feet and a light (or guide) unto my path."

The hunger of this fire of the soul can only be fed by the strongest words you have ever heard.

In science we learn to face all the feelings with right Words till the Whole body glows and the whole character flames with good health, good judgment, and hospitality along every line.

Now the world has the words that will fan the vital spark through all the being into a health out of the reach of sickness, a peace out of the reach of pain, a life out of the reach of death, a success out of the reach of defeat. The world must not deny this. The world must not listen when the most popular magazine of the day tells us that all mankind now rests under the era of bafflement and despair. It must not believe the scholars when they tell that only those plays and songs and preachers describing defeated man are popular. The world must not believe anybody who says that the Omar Khayam pictures of the soul flying desolate are more popular than the songs of deliverance and the teachers of triumph.

When the actor impersonating the potter struggling to revive the lost art of the Tatswood pottery is at the last day likely to fail because no one will even give him a hod of coal, yet the fires of his ever — young soul springs up crying, "I will begin again!" And if then you fail?" "Begin again!" Why does the audience, away to the galleries, applaud if to be defeated absolutely is more popular than to rise on the wings of the words of the soul? "Success and not failure is my birthright."

Isaiah understands how to teach a nation, a religious body, a man, what is true, better than the teachers of today, for he sees the Man whom we, 2500 years after him, call Messiah, smite the whole earth with the words of His twelve lessons of life science, and that the profoundest doctrine ever enunciated is, "Judge not after the sight of the eyes, nor after the hearing of the ears," for so shall thy Master teach thee, Himself fulfilling the law. When ye shall "judge not according to appearance," they shall not hurt nor destroy in all My holy mountain.

The prophecy reads that they that shut their eyes and stop their ears from evil shall dwell on high. Their bread shall be sure. Their waters shall not fail. They shall partake of the living substance, even the word of God.

"There is a substance pervading all the worlds of the universe," said the philosophers of antiquity. It fills all things. It is too fine for the senses to recognize. It is only handled by the words of the mind. Nay, the words of the mind are too coarse to handle this substance that pervades all things; it must be touched only by the understanding of the mind. And the understanding of truth is the only touch fine enough to mold this substance, which is truth itself.

Out of it is made happiness, peace, delight. This substance is Truth. Truth is God. God is the only substance. Only they who know that it is not truth which call us bones and flesh and nerves; only they who know that it is not truth which says that there are any thoughts or any substance out of which to make evil, can touch the mount where there is nothing to hurt or destroy.

How fine is the writing on the "ensign" Isaiah saw should be lifted up in these days!

Is not this the acme of "judging not according to the sight of the eyes nor the hearing of the ears," when we know that it as bad for the preacher of the wickedness of killing as it is for the slayer to slay, for

He who thinks that he can slay a life —

Or he who thinks life can be slain —

These both do err, for life is God,

And God cannot be slain.

There is no substance out of which to make one who can kill. There is no substance out of which to make one who thinks such things can happen.

There is only God.

Isaiah says that the gentiles will hasten to rest under this banner.

"And its rest shall be glorious!"

Ho! Ye Who toil and labor to earn your bread; rest under this teaching. Your rest shall be on the topless mount of the living God. Christ Jesus has come.

Rest, pale mother, under the ensign of the truth Jesus Christ taught-- there is only God - and the reviving winds of the hilltops of Paradise shall fan your white brow and set your tired feet among the green fields of love, and your "rest shall be glorious."

Come, world-Weary traveler, drink from this water of the life Christ Jesus preached — listen not to the noise of the teachers of bafflement and despair — the triumphant song of your own soul defies them. Captivity is led captive. Christ Jesus has come, and they that come under His ensign know no evil. For them God the good is all. January 3rd, 1892

BIBLE LESSON XXVI. Isaiah 26:2. THE TWELVE GATES

Here is a lesson in prophecy. Isaiah sees ahead from his own time into a period never yet reached (externally) when all the nations will speak truth. And with their speaking truth there should be salvation in the very stones of the walls of the city.

All the time Isaiah is writing you will notice that he believes intensely in time. He foretells the good future of the race. He sees the golden age to come.

Such men as Isaiah have had a great deal to do with the civilized world's looking forward to the coming of God as Father, Son and Holy Spirit, instead of knowing and realizing that God, as the Giver of every good and satisfactory condition, is always here in His greatest power and greatest beneficence, ready to pour out into visible gifts what lies so closely around us.

Any strong mind with intense conviction can set the current of the world's thought flowing when it speaks.

So Isaiah set the current of the World's thought consciously where his words were read, and unconsciously where they were only felt, into the belief in a far-off future for its good. The very best kind of men the race has had, with only one or two marked exceptions, have believed in future good instead of insisting upon all things now.

Your bodily health should be perfect now, whether Isaiah believed you should wait for a golden age for it or not. Your mind should be perfect in its judgment so that you should speak no error and make no mistake now,

Isaiah and all the rest of the prophets to the contrary notwithstanding. Your prosperity along every line of effort should be delightfully satisfactory ever minute now. All the prophets of Israel and the preachers of the ages should be rejected if they speak contrariwise.

Jesus Christ says, "Now is the day of salvation." He is not pleased that John the Baptist is always telling of what is to come. He says that the very least spiritually-minded to be in the kingdom (not going into it), is greater. The kingdom of health (health is God) is here Waiting our seeing and loving it. The kingdom of judgment (judgment is God) is here waiting our seeing and loving it. The kingdom of prosperity (prosperity is God) is here waiting our seeing and loving it. One is no more material than another.

In the old high Jewish science of God, prosperity was always a sign of God's recognized presence. There must be also good health and noble judgment to accompany prosperity, else we will be one — sided.

If you are afraid to lay hold on prosperity as a marked sign of favor from the Most High, you show that some great error of a man or set of men struggling to be spiritually — minded has got hold of your thoughts to push them his or their Way.

Jesus Christ owned all the kingdoms of this world and the riches of them. "Know ye not that Jesus Christ is in you?"

Take special notice that Jesus Christ assures you and all the race that being spiritually-minded you are sure to have a hundredfold more in this sphere of experience and in the realm of high thoughts where you go. By continually keeping His name you have everlasting rest in delightful companionship, unbroken family life, abundant blessing greater than you can ask or even think.

The kingdom of God is an everlasting kingdom lying around us. To speak of it as here and now is to open our eyes to see it. Many a man has grown old still hoping to be prospered when he might have taken the prosperity held out to him from the first by saying, "I am prosperous now and I am awake to see it. I do not believe in waiting to get what is my right today."

It is about time the world got out from under the swing of people's thoughts of futures. The Buddhists teach, and so did the Egyptians long ago, that we ought to cry "IT IS! IT IS!" to the good.

A good physician is one who believes that his powders and pills will work now. If he hands his successful pills and powders to a man who believes that maybe sometime he will be a successful doctor, those pills and powders won't work through the future kind of mind unless that mind yields absolutely to the now feeling of the successful one.

You can take the successful note of now from your own reason, or you can get near some successful man or woman and get a treatment from their confident mental quality.

I do not believe in poor Christians. I have seen people get quite Well of their crooked limbs who lost all their means after being quite subservient in mind to one who thought healed legs were a sign of spiritual life, but who felt that prosperity was not a sign of spiritual life.

Elisha, who lived about a hundred years before Isaiah, did not speak so powerfully as Isaiah; if he had we would be much more prosperous now than we seem to be. Elisha picked up dead people and said, "Live now!" He fed hundreds of people out of small provisions right when they were hungry. He saw how mean it would be to promise pottage to starving people in a golden age to come.

Once when he was living in the little village of Dothan, the Syrian king sent a host of soldiers to slay him. Elisha's servant was terrified, but Elisha calmly said, "They that be with us are more than they that be with them." And looking around about towards the hills of Samaria the servant saw chariots and horses and majestic horseman fighting their cause, and there was no army of Syrians could hurt Elisha.

Do you believe this? It would be a good plan for you to believe that if you think what is true with all your might that all the supernal beings of the World of God are on your side.

Do not wait for danger and privation and sorrow to swoop down on you like a wind from the strong errors of the prophets and priests and ministers of the past in conjunction with the present overpowering belief in the reality and law of such things. Rise and think for yourself and then when the day of calamity seems to be about to destroy you, you will find the thoughts you now take up will encamp in the hills about you and put all evils to flight.

I suppose you understand that those majestic horsemen and chariots of fire were the outpicturing of Elisha's affirmations.

"Have your feet shod with the preparation of the gospel."

Today think the bravest and noblest and richest thoughts you can speak. Think them Well. They will come back as good health, good judgment, prosperity.

"He createth the fruit of the lips."

Words come back in fruits of all kinds. Just hear the beggars scream. Who made them beggars? Isaiah, John the Baptist, the pulpits of modern times and all such as agree that good health, good judgment, and prosperity are going to belong to mankind in the future.

"Now is the day of salvation," says Jesus. "Open are the gates," said Isaiah. He meant open your mind to speak boldly the twelve words of science.

The twelve gates of revelation and prophecy and science are the twelve knowledges you already possess. The moment you hear from the roar of without, the words that are not true, you begin to close your gates. Open the twelve gates boldly. Swing open the gates of that wonderful wisdom given you from the foundations of the world. Regard nobody's teaching who believes in the power of evil. Avoid books that describe evil. Ignore people who believe in evil. Open wide the twelve gates of your noble city and shed abroad the glory of health, strength, joy, prosperity.

Do you know the twelve laws that are shut up within your wonderful mind?

You had better hear them spoken boldly by somebody who knows them and believes in them, but I will give them briefly for you to speak either silently or audibly:

Remember that what you think is a wave of light going through the mental atmosphere of the world, and where ever your true thought strikes, somebody will be lifted off a bed of pain or healed of some sorrow.

There is good for me. My good is my God, my life, my truth, my love, my substance, my intelligence, omnipresent, omnipotent, omniscient.

There is no mixture of evil in my good. There is no opposition to my God as material conditions of any kind. There is no absence of life, substance, intelligence. There is nothing to hate. There is no presence of sin, sickness, or death in my World, where God is the only presence and power and Wisdom.

God is all. God is the omnipresent, omnipotent, omniscient good, as life, truth, love, substance, intelligence. I am my own idea of God, and I live and move and have my being according to my idea of God. I am spirit, mind like my God, and shed abroad wisdom, strength, holiness. My God works through me to will and to do that which ought to be done by me. I am governed by the true God and am kept from sin, from suffering for sin, and I cannot fear sin, sickness, or death.

I do believe that the true God is now working with me and through me and by me and for me, to make me a living demonstration of omnipresent, omnipotent, omniscient goodness.

As spirit I can preach the gospel. Heal the sick, cast out demons, raise the dead.

I understand the secret of instantaneous spiritual demonstration.

I hold no accusations against the people of God. I do not believe in lustful passions or sensual appetites. I believe that all these are the hunger and thirst after righteousness, given a false name.

I do not accuse the people of God of deceiving each other or of being deceived. There is no opposition to truth.

I do not accuse the people of God of being sinners. It is true that all things were made by the true God and are now very good.

I do not believe in a mixture of good and evil in the universe. I stand to my confidence that all is good. All is good in truth. According to my faith so it is now unto me and unto those about me.

I cannot admit that there is any foolishness or ignorance or weakness or old — age failure in omnipresent, omnipotent, omniscience. There is but one mind, and that is God — one substance, and that is God.

The white soul of every creature stands out ransomed from sin, death and sorrow by the words of truth. The whole world is awake to righteousness. Time is no more. All is well now.

Judging not after the sign of the eyes nor after the hearing of the ears, these twelve gates will open and you will surely see things as they are and not as has been believed they are.

To live and think these thoughts is to shine as the sun with love and wisdom. This was the truth as lived by Jesus Christ. This is the truth Jesus Christ lives. This is the truth everlasting.

High over all principalities and powers of unbelief in the allness of God, high over all memories of your past, high out of reach of your fears of the future, live and reign in truth with Jesus Christ in you and with you and by you and for you.

Do you not know that this truth is Jesus Christ in you? Do you not know that when you speak this truth it is Jesus Christ opening the gates of glory for your world?

Poor Isaiah looked forward to a time when the world should know it. We rise in triumph of knowing that the kingdom of God is within us all now.

January 10th, 1892

BIBLE LESSON XXVII. Isaiah 28:1. WHO ARE DRUNKARDS

The lesson for today is all about woe, according to Isaiah and the religious world that has let its thought currents be stirred by Isaiah. It is, "Woe to the crown of pride, to the drunkards of Ephraim'," and the Golden text selected is, "Wine is a mocker, strong drink is raging, and whosoever is deceived thereby is not wise."

According to absolute truth, who are drunkards? Those who have swallowed the idea that there is another power besides spirit, another substance besides spirit, another law besides spirit.

What other power besides spirit is there? None. "Is there any besides Me? Nay, I know not any."

What other substance is there besides spirit? None. "Do not I fill heaven and earth?"

What other law is there besides the law of the spirit? None. "The law of the spirit maketh free from sin and death." "There shall be one Lord (law) and His name one."

Then who is there to swallow the idea that there is more than one power, presence, law? Nobody.

There is but one being. "There is one God who is above you all and through you all and in you all."

Then who is there to be a drunkard? Nobody.

Then what is Isaiah talking about in this twenty-eighth chapter? Nothing.

How, then is it profitable to read and study the chapter? Simply as the observation of contrasts — opposites. To look his words over from the standpoint of one who knows what is real and what is supposition is worthwhile.

If there were anybody to believe in two powers and the results of the belief were to confront us this would be the way the results would look.

But starting out with the belief in evil and good would not make both evil and good true, any more than it would make it true if you should suspect a good man of having stolen your watch when he was utterly incapable of such a thing.

God is the only Presence, Power, Law. You may agree with Isaiah and the kings and queens and college presidents of the world that drunkenness and poverty and sorrow are realities and are permitted within the omnipresent good, but it is a lie from the beginning just the same and you will only demonstrate freedom in yourself and for your world by rising out of the clutches of Isaiah and the kings and queens and college presidents by speaking the truth.

"You shall know the truth and the truth shall set you free."

If there were any being to get drunk then he must have first swallowed the belief in two powers, two substances, two laws. Then he would get afraid of the other power and get to hating the other presence. Then his hate must rest somewhere and on something as the magnetic belts that are supposed to circle the earth find some stones, some plants, some animals that will catch and hold their quality of magnetism more than others.

If a person keeps saying, even casually and carelessly, "I hate it," or "I hate him," his words must go over the airs like dandelion seeds and drop somewhere, and whoever comes into the spots where the words are lying will pick up the harmless little nightshade or tobacco plant and find poison in it. He will find the word hate dropped into the plant and will say it is poison.

But it would never be true for a moment. For "God saw everything that He had made and, behold, it was very good." "And Without Him was nothing made that was made." Ephraim in this woe of Isaiah is Samaria which was named after Ephraim. Ephraim means double fruitfulness — that is, both evil and good thoughts should have their fruits in this city. They should have their crown here. They should be very apparent.

Isaiah falls directly into the sight of both good and evil, and one moment triumphantly prophesies the double good to be demonstrated when people shall not judge after the sight of the eyes, and in the next moment judges entirely after the sight of his eyes by seeing where the hate thoughts of Esau had stopped in the vineyards and among the people of Samaria. Ephraim or Samaria took the hate thoughts of Esau and the fear thoughts of Jacob, and Isaiah saw the feeling effects of such notions so vividly that he caused the hate and fear to come quickly to a head, like a great boil, and break over in to a terrible rage of misery. For Isaiah believed greatly in the active operation of evil now and the future active operation of good.

His mind had great power. At Samaria he might have pronounced the omnipotence of the good with such intense spiritual and mental efficiency that the reeling priests and drunken princes would have shouted praises and hallelujahs to Jehovah Nissi.

The banner over them was love. The belief around them was hate. Where did all the hate come from? It had slipped over the head of Ephraim himself from Esau's hatred of Jacob, had rested temporarily on poor

Joseph, sold by his brethren in to Egypt, and had come down to reach its ultimate or crown of pride in Samaria.

Isaiah ought to have realized how powerful — how doubly powerful the Word of good would be in Samaria, just as Elisha had so long before him.

Just at the moment when the hate thoughts of Esau and the fear thought of Jacob were festered into What was called the siege of Samaria, Elisha had risen in the power of his mind and spoken such words as had turned the Syrian army aside, and fed the starving inhabitants of the city where forever the signs of evil and of good together should distract the mind to see double, as the Iceland spar doubly refracts light, and forever makes two images of one substance — till we withdraw our hate thoughts from the earth.

Whoever sees both good and evil plays the part of a double refractor, and is typified by the Iceland spar. He is well represented by Isaiah if he feels dreadfully about the evil and works himself sick in the slums, supposing that to mourn and wail and pronounce woes on governments, preachers, teachers, for not stopping the same is Wise. Such ragings are deceptions, and "whoever is deceived thereby is not wise."

Back of all that the senses tell, and back of all that the mind believes, is the truth. Whoever started there, and believed in something not true, he caused a Jacob to be both mean and noble. There are two Jacobs now. Jacob stole his birthright and earned Rachel. These two trains of character fought within him near the brook of Jabbok. He was trying to believe in the triumph of love while his mind was half believing in the power of hate.

The confidence in the power and presence and efficiency or law of love is never absent from anybody's mind; but not everybody rallies that idea (which is his angel], and causes it to face the fear of hate, or fear of evil, as Jacob did just before he met Esau.

His confidence in the power of love prevailed, and love spoke boldly as his noble friend, "As a prince hast thou power with God and man."

Take your two states of mind and settle the question today whether you believe in the presence and power and working of the love of God to stop all the fruits of hate and fear now. See how Jacob prevailed. Esau met him kindly. Your mission is greater than Jacob's. He settled it for himself, but not for his children nor for his world. You and I will take the question for all the universe.

I do believe in the good only as now working with me and through me and by me and for me to make me a living demonstration of the power of goodness for all the world. I do not believe in the signs of evil. God is all. God folds and keeps all this world in love. I pronounce all evil sights and sounds absent, and declare love and joy their rightful inheritance of every creature, from this moment.

If the absurdity of such a prayer comes up it is your Jacob experience. Rise and wrestle to believe in the good. Miracles are wrought by prayer, child of God.

When fear of evil or hate of evil sights or belief in a law of evil comes up within you, Wrestle; wrestle all night till the morning. You will see great corporations wither and drunken officials cease from power and proud magnates get meek as Jacob's thigh — which was the part of him that stood for his fear of evil — as these are the part of the world that stand out as your fear of evil or grief at evil.

Jacob was most interested in his own fortunes. You are interested in a common humanity. What you have you wish all the world to have. They may receive it at your hands. If you believe otherwise than this, Wrestle with my message for it is sent to tell you that our God reigns and you will see His loving kindness when you believe He is the only presence, the only power, and the only efficiency.

At Samaria, Elisha decided for the loving kindness of Jehovah. At Samaria, Jesus announced the presence of the Messiah. At Samaria, Isaiah pronounced for the power of evil as ending in death.

The noble vineyards, the beautiful olive groves, and the bountiful fields of Waving grain in Samaria were the fruit of the word of the loving kindness of God believed in. The intoxicating wines, the reeling priests, and profligate princes were the fruits of the Words of hate and the belief in hate.

As there is only one presence and that is omnipresent, only one power and that is omnipotence, only one science or knowledge and that is omniscience, any other idea of anything must be no idea at all — just delusion.

Whenever one has tried the ways of the world and learned the law of the spirit there comes a time when he must choose positively which he will believe in. It will mark itself on his face from that moment, for he has met his Samaria, and the watchpost thereof is in him from that time on. Samaria means "watchpost."

The Woman at the well still under the dominion of the Isaiah type of a future Messiah heard Jesus Christ tell her that the Messiah was already here. We who have been believing that the good is coming to us now rise to shake off the belief in time and the belief in the presence of evil and declare that there is nothing to hate. We declare from the coiling cobra to the flowing bowl of the reeling statesmen we withdraw our accusations.

There is nothing to hate. God made all things and pronounced them very good. We will not fill them with our fear of them. We know that this is the only law of safety there is. It is the law of non — condemnation practiced by Jesus Christ. "Neither do I condemn thee." So shall it be fulfilled of which He promised, "They shall drink any deadly thing and it shall not hurt them."

We will remember how God made everything good, even all mankind, and will not accuse anybody of anything. There we will see our high thoughts come around us instead of our low thoughts. The high thoughts of Abraham came and sat in the door of his tent like men. The high thoughts of Elijah took him up in a chariot of majesty. The high thoughts of Elisha encamped as Majestic horsemen and descended the walls of Samaria to tell him how to feed the besieged city. The high thoughts of Jesus fed Him, as an angel came and ministered. All the people round about us are majestic, noble, beautiful, happy.

If we have covered them with mantles of meanness, with veils of dishonesty, with skins of ugliness, with talks of misery, we hereby Withdraw all the thoughts which have caused them to look and act quite different from their true selves, and we know that so shall the supernal beings God keeps in this world — the angels of whom we are unaware — come into our sight.

All is good. All is beauty. All is love. Here, on the hilltop of Samaria, we lift our eyes to God and pronounce no Woe on mankind, no denunciation on the creeping things, nor on the growing plants or fruit.

There is no process by which any man can hurt his neighbor according to spirit. And spirit is all. There is no way whereby man can defraud his neighbor according to spirit. And spirit is all. There is no law whereby anything that lives or grows can cause our young men to reel or stagger as drunken. There is only God. There are no words given under Heaven for anybody to eat save the Words of Jesus Christ. "They shall have no power to hurt."

Do you not see that if you must rise today and announce to your own self whether you accuse anything or anybody, or withdraw your accusation, that there is but one thing to do?

If you have noticed how no other plan Works you may be more Willing to withdraw your accusations for a new plan. Whosoever is deceived by thinking that it is wine that causes men to reel had better withdraw his accusation from the wine and see it "have no power to hurt." Whosoever thinks that strong drink is raging as a Wild enemy to peace and prosperity had better withdraw his fear of evil and his belief in hate and his sting of accusation from the air where they have wondered and dropped into the fermented grains, and strong drink shall have no power to hurt even when mixed with the deadly drugs that represent our hatred of people.

"They shall drink any deadly thing and it shall not hurt them."

The stings of our false notions we now withdraw. We love truth and good substance. "If this be not true then is my preaching vain," and I must enter the gates of despair with the rest of the philanthropists of the world who believe in fighting the evils their own beliefs have projected on the canvas of humanity.

But I do not believe in the power or the presence or the action of evil. At the highest point of its crown of pride I name it delusion and put there the triumphant healing name — Jesus Christ.

"There is, therefore, now no condemnation."

There is nothing to hate. All is spirit.

This is the teaching prophesied to come; "Hear and your soul shall live."

We feel the air blow o'er us,

And the glory shines before us

Of what mankind may be,

Pure, generous, brave and free.

"Am I my brother's keeper?" Yea, verily.

But the beasts of the field were made to love me, the storms were made to praise me, and I was made to love them all. There is nothing to hate.

January 17th, 1892

BIBLE LESSON XXVIII. Isaiah 37:1. AWAKE THOU THAT SLEEPEST

Here is a lesson that tells religious people — truly God-loving people — what to do today with the great trust combinations, the soulless corporations and unequal opportunities of human beings on the plant.

Now, the naming of these things does not make them realities by any means, any more than naming and describing a nightmare makes it a reality, though all its Gorgons have seemed more real than the presence of your loving mother near you all the time.

We name what seems evil in order to take away its appearance, or seeming.

It is a great nightmare which insists that in a world occupied by the good entirely, any other actions can be going on except good. Then the whole business of those who know that it is only a dream is to awaken the World to truth. Paul cried, "Awake, thou that sleepest!"

The object lesson which is here presented from Isaiah Chapter 37, is the explicit direction to us, and by following it we can stop this great amassing of riches at the expense of the helpless (so described) and the strange situation of a few able to withhold opportunities from the many.

Historically the object lesson was placed on the boards 712 B.C. Hezekiah was a good and pious King of Judah. Sennacherib was the idolatrous King of the powerful Assyrians. They met in battle in exactly the same way we will meet in battle the Assyrian monarch, capitalization of today.

Hezekiah set his idea of God out plainly before all the people in the temple. You will notice that he never compromised his description of God by admitting for an instant that it was God who permitted the Assyrians to get such powerful odds against Jerusalem.

In the science of mind it is very important that we speak accurately, just as it is very important that we say four and two are six in a great problem in trigonometry. Mind builds all conditions and circumstances. Then, of course, we must have truth in the mind to build true conditions and circumstances.

If Hezekiah had said once that it was their duty to be "resigned to the troubles God had in His providence assigned to them," the silent victory here recorded could never have taken place.

It is no credit to our reason to be setting up a straw or stone Gorgon to knock down; so it is no credit to our judgment to be setting up such errors in our minds as that God in His providence has seen fit to do this or that which has hurt so sorely.

Only by the accurate description of their God could Hezekiah have defeated with his little handful of material power the army of 185,000 Assyrians pitted against Jerusalem. Only by the accurate description of God can we defeat the solid phalanx of material riches pitted against the just rights of mankind today.

Fighting the princes and magnates of the planet will not make them less. It will only put the power from them into the hands of ruffians, who will not be half as wise in dealing with it as those already in power are.

Hezekiah, with his kingdom, had been having a long, hard struggle to live against such a state of affairs, just as the good and honest people of today feel that they have a hard time to get on in the world with such great corporations chewing them up and Working against them all the time, while dishonesty seems to flourish and goodness is laughed at.

Sennacherib, the king of a great corporation that has swallowed all the smaller enterprises of the whole country round about, sent Word to Hezekiah that if he would work in his interests he would feed and clothe and house him well. He told Hezekiah it was no use for him to stand up and declare that the invisible Lord Jehovah would or could defend Jerusalem against him because so far everything had been obliged to yield. He mentioned the mining interests, the manufacturing interests, the political machinery, the shipping interests, educational efforts (under the term "gods," of course) that had already succumbed entirely and now he advises religion to do likewise.

Hezekiah never answered Sennacherib in words face to face. He took the letter that described how everything was yielding and "spread it before the Lord." Then he said, "It is true that all these interests," under the symbolic names of "kingdoms," of course, "have succumbed to Sennacherib whose god was Nisroch (Monopoly) but none of these interests of humanity have stood forth and declared themselves under the unfailing protection of the Lord God Almighty."

"No, they had all hoped to fight materiality with materiality (mentioned as material God against material God, of course). But as for me, I do not believe in meeting evil with evil, matter with matter. I do not believe that there is any need of martyrdom or suffering or failure or defeat of any kind for those who trust in the true God."

Then Hezekiah declared his highest ideal of God. Hear him. There is no "flinchy" speaking of yielding to Sennacherib's hosts, "if it be the Lord's will." He knows, if he knows anything, that his highest ideal of the Divine Being is not of one who has to do evil that good may come. If he had admitted that idea into his description of God he would have been setting up a less than the true God, and an imaginary God cannot meet Sennacherib's host. Mind that.

Today we cannot try any halfway God on the situation. This description of Hezekiah's is the only true one: "O, Lord of Hosts, God of Israel, that dwelleth between the cherubim (of love and protection), Thou art the God, even Thou alone, of all the kingdoms of the earth. Thou hast made heaven and earth. Save us that all the kingdoms of the earth may know that Thou are the Lord, even Thou only."

As he thus described his highest ideal of God, the thought went over to the camp of the Assyrians, whose soldiers were the personified beliefs in the power of trusts and monopolies, and 185,000 men lay "dead corpses" without the sound of a battering ram, or arrow, or stone.

The greatest fight of the ages was in idea. And the two ideas that fought were the perfect description of God and the imagination of what God is.

The might of the gentiles, unsmote by the sword, Hath melted like snow in the glance of the Lord.

"For the weapons of our Warfare are not carnal, but mighty through God to the pulling down of strongholds."

And now, who is there to arise in the power of his might for the honor of the good, and describe his highest idea, of the good as having the right to reign? The only reason Sennacherib and his hosts have come down upon the world in spite of religious teachings, is because the highest idea, of What ought to be, has not been described as what is.

The speaking out from the silence Where the ideal has always been hidden by the repetition of the nonsense that "God, in His inscrutable wisdom, permits evil, to which we must bow our heads," is the divine "glance of truth" which will lay every trust company, every unjust corporation, every unrighteous scheme, low as Sennacherib's host.

On even a small scale of human experience this principle will work. It is better for those people who have been threatened with poverty and want through any sort or kind of combination of hard luck against them, to make up their mind what their highest ideal of God is and talk to it and tell it what they expect of such a character.

Write down your highest ideal. Read it over. If you have cut under the truth of the true God you must erase that part and make it right. Only the highest idea can come against the culmination of the series of errors in the algebra of human experience wherewith no value stands for soul, all value.

No preaching but the highest ideality can meet Sennacherib's host of believers that the god Nisroch (monopoly of the goods of the world) is in rule.

The highest ideal is the only real. It has been kept silent by our not speaking it forth. We are the Word. We speak as we please — that which we speak stands forth. No compromise. The true God is that "Thou Only" of Hezekiah.

The actual conscious speaking or thinking of truth has an astonishing effect upon hosts of minds. Any idea that is right will accomplish wonders of good by laying hosts of nightmares low.

For instance, a few years ago somewhere a man or woman who had believed in sickness and disease as a part of their inheritance, and had tried every material thing in creation from foreign travel to honeybees' stings and southern flies thought suddenly as all these things had failed there was nothing more to do but to do nothing. Accordingly that hitherto unsuccessful invalid determined to do nothing. The same idea went on the wings of the winds and simultaneously all over the planet chronics of a certain type of mind determined to lie still and see what would become of them.

That was a beautiful state of mind. The silence into which they committed themselves is the ideal where all good lies waiting. They all got Well. Their old maladies dropped down like Sennacherib's host.

Afterwards certain of them said they thought of God as a healing presence while they lay there. It came to them that God is health and not sickness. Others said they felt that the silence is nature's restorative: vis medicatris naturae. "In the silence, in the silence, God speaketh to my soul."

In great sickness or pain or trouble lie very still. Lie still as death. Down through your mind will fall the healing God.

In such cases as this, however, carefully describe your highest ideal of God and tell it what you expect of it. Don't compromise. Don't give in because you remember What good people have suffered. I tell you they need not have suffered if they had believed in the true God. Cut out of your mind such memories. Cut out of your mind that you Want the will of God to be done. The will of your old trouble-sending deity isn't Worth remembering.

Just read how unconditioned Great Hezekiah's God Was, and, bearing in mind what great things the unconditioned God accomplished for him, insist on His doing the same for you.

There is a little side lesson in this one of Hezekiah's demonstration which is useful as showing how lovingly there is a goodness shaping our ends for us which we may have demonstrated in the smallest items.

Hezekiah's name meant "Strength of Jehovah." Thus he had all strength on his side. He ought to have just given thanks for his strength just as Jesus Christ always did before a miracle. You will see that Hezekiah was a trifle afraid of the strength of materiality — of the opposing conditions. Without entering into any explanation of how this shows that "in our greatest strength," we cannot help seeing that each person's name stands for his easiest honors and also for his greatest errors or weaknesses.

If anyone knows the significance of his own name he knows what it is he can demonstrate most quickly.

The shadow of that great good is always the fear that things are exactly the opposite. If your name is Rebekah you are chained to prosperity, and by pulling on the principle of bounty by your giving thanks that you have such great possessions belonging to you, they will come flying into your sight. Very likely you are complaining of poverty and crying with longings the very moments when you ought to be giving thanks that your highest ideal of prosperity is yours now.

Suppose your name is William. Whatever you put after the two words "I am" will demonstrate promptly. Very likely you will have very intense experiences, because you speak well of yourself sometimes, and ill of yourself sometimes. You should identify yourself with the highest Name you know. You should be like Jesus Christ, and be so at one with truth that you cannot distinguish between truth and yourself. You remember that He said, "I am truth." The highest ideal you can conceive — you are it. You can say "I am Omnipotent Spirit," and prove it.

Suppose your name is Francis. Your birthright is freedom. You should say often "I am free." Probably you have a great habit of getting under the personal influence of other people. The instant you get under them your judgment gets biased.

Your name may be Mary, and your affirmation ought to be, "I am honored and glorified." But very likely you are given to mourning because your human experience is bitter.

This is one of the little side lessons off from the main one of the Hezekiah prayer for deliverance, but the good that folds us around, waiting to be announced, blesses even the tiniest item of our life when We acknowledge it.

"Acknowledge Me in all thy ways (in the smallest transactions and situations) and I will direct thy paths." Set your mind steadfastly to the name and the character of the good according to your ideal.

That highest good is the real. The ideal is the real. No matter how silent you have hitherto been on the subject now is the time to rise with the right description of the true God.

There will be no more pain, no more poverty, no more discord in your life, with the acknowledgment that is right. What is your name? You were not named carelessly. The word that you bear is your word that will come flying to demonstrate itself when you speak it and bravely refuse the easiest error into which you are habitually slipping.

Who is a God like the true God? Who redeemeth all life from destruction, who healeth all diseases, who crowneth with loving kindness everything and everybody, every instant, wave only the true God? How great and efficient and kind is your God?

That one whom you have been describing is the one who dealt with you up to date. January 24th, 1892

BIBLE LESSON XXIX. Isaiah 53:1. THE HEALING LIGHT

"Who hath believed our report? And to whom is the arm of the Lord revealed?"

If We were the least bit under the spell of Isaiah's powerful mind, we would be just as majestically mournful at the apparent unbelief of this age in the teachings of Jesus Christ as Isaiah was at the age he anticipated.

But we will not be biased by Isaiah's belief in evil and the power of evil. We will take his own words that the highest possible doctrine is refusing to judge after the sight of the eyes and after the hearing of the ears. We will look straight into the meanings of the words of the Messiah Himself, when He says "I am Truth," and "According to thy faith be it unto thee;" also, "For the lightest Word thou shalt give account." Therefore, "Judge not according to appearance, but judge righteous judgment."

People often have premonitions of evil. They do not know the law of the annulling power of their own words, and so they wait until the premonitions come to pass, and tell the papers and magazines What a mysterious faculty they have for prophecy.

That premonitive instinct which they have is the signal that it is at that moment time for them to use a power they really do possess, which is that of preventing calamities. If you have a foreboding feeling, it is the sign that you ought to speak certain words.

Knowing the power of words you can speak the right ones promptly and heartily. "Thou shalt decree a thing and it shall be established unto thee; when men are cast down then thou shalt say, there is lifting up."

A clergyman of the recognized and dominant faith (that is in school and satan and afflictions from God] was a very beloved pastor in sickness. He had a cheerful face and fatherly manner that comforted all kinds and classes of people. He had been many years accustomed to visiting his parish sick and had learned to be quite wise in detecting symptoms and advising precautions. There was always one sign that he knew as the foreshadowing of What is called death. It never failed to herald that strange belief of mankind. When he realized an imperceptible [to the eyes) purplish haze he knew its forewarning.

After a while he heard of this law of the right word as able to destroy sickness, sin and death and once when he saw the hitherto unfailing signal he determined to speak it away if there was such a thing. So he said to the purplish haze, "Once I knew you as the sign of death, but now I do not believe in death, nor in the signs of death; I believe only in life and the signs of life. Life is God Omnipotent. I pronounce you the sign of renewing, vigorous life for this man, in the name of the Father, and of the Son and of the Holy Ghost." The purple haze lifted and the red blood tinged the cheeks and fingers of the sick man.

Isaiah saw the rejection of the Redeemer as a coming state of affairs under the law of the fruitage of error. But why did he not blast the fruits of error while they were in the leaf — time of their spring greenness, 712 years B.C. just as Jesus blasted the fig tree before the figs ripened, to illustrate the power of truth to stop error before it comes to fruitage?

Did not Isaiah know enough of the meaning of the passage, "and the Lord repented," to know that the law of the good (or the Lord) can always be spoken in time to turn back [or repent) anything not good?

It is perfectly astonishing how much power of vision Isaiah had to see both evil and good fruits, like a helpless spectator. If he had spoken vehemently that according to the law of error the world would reject Jesus Christ first and His teachings afterwards, but he pronounced error null and void and its results nothingness, his stupendous mind would have drawn the curtains of darkness to the right and the left from the age when Jesus came, and they would have seen Him in His true light. Then again, Isaiah ought to have told our age that we should see the reasonableness of the ideal and would not reject it when it should come announced as plain judgment of goodness.

It seem verily as if we had no mind so manifestly powerful as Isaiah's now, because nobody has seemed to rouse out of the belief in future as strongly as Isaiah rose out of his age when destruction lay upon it and announced coming prosperity.

"To whom is the arm of the Lord revealed?" That is, who sees this law not that Jesus Christ has taught it, so plainly that he can demonstrate the power thereof? Arms are symbols of power in the scriptures. Who sees plainly the power of the good over all evil, even to the annihilation thereof, present, as Isaiah saw the future demonstration of the good? So this lesson teaches us over again the necessity of declaring that the truth about things is now just as much as it ever was or ever will be. Heaven is now and here. It never will be any more here than it is now. But who says this strongly? So Isaiah mourns because he saw us speaking in our dream of error very feebly like people asleep and muttering.

There used to be a theory that this world is all asleep. While we are lying still on our beds in dreamless sleep We are in the normal and natural condition, as we noticed that the sickest, most pained or troubled creature is well enough if he is asleep in dreamless peace. That all what we call waking is not true waking, but nightmare — pure nightmare. That all this time we are at home in our "Father's house where the many mansions be," and only need to speak the right word in this our nightmare (which we have foolishly called our Wake state), to look around and see our home.

Suddenly by the speaking of the right words you will find that you are not teaching school, not running engines, not arguing law points, not translating hieroglyphics, not fighting monopolies or making them — no, you are awake at home.

Oh, Such a home! 'Tis there that never remember
When from earth thy proud soul is set free,
That cold chilling winds of December
Stole all thy companions from thee.

No. Paul told people to awake. David said he should be satisfied when he should awake. Paul wished the people of the past had been mindful of the country from whence they came out.

Hosea said, "Take with you words and return unto your God." Note your God. Paul did not feel the necessity of himself being mindful of the country from when he came out.

We will not split the rock that foundered Paul. Let us remember the country whence we came out. We will speak vehemently with the hot fervor of joy at being told that words will Waken us to see What this kingdom is to which we are so asleep.

In philosophy we are told that whenever in our sleep we dream that We sleep or dream, we are dreaming, that then We are on the point of awakening. So now that we dream that we dream or are told that this is all a nightmare reminder of our home, we must be near awakening.

And that is what all the religionists and astronomers and geologists are trying to stammer about when they tell about the coming end of the world.

According to the gospel, Jesus Christ was supremely awake and is now awake. And as children and grown men and women have to be awakened out of the palsying nightmares, so Jesus Christ awakens us with His words if we speak them.

Strange about it that We must speak His words ourselves. It is just as the mother cannot hold the child's eyes open, but it must open its own eyes, that Jesus Christ tells us, "Keep my words." Whoever realizes this, to him is "the arm of the Lord revealed."

If it is the law of health that the sick woman or man must say positively, "I am well," before he sees himself well, you can see why it is that we must declare ourselves wide awake and not dreaming in order to see our good that lies here. Isaiah insists that the doctrine of truth will "have no form or comeliness."

Some people do not like music; some people do not like paintings; some people do not like sculpture; some people do not like to be told the truth about the power of their own thoughts to get them into scrapes and to get them out of them. They do not see what majesty and dignity that confers upon us, and how kingly we reign over our realm of ideas. It is the law of mind that if we refuse to think certain thoughts we shall never see certain kinds of people. It is the law of mind as related to life that if We positively refuse to think certain thoughts We shall never experience certain conditions of body. It lies in the power of mind as related to life experiences that if we choose we can shut down squarely on thinking such thoughts as are simply shiftless and frivolous and only the rehearsal in memory of some past experience far from ennobling. It is a good plan to shut down on them, for they bring around us their own kinds of people and conditions.

You will be surprised how speedily a certain class of people and conditions will drop out of your life when you stop thinking certain thoughts which they personify. The early morning is said to be the time when the mind is most efficient to cut off useless branches and dead sticks by speaking silently, "I hereby cast out of my mind all such thoughts as have kept me from healthy judgment and prosperity." Then give the mind the good tonic of a strong statement like, "I am sound in health, able in judgment and satisfied with prosperity."

Now, Isaiah herein proceeds to tell us that the Lord laid upon Jesus Christ the iniquity of us all. That was true in this sense, viz., that He took the cup of our experience, which we have forced upon ourselves by imaginations, and tasted it to see what it is best for us to do under such circumstances. He has left the word that it is to be refused as the cup of nothingness.

It is no use for you to bear poverty. You can say positively, "I refuse to be poor. I refuse the cup of poverty. Jesus Christ told me that there is enough and to spare and God is my bountiful supply from this time on."

It is no use for you to cry over anything that has happened to you. Refuse the cup. It is all a nightmare. You do not need to bear anything. It is sheer nonsense for you to get down on your knees and ask God to help you bear what you were never made to bear. You can be noble and good and powerful and wise without suffering for it. It is better to cure a tumor than to carry it around with you. So it is better to dissolve a grief in the cleansing acids of right words than to lug it around.

Martyrdom is only the belief that it is pleasing to God to have us suffer. What kind of a God would that be who could create certain beings to suffer into strength? It is not any use to try to make even the meekest of us believe in and adore such a being. If Jesus Christ chose to go through all our experiences in order to tell us what to do, We will love and bless and obey Him, both as principle and demonstration of principle (which means a right-living character). In this sense only did the Lord lay on Him our iniquities. We can all choose our own thoughts, and thus choose our own companionships, such as those thoughts attract. It is very common for very gently, courageous girls, especially schoolteachers, to think very depressing thoughts, and then wonder why they are so shut off from everything they would like to have. Cut off the depressing thoughts and spend every instant you can get deliberately refusing the cup of trouble, deprivation, pain, and announcing your God-given rights.

Jesus Christ felt called upon to test everything and let us see for ourselves that the Whole material world is under us, not over us, nor in our arms. You will see by this 53rd chapter of Isaiah that there was nothing of suffering which we dream of in this silly nightmare that He did not test.

It is told that God hath given Him a Name above every name. That Name is the quickening principle — the awakening power. You are privileged to do with the Name as you please, but it is very evident that it means all that you wish to have and to know concentrated.

Now, because the science of satisfactory living is so simple do not turn away from it. The more simple the machinery the greater its executive power. It is written that at the name of Jesus everything shall bow. If this word be in our mind this power will be in our life. We shall be surprised when We Wake up to find how simple the law of masterful success is. And there is no doubt about everything depending upon a state of mind, as there is no doubt about a state of mind being induced by words or thoughts.

We often wonder why a small deformed-appearing man has such great powers. It is because he suddenly betook himself to some new Way of thinking. Agesilaus II, King of Sparta, was deformed, short of stature and lame, yet he was a brilliant general. In his 18th year he went to assist the Egyptians against the Persians. He made such a poor appearance that the King of Egypt refused his alliance. Of course the King of Egypt was defeated.

There is a story of a man who had been told that the philosopher's stone was in a pile of stones, and he began to examine them throwing them away one by one after examining them. He got so in the habit of throwing them away that he got careless in his examinations and carelessly threw away the philosopher's stone with the rest. As he threw them into the sea, he never could reclaim them and lost his chance.

Here is a doctrine that is the true philosopher's stone. It is the only doctrine on the face of the earth that has any practical efficiency. But it has nobody and nothing of riches or fame or name to gather its adherents with. This is exactly according to prophecy. This is therefore something to commend it, as the reigning religions have all these things on their side. Yet can you not see how the silent forces of its great truths are permeating, overturning, changing dynasties, religions, political, ethical?

It is one of the denials which every mind should make for its own advancement into its greatest power that it holds no prejudice of any kind. Prejudice for or prejudice against anybody or anything in all the world.

The grand jury disposed of the case of Charles Wesley in the time of an Irish mob by the following verdict: "We find Charles Wesley to be a person of ill fame, a vagabond, and a common disturber of his Majesty's peace; and we pray that he may be transported."

How much do you think Homer got for his Iliad or Dante for his Paradise?

According to this prophecy of Isaiah, this is exactly the verdict people will make while the greatest doctrine ever enunciated is being taught by those who see its truth and its majesty and are willing to stand by till it demonstrates itself.

They shall see of their travail and be satisfied. They shall see that it is greatly Worth while to say, "I am not prejudiced for or against anybody or anything in all the world. I am satisfied with the truth of God." For they shall see that state of mind is like a clear transparency through which the Redeemer's healing light shall stream.

This is the dawn of noble faith,
The day doth follow soon.
When hope can breathe with freer breath,
For night is lost in noon.
January 31st, 1892

BIBLE LESSON XXX. Isaiah 55:1. TRUE IDEAL OF GOD

"Ho, everyone that thirsteth," writes Isaiah. He knows enough of mind to know how it hungers and thirsts all the time for sustaining ideas.

And if he knows anything he knows that an idea which will refresh and satisfy one mind will just be brackish drink and husks for another. So when he is speaking of those waters that will quench the thirst of everybody, old and young, rich and poor alike, he must mean a different kind of waters from the ideas then being taught among men even in the schools of the prophets of Israel.

Moses had been taught years and years before Isaiah that man himself is the "I AM THAT I AM." David had taught the God-nature of humanity. I said ye are gods." It has been running in the minds of many that as with the forward the Lord had shown Himself forward, and with the merciful had shown mercy; that there was therefore no God at all except as we should imagine one, and therefore that there is no God.

It had been strongly intimated as practical doctrine what Isaiah had written in his Chapter that "We are all nothing and our works are nothing." Therefore there is nothing at all. Again, many had practiced cold, hunger, nakedness, self-tortures, hoping to find the nature of things that they might satisfy their thirst for knowledge of what is the true way to be masters of human destiny and not slaves to it.

None of these ways of believing or performing had quenched the thirst or satisfied the hunger of anybody. Isaiah believed there was a way to get our thirst quenched, however, just as Abraham and Moses and the Egyptians and Brahmins had been believing for thousands of years. Some called this strange and unceasing hunger the call of the Wick of life for oil. What the oil was that would keep the life-wick burning they could not really settle, but they finally concluded that it was the call of the mind for truth. So they practiced telling that all is God and there is no God. They practiced telling that we are all and We are nothing. They practiced telling of the interior spirits that keep record of our actions and motives as long as we live, one keeping record of the good motives and actions and the other of the not good actions and motives.

Still the hunger and the thirst kept on, and have kept on ever since.

A prophet used to be one who kept his mind on things not perceptible to the senses; and he every now and then uttered absolute truth along some line without at all realizing what he was saying. Then he Wrought some miracle by what he said. Trying again to work the miracle by using the same

Words he would find that they would not work and then he gave up the effort to do his Work by those Words.

If you should go into a room, as Edward Irving did Where a boy was supposed to be dying, and should cause him to spring to life again by saying, "My boy, God loves you," you might be chagrined to find that the next case would not pay the slightest attention to your words.

It ought to be of great importance to you what cured the boy in the first case, and then, of course, you would readily know Why the next one did not respond. You would not have to find out by study why the second did not recover, but you would turn your attention to why and how the first one responded. Here Isaiah utters a profounder truth than has been written down, "Expede Herculem." That is, if you see a foot of Hercules how can you help judging of his Whole stature?

Here when Isaiah tells us that he can have no hunger and thirst of mind satisfied at this wonderful spring "without money and Without price," he means first that we need not slay lambs and young bullocks hoping to get any satisfaction from a propitiated God of supply. He means also that there are no works we can do that will earn us favor with the first cause of good bounty. He means that there are no thanksgivings we can offer, no praises that we may utter, no faith we can give the Source of every blessing hoping to buy satisfaction thereby.

If one thing won't buy us any favor with Goodness, nothing will.

Isaiah rose on the wings of a mighty truth here and spoke of the Divine supply as now at hand, not to be cajoled or bought off or propitiated by anything we can do.

What a lovely Being this is whom Isaiah brings near! He already is able and ready to provide us with all things without our praising Him, hoping by praise to cajole Him. He gives us bountifully of what will feed and delight us without our begging, hoping by such gyrations of mind to please and flatter Him into rewarding us. He does not demand of us the exercise of a great faith in Him before His goodness will vouchsafe any manifestation of itself.

No, the true God is your highest ideal of supreme goodness. Spread out boldly with your words what you think the best kind of a God would do and there you have what is true of God.

Why haven't you got the gifts of the true God?

Why, we always have the gifts of that God we have described. The gifts of the true God are here. We may have them without money and without price. When you have described the untrue God you must get untrue conditions. The true God folds us around with exactly the life we like. When poverty strikes you it is not what the true God sent, but only what your former description of God has brought around you. Therefore you ought to say, "My God never sends poverty or trouble to anyone; my God supplies all my needs." This last affirmation was one that David used.

But there is a higher ideal of God than one who supplies needs. The higher ideal is of One who never lets anybody or anything need anything. There is even a higher ideal of God than of One who never lets anybody or anything need anything. The higher ideal is of One who never permitted anybody or anything to ever imagine a need.

Yet there is a still higher ideal of God than even that; it is of One who shows us all without our paying any price of praising Him or trusting Him that we are here and now safe at home in our Father's and Mother's house with the fair hills of Paradise in full sight.

Our highest ideal of God is of supreme, generous, universal, bounty, goodness, love, bliss.

Is this, then the highest? Yes. How have we found out that it is by the description of the true God that we see the true God? By reading the lessons in Isaiah. But what illuminated our minds to see these underlying lessons? Holding the name Jesus Christ.

What is it to hold this name in our heart? Simply to speak it silently with the mind. But is not that ridiculous gymnastics? No. By knowing the nature of mind we see how much more potent with power over our life experiences some words are than others, and it is proven as an actual result that holding this name steadily illuminates the mind to know new statements of truth and to increase in strength and power and judgment. The Name means demonstration in daily life of the power and presence of the true God.

Holding the name teaches you that you need not say that you yield to the will of an imaginary God who is said to be capable of sending pain and affliction and poverty into your lot or into anybody's lot. Holding the Name causes you to see that in truth it is just as much idolatry to lay down your praises upon the altar, or your thanks, or your Will, or anything, expecting to earn any favors by such offsprings, as it is to offer young lambs or doves.

You are one with the true God by describing Him, and praise and thanks and will and faith are then natural expressions of your delight. Here Isaiah tells how surely all the Words that go forth out of his mouth shall prosper in the thing whereunto they are sent. But he has shown already that the thoughts we have been holding have been lower ideals than we need to have held and prosperity is the thing which we please to see prospered will only be manifest by our stating high ideals.

As to the demonstration of God with us we need only to say to the unhappy Woman, "My God does not allow you to be unhappy. My God makes you supremely glad with the bounty of His goodness." We need not watch her to see if her state of mind changes. We may chase ourselves up closer than that and say," My God does not expect me to watch to see if He is Good." According to this lesson of Isaiah we have not given our God credit for common honor.

"As the Heavens are higher than the earth, so are my thoughts higher than your thoughts." So we will describe a Good Being without human foibles or characteristics.

All these lessons carefully noted will discover to you what is called in this chapter "fatness." That is, some one of them has healing instruction for your mind which will take you right out of the place which you do not like and set you down into the place which you do like. It is intended for you that you should be doing what pleases you every minute. There is not a single tramp on the streets who has not the same ideal of God that you have if you push him step by step to tell it. Expressing it would please him.

There is not a convict or pampered prince but what has the same ideal you have. He who has covered up his ideal with many imaginations is acting basely to show how he has covered his ideal of God. But it is all there. Let him express it and be satisfied with bliss.

The same is true of everything. There is a region of the mind that knows all things. All language is understood by you already.

Lift off the rubbish and let the spring of your knowledge burst forth. Get in league with your own nature: "Thou shalt be in league with the stones of the field."

So here the lesson teaches that by a certain procedure every mind that is thirsting and hungering for wine and meat that will satisfy can find the spring of enchanting liquids and delightful viands somewhere in his own nature, in his own mind.

This procedure has been hinted at and touched upon in its various steps by every religion and by every age, but all the steps have not been given till now.

And there is so much rubbish of false notions covering the beautiful message that is meant for us alone that we have to refuse everything we have ever been taught and begin over again like little children to think What is true.

Each religion has some gem of truth in its bosom. So we must not hold any accusation against any religion. Each man and each woman is sent forth with some divine motive, and so we cannot accuse them of anything because that shows at once that we are not thinking of the divine motive of their being but are only thinking upon the nonsense that shadows them.

It is ceasing from accusation that is lifting off rubbish.

Swing to the right and the left,
Gates of sorrow and pain,
Let the glory of truth and her peace
Over earth's children reign.

The highest wisdom of Greece was expressed in the words, "Know thyself." In the oldest religious philosophy of the World, viz., the Vedanta, the highest instruction is, "Know thyself." That which you are already within your own self is that which is your own delight. That which you are already Within your own self is the divine purpose which sent you forth. If you will chase that purpose up face to face with itself you will have uncovered the true God. Suppose you find that you are working today for money? For what purpose do you want money? For easier, more pleasant living. But why do you want easier, more pleasant living? So as to be free from pain of any kind to the body. But why do you want to be free from pain of body? Because I do not like it. But Why do you not like it? Because it is not my nature to like it.

There you are, face to face with your nature which you find is opposed to pain. With what does your nature feel like and dislike? With the mind. There you are, face to face with your own mind, which is exactly like everybody e1se's mind in the universe. It is the universal mind. And the universal mind is omnipresent mind opposed to pain. Thus God is not the giver of pain, but the opposer of pain.

"As I live, saith the Lord, I know the thoughts that I think toward you, thoughts of peace and not of evil." "Why have ye made the heart of the righteous sad whom I have not made sad? saith the Lord." Therefore all imaginations of pain of any kind as sent by God or pleasing to God are pure nonsense. They are accusations against God and not truth of God.

John, the Revelator, saw the time when the red dragon or the accuser should be destroyed by the testimony of the saints. Just testimony of your own mind at its starting point is sufficient to put you to drinking this wonderful water.

It seems there is no slaying, no ending of that opposition to pain within your mind and all mind. It is God himself.

There have been quite a number of miracles wrought for the planet by some strong minds knowing the truth. One miracle has been that those who believe in the pain of the world as permitted to exist by some mysterious inefficiency of Jehovah have felt the stir of their own opposition to pain, and have actually gone to work to shut up some hard actions that have brought pain. They have waged war on some places where pain was made.

Those who did not believe that pain of any kind is forced upon us by the true God were the instigators of the actions against pain by those who believe that the true God originated pain.

They are very young in their instigations against the accusers of God — or very young in their convictions that God is opposed to pain, but the growth of their strength is marvelous, and the places where pain is going on are soon to feel the same revulsions against what is not originated by the true God as the best of thinkers.

For mind is one and he who thinks truth stirs all minds to think truth. "Think truly, and thy thoughts will the world's famine feed." "Ho, everyone that thirsteth." "Buy satisfying powers without price." "My thoughts are higher than your thoughts," and "my word shall prosper in that which I please;' therefore "seek ye the Lord While He is near," for the words of God are the joy of every heart.

The most cogent instruction conveyed esoterically here in this 55th chapter of Isaiah is that the nature of every mind is opposed to evil of any kind. That the expression of this nature is feeding and watering to the mind. That there is nothing this nature, common to all minds alike, does not know. That what is called genius along any line is simply the uncovering of some one word against limitation. That genius along every line is the birthright of every creature. That genius along every line may be demonstrated by describing the true God. That holding the name Jesus Christ teaches new powers, new faculties, true Ways of uncovering the brilliant possibilities of each mind by a short, easy method.

"My yoke is easy and my burden is light." That knowing all this sets those who still believe God is in league With evil by permitting it, to squirming and struggling to stop it; for if they believe in it they must Work in it. "Let the dead bury the dead." That it is better to know the true God and not have to fight than to imagine one and fight like heroes.

The South Winds are quick witted,

The schools are sad and slow,

The masters quite omitted

The love we care to know.

The end of all that the senses cognize is at hand. "Arise, let us go hence."

February 7th, 1892

BIBLE LESSON XXXI. Jeremiah 1:6. HEAVEN AROUND US

This lesson is from Jeremiah, Chapter 31. It explains the life of man under law and the life of man under grace. "The law was given by Moses, but grace and truth came by Jesus Christ." When we come to appreciate the difference between what are our experiences while subject to the law of matter and its mind, and our experiences while under the gospel of Spirit we see the Work which Jesus Christ wrought. "Christ has redeemed us from the curse of the law."

This lesson explains two other points, namely, what it means to acknowledge God in all our ways, and what it means to "look unto Me and be ye saved all the ends of the earth."

When shrinking, timid, young Jeremiah hears the truth of God he feels that he cannot preach it, so he says, "I am only a child." Then the God rises within him and sternly commands, "say not thou I am a child; see, I have this day set thee over the nations and over the kingdoms." This command to Jeremiah is commanded to all who have heard that their substance is God, their life is God, and their intelligence is God. It completely takes away from us the pleasing delusion, "I am only a child who is lying on the bosom of Infinite love," and puts it in its place, "I am infinite self-responsibility."

The command to look unto God in all words and ways is the same as "Stand thou upright on thy feet," and understand the atonement! Or that thou and God are one and inseparable spirit. For we understand distinctly that only spirit can look at spirit and thus as we are of the same substance God is, we are looking at our own substance when we realize salvation. It is another way of putting the doctrine that to know ourselves is the highest knowledge.

Jesus Christ found men under both the physical and metaphysical law. That is, He found them looking at matter as reigning over them, and also at carnal mind as reigning over them. He ignored both the physical and metaphysical bondage of mankind, and showed them free grace. That nobody has ever accepted the freedom He offered, so they also are free as He was, does not make His less.

He found them believing that they must Wait for summer and winter, seedtime and harvest, grinding and baking, for their bread. He showed them that this was not necessary, and increased five loaves without any material procedure into quite enough to feed 5,000 men, besides Women and children. "I have meat to eat that ye know not We do not need to spawn and hook fish, He explained, and He ignored physical law and multiplied fish with the bread.

He showed that no man with cataracts on his eyes need go into a dark room and lie waiting, after a skillful operation by some sharp instrument in the hands of a surgeon, in order to see clearly. A word is quite sufficient. "I came to bring recovery of sight to the blind" by the gospel.

He ignored grape culture, and yet produced reviving wines. "Buy wine, without money and without price," by turning water into wine at your Word was His instruction. He spoke to the gold in the fish, and it precipitated at once. He proved that it is not by might or power of horseman or steel that one is best defended from earthly foes, by causing the officers and soldiers to fall backward and upon their faces at sight of Him.

There is something surpassing all things in one who holds true ideas. The name of Jesus Christ when held hard in mind will quicken all our powers — quicken our signs of greatness. At the information of the seventh angel in Revelation, that the kingdoms of the world were to become the kingdoms of Christ, the four and twenty elders fell down on their faces. These four and twenty elders represent the statements of the law under which mankind has had its neck — the twelve laws of matter and the twelve laws of mind. You will find these laws as related to human experience, put together in what are called the twelve lessons on Christian science.*

But while they are very good to announce God with, they are finally to fall down on their faces and yield the point that free grace is divinely more tender than salvation earned by obedience to law. The seventh angel is the seventh definite teaching concerning God. The seventh angel is now sounding. There is no uncertain sound in this last doctrine of God. You will find a perfect description of this hour and the way this teaching of the truth that God is all and there is none else, in Chapter 11 of Revelation, commencing at verse 15.

There you will see that heaven is all around us. We are the temple of God. We open our mind to speak truth no matter what seems opposed to us, and we find that on our heart is written the covenant with God whereby we are to never hear of, or know trouble any more forever, and that all the miserable people on the earth are really waiting for the truth concerning God to be told them.

This truth is written within them, but what is called religious teachings have hidden their heaven and their covenant with God.

Robinson Crusoe felt that he must teach Friday about God and the devil so as to be doing his Christian duty by that child of nature. Friday understood readily about God, but why the good God who was so strong didn't "kill the debble" was a mystery that confused him. This convinced Crusoe that a supernatural and revealed religion was absolutely necessary to salvation.

The supernatural and revealed religion that tells of the Supreme Good as authorizing or permitting evil is that which closes the temple of mind. Now the seventh angel sounds and we hear that that was not and never will be true. Jesus Christ annulled the metaphysical laws as utterly as the physical. The metaphysical law is that "He that leadeth into captivity shall be led captive, and he that killeth with the sword shall be killed by the sword." "This was the patience and the faith of the saints." But there is to be no sword — no vengeance; mankind are all to be told the truth. "The truth shall make them free."

Under the law of metaphysics, "for the lightest word thou shalt give account." Under this law the physical body registers all the mistakes of the mind in disease, sickness, poverty, pain. But with the knowledge of Christ or Truth we are set free from the results of words and thoughts. To accept the freedom of Christ is to accept immunity from the law of cause and effect.

All the lessons in law fall on their faces with gratitude that the highest truth has taken to itself its great power and will now reign. This law of cause and effect has for its teaching many strong clauses which have made people almost afraid to think and to speak. Under this law to say to a child, "Poor little thing," is to cause it to grow up poor in purse, poor in flesh, and timid and shrinking. Under this law if one gets a counterfeit dollar into his possession by mistake he knows he must have sometime let somebody pay him a few cents too much change and did not rectify it. The few cents have come back with interest — out of hand. Under this law every blind person we meet is the outpicturing of some refusal on our part to see the justice done ourselves or somebody else. Under this law we have Karma, that is, repeated returns of the consequences of our deeds and thoughts.

According to early metaphysics it was considered unpardonable ignorance not to be able to quickly detect the errors that had caused the troubles suffered by people. But "Christ redeemed us from the curse of the law." "Let no fruit grow on thee," He said to the most vigorous and flourishing signs of the powers of evil. For you must bear in mind that He was giving a lesson in the annulling power of the gospel when He blasted the vigorous fig tree.

"Thy sins be forgiven thee" — this is the gospel. It is possible for us all to say and have the words come true, I refuse the consequences of my past words and thoughts. I do not live under the law but under the gospel. I am free from the law.

Under the gospel there is no heredity of body or mind. Under grace there is no deception or consequences of deception. Under grace there is no discord. Under grace there is no foolishness or ignorance or consequences of foolishness or ignorance. Under grace there is no death, there is illumination. One can keep under the law as long as he pleases, and one can accept grace when one pleases.

There is a mystery or secret about Jesus Christ and free grace which cannot be communicated. It will come by speaking the name Jesus Christ. Nobody can tell the way he feels when he sees himself no longer under the law but under grace. He can only say that the name is the "name overall victorious."

The atonement here taught by this chapter where God and His people are One is sometimes expressed by "seeing God." We must know that We are exactly What we see. To see is to understand. To understand God is to be God. This is Written in the heart.

"Look unto Me" is a command that has almost escaped the notice of mankind when studying Scriptures. There is a mystery about looking steadily at anything that has escaped the mention of philosophers.

The Germans of ancient times used to heal by looking straight at their patients and saying, "God looks you quite away." They thus really looked straight past the appearance to the reality or spiritual man and caused it to stand forth as health. It was their own spirit looking at the spirit of the other and the twain being one, that which was nothing fell away. Great healing was wrought this way.

It has been found out that by looking at some one proposition of any language anybody can catch the clew to the language and without study know it by the instruction of spirit. Heaven is around us. There is only heaven around us. To look steadily at anything around is really to be looking into heaven. Keep on looking until it is plain.

A young man was told that certain envelopes in a circle of sealed envelopes contained money. There was no clew to those with money enclosed and those without money. But he found out every one that contained money by looking at them a long time, till those containing what he Wished for seemed to have a mark on them and be the only envelopes there at all. See what small issues confirm great ones.

All that you can ask is lying near you. "Look and see." There is a substance within us akin to every other substance. There is a divining rod or touchstone Within us to draw all that we can think of.

The Chinese have a habit of placing a shining stone on a high stand in the middle of the room and sitting down in a circle and gazing steadfastly up at the stone, expecting it to hand them down blessings. They who look steadily enough always get their blessings.

There is a cathedral in the East where there hangs in a darkened room a picture of the Virgin Mary. The sunlight strikes across her face, and all the lame, palsied, and deaf go there and gaze steadfastly up into her face. There have been thousands healed by thus looking at the picture till the symbol quite faded and the healing spirit smiled answers.

All obstacles may be looked away from the spirit of success. All obstacles may be looked away from the bounty of God. It is the Spirit bearing witness with our spirit that we are one. This Witness of spirit with spirit is atonement — one mens or one mind.

The highest good you heart can conceive is the good that lies Waiting to bless you. It is going to be utterly impossible for combinations of men or single men to keep the success and the substance of other men from them as it is impossible to keep God from God, with the catching sight of truth.

Drop your supernatural and revealed religion, so-called, and open your mind to describe what you think is bliss. Look all the obstacles away from your idea of bliss.

That which is written within you is truth; that which you have been told is false. The kingdom of heaven is at hand, not trouble and despair and misery; these are the fruits of revealed or supposed religion. Look past them as you would look past a mask hiding the beautiful face of your child. You can make the sun look pale and murky at noonday with a piece of smoked glass. Take away the glass and there is the sunshine. Take away your former religion, which had so much about death and sorrow and sin, and see what is true.

See! Look! Thou and God are one and inseparable. This is truth. No other truth will Work miracles. If you know all about the stars and their orbits, can bind the Pleiades and loose the bonds of Orion, it is not worth while unless your heart has opened and recognized truth.

Read over this 31st chapter of Jeremiah and see how all the ordinances of the earth are made naught by the gospel of grace. Read over the last verses of Chapter 11, Revelations, and see how these times confirm the prophecies. Realize what is now being taught and see if you are among the voices of opposition, the thunders and lightnings of holding on to the old ways of thinking, or among the bold and redeemed and fearless under grace.

Remember that what is true of principle is true of practice. Practice and principle are one. If you cannot prove that God is your provider, your defense, your health, your inspiration, what comfort can you be getting out of your religion?

These things are not waiting for proof till after death. They are now. Look! Look around you. Look steadily. The kingdom of heaven folds you round. There is no law under which you need keep your neck. You are free under grace. "I will forgive thine iniquity and remember thine sin no more." "I will watch over them to build and to plant." "Look unto Me!" "I am nigh thee."

All things are passing —

God never changeth.

I fill those objects near thee. I fill those circumstances near thee. Look steadfastly. I will reveal myself to the steadfast seeker. "I in thee and thou in Me." "Is there any beside Me? Nay, I know not any."

"Say not thou, 'I am a child' — see! I set thee this day over the nations and over the kingdoms." Take thine inheritance. The law is under thy feet. "Old things are forgotten." "All things are made new."

February 14th, 1892

BIBLE LESSON XXXII. Jeremiah 35. BUT ONE SUBSTANCE

This burning of the prophecies of Jeremiah by Jehoiakim, King of Judah, brings to remembrance the old Latin proverb, Qui vult decipi, decipiatur, which means, "Let him who Wishes to be deceived, be deceived."

Jeremiah had written to Jehoiakim that there were two ways for him to save Judah from destruction — one was by yielding to Babylon which, though under the horizon of power (that is, not apparently the coming power), was yet going to conquer all nations; and the other way was to call a great assembly to prayer as Hezekiah had done about a hundred years before.

There were no signs of Babylon attacking Jerusalem and Jehoiakim burned the roll containing the advices of Jeremiah. They seemed to him nonsense. As a king he felt that his words and actions must be worth more than a prophet's impressions, and he felt a pompous certainty that he knew his own business best. At any rate he wanted not to believe Jeremiah, and it was his choice to set up a scheme defying the defense of prayer and the defense of horsemen. Babylon stood for the intelligence of worldliness, and prayer stood for the intelligence of spirit. Jehoiakim did not want to use intelligence in being safe. He just wanted to be safe. So he burned the instructions of Jeremiah. It was as though a man should burn the bill of goods purchased by him at some store, thinking that would end the matter.

You have heard before that "the letter killeth." The kingdom of Judah stood for the letter of truth. It lived longer than the kingdom of Israel, which stood for the feeling of truth. Hoshea, the last king of Israel, Was weak and irresolute, though good enough, and was overthrown.

That is the way with all feelings not headed by judgment. Feeling causes people to do things because they like or dislike. They love somebody sentimentally, and no matter what that one would do in a position of trust they put him there. They dislike somebody and no matter what his fitness for a position they would not let him have it. So their kingdom wanes. All things get to running intolerably, like the watch which the owner cannot use and the watchmaker cannot see why it will not run when its works are so perfect, till they find its balance-wheel is magnetized.

Judah stood for the word or letter which also kills itself. When once Word and feeling are married they give good judgment. Jehoiakim said exactly the right words but he said them without intelligence. He was like one who says that the child with typhoid fever has nothing at all the matter, because he never saw such a case and hasn't the remotest idea What he has to meet, but has heard the scientific statement that all claims of evil are nothing at all. So he says the Words and goes to sleep to wake and find the child dead, and himself condemned for criminal carelessness. As Jehoiakim refused both the intelligence of spirit and the intelligence of armies he was wound up. Zeal without judgment, and word without judgment, are equally self-destructive.

Both Jeremiah and Jehoiakim believed in law and so both had to fulfill the law exactly as it demands. Of course, there is a higher than law, under whose wings one can throw himself and come out unscathed, but neither of these men recognized this in a way to save their kingdom.

Jeremiah did not appeal to the highest nature of Jehoiakim; Jehoiakim did not permit it to speak.

We get the rewards of that principle we serve. If we believe in Spanish flies as the cure for neuralgia we must use Spanish flies till they fail us. Jeremiah believed that the children of Judah had done evil and so, of course, he expected evil to reward them. It was Hahnemann's similia similibus curantur.

It goes with the belief in the law of evil that punishment must follow offenses, and what sort of seeds We sow those We reap. There is an intelligent repudiation of this law which will set anybody free from the consequences of his own past foolish or ignorant words.

But neither the Israelite nor the Judahite performs intelligently except when turning his annulling words toward God. Jeremiah, Isaiah, Stephen, Guyon, were all martyrs to their belief in evil as belonging to them. Looking into material things for their own sake, they will be sure to give you their kind of fruitage.

The man who invented the telescope was put into a dungeon. The man who constructed the microscope starved to death. They had no intelligence of life. If you feed a man who tells you he is starving While you know he is not honest, yet your principle of conduct compels you to do kindly by him, he will be the means of bringing you some good in some way unintentionally. If you feel tenderness and mercy some way he will get you a merciful return for your action.

Say never affection was wasted.

Affection never was wasted.

If it enrich not the heart of another,

Its waters returning back to their fountains

Shall fill them full of refreshment.

That which the fountain rejected

Returning again to the fountain.

Probably the point that will strike the intelligent metaphysician as strongest in this lesson is that there are two ways of denying evil and matter: one intelligently, and the other blindly.

One of the first propositions of Christian doctrine is that there is but one substance filling all space, all places, all things. There is but one substance.

As there can be but one omnipresence of cause this substance everywhere present is God. God is good. Thus all is good. Then there follows the necessary negation to such a promise, viz., then there is no evil.

The intelligent acceptance of this reasoning has the most straightening and purifying effect upon character. All appetites, passions, tempers, diseases stop as if by magic. The blind acceptance of this reasoning causes people to act exactly like Jehoiakim. Whatever appetite or passion or temper they had before they now say it is good because there is no evil. Now that one little turn of metaphysics contains all the law and the gospel. It makes all the difference between intelligence and ignorance, light and darkness.

The one who says his conduct is good when it is manifestly bad is as much a believer in evil and will take as much punishment for evil as he did before he spoke the words. For demonstration is the accompaniment of truth understood. Whoever says there is no evil because good is all will show forth good only, else he does not believe a Word he is saying. He really is thinking that evil is all. So he shows forth What he is thinking. It is just the same with sickness. Unless we show out health at once when We say there is no sickness because God is all and God cannot be sick, of course we are believing within our minds that sickness is real. It is as plain as the sunshine What we believe in. We show it out.

Remember the words of Jesus, "According to thy faith be it unto thee." A blind woman believed that she could see, no matter how she had been deceived by teachings about matter and evil, because God has made her. She held onto her conviction that if God made her perfect she really must be perfect, until suddenly her sight came as clear as crystal. There have been many such cases where the conviction was based on intelligent reasoning, which suddenly showed forth in health, even in straightening crooked bones.

Truth understood is as straightening to character as to bones.

This is Christian science.* We do not understand the science unless we demonstrate it, so Jehoiakim had no intelligent conception of his denial of evil and matter. It is intelligence that is God. It is the word of intelligence that is God manifest.

It is here that the presence and office of Jesus Christ come in. The mind has been so accustomed to sophistries that it seems to be easy to lead even quite bright-appearing people off into byways and hedges and blind alleys. This name holds the mind to judgment and to demonstration of goodness.

It is at this point of statement that students of science halt and begin to think that it is license to evil and not power of good the science effects. Here they stop to accuse each other and to draw off from each other. Here at this juncture they have to start their reasoning over again, clinging fast to the name that stands for wholeness and goodness. At this point many sorrowful experiences face the student. He will take them into his talk and reasoning or refuse them. Here he feels he is right and everybody else in the wrong, and he refuses to let any man buy or sell save as he has "his mark on his forehead or in his right hand."

This is the place where those who choose to declare that God is not respecter of persons and has filled with His substance and power all men alike, begin to create or enter into the new heaven and the new earth, where they hunger no more, neither thirst any more, and their joy no man can take away. Here is where intelligence seems to fail and one has to rise and announce that intelligence is God, and as God cannot fail so intelligence cannot fail. Here is Where provisions seem to stop and one has to rise and announce as God cannot be cut off so support cannot be cut off or stop.

There are times when the mind has to see only one side of the question on intelligent principle. There have been many examples of this sudden rising to announce truth from the Jesus Christ standpoint and the effect has been wonderful.

It is not sentimental wishing and it is not simple denial and affirmation that work when the forces of the claims of evil meet the scientific statements. It is honest conviction. And "conviction is not properly speaking conviction till it develops itself into action."

Looking over the young people just starting out upon the voyage of human experience, strict science says to each one: "Rise, when sorrow, pain, disappointment come to you, and say with all the force of your mind, I refuse them! Jesus Christ told me not to experience this and I will not."

Whatever came knocking at your door will fall away from your lot. The next test will be easier. And so you will demonstrate God in life. You will be a living glory to the World. You will bring the new heaven and the new earth, and the former will be forgotten.

Look at the gray-haired, deeply wrinkled faces of the people you meet. What aged them thus? Drinking the cup of sorrow, pain, disappointment, supposing that it was the common lot of mankind. Never. If they had refused to feel badly, refused to think of the pain, sorrow, and disappointment, because God never intended it for them, they would be beautiful as the archangels, living lights in the dark places, healing to the nations.

Now that the science of good has come we will accept the glorious offering.

There is only one beauty, health, bounty, buoyant youth in truth.

The letter of denial must be united to the conviction that it is a truth. The feeling of denial must be united to do the Word of right reasoning. Then we enter upon our rightful kind of life. It is just beginning to be proven how foolish the sufferings of good people have been through mistaken notions of God's intentions towards them. February 21st, 1892

BIBLE LESSON XXXIII. Jeremiah 32. JUSTICE OF JEHOVAH

This lesson suggests two points that have been brought up again and again, but are ever good to be brought to mind. The first is that, so far as our own self is concerned, in this training process we must take the position of non-resistance to both good and evil. The second is that in dealing with the great problem of the world, the sending forth of true words from the heart is more efficient than all the personal hand-to-hand efforts We can make.

Then, too, the lesson brings up the old, old question as to why it is that those who love God best and give life and time and heart and all things to the service of God after the highest dictates of their convictions have always been the persecuted and abused and tormented of the world.

Here it is over again, rehearsed in the imprisonment of Jeremiah on an unjust charge, made by the princes against him through spite. The siege of Babylon against Jerusalem is now raging. Zedekiah is now king over Judah. Jeremiah had foreseen it when nobody else did and warned them of the only safe course, but, being disregarded, the siege is now on.

Zedekiah means "Justice of Jehovah." There is a sure working of cause and effect on the side of human experience that has been called the justice of Jehovah. It is the way the good looks to those who believe in evil. The good does not look at all that way to those who do not believe in the reality or power of evil. This justice or logic of events is shown by the downfall of Israel and Judah.

Israel refused to lean upon spirit, and turned to Egypt for assistance. Egypt failed her. Egypt stands for materiality. The most sentimental minister must not lean upon material things to brace up his Work with. Neither must the most formal one. Judah was now looking to Egypt for aid and Egypt was failing him. The minister who goes from Methodism to Congregationalism, from Congregationalism to Presbyterianism, etc., to comply with the salaries offered, is a preacher of the letter of the law and has no noble principle which will keep him from extreme poverty of health and purse and brain one of these days.

He depends on Egypt's materiality. He must look at Zedekiah's fate. He represents the minister of God who preaches the letter even though very ably and his heart is not in principle.

Jeremiah told them to yield to Chaldea, which as a lesson to ministers means, go into some Work besides preaching and meditate upon what you do believe before you attempt to publicly preach God.

Of course a still higher way is to call halt and cry mightily unto principle till you are united therewith demonstrably enough to be cured and well provided for by the grace of spirit.

But Israel and Judah do not do that.

The ministers of God who preach that "the earth is the Lord's and the fullness thereof," must be careful not to give the world over to Satan in their preaching, because it shows letter and not consistent principle. We must be careful not to remark that the reward of St. Stephen for serving God was paid by the world with stones, without adding that Stephen believed in stones, else he would not be stoned. We must know that what we believe in is what we are serving. We might believe that there is a satan and that would be quite service enough to get satanic dealings. Guyon loved God and asked particularly that the usual torments and hardships and martyrdoms of God's people be given to her. She got them. But God did not send them. It is blasphemy of Divine goodness to say that Divine goodness ever sent evil. Can a sweet fountain send forth bitterness?

They who have Washed their robes white are those who have spoken high, clean truth unmixed with error.

The high clean truth of God is that all evil experiences are just beliefs and not realities. He who believes in limitations will be finding limitations constantly. He who believes there is an open door as Jesus taught will find limitations broken down more and more. People often notice that Christian scientists* are limited in powers and abilities like other people. If so then they believe in limitations just as they were taught in youth and pay little heed to the actual teachings of Jesus about unlimited good. By repeated instructions We may be sure to feel all that we say and thus drop our palsied hands, lame feet, rheumatic limbs, and poor eyesight. It is our privilege. It is not by leaning on Egypt that we get our health, strength and happiness, for that has been a demonstrable failure after ages upon ages of trial thereof.

In the management of those things that seem so bad in what is called the eternal world We see by this lesson that more good can be wrought by thinking and speaking unadulterated truth than by physical efforts. For illustration, think of Peter in prison under Herod under strong guards and behind stone walls, with heavy chains on his hands. Could the Christians of his time hope by pounding the walls or cajoling the jailors to get Peter out?

That is exactly where millions of people are now placed by the Herod belief in poverty and trouble. By going down in the alleys and carrying flowers and salves do you touch poverty so as to cajole it out of the notion of hedging millions behind its bars? Do you pound the walls built by trouble so that they shake a bit by all that you have done with your missions? Well, that is because you do not understand the principle that leads captivity captive.

Peter kept speaking truth; so did Mary and the rest of the Christian church at home. By and by one of them spoke the very truth that had the setting-free power. This truth appeared as an angel and touching Peter the chains fell off his hands and the prison doors opened.

Truth is mighty. Elisha spoke so many noble words of truth that many angels appeared to him. Jesus had angels come and minister unto Him. Angles are true words. About two hundred years ago a priest who loved truth found that he could heal the sick by speaking certain words. Thousands whom pills and poultices and surgery and other material methods would not cure were cured by these Words of truth. Maxwell, a Scotch physician, cared a great deal about healing people, and while he was thinking over the need of healing by some other way than the failing methods of materiality, he suddenly saw that the universe is filled with bright, fleet, ethereal light.

All things are radiant with this light. But not unless we get into a certain state of mind can we see this light. He said We could store up a fullness of this light and pass it along over the fleet light that spins through all space, and wherever our light should shine those people would be healed no matter how far away they might be.

All things seem to be so dependent upon states of mind that it is a mystery why there has not been more notice of the effects of states of mind and the process by which to attain correct states of mind.

When you are cold clear to your marrow bone all of a sudden you feel Warm. Do you know what made you warm? It was a thought you thought last week just got ready to work while you were cold. Sometimes you are tired and discouraged and suddenly are cheerful and rested. It was a sudden thought that flashed through your mind that rested you. Maybe a line of a loving o1d hymn. One may be hungry and suddenly not hungry. A loving Word spoken to somebody else who did not appreciate it went over and lodged in the mind of the hungry one and he felt fed. "Thy words were found and I did eat them."

Now and then people Wonder why the Christian scientists* wear warm clothes and eat and sleep like other people if they believe there is a mental state equal to warmth, food, and rest. Christ, their teacher, told them to take no thought about eating, drinking and sleeping, but take such things as should be provided naturally according to their time and station, but to be sure to preach all the time the good word, heal the sick by their word, cast out tempers by their true words, raise the dead by their true words and then that all the rest would come to them. So they obey His orders, and they do indeed have things right and good.

You remember that He and His yoke were so easy and His burden so light that people would have one hundred fold more in this sphere of experience than before obeying Him, and that in the next higher state of mind they would not have to consult or confer about death at all.

According to this it is in no sense pleasing to Him, to have anybody shutting himself up within a cell or starving or freezing himself. Such things show foolish misunderstandings of Him and His doctrines. This lesson teaches that success in your own state of mind is best secured by an attitude of non-resistance to both good and evil.

When Jesus Christ felt the touch of the Holy Spirit and heard the voice say, "This is My beloved Son." He answered never a word. When they accused Him of being a glutton and a Wine-bibber He answered nothing. "As a sheep before her shearers is dumb so He opened not His mouth."

But when the voice gave a noble message to Moses he shrank muttering, "What will people think of me?" When Jeremiah heard the voice giving him the great honor, he shrank murmuring, "I can't, too young."

These both resisted the good. But when evil shows its intentions Jeremiah resisted nothing but stood back a helpless spectator of the panorama. He though if Judah had sinned Judah's punishment was unavertible. This was natural effect, he said. Jesus Christ told us that that idea of eye for eye and tooth for tooth was entirely Wrong, for we should not meet evil by fighting it with its own weapons. "The weapons of our Warfare are not carnal but mighty through God to the pulling down of strongholds." When He said, "Resist the devil and he will flee from you," He knew how everything that claims to be bad also claims to have its own way of proceeding and thus claims its own amount and kind of intelligence. Rheumatism claims a way of its own. So does softening of the brain. So does poverty. So do all so-called bad things.

When Martin Luther threw a material inkstand at a phantom Satan he showed he did not understand scientific handling of phantoms, for this phantom was much with him afterwards. Two men were suddenly set upon by an enormous bear in a field. They were both unarmed, and when the bear began hugging one of them the other man, by that sudden flashing of the weapon of defense which every creature carries, began to talk to the bear somewhat like this, "I'm ashamed and astonished to see a great, noble bear like you spring out in this Way on two men who just now have nothing to fight you with. You ought to be ashamed of such a mean action and get down at once from my friend and get you gone to your lair where you belong." That bear actually got down in a shamed way and slunk back to the forest where he came from.

A man hurt his hand between two stones, and as he felt he must support his family and could not take time to nurse a mangled hand back to health, he held the hand up and said to the pain and blood, "Now I cannot spare my hand. You must not stay with me hanging on to my hand and keeping me from doing my work. You must get right away at once." Within a few minutes the hand was hardy enough to use.

A Woman had inflammatory rheumatism coming on. She was a good Catholic, so she made the sign of the cross on her limbs several times, Wetting her finger as so many of the good Catholics of the past used to do. When the pain did not stop she suddenly spoke to it as if it was a live thing saying, "Look here, now; I have done my part. I have crossed myself as many times as ought to satisfy a decent pain that it was time for it to go away. Now you do your part and get away from me to where you belong." Sure enough the pain left her at once.

Any position you take of mastery is your self-empowering to victory. In Christian science* people use a reason for the hope that is in them when they name a pain or trouble to unname it by saying that its name is all there is to it.

Jeremiah had a Wonderfully executive mind. He might have faced up all the horrors of Chaldean warfare and stopped them. But to him they were real, and Zedekiah's weak character was so in need of punishment that he focused to the teachings he had formally received about eye for eye and tooth for tooth. There is one thing that a strong mind generally does if it does not look well to its Own independent reasoning, and that is to cohere to a prejudice. Then it speaks forth from that when its mighty possibilities are to gather a store of truth and heal all things. Poverty, trouble, warfare, injustice, may all be met by a reasonable argument, and reasoned out of the universe, as the bear was reasoned away from the man. Jeremiah saved himself from death at this siege by believing one passage of Jewish teachings, viz., "I am with thee, saith the Lord, to deliver thee." Almost all good "Christians believe in a God who crowds them down into the most dreadful straits and then picks them out at the last minute. They keep forgetting that if they make up such an idol it will do so by them according to their faith.

We had better not take any preconceived teachings or strange notions to the Bible when we study it, for those preconceptions act like smoked glass before the eyes of the mind.

Jonathan Edwards got from his father a notion that the universe is nowhere save in Divine Mind, and in this mind God is holding His children over lakes of fire by threads.

A great thinker got a prejudice whereby he felt that Jesus Christ taught a lower system of morals than Juvenal, the Roman poet, who lived about 40 A.D., inasmuch as Jesus taught behaving one's self for fear of hellfire and the council, While Juvenal taught that good men love virtue for its own sake, while bad men act virtuously for fear of punishment.

Eckart, the Vicar of the Dominicans about the year 1300, got out of his study of scriptures that his greatest prayer must be to get rid of God. Maitland got out of his study of the Bible that "God is the bogie of the nurseries." Tyndall, who in 1526 distributed 150,000 Bibles over England, got the idea that he must be burned for doing good.

The Christian scientist* gets out of the Scriptures that this is the day when the sun shall be darkened and the moon refuse her light for the Lord God and the Lamb are the only light we need.

Reading carefully we find that all the lights of the past fade under the glory of truth believed untrammeled by prejudices. We see that all the nations are stepping their feet into that country where there no more pain, neither sorrow nor crying. This country Where "there is no evil at all" is in the mind that looks unto truth as its light and its salvation, its defiance and its provision.

And out of the Scriptures we read that whatsoever the mind believes is true and real, that the body shall experience. Out of the Scriptures We read that when we believe what is absolutely true then indeed is the Kingdom of Heaven come and the prisoners of human experience are set free.

February 28th, 1892

BIBLE LESSON XXXIV. Jeremiah 39. GOD AND MAN ARE ONE

Jeremiah wrote this history. All human history is but the transcription of a dream. It never happened at all. If the circumstances and events and laws and phenomena of human experience ever did take place — ever were set going by any being — then there is no telling what may lie in wait for us after this experience and no supposing of What happened before this was set going. Also there is no possibility of admiring or loving their origin.

Strict investigation of Scripture and strict logic compels us to see that "as from a dream one awaketh," so may we arise from all this phantasmagoria now. "Now is the accepted time. Now is the day of salvation."

The "I" of every living thing is the maker of its own experiences. The "I" stands at the center of being and thinks its thoughts. A11 thoughts are thrown outward into forms. Thoughts that are true make substantial and enduring forms. Thoughts that are only suppositious shadow the substantial and good.

Many a thinker has felt this truth and spoken it. The best words seem to have been spoken by good physicians. This was because they were enamored of the idea of helping others.

Descartes, the French philosopher, thought that the key to the understanding of the mystery of life lay in understanding how to heal. Sir Thomas Brown said: "The severe learning of the schools shall never take from me the conviction that what we perceive with the senses only shadows some substantial realities which the sense cannot cognize."

Whoever shall learn to recall all the thoughts he has ever thought home to himself, and start them over again as truth only, without supposing anything will find his world transformed. We do not need to see the world as we have seen it. We may learn to see it as truth expressed by thinking truth. When we think such things as this 39m Chapter of Jeremiah tells, we are not thinking truth unless we look to the esoteric significance. The esoteric meaning of all this is that by supposing what is not true we are likely to get into just such a situation as Zedekiah did. It would not be a real situation.

Nothing could make it real, but it might seem very real to us. The Whole lesson may be resolved into a state of mind showing itself outwardly.

Nebuchadnezzar, King of Babylon, is our most determined belief in the reality of the world as it appears to the scholar. The scholar is always proudly certain that he knows all that the world has taught, and what has been accepted by scholars must be accepted by the church which he attends. The letter of the church must be besieged by the school till the minister of spiritual messages cannot be listened to if his worldly education has been neglected.

Then the church runs out upon the plains of blank fear and yields the question. The single mind does the same with its thoughts. If ever you have a thought you had to study Latin or Sanskrit or Greek roots or logic in order to know highest good, you also are Zedekiah running out on the plains of blank fear. Nebuchadnezzar is after you. For the fact is you do not have to study these things at all. Jerusalem is yours. You know all things within your own mind. This is truth.

Wisdom is yours. At the center of your being you are identical with wisdom itself. This is the truth. At the center of your mind you can stand and refuse all the notions of Babylon (or the world). Always your neighbors will be exactly like those you now associate with so long as you stand at the center of your mind and suppose the things that you now do. Always you will be forgetful and inferior and depressed and snubbed, so long as you stand at the center and load and fire such suppositions as you do now.

It is your privilege never to yield a point to Babylon, but instead to dictate to Babylon. Society should not dictate to you that there is any difference among the sons and daughters of God. You should ignore such errors and transcend society with the words of truth. Babylon shall be cringing to Jerusalem. Society shall cringe like a shadow under the words, "There is neither Jew nor Gentile, Greek nor barbarian, bond nor free," in truth. It is only in error there is difference.

But then you must never forget that society is something that you make for yourself by your thoughts. You must not be led by any experience of any sort or kind to believe that by nature you are not divine. If anybody tells you that you are a miserable sinner at heart, who empowered him to tell you that and why should you believe him?

Why not stand upright at the center of mind, quite ignoring him and his words, and look into your own nature for yourself. Any yielding the point of your own central Wisdom and divinity is being chased by the King of Babylon.

For the highest teaching of Babylon is that you know nothing and must be taught everything. This is not truth.

Here where it tells that the Chaldeans broke down the walls of Jerusalem you may see how your stronghold that the "spirit shall teach you all things" must never yield the point in the first place that schools are necessary to your knowledge. This does not argue against schools, but only against dependence upon them. Self-knowledge is the knowledge of God, which is mastery of all other knowledge. If there is a way of thinking about God that has the effect of healing the sick, that is surely the true way to think about God. If there is a way to think about God that will strengthen your judgment, that is, without doubt, the true Way to think about God.

It is practical. Do not believe a single thing that very learned men tell you, if they show no sign of truth in their conduct or bodily states. If a man must of necessity show forth his own thoughts upon his body his thoughts must be erroneous if he has sick spells, lameness, blindness, rheumatic pains, or nervous exhaustion.

There must be some great error in the mind of that learned man who finally has softening of the brain. There must be some great mistake in that preacher's doctrine who has to recuperate from overwork. "My words are life to them that find them and health to all their flesh."

There will not be the least studying of Dante, or Goethe, or Shakespeare when it is found that their errors of mind are silently communicated to all those readers who have not been so steadied by knowing truth but that unhealthy ideas can chase them and break down the walls of their safety (Jerusalem). There is mighty error of mind which each one of these communicates to his readers.

Many a young man and maiden has disappointed his or her friends' high hopes because they caught the infliction of the false ideas held by the brilliant authors and mighty scholars whose writings they read with delight. Every child is supremely above his books.

There is a way of teaching, or drawing forth from the Wonderful love possessed by children. But nobody has learned that way so but that the walls of Jerusalem, or the beautiful gates of the child-mind are always broken down by worldly insisting upon knowledge from without. This knowledge, as all the scholars know, is constantly varying, constantly being upset. There is only one knowledge that remains eternally changeless. Cogito, ergo sum. This is the innate knowledge of the "I Am."

Whoever can get the child to stand by his own self-conviction quite independent of any instruction whatsoever from without has the secret of education and starts the demonstration of genius. Jesus Christ would not be taught anything. "He needed not that any man should teach Him." Do you suppose that any child is different from Jesus Christ? Not at all.

If you think that any child is different from Jesus Christ you think a falsity and simply show that your walls of Jerusalem have been broken down.

Mary and Joseph showed great wisdom in letting their little Jesus have so much freedom. Of course He was not constantly told not to do this and not to do that, and He was never scolded. They knew what all parents ought to know, viz., that every child's "face always beholds the face of the Father."

In speaking forth that truth which the child always knew from the beginning, He urged upon men not ever to judge from appearances but to start judgment from right reasoning.

Right reasoning is like a wind that blows great trees down and sends the chaff flying off the earth. Right reasoning held by a few minds will blow all the errors out of the mind of humanity. Right reasoning gives the metaphysical purport of all the historic records of Scripture. And purely metaphysical reasonings dissolve all materiality. "The earth is clean dissolved."

You have heard that absolutely pure water would dissolve everything it touched. Pure reasoning is pure water. It is that pure reasoning that is now turning the steam loose over the world mind. The elements cannot help melting. If a little child should stand up and speak forth its own inner knowing, nothing abnormal or untrue could remain in its presence. The abnormal and undesirable will dissolve first.

Sickness falls. Death stops. Tempers and passions flee. These things follow the preaching of truth. Then the visible heavens will roll away like a scroll and the material earth is clean dissolved. Just unadulterated truth will finally effect this.

Do you notice that Nebuzaradan gave the houses and lands of Jerusalem to those who had not had anything at all before? Well, you must be Wise enough to notice that the old ideas that have been snubbed in the past are coming to the front as the most powerful ideas to hold. One of these snubbed ideas is the reality of matter. It is going to be one of the richest ideas of the future.

Another snubbed old idea growing into rich favor is, "there is no reality in sickness." Another one is, "we are already at home in God. There is no future."

Kingdoms of matter rise and fall, philosophies stand high and sink into disrepute, the wise old alchemies are held in derision, but that only the good is true shall increase in favor till all is seen as good indeed; that human history never took place shall be the noblest religion; that God and we are one and the same, the only substance Spirit. This is the last trump of Gabriel — ultimate truth.

March 6th, 1892

BIBLE LESSON XXXV. Ezekiel 4:9. SPIRITUAL IDEAS

This lesson was written down by Ezekiel as concerning the miracle-working nature of God. He hereby shows what is quite true, viz., that you do not have to deserve great and unexpected blessings before getting them. They are likely to be showered down on heathen-minded people (those who know nothing of spiritual ideas); on carnal-minded people (those who know that there are spiritual teachings, but they like money and food and clothes better); on hard-hearted people (those who care for nothing and nobody), and upon the spiritually-inclined alike.

The law of cause and effect deal with the fruits of thoughts. "He that createth the fruit of the lips." The grace and mercy and bounty of God transcend law. You will receive all these anyhow. It is a great rest for the mind to know that it is blessed with some wonderful gifts whether it deserves them or not, and that it is likely to have splendid signs of the good bounty of Jehovah any minute.

Pious people have often regretted this mystery, but they have not been able to stop it. They verily have wished that the sun did not shine quite so brightly on the circus tent as on the camp-meeting, but it did. They have often Wished that such gambling and speculating kinds of people did not get all the money and things, but they did. Sometimes quite undesirable kinds of folks have been empowered to do beautiful healing, while the highly moral have been slow at such "Works." No matter how exasperating to those who think they ought to be rewarded for being better than their neighbors, it still keeps on.

Ezekiel feels the transcendentally — good God speaking through him in this lesson, as, "I will call for the corn and I will lay no famine upon you, not for your sakes, but that they shall know that I am the Lord."

All good things, from shoes to synagogues, from the Gospel to the baby's prattle, are from the Lord.

Such a rest to know you do not have to be good in order to get good things. So the father and mother who refuse the boy his breakfast or dinner of supper or bed because he has been naughty are far, far from God-like.

Such a rest to know that the ravens and robins do not have to pray and praise and have faith in some kind of a god in order to get their breakfast. The good Father feeds and suns and warms them whether they praise and pray or not.

This is what makes God the Lord so beautiful. He asks you to merit nothing. There is a law of cause and effect whereby, if one keeps refusing good, he need not have it by and by, as, for instance, the mind refuses honor, integrity, and the respect of friends, so he need not have them; but these blessings are scattered thickly. He may keep throwing away his money and home until they are gone, but he had them sent to him whether he deserved them or not.

Anybody may expect Wonderful miracles of good any moment. One may be so hardened in heart that his neighbors are afraid of him and suddenly have a "heart of flesh" come into him as he tells here.

Just at the moment when he feels hardest the lightning of spirit makes a rift in the mental sphere round him and he sees how good God is (not how angry He is) and suddenly loves Him. Just when the heart is most bitter and despairing a rift is made in the cloud of ideas, and the tenderness and mercy of God [not His hardness and absence) are realized, and love and adoration quicken us. It is no use to try to scare people into being good for the sake of the rewards of goodness. Rewards do not come for being good. The stake, the rack, the jail, public scorn have always been doled out to those who have urged being good for the sake of the rewards of goodness.

Come, let us tell how bountifully indulgent God is — how He is love, whether We love or not; how He feeds, whether We praise or not; how He clothes, Whether we pray or not; how He inspires us with genius, Whether we have faith in Him or not. The constant description of the goodness and bounty, and mercy and tenderness, and love of God has the most marvelous effect upon the atmosphere. The cold, feeling mind alone in some splendid room, suddenly feels the vibrating mental messages and is moved with compassion. "I love Thee for Thy goodness; forgive me. I will help my brother's children whom I have ignored. Help me to be merciful and kind."

Nobody had need to preach about how that cold, unfeeling mind had stiffened the joints, and show the rigor of cause and effect in order to heal them. They are now healed.

Ezekiel here gives one of those "treatments" to the captive Jews which, if we will read over often, will hasten the loosing of the bonds of captivity for all the earth. A11 men will feel their minds break open and warm at such mental messages. We might cross out his ideas of remembering our badness and "loathing our sinfulness," for God, you know remembers nothing. "Their sins will I remember no more against them forever." "They shall forget misery as Waters that pass away."

All those prophets of ancient times were tinged more or less with their past teachings. Shake off everything that you have been taught. Stop remembering anything. It is one of the best practices you can undertake. Forget everything purposely for a few minutes every day. When you come to recollection again what do you suppose you will remember? That which is good. Try it. Try again. Keep it up for years. It is natural for you to remember only just the good. It is artificial to remember the bad. You must be very world-taught if you cherish the past, and so forgetting on purpose may be the only healing practice you need. If you are in trouble and have tried many ways to get out, sit down and forget everything, good, bad and indifferent. The nature of your mind unclothed by ideas is clear with intelligence, bold with understanding, able with right action.

Success and prosperity are your divine nature. The ideas that you are clothed with are very unnecessary. Strip yourself of them at once. Carlyle said that the ideas We are clothed With are "a shadow system gathered round over me."

Ezekiel here holds up a few of his old pieces of his old shell, a few rags of his old teachings, which we will draw our pencil through, for as God never said any such thing we have no time to waste believing that we have to be hunting up how bad we used to be.

There was a man in India four years ago who could cause you to forget everything. He could hold you still in the cleansing solution of forgetfulness till you should touch mind to mind with God. Then suddenly you would spring from this mental "bath" (such as Ezekiel speaks of here], and every bone, muscle, nerve, convolution, would be smiling and dancing with health. Every thought would be entranced with its own beauty and wisdom.

People flocked to him to be healed. One Woman spoke to God in such a fashion that she forgot everything except His presence and was cured of dropsy by so doing.

This Washing and cleansing that Ezekiel promises we are all to have at last along with Jewry, are simply forgetting everything which the man had such a knack at making people do. Have your ever tried forgetting everything? No. Then it is time you tried it. If you are very busy all day, take the time just as you are about to sleep at night. Think nothing — nothing, on purpose. Sleep will help you. Sleep is an effort on your part to forget. Descartes, the Frenchman, learned to forget when his mind was just loaded with items. So can you.

Of course you will find written in indelible characters the good and so when you first open your eyes in the morning there will be a thought of "something good is coming to me."

If you are awake in the night, practice forgetting. People are always kept awake in the night for their own good. "The Lord holdeth mine eyes Waking." Their whole affairs can be managed by night thoughts. By day they are tangled with other people's ideas. By night they are alone with God.

God is their friend. "There is a friend that sticketh closer than a brother." Talk with this friend. Tell Him all your needs. Tell Him your plans no matter how bad your purposes are. Tell God with whom you lie awake.

Wisdom and greatness will awake in the morning with you. If you have changed your plans by morning you will still be successful. By this lesson you may know that you never made any mistakes. God was your past.

"I am Alpha." By this you may know that you never can make any mistakes. God is your future. "I am Omega." By this you may know that nothing can hurt you.

"My presence shall go with thee." By this you may not think that it is by any fault of yours at all that you have evils fallen upon you. And it will be no virtue of yours that your blessings come to recognize, "Not for your sakes."

This God who asks nothing and does all is the kind to describe to make the airs warm and the earthquakes cease; the heavens drop down kindness to every creature Whether he deserves it or not, and violence to cease forever; the winds to bring you good news from a far country and youth to come again to your wasted heart: home to fold you round and right Words to distill as dew from your lips. It is not the deserts of the Jews but their being that is blessed.

It is not your worthiness (praise be to the true God) but the fact of your being that shall cause you to feel this treatment of Ezekiel in its fullness. The planet is being treated to forget. The nations are being treated to forget. So the planet will cease from cyclones and the nations from carnage. "Nature abhors a vacuum." When you forget you are a vacuum, what do you suppose wishes to kiss your divine nature if freed from its memories? All good wishes toward you. What do you suppose will wish to kiss you if you forget the good and forget the good only? Why more bad things, of course, will hasten to greet their own. So it is Well to forget everything. At the uncovered center is God. God is good! And thus, My own shall come to me."

March 13th, 1892

NOTE. BIBLE LESSON XXXVI, FOR MARCH 20, 1892, WAS NOT AVAILABLE IN THE ORIGINALS CONSULTED, THEREFORE IS THE ONLY ONE OF THE FIRST SEVENTY FIVE LESSONS NOT INCLUDED IN THIS COLLECTION.

Bible Lesson XXXVII. Isaiah 40:1-10. All Flesh is Grass

There are four verses in this lesson which contain all the Science of God ever announced to the world. They are the first twelve lessons of the Science, and the second twelve also.

The first set of twelve lessons has already been given very plainly, and is beginning to work its way in the world of sense and intellect. The second set of twelve lessons can come clearly apparent only to those who accept in understanding the first twelve.

If a student finds himself suddenly in possession of the second set of lessons and then goes and tells thereof, he is soon hushed up, and finds himself obliged to go tenderly over the first lessons line upon line and precept upon precept, because his hearers tell him he is annihilating their God, destroying the office and character of Christ, denying the Bible. He must then patiently tell them that God is indestructible, irresistible Substance. Christ is Eternal Truth. The Word of God is infallible.

He does not insist at this point upon telling what he knows to be true, viz, that their God is nowhere, their Christ is a hoax, their Bible an imagination. It must come to each mind by itself that the true God, the true Christ, the true Bible are infinitely incapable of such dealings as the outward wordings of the external Bible proclaim or human observations argue.

The verses that tell the whole story are: "Speak ye comfortably unto Jerusalem that her warfare is accomplished, for she hath received of the Lord's hand, double for all her sins."... "Make straight in the desert a highway for our God."... "All flesh is grass" ... "The Lord will come with a strong hand, and His arm shall rule for Him."

Any mind that has ever listened to the voice of God at its center, and has pledged itself to love and believed in God, is Jerusalem. Unto this mind with its body and human lot, it is promised, "The Lord will take away from thee all sickness, and will put none of the evil diseases of Egypt upon thee." "In famine He shall redeem thee from death, and in war from the power of the sword." "Bread shall be given him, his waters shall be sure." "He will cover thee with His feathers and under His wings shalt thou trust." "The Almighty shall be thy defense, and thou shalt have plenty of silver." "Thou shalt run and not be weary, walk and not faint." "He shall give His angels charge over thee to keep thee, lest at any time thou dash thy foot against a stone."

The Egypt mind gets no such promises. The Egypt mind is the mind that dwells in the senses and has never listened to the voice of the Spirit. It has never pledged itself to live after the dictates of righteousness. Here Jerusalem has been suffering great tribulations in spite of the wonderful promises. How is this? Because she has entangled her mind with imaginations of ways of getting a living, of learning, of happiness, not in accord with the teachings of the Spirit. Looking at the ways of the world, she has felt that she "must do in Rome as the Romans do." She speaks of God as her rest, and fears accidents. She speaks of God as her health, and looks to material things for her healing. She says: "The merciful man is merciful to his beast," and cuts off the helpless horses' tails to do like the world. Thus is Jerusalem taking at some point of her experience, the fruits of compromise.

But the Truth works also. The Truth the mind tells comes unto its fruitage as well as the error the mind thinks. Then, when error has reached its highest point of pain, the Truth comes like a healing balm, "Speak comfortably unto Jerusalem."

If in your childhood, some true word kept conning itself over in your mind, it will come to you at your sorest need as a healing. This is what is meant by "Man's extremity is God's opportunity." But it is the mind pledged to faith in such Truth that gets the healing by its own words, not the mind living in its imaginations. The affairs of your life are met at their direst extremities by certain words you once spoke, just as your bodily health is overtaken. I hope you believed this passage at some period of your life: "Call thou upon Me in the day of adversity, and I will deliver thee." It will come with unexpected successes at some least probable moment, "In such an hour as ye think not."

All this is taught in the first lessons of Science. The idea of Jerusalem receiving double for her sins, is the same as the idea of sixty and an hundred-fold fruitage for Truth told. Seeds make more than themselves. The mind always cries, "My punishment is too great for my mistakes." It rejoices in the "exceeding weight" of its successes.

The third verse, commanding mind to make straight in the desert a highway for God, has also an intimation of the highest lessons of Science. But the simple information will strike you as extravagant enough, so you may get the profoundest one out by yourself. This is the simplest metaphysical interpretation allowable, viz, that every mind has its Sahara spot - its desert place. This desert spot is your dead hopes. It is that place in your mind where you expect nothing though such things as you would most love to have are the very ones you do not expect.

Why do you not expect them? How dared your teachers teach you that you must not expect those things here and now? You do not expect to dwell here again with your beloved? You do not expect the renewal of youth? You do not expect miracles to be wrought for you?

Why not? Make straight through that desert of non-expectation for the fulfillment of each one of them. "The desert shall blossom as the rose." "I will satisfy thy soul in drought." The most marvelous things you can think of are the things to expect in the Science of God. In a certain city, where the rich have everything and the poor have nothing, there has arisen a meek sect of people who say they can call upon the Father-Mother God for everything, even to money. They do not seem to have any visible means of getting their living, yet they are honorable in their dealings and never run into debt. The people of that city have stoned them, thrown mud at them and broken their windows, though they are harmless and un-retaliating.

Would not you rather know how to call upon God, in whose hands are all the treasures of the hills, than to know how to make a deal on the Board of Trade that would cost every starving child one penny more for his supper, which penny he cannot get? Why do they not stone those who gather the productions of the generous earth into corners and make it so hard for the poor, instead of those who are making a path through the desert of hard times for the marvelous God to walk through? Would not you rather know the process by which the noble Ram Lal called down the white fog on the hills of Keitung to defend his friend from the would-be murderers, than to know the latest device in electric alarms for burglars? There on the hills of desolation in the desert mound of no prospect for help, was the marvelous God of defense.

Would not you rather know the mystic language by which the three wise men met on the plains of no fruitage under the white stars of midnight, never having met before, coming by sure steps, unsought by cablegrams, telegrams, letters, to find in each other friendship unfailing, comradeship in all things, than to know how our ministers to England or France, or our fair women delegates are received at foreign courts? There on the sands, with only the moon for a light, the marvelous God taught His friendship for man.

Come — desert spot in the heart where you do not expect love, do not expect home, do not expect fulfillment — awake! The God of the nations commandeth, expect! This is the hour when the desert must bloom. "Is anything too hard for Me?" saith our God. Let them keep their gold, God will provide. Let them corner our bread and meat, God will provide. Let them preach death and sorrow, God will bring to life, and comfort them that mourn.

All the riches of earth shall be no more counted in that day when the desert lifts up her head than the air is now measured out. We do not hold our breath lest the air fail us. Here on the desert we hold fast no riches. God will provide. Do you rise into faith as this simple text opens its loving meaning to you?

Here on the lap of our mother we rest;
God is our home.
Here none shall pursue us,
Here none can undo us.
We walk with the blest,
God is our home.

The next text is: "All flesh is grass." That is the second lesson of Science, the second lesson of the first course. Here we count it as true that all earthly things are symbols only. Thought is the substance. Then we push the meaning still further and say that the thoughts that show forth in material things are as *non est* as the material things themselves.

Is that too metaphysical for you? Oh, no, it is not. You already believe that God, the Mind of the universe, fills all space and place and where. "Am not I God? Do I not fill heaven and earth? Is there any besides Me? Nay, I know not any." Then there is but one Mind thinking thoughts. So the thoughts that produce material things with their clashings and sorrows are no thoughts at all. It has a very uplifting effect upon the mind and a very enchanting power over your affairs to understand this text. Down through the walls steps the transcendent Jesus into your presence. The granules of matter offer no resistance to the Mind that knows them not. Spirit will bear witness with Spirit that there is only one substance at all, and that is your soul. "The flesh profiteth nothing," speaks the entrancing Friend as He lifts you out of the memory of the past — out of the pain of the present.

Alone with Thee, my soul walks fearless,
Mantled by Thee, I rest in happy peace;
Standing 'mid scenes I once mourned as cheerless,
I now joyous smile, proclaiming swift release.

The fourth text takes us by one touch of inspiration to the unspoken top of the Mount of Paradise, where in the workshop of Jehovah we watch the Christian doctrine redeem the race.

"The Lord God shall come with a strong hand and His arm shall rule for Him." This is prophecy. John the Revelator saw the same moment and on the friendless isle of Patmos, rejoiced in our day. In the great pyramid of Gizeh, the north star looked down the mystic shaft of ages ago and wrote across her golden breast that the line where it is intended history shall end and prophecy be fulfilled, is today.

John spoke it by a figure. He saw the holy Science as a woman. Take your mind away from men and women and think only of the Holy Spirit as you read how he saw the woman clothed as the sun, having on her head the crown of twelve stars, and the moon under her feet. This is the Science of God, and it gives to the world the Man-Child who shall rule all nations with a rod of iron.

The Man-Child of Science is the strong teaching of Science, the strong and invincible idea that springs forth at its highest point of instruction, viz, that man is God and God is man. The Spirit of man and the Spirit of God are one. The Spirit of man may say: "I am that I am, as the Spirit of God my say, "I am that I am." "There is a Spirit in man, and the inspiration of the Almighty giveth him understanding." Who told them to change the royal arch word of God ever speaking in the soul, "I am that I am," in Masonry to "I was, but am no more?"

Am not I "Alpha and Omega, the beginning and the end?" Who said that the flesh might speak? Shall any have voice save God?

The "strong right hand" of this text means the efficient thought, or strong idea of God. The idea of mind is the son, or man-child. The idea that the "I am that I am" in man is the "I am that I am" of God shall rule nations with a rod of iron, though the Science that gave it birth may have to be driven into the wilderness of the scorn of the world.

Now think of all those who teach the Science, as the Science itself, and with the twelfth of Revelation, follow their experience after they give forth their noblest conclusion. The chased black in the everglades was no more at bay than they, as the very abstraction of evil hurries them into poverty, pain, tribulation. At this point, they are met with the strange information that holding the name Jesus Christ in mind, forces all the issues between Good and evil, into their own experience.

If Jesus Christ "had not where to lay His head," neither shall they. If He was "despised and rejected," so shall they be — by holding His name in mind. But "the earth helped the woman." The very wilderness shall yield you the corn, and the wine of dominion over all the ways of the flesh. "His own arm shall get Him rule." Throw your highest truth into the arena, and let it fight for itself. Jesus Christ teaches you dominion. It is Jesus Christ in you that is the "I am that I am."

"He shall rule from sea to sea, and from the river to the uttermost parts of the earth."

John, speaking in a figure, saw the holy Science fly away with the "wings of a great eagle." The two wings with which you who enter into the Science may fly, are two words: "within and without." God is both within you and without you, the here and the there, the beginning and the end. To you forever the breath comes, "I am satisfied in Thee," and from you forever the response must go back, "I am satisfied in Thee."

From far beyond principalities and powers, from farther than angels and archangels fly, drops down the message into your heart, "I am satisfied in Thee." From your breath in the wilderness of earthly seemings, the triumphant response, "I am satisfied in Thee." From the heart-fires of the earth, from the crawling things and the stones comes the nourishing message, "I am satisfied in Thee." And from your wise heart, no timid answer steals; like a radiant light your word lets fall, "I am satisfied in Thee."

Thus, they that know the Science are "nourished." Its arm gets them rule. "Thus shalt thou be in league with the stones of the field, and the beasts of the field shall be at peace with thee." March 27, 1892

Bible Lesson XXXVIII. Psalm 1:1-6. Realm of Thought

Here in this first Psalm, we have a lesson in contrasts. The mental processes starting from the choice of the will, or the choice of the affections, gather ideas on their way, and are confronted by and by with the results of holding those ideas they have chosen.

It is not at all necessary that one should think as his neighbors do, nor that he should think as things and circumstances around him would like him to. He may think what he pleases. And what he pleases to think will make up his destiny of human experience.

One may insist upon thinking lightly of misfortune till his mind becomes so buoyant and joyous that he has actually lost the power to be downcast or depressed. Then, of course, he will draw to himself people and circumstances and affairs buoyant and joyous. For we draw a "congregation" (as it is here called) of things about us exactly like our mind.

As the magnetized bar draws steel filings, so does your determination to be cheerful draw cheerful conditions. This is as true of the wretch in the slums as of Victoria. This is the gospel. Not admitting any idea that can draw misery as its out showing, one might come up out of the most depressing situations, like a. cork out of water.

Mark Antony said: "But I, unless I think what has happened is an evil, am not injured. And it is my power not to think so." So the psalmist tried to paint the discomfort of the mind that chooses to think how dark the world is, how dishonest people are, how unfortunate innocent creatures are. It is an idea of his that you can scare people into being good by painting the torments of the bad. It is a wrong notion. For, if you cause the mind to imagine anything, the body and surroundings will scramble to carry out the imagination.

Many times children are imagined to be doing something, or to have been doing something, which they had never thought of. They stand out as expressions of our ideals, and feel a masterful impulsion to carry out our imaginations. So the next thing we hear of is that they are doing just as we imagined. Then we praise ourselves for our intuitions. Nay, let us cleanse us of unrighteousness rather, for we pushed them into the doing. We thought and they acted as:

"My friend and I were lovers;
It was good for us to be together.
We were companions in our trust;
But one day I suspected him — my friend,
Of doing that which he had not.
I did not tell him of my suspect,
But his unconscious eye looked grief.
I kept on still suspecting him, while he was innocent,
Till by and by he looked askance at me,
And was afraid when I was nigh.
And I went on still holding my gnawing worm of suspect,
While he, my friend, was innocent,
Till by and by he caught the word
That haunted me, and it tempted him
To do that which in my heart I thought.
He tremblingly went towards the action,
I all the while determining he had done it,
Till in an evil hour my friend,
Who formerly was innocent,
Was guilty of the deed I had thought in my heart.
And now he walks a sinner

Who erstwhile was righteous,
Made sinner by my suspect
Who, my God, is guilty in this case –
My friend who once was innocent,
Or I who thought him guilty?"

When one thinks oppositely of friends, children, events, purposely, on principle, one can get his mind so trained that it will never walk in the "counsel of the ungodly." It is not in the slightest necessary for anyone to think anyone or anything is not good. When one sees how a man ill uses another man, a prompt metaphysical process will cause his hand to drop and his heart to forget even its intention to do wrong. The fountain of kindness and nobility will spring forth. This fountain is the living spring within everyone and everything. It is the Real Self. It has been hidden by a mass of rubbish. Our thoughts have been part of the rubbish covering men and women and children and things. To remove our thoughts is to take off part of the rubbish.

In the Science of Mind we find what thoughts have most potency at removing rubbish.

We need to keep ourselves free from the rubbish of false notions. The second lesson in Spiritual Science deals entirely with the process of self–cleansing — setting free. The only thing to be rid of, is one's own thoughts. These thoughts are gathered from people very often. Take the man lying on his bed of sickness. What put him there? Thoughts. Whose thoughts? Those his neighbors gave him, that his family gave him, those he has imagined on his own account.

The neighbors' thoughts lie down on him like dead weights. They say, "You must not sit up. You must not eat. You must not drink. You must have this done. You must have that done." On what compulsion must he? If he will think within his mind, "I put away your ideas, they are nothing to me; I am able to do what I please," very soon he will rise buoyantly out of their notions, and even they will admit that he is right. He need not open his lips. Mind is master. If he should say that aloud, he would get into controversy which would irritate them all. He would make more work for his mind. No need of piling Pelion upon Ossa to get free from his ailments.

To get to thinking as other people do, is to "walk in their counsel." The mind walks around among the kingdom of thoughts not seen by the eyes nor heard by the ears. Just as we are celebrating the discovery of America, another unknown kingdom spreads its angled wiles and wonderful rivers before our gaze. It is the kingdom of thoughts. To understand thoughts, is to understand things. Everything is made up of thoughts, governed by thoughts, moved by thoughts. We ought to have someone arise with a genius for managing thoughts. Only one has ever understood the realm at all. That was Jesus of Nazareth. The rest have been trying to understand it. They have improved sufficiently to ward off those wild ideas, which make sickness. They are hastening so as not to be at all afraid of the thoughts of their neighbors.

That is a great advance on the fears they had not so very long ago that other people's thoughts were bad for them. They are rousing to understand dominion over conditions of all kinds now. The knowledge that "Thou wilt keep him in perfect peace whose mind is stayed on Thee," is the call to understand how to have peace by taking the right staff as we walk through to this country.

We get to "sitting in the seat of the scornful" by thinking that there is so much greed among rich men that there are starving millions for us to be anxious about. This scorn is not healing for bruises. There is an idea that is healing for bruises made by the grasping and over-reaching of the men of the world. Ignore the physical shadows dropped down by thoughts, and put over the country of causation the right idea. Here it is: "I pronounce all greed and dishonesty finished — ended. The good now reigns supreme."

Pay no attention to material things that look impossible to be ended. The God whose word spoken is the redemption of all hearts said definitely: "Thou shalt decree a thing and it shall be established unto thee." This giant idea sent stalking through the realm of mind will knock down everything not like itself. The man who had thought of cornering the wheat says, "I shan't do it; I cannot." The woman who was trying to get the advantage of her customer stops suddenly. The man who was sick with discouragement lifts up his head. He goes out and finds a position. Your giant cleared his mind's eye and sent him straight to the right place.

In this realm of mind, it was said by one who traveled over a certain patch thereof, that it is possible for one to shut his eyes and stop his ears so entirely to what is going on in the streets and in houses, as to hear the voice of the King saying: "This is the way," and then, that everyone who so hears will go right into the line of prosperity.

By the understanding of causes and how to govern causes, we find the way to our own prosperity. By the knowledge of Truth, we discover that everyone has his own way of being prosperous. There is prosperity for every creature. It will not come by worldly dodges nor indeed by following out the lines of theology announced by the most popular preachers. It seems hard to tell this Truth. It looks as if one were trying to speak ill of good preachers. No, it is good to tell what is true. It is good news to say that you need not believe one word about hades or Satan, or the dispensation of Providence, or the visitation of God through sickness, weakness, death, calamity, poverty. All those things are the shadows cast by ideas. Change the ideas and the real dispensations of Providence and visitations of God will shine like the smiles of those you love best. The rich revivings that come with true ideas are here likened to "Trees planted by rivers of living waters." This is like the talk of Jesus Christ. He said: "To him that bath, shall be given; and from him that bath not, shall be taken even that he seemeth to have."

The Scriptures are a unit in telling that you attract more and more of things and people and powers like your thoughts. Both these texts prove this. If you keep your mind on prosperity, you will have that idea enrich and revive as a tree planted by living waters, or, as Jesus Christ said, more "shall be given to him." So then, what little idea of misery he did have or you did have, will drop away. "From him shall be taken that which he seemeth to have."

Here we are told to stand in judgment and also in the congregation of the righteous. Our thoughts are our "congregation." We must stand up and hold our own with our own congregation. The platform on which we stand is God, the life of the universe. It is not the will of God that anyone or anything should ever die. Did you ever make the erroneous statement, "It has pleased God to cause our good brother to be taken from us?" Well, now, your judgment has not been exercised by such a lie. It has leaned against nothing and so when your child or mother was exposed to your presence, she felt faint. Tell your congregation of thoughts that the great poets and theologians may enjoy their sicknesses, misfortunes, disappointments, if they please; you propose to have some judgment of your own. So you say: "My God is the Giver and Keeper of the life of all things. He never sends death to anything or anyone. Hearing cannot end. Light cannot fail. Peace is unbroken. Joy is endless. Buoyant vigor is increasing. This is my kind of God." As this is the true God, you cannot have any of the dying gifts of that old imaginary being, your judgment used to lean against.

Your congregation will revive with your words. That is, every idea that you have will be happy and vigorous. Then your acquaintances will grow healthy. Every old person is a trait of yours that is getting towards its end. Notice the peculiarity of him or her and see your odd conceit standing forth. Every lame person is the walking image of one of our ideas. Get well grounded in the four propositions of metaphysics or Spiritual Science, and you will cure lameness. These are the four propositions. They are better than anarchy, or nihilism for want, unrest, hate. "It is not God's will that anyone or anything should ever be sick or diseased; God is the health of the universe. It is not God's will that anyone or anything should be feeble or weak; God is the strength of the world. It is not God's will that anyone or anything should be hurt or frightened; God is the defense of the world. It is not God's will that anyone or anything should ever know want; God is the support of the world."

This is a lesson in will. While you are silent, with the wills of millions of creatures determined to get their advantage whether you are advantaged or not, crossing and re-crossing over you like a network, look calmly, coolly, at the situation.

You cannot manage all those wills by any will of yours bent on the same purpose. This is what Jesus Christ meant by saying, "I can of mine own self do nothing." The will that is like that network of wills is quite unequal to the Herculean task of fighting them. Breathe deep now. That will lies deep. Your breath is your dominion. There is a will that is God. It is your true will. It will, snap all those wills crossed over and against you. Now choose deliberately the true ideas of God to live by and you will find life will completely change. That will is acting. Sometimes you may say, "I can do nothing with these things. Jesus Christ can manage them easily. To Jesus Christ I leave them.

As Jesus Christ is within you, you will probably do or say something yourself which will be strong, positive, dominant. Yet the old-fashioned domineering human will, will not be in your words or actions. It is Jesus Christ's will speaking and acting. Jesus Christ is dominion. "Be not afraid," He said, "I have overcome the world."

There have been people so feeble they could not sit up, who breathed their breath deep — clear to the foundations of their body, knowing that the breath was dominion, and they burned as with fires while the hot blood tingled through them. Then they arose new creatures. This was after many people who did not believe in the breath of dominion, but did believe in the breath of death, had given them up.

The will that keeps so still is the silence of God, waiting to rise like the lion of the tribe of Judah, with your word. "Without the word 'was nothing made." You yourself are the Word. You speak when you please. You speak what you please. The psalmist notices how miserable people are who look at human experience with the idea of meeting it with human methods. He also speaks of the conquering shouts of those who ignore the wills of the world and speak from the deep places where the Omnipotent Will within us all rests. It rouses like a strong lion from its lair. To all the purposes of the world set against life, health, strength, judgment, supplies, it says, "It is finished. The kingdoms of this world are now become the kingdoms of our Lord and His Christ." April 3, 1892

Bible Lesson XXXIX. Psalm 2:1-12. The Power of Faith

Before noticing today's lesson, make the connection in this course which last Sunday's text suggests. That can be summed up in the four propositions distinctly announced by the Second Psalm explained esoterically.

They are these:

1. I stand by the Omnipotent Truth that God is the Life of Omnipresence and as God is Life without any death there is therefore no death at all to Substance or Strength.

To believe in death is to be what this psalmist denominated a "heathen imagining vain things." By this statement, we come into clear knowledge of what the eastern sages meant by saying thousands of years ago that:

"He who thinks that he can slay a life,
Or he who thinks life can be slain,
These both do err;
For life is God, and God cannot be slain."

We understand that it is as great an evidence of heathenism or ignorance to strike down one's neighbor with intent to slay as to preach that it is wicked to kill, or vice versa. For there is only one life in the universe. It fills the universe full. There is no place to take life from and none to take it to — save itself.

The out-showing of belief in death is the raging of anger, man against his brother man, supposing that his brother has gotten something away from him; or against fate, thinking "imagining" we have been defrauded of something. We are here shown that "according to thy faith be it unto thee," is wholly in reference to human experiences. Faith is here shown to be that persistent way of thinking which is peculiar to every man, woman, child as distinct from his neighbor. It is what we think within our hearts independent of our speech and independent of our true Spirit, which determines our destiny.

For illustration, take Napoleon Bonaparte; he was always calculating what he should do in case he were defeated. This was his persistent thought. He was not born for defeat. There is a spring of the conquering Spirit buoyantly rising within the bosom of every child. It was so buoyantly near the surface in the little Napoleon, that at six years of age, he would fearlessly fight with boys twice his age and always whip them, because he had not then begun to calculate what he should do in case of being himself whipped.

He who knows the laws of the esoteric as related to the exoteric, will easily trace the teaching that "as a man thinketh in his heart so is he," is written on the scroll of Napoleon's destiny. By and by that subtle river encroached upon the firm intent of his victorious mind, and though his voice was as rallying and his limbs as agile and energetic as ever, the time for the fruitage of his secret thoughts had come, and nothing could stay the signal and irredeemable defeat of Waterloo.

"What we are by thought was wrought and built." The belief that "man is born to die," will show forth in death. But death will not be true because we believe in death by any manner of means. Would it make any difference to the fact of there being a principle of righteousness if you should say that you did not believe in righteousness? It would change your conduct and darken your hopes, but that right is right would go right on regardless of your nonsense. So Life Omnipresent goes on forever filling all the spaces of Omnipresence with the living God though all the kings and preachers of the world proclaim how real death is.

In standing to pass along this first spiritual teaching of this psalm, rejoice in the discovery that it has an exoteric or practical effect to speak this great truth forth as a conviction of mind. Those who speak it as real conviction act as if they had been pushed into the current of living, instead of struggling across it. Life flows visibly through them. Their blood bounds as if some obstruction had been suddenly removed. Their ears quicken and the hearing they bad supposed was dead they find to be as alive as in the days of boyhood before the mind had calculated about death.

Many a supposed dead faculty is waiting for the honest conviction of the mind, that this is true, viz. that all death is an imagination; all old age is the winding up of much believing in the reality of corpses, and all paralyzed or stopped faculties are the hints of truth that the persistent imaginations of mind are marshalling their forces. Imaginations show forth to all those who believe them. Sometimes those who are called Spiritual Scientists are scolded and abused for having death near them, which they do not seem to be able to stop. Do you suppose Napoleon's sudden declaration, "I do not now believe in defeat," would have worked with sudden success against the marshalled armies of his years of mental calculation of defeats? No. Only the fires of the faith of God Himself work with instantaneous demonstration.

If you should look straight past all exteriors into the persistent expectations of death, and calculations about death which those young faithists (called Spiritual Scientists) have, you would see their callused minds striving to believe in life, but solidly determined upon death since their childhood.

It is for the fire of God-faith, the cold mind yearns. God does not believe in death. So Jesus said, "Have the faith of God." Paul said, "By faith the dead are raised." He means that faith, which is the way the mind persists in thinking, will make life visible where it has been hidden by "heathen imaginations."

2. The second proposition here made, as you will see by reading the first twelve verses of the Psalm, is: "God is the health of the universe. As God is the Omnipresence, that which is not God is the nowhere present. As disease, imperfection, sickness are not God, they are nowhere present."

This reminds us of Plato's saying, that when we "discover the one in the many, we have penetrated to the secret of existence." This proposition is universal. As the mind throws its free reasoning afar towards the horizons of the infinite seas, it feels the splendor of this truth that in Omnipresent Holiness, there is no imperfection, and if the mind is honest and docile, it will know that as we live in God, breathe in God, and move in God, so for us also there is no sickness or disease, or imperfect substance.

That which is true of the large is true of the small. That which is true of the all is true of the one. All and each may say truly, "What God is, that I am." Just as soon as this wholesome doctrine gets the consent of the secret heart, the cheeks redden, the flesh glows, the breath deepens. "I am well."

Here we are brought to face the question of where God is, and we must bring Science, revelation, and practical experience to confirm one another.

It is according to the Science of Christ that for the lightest word we give a demonstration. The text is, "For the lightest word thou shalt give account." The Science teaches that the words of Truth are "Life to them that find them and death to all their flesh." Revelation came to the spiritual hearts of the Brahmins ages ago, that "It is by the divine word that the sick are surely healed." Whoever speaks Truth with his secret heart in league with it, is healed. Let experience teach you. The experience of thousands upon thousands testifies that Truth is a healing principle. The cheery refreshment of eternal Truth comes sifting its perfumes of youth and vigor through the tangled threads of our substance, and the promise is fulfilled. "Thy light shall break forth as the morning, and thy health shall spring forth speedily."

Is the substance of God here? Yea, God is here. Is the substance of God there? Yea, God is there.

Early in the study of the Science of God the students said, "We must look for God without us. We must think of Spirit as exterior, there, beyond; never within us." The practical effect of that divorcing of the without from the within in the thoughts of the heart, was that while as a ministry they performed much healing of their neighbors, and made bold to dictate to the universe its mission as the substance of God, they were remarkably unable to cure themselves of their ailments. Palsy, blindness, lameness, pain kept their relentless hold upon them. Then there arose a message among them that, as their own substance was Spirit or God, they must look within for God, never without. They practiced according to the injunction over the Delphic temple — "Know thyself."

The practical results of this insistence upon the God within and not without was to make their eyes keen of sight, their bodies sound and wholesome; but they had not so much effect upon their neighbors' bodily health or physical faculties, and they were always finding their experiences with men and things and affairs disastrous.

They divorced the God substance within from the God substance without. Looking back over the history of mystic or religious teachings we see that all divorce of every sort and kind sprang forth from the one-sided message, "God is within me, not without me," or "God is without me, not within me." All wars are the belief in divorce externalizing, the belief of life apart from Life. There was an ancient sage who made the beautiful announcement, "There is no apartness." They who do not believe in apartness will never have their homes broken by death or divorce or infidelity. They will never fear accidents or hurts or calamities. They will see their safety in the depths of the sea as in their mother's home. "Is He not yonder in the uttermost sea? The sea is His, He made it."

3. They will easily receive the third proposition of this psalm, which interpreted, is, "God is the defense, the protection, the surety of the universe, and as in God there is no danger, so in the universe where God abides, there is no danger forevermore."

This is a Truth. Do you know what Truth has power to do when it is spoken? It can still the tempest, stop the earthquake, intercept the lightning, ward off accidents. Truth is Omnipotence.

"On Truth the worlds were founded. By Truth the worlds were made. Truth is Lord over all and there is nothing higher than it."

If you dare to turn your mind's eye over the accidents and calamities of the ages, you are what this psalmist holds in derision as not having yet learned that imaginations of evil bring experiences of evil. How can evil be in the substance of God? Maimonides said, "When thy senses affirm what thy reason rejects, deny the testimony of the senses and listen to reason." Truth is reason. "God is our omnipresent defense forever." To say this will prove it. "There shall no ill come nigh thy dwelling."

4. The fourth proposition that can be demonstrated as Truth is here brought out as, "God is the support, the provider of the universe and all things in it. As God is the substance of all things and God is self-providing, nothing can want or lack or famish in all creation." So many, who imagine lack, want, indebtedness, poverty, should speak this truth. They must learn it by rote and have it for the secret run of their hearts till they forget that they ever imagined such idle tales as the failure of their substance.

Where it says here that we must "Kiss the Son lest He be angry," it means that we must greet all creation as good to us. There is nothing to hurt us, or rob us or defile us. Greet all things as God — as the Son, or message of God to us that even the stones tell us where there is gold with which to buy bread. The beasts call the direction from whence our success comes quickest. This moment the winds whisper the secret of our prosperity. Everything tells of universal bounty for each creature.

Love them. Condemn them not. It is as our mind secretly thinks that our world returns its dealings to us. But though we create our experiences by our mind's subtle thoughts, we do not create Truth.

Forever these propositions which this psalm repeats woo us to speak them till God in His love is visible, not hidden. God is Truth. Truth is God.

April 10, 1892

Bible Lesson XL. Psalm 19:1-14. Let the Spirit Work

This Nineteenth Psalm causes us to listen to every voice and watch every action as a message from Jehovah full of truth and inspiration for us.

The influence of taking literally such writings as this has always made people inspirational. To such a one upon hearing the propositions of Spiritual Science stated, while the mind was exercised to its highest point of perception of its message and instruction, the great conviction came that — "Christianity as taught today was never the Truth of God nor the Truth of Life, and that the Science called Christian can never galvanize into the living faith of mankind the lifeless hoax, but out of its approximate truths the true doctrine can spring."

"Day unto day uttereth speech." It is the eternal renewal of Truth. When one speaks from honest conviction after much study of religious teachings, — his highest conclusion is that Christianity as at present taught, and as understood by the early church fathers, and explained by the latest phase thereof, was never the Truth of God nor the Truth of Life, — we will listen. For only so far as a religious faith can practicalize, is it worth while. And only so far as it demonstrates what we all recognize as good, is it true.

There must have been some total misconception of Truth in the minds of the early church fathers to have resulted in such savagery as they exhibited toward women and children. There must be some total misconception of Truth in the minds of those church people who are keeping such savage watch over the actions of that little child lest it steal, or overeat, or be too joyous. It must be some total misconception of Truth in the minds of those metaphysical exponents of Christianity who are sick, lame, blind, unfortunate. Let us be meek and lowly, and reason together to drop our faults, though in so doing we drop our seeming virtues. We will not pride ourselves on our piety or moralities while we are not manifesting the works of Jesus Christ.

There certainly are doctrines enunciated by Jesus Christ, which are not now taught as He meant them. He was Spirit and His words were Spirit. He taught a spiritual doctrine in words suited to lift each grade of mind a step higher "day unto day." The profoundest mystic will find himself outstripped by the mysticism of Jesus. The most formal Puritan burning with pious self-righteousness his helpless neighbors, will find a. text easy to interpret: "Do good. Forgive."

There have been certain works laid great stress upon in the most practical interpretations of Christianity. Those works are healing, teaching, reforming, raising from death. There have been certain ideas insisted upon as true, viz., that faith in God is necessary to our wellbeing; that understanding of God would make man one with God; that praise and thanksgiving to God would cause the heavens to drop down blessings. All these ideas are the rounds of Jacob's ladder to us. We take them and rest on them just long enough to spring on to the higher round.

While at first there was great stress laid upon the practical fruits of right faith, healing from sickness and reforming from vicious habits were looked for as necessary "evidences of Christianity." This was a higher round of the ladder of thinking than that one where we thought ourselves very well pleasing to God to accuse Him of sending us sickness and buffetings of Satan.

Then it was a higher round of the ladder of thinking when they who were healed and reformed refused to stop at such simple demonstrations, and boldly proclaimed that no one ever need to be poor, no one ever need to be hurt, no one ever need to make any mistakes.

It was still a higher round when we were taught that a line of thinking would place us so in line with righteousness that we could be health and peace and bounty to all the world with whom we should come in contact without even trying to help them. It is still a higher round of the ladder of glory for the feet of our mind to stand upon, to proclaim that there never was any healing to be done, never any suffering to ameliorate, never any sins to pardon, for "there is no speech nor language where the voice of God Himself is not heard," exactly as the mystic sense of this psalm proclaims. And so when one tells us that it is no use to try to galvanize into life the miracles of Christianity, we understand him as meaning it is Christlike to declare there never was any necessity for miracles because God is all.

When one tells us that it is nonsense to teach that faith and praise and prayer are keys into the favor of God, we understand that it is truly Christlike to proclaim that Truth is true and Good is good whether we have faith in it or not, or whether we praise it or not. It is the highest doctrine of the rounds thus far, that we are already in heaven in the glory that was ours from the great forever without beginning of years or end of days. The higher the round one steps his thoughts upon, the more delightful he finds life.

"The sun" is always the headlight of Truth in these lessons. It has a "tabernacle." That is, there is always a place where someone speaks fearlessly one higher statement than is popular in his age. It is the sum total of all the teachings of the ages, which interprets aright the Moslem marching song, "There is no God but God." It causes you to give up your former idea of God and to think not at all of God, but simply to rest while He thinks for you. It is the mind that ceases to project any thoughts at all which makes itself a vacuum into which Truth rushes.

While we are projecting our imaginations we are describing unrealities, because while we are projecting our thoughts, we see only our own creations.

"There is no understanding of errors," as it tells us here in the twelfth verse. There is only stopping our thinking. The great vacuum of silence, of stillness, of ceasing from thoughts is a suction for the strength and understanding of God. He who stops thinking is greater than he who thinks the highest doctrines he has ever heard. He who does nothing is the greatest of workers. He lets God work. He who loves nothing and no one is the greatest lover, for he lets God love. He who wills nothing is the divinest demonstration of will, for he lets the will of God be done. This is Science. It is revelation. It is practical. Rest from seeing will give your eyes strength of sight. God is rest. Rest from thinking will demonstrate perfection of Mind. God is Mind.

One who was writing of the rest of God as revealed by John the isle of Patmos felt the material objects of his room moving away him; felt the ideas of his mind slipping from their cells into the abysses of nowhere; felt the rush of the Shekinah of God through his being; heard himself called by his own name as it is written in Paradise.

They who watch the quarreling of nations may watch no longer. "In such an hour as ye think not, Jesus Christ cometh." Let drop your notions of responsibility. God is the responsible. Let fall your imaginations of duties awaiting your efforts. God is the worker.

This is the Divine baptism of the water of Life. Keep still. Stiller yet. Far stiller than the world ever thought of. It is now the hush of the morning of God. Now each one can be sure in himself. I do not work, I am worked. I do not think, I am thought. I do not will, I am willed. I do not love, I am loved. I do not move, I am moved. I do not need, I am needed. "I came not to do mine own will, but the will of Him who sent me."

As I let the true will be done, I see heaven opening and the angels of God feeding the hungry, healing the distressed, exposing the souls of mankind, all white and gentle. As I keep still, I find that all heaven is contained in the doctrine of "Let." This is the mystic influence of the nineteenth psalm.

April 17th, 1892

Bible Lesson XLI. Psalm 23:1-6. Christ is Dominion

According to the scientific or absolute interpretation of the Bible stories and descriptions, we have such a teaching of life that actually we can understand all the material earth to be optical delusion. This psalm of David reminds us of how safely the three wise Hebrews sat in the furnace unhurt. Why were they unhurt? Because they knew that fire cannot burn Spirit. Were they Spirit? Just Spirit, and nothing else.

Does it make any difference to the power of fire to burn your flesh if you know you were made of God Substance, and not material substance? "Ye shall know the Truth, and the Truth shall make you free." "When thou walkest through the fire thou shalt not be burned."

Is this explanation of the Scriptures common? No. The Scriptures are usually described as lessons preparing mankind for a future state, instead of as actual information of immunities from every sort and kind of misery here and now.

The psalm reminds us of Daniel in the den of lions unharmed. How could Daniel be so safe in the lion's den? Because, as it is explained in Daniel 1:4, he had "understanding of Science." What Science was that which Daniel, Hananiah, Mishael, and Azariah had? The Science of "Om" — Omniscience. They had great wisdom in this Science. Is that Science understood in our time? It is understood just so far as those studying it can save themselves from drowning by their understanding of Spirit, and not by their ability to swim or build rafts; by their safety in the midst of fires and swords through their knowledge of God, and not by their ability to run or fight back; by their never knowing pain, or sickness, or poverty through having the "Lord for their Shepherd."

What does it mean to have the Lord for a shepherd? It means having the law of the Spirit in the understanding so that material processes count for nothing. Can that law be understood now? Law of Spirit is eternal. Is this law in any respect like the law of matter and evil? "My ways are not your ways," saith the Lord.

Why was not the thorn removed from Paul if understanding of Spirit redeems one from trouble? There was no thorn to remove. If Paul persisted in imagining a trouble and in declaring that he was able to bear a trouble, he would find himself able to bear his imagination. "By thy words thou art justified," saith Jesus.

Then it is not noble to endure great sorrows and afflictions with fortitude? It is the nobility of one who sets up a straw image and fights it, or of one who builds a pond of iced blood and walks through it, praising himself for his ability to endure cold and pain. Would it be nobler to understand that according to the law of the Spirit of life there never was any reality in sorrows and afflictions only such as we have imagined? It would be the nobility of one who understands the Science of God and chose to live it rather than one who kept on insisting that there is no Science of God.

"For this is Life eternal, that ye know the true God." What does eternal Life mean? It means that there is no end to any faculty. Seeing is an eternal faculty. To know the true God will keep the sight strong forever. Hearing is an eternal faculty. To know the true God will keep the hearing good forever. Self-providing is an eternal faculty. To know the true God will make us self-providing and self-sustaining forever.

This is what the first verse of this psalm means: "The Lord is my Shepherd. I shall not want." To know the law of God is to know the law of Spirit, for God is Spirit.

If one should sit right down in the midst of this sordid age and determine to get his provision from Spirit, and not by any material process whatsoever, would he be provided for? Yes. He would help to open the gates of the golden age, when no one can get anything away from anyone, and no one can get any power over any one. It ushers in the sight of Truth and we are ashamed of our barterings and calculatings. We can see that all ideas of buying and selling, giving and taking, borrowing and lending, had their rise in our covenantings with God to give us life, and health, and home, and heaven, if we could give Him faith, or praise, or penance. We should not attempt to barter with the true God for our blessings. "He giveth to all men liberally." "The gift of God is Eternal Life."

Eternal Life must be applied to our blessings as well as to our being. If you will not agree with your God to give Him anything or do anything for Him, you will feel a thousand times more grateful when you see your safety and pleasure increasing day by day, than if you should agree to praise, or acknowledge, or give thanks, for there is always a sneaking feeling of not having been half thankful enough or half-conscious enough of the goodness of God if one has agreed to give thanks and praises for blessings received. And this sneaking feeling of not having half kept your obligations is very hardening to the character and irritating to the mind.

Many a man or woman is ugly or cross, because he or she feels as if there were something they ought to have done which they have not. And the hidden idea, that you have not half performed your obligations to your God, will end by your getting into debts which it will seem impossible for you to pay. Indebtedness to your fellow men is an awfully uncomfortable feeling. So in Science you are taught to go and make it right with your God and you will find it easy then to make it right with your neighbor. Tell the true God that you never owed Him anything and He never owed you anything. Speak boldly that as God cannot owe God, so you cannot owe God, for your substance, your life, your mind is God, and God is your substance, your life, and your mind.

Jesus taught this lesson of getting out of debt by a saying that has been translated this way: "Forgive us our debts as we forgive our debtors." Looking at the text from the scientific standpoint of David, as found in the sixth verse of this psalm, we see that "forgive us our debts," means: "give now into our mind Thy knowledge that there is no debt." As we now pass along the lines of mind that there is no debt, we hereby drop our imagination that we could owe God anything, or that God could owe us anything. As God is the substance, and life and mind of man, so man cannot owe man anything.

Will such reasoning make you careless about paying money you owe? No. It will provide you with easy abundance to pay what you have promised. It will "anoint your head with oil." It is the self-treatment farmers and working people should use. Talk to God that He owes you nothing and you owe Him nothing. There is no deal and barter in Spirit. There is no four and five are nine in Spirit. While anyone is hugging on to the idea of obligations to God, he will be constantly getting into some sort of obligations to his fellow man. The burden of his family becomes a disease. God provides abundantly. "Goodness and mercy shall follow us all the days of our life."

When you see the wolfish faces of the anarchists, nihilists, communists, pass the Divine Truth along to them that they owe no one and no one owes them, for God cannot owe God. Their thwarted hearts were first crushed under the heel of the religious teaching that penance was due God, faith was due Him, praise had not been half rendered, acknowledgment had been a failure on their part.

There is a loving truth shining up from one line in this psalm that makes me think of the way a diamond throws its sunshine from its angles and facets. It touches a dark corner of your mind with glory, precious child, if you look at it steadfastly. You cannot look at one of these texts, or even at a single word, but that finally it will shine with a loving meaning. But this one about "dwelling in the house of the Lord forever," is greatly bright for that hidden chamber in your heart, where the curtains are drawn so close that you will not admit to yourself that there is such a chamber — you keep it so dark. Let this light shine into it with me while we hold the candle of Science in our hand.

It is that chamber where you keep the silent thought, "I made a great mistake; I wish I had not done and said what I did." The outcome of having such a dark chamber in your heart is vicissitude of fortune and friendship. Let us deal with it scientifically. There is no advantage in vicissitude. Religious people may tell you there is, but Science shows you plainly that there is not. To "dwell in the house of the Lord forever," means to dwell in that state of mind that keeps you prosperous, and happy and beloved always. You cannot be prosperous, or happy, or beloved steadfastly while you have a place within you that repeats within itself, "I made a mistake, I made a mistake."

As God cannot make a mistake, so you could not make a mistake. There are no mistakes. "But," you say, "I did make the mistake and now I am desolate and unhappy in consequence." You do not need to speak from that standpoint just now. Speak from the spiritual standpoint a few minutes. You have spoken, and thought, and acted from the standpoint of having made a. mistake, lo, these many years, and now it is only fair that you should speak from the standpoint of this text, which is Absolute Truth, for the few minutes we are together.

In Spirit, which is your true nature, you are utterly incapable of making mistakes. In Spirit you are God. Ignoring the shadow nature with its dark claims, speak now with Truth from your spiritual nature saying, "I never made any mistake; therefore I never took the consequences of any mistake." You had better speak often and much from your spiritual nature. Its name is, "I am" or its name simply is, "I." Let that "I" tell its tale of goodness and peace over and over till the old "I" with its tales of woe is never heard speaking or felt thinking any more at all. This "I" of you that never made any mistakes is Jesus Christ in you.

Jesus Christ is dominion, and light and joy. How much of your time have you spent speaking from your spiritual nature? Pass your knowledge along over the airs to the unfortunate. They will stop speaking from that "I" of themselves which is so miserably sorry it made such mistakes in the past.

Job caught sight of the "I' that is not wicked, and though his best friends urged him to acknowledge his mistake, he declared he had never made any. So he came off victorious and unscathed. You must not let that nature speak now for you which says, "But it cannot be made up to me, now that the friends are gone and the home is broken up forever." In Truth, they were never taken away. By Truth, you are able to understand that it is all to you "as a dream when one awaketh." You must spend your time with Truth and see what it will bring. If you have never tried this way, of course you are not competent to shake your head unbelievingly.

There are many witnesses to testify to the satisfaction of speaking from the spiritual standpoint, instead of from the material standpoint. Material experiences are ceasing to a great many people. They used to be careful and troubled about many things and they had to work fearfully. Today they are relieved of care and trouble and they do right works easily. They are living witnesses of the promise, "My Presence shall go with thee and I will give thee rest."

There are many tired mothers to whom you may pass the Truth that they are Spirit and not matter. Their pale faces will brighten when to the Divine in them that tries to speak and waits to be spoken to, you proclaim, "You are Spirit, and Spirit is free." As the ocean breeze refreshes the heat burdened traveler, so your breath renews the roses and the smiles of the youth of the motherhood on earth. To the friendless, you may be friend though you never speak to them or meet them. They are thinking perpetually from the standpoint of loss. In Spirit, nothing is lost or wasted. That which is in God goes to God. There is no loss. There is no loss even of your simplest possessions. There is no waste even in your kitchen.

Sit down by the river of that Truth and speak from the Spirit entirely for as long as you can. "There is nothing lost in Spirit. There is nothing wasted in Spirit. There is nothing lacking in Spirit."

As you preach this mysterious gospel in the silence of your mind, you will, be told exactly where and how to restore unto yourself that which you seemed to have lost. Even your possessions that have seemed lost or wasted will come into your sight, and you may take them into your ownership again.

And speaking from this standpoint, your friends and your possessions will take on a new light. At first, the result of saying that there are no mistakes or losses may not seem to be restorations. Some breakings — up may begin, breakings — up of the present states of affairs as they look. Even your present friends may change in the seeming. But your true words going forth from the Spirit will stand to the setting up in right order of all things. Restoration is sure. "I will restore unto thee, all the years that the caterpillar hath wasted." Caterpillar means the speaking from the material standpoint. It makes you so hungry all the time, gnawing and wishing and longing and waiting. The "I' that restores and satisfies like a shepherd, is the Spiritual speaking, letting the Spirit tell its tales in your mind.

Pretty soon all, the Science of God will be clear to you. Then you will be as bold as the rest in proclaiming that all study of material things is vanity, while the study of Spirit is the very powder of God in you "all the days of your eternal Life."

April 24, 1892

Bible Lesson XLII. Psalm 51:1-13. External or Mystic

The fifty-first psalm is both external and mystic. We will heed its mystic sense. In Science we learn that to study the external is to be baffled at every turn, — to finally end by the well-known saying of the physicists: "The most that we know is that we know nothing." We are always like what we are studying. The conclusions of the materialists are right. He has been studying nothing when he has been studying matter, and so he must know nothing. In Science we learn that to study the mystic or spiritual sense of all things is to glow and brighten with substantial understanding. For the mystic or spiritual is the real. To study the real is to show forth reality. This fifty-first psalm is called the prayer of the penitent. It is David's misery because he has so speedily found out that he had believed falsely when he believed that adultery and murder would satisfy his heart.

All penitence has been discovered to be simply the howlings of those who are disappointed because mistakes have not made them happy. Some harden their hearts in anger. Some feel penitent.

Penitence is a quicker road back to a chance to begin over again than hard-heartedness. But everyone goes back to his chance to begin over again somehow. There are none lost. They may sleep profoundly in hard-heartedness, and so be longer going back in mind to their first estate than the penitent, but they will wake up somewhere, somehow, sometime.

"Blot out my transgressions," cries David. This means make them nothing. "Against Thee, Thee only, have I sinned." As one cannot sin against Omnipotence, this was the noblest self-treatment David could have spoken. Omnipotence is the only power. There is, therefore, no power in sin. Omnipotence is the only Being. There is, therefore, no being to sin against the only Being. There is, therefore, no place, or space, or where, that sin could be committed.

Does this seem to be true reasoning when we look out upon the phenomenal world? Oh no! It is pronounced in the highest sense ridiculous. Why, then, do we reason along lines that bring down so much derision and contempt? Because they are the lines that bring freedom from what seems to be sin. Because they are the lines that bring freedom from sickness and misfortune. The moment one declares that his sin or his crime is against Omnipresence and Omnipotence only, he feels inwardly that it is blotted out from that moment. He is touching heart to heart with Spirit. He pays no attention to material men and women. He is a mystic and is happy. The first taste of the bliss of the mystic makes a difference in the actions of the individual. If you get this taste by clear, careful reasonings, you will be able to explain the way and others may reason exactly as you do and taste the bliss and change their actions. If you stumble upon the taste, you may not be so good at explaining the process by which you were made so happy.

Take these cases to illustrate. They explain the real meaning of the text, "Cast all your care on God." One woman was left a widow with a family of little children. She sat down with her babies around her and said positively that God must provide for her and her children. She held firmly on to this position in mind and though her neighbors called her shiftless, she would not yield this point. They pointed out women who had opened boarding houses and shops. She held her ground. They told her that "God helps them that help themselves." All to no avail. She could not explain that she was taking literally the deepest meaning of the words of Jesus Christ, "Cast all your care on God."

She took the word "all" to mean all. And it turned out wonderfully. From the most unexpected quarters, beautiful gifts and bountiful provisions came to her. The neighbors said it was lucky that so shiftless a woman was so lucky in having presents, which she had not earned. According to the Science of Jesus Christ, she had earned them in the only way that is legitimate. It is not scientific to order your life by the proverb, "God helps them that help themselves." It is not true. It is absolutely true that God helps them that let Him do everything. There was a beautiful church lately built by men who believe that "God helps them that help themselves." Every man who contracted to do any part of the building lost money, from the digging in the earth to the tipping of the spire. It was a wrong principle of action, you see. It was not easy for the woman to explain her feeling of "rest in the Lord to bring it to pass." It is easy for those who study the second series of lessons in Spiritual Science to see and to put into practice, that God is the only provider, the only caretaker, the only worker.

David was mourning about his having thought he should be happy if he committed two crimes. By mourning over them and talking to God about them, he suddenly struck the treatment that will unburden anyone of the greatest sort or kind of mental weight. He looked right straight to God. He laid it all upon God. He in that moment felt how utterly nowhere is sin, suffering, death, because God is all.

"Is there any besides me?" saith the Lord "Do not r fill heaven and earth?" The millions of unemployed laborers are here today the visible result of the religious teaching that the Lord helps those who help themselves. The planet is convulsing with the conflicts of labor and capital because of that proverb. Their ancestors worked like galley slaves, and from their tired energies put forth these offspring. Our rich men work like galley slaves, and from their harassed forces put forth their, incompetent offspring who will be the unemployed grumblers of the next generation. This is the process of generation according to the flesh. David says it is the being "shapen in iniquity." Jesus Christ put his finger back to the error in the mind which says that because we came forth from the flesh we are full of trouble, therefore we must earn our bread by the sweat of our brow, and he said, "Call no man upon earth your father for one is your Father, even God." Then He erased the idea of laboring for your living with the words, "Labor not for the meat that perisheth."

It would be a divine treatment of yourself if you would stop this moment and take Jesus Christ at His Word by proclaiming mentally, "I never came forth from the flesh of the material world. I came forth from God. God is my Father and my Mother. I do not have to be anxious or careful about my living. God is my provider. I do not have to labor. God works for me. I do not believe in anyone's laboring for the meat that perisheth. I believe that God will clothe and feed all the world without their struggling any more than the lily struggles. From this moment I believe that God does all and everything. Amen." You must take all the texts of Scripture and push them to their extremest meanings. No matter how many fences have been put up by theology, so called, be bold and reckless in taking inspirations of Spirit to be practically true.

David speaks of being restored unto the joy of salvation after he has mourned at his mother's having been a material woman. By a sudden gleam he found that he had been a child of God from the first. It is easy to erase the idea of material parents and wake up in "God our home."

We erase ideas from our minds by words. "Let us take with us words and go unto our God." It is a bath in the waters of Paradise to wash our old ideas of these Scriptures out of mind and take the texts just as they mean.

This planet has been called by poets and geniuses, "The sorrowful star." It has also been called the planet of doubt. It was found to be the only star whose inhabitants doubted the goodness of God. It is certainly a globe where it is written plainly that it is what we believe in our hearts that we show out in our lives.

We believe in heredity in the flesh and we show out that belief in inherited foolishness and inherited disease. We take Jesus Christ at His word and deny heredity in flesh and proclaim our heredity from God. As soon as the new idea gets any hold on our faith, we show healthy bodies and wise minds. There was an African king who believed that poisons were good to eat. He got to eating poisons all the time and flourished on them. Those who came near him did not believe that poisons were good to eat, so when he embraced them much, they died. His faith was death to his neighbors because it was not based in the principle that God is the life of the plants and the life of the world. He just believed in poisons as good for himself.

There is a man who has thought about force so much that he believes in force more than anyone in this country. This confidence in force makes him able to set immense masses of machinery into action. Another believes so intently in curing drunkards that he cures them at once. Both these men have limited the range of their ministry, though they do wonders as far as they go with their faith. You must have the faith of God, every one of you. You must eat Omnipotence. You will never be satisfied with anything less than Omnipotence. It will not take away from your neighbor's Omnipotence if you have eaten Omnipotence, any more than it could take away from your teacher's knowledge of Euclid if you should know as much as he does.

You must have all the riches of God, every one of you. Nothing will satisfy you short of all there is in creation. It will not take away from your neighbor's riches if you have all the riches there are in creation any more than it would take away from your neighbor's health for you to be healthy.

This is the "glory you had with the Father before the world was." David puts it here in the word "restore." Such a faith as this emanating from you will heal and uplift and feed the world. To believe any less than this is to show out less than perfect healing power, perfect helping energy, perfect judgment.

It is believing less than we have a right to believe, that makes us a sorrowful star and a doubter of the goodness and impartiality of God. "Uphold me with a free spirit," sings David. Last week the lesson was that men are anarchists because they are the product of the idea that we must pledge ourselves to give something to the Almighty if He will answer our prayers. We found the interior meaning to be that no one should ever pledge himself to do anything or to give anything or owe anything to God Almighty, but should agree with Him to do everything Himself, and give everything Himself for nothing, just as it is written, "He giveth to all men liberally," and never scolds nor complains nor lays it up against anyone if she or he has not done penance nor given alms. This week the idea that reigns is the free Spirit. We see that there is no limit to our possession and powers, every one of us, without interfering at all with our neighbor's possessions and powers. We find that it sets all minds free from the idea of earning bread by the sweat of the brow.

We find that the belief in earning wages of our fellow men is the curse, or the serpent upon whose head the woman shall set her heel in the last days of the material earth.

The Science of God is the woman. The belief in earning our living by the favor of our neighbors is the serpent of belief in some of our neighbors being wiser or richer or stronger than we.

Upon this idea that has wound its smothering coils around the earth the Science sets its heel of denial. No! There is no respect of persons with God. Each one owns all of God, and none can take from his neighbor's all. Each one knows all of God, and none shall be able to teach his neighbor, "Lo, here is God, or lo, there," for all proclaim they know Him, from the least unto the greatest. None shall earn his rights from his neighbor, but each shall receive without labor the gift of God. "Labor not for the meat that perisheth." God shall uphold us with His free Spirit forever. "We trust in God." Such a doctrine as this held in the mind will fruit practically in new avenues of subsistence being opened up to those who by long belief in superiority and inferiority and earning from neighbors, are now our restless unemployed and our angry employed. There are metaphysical powers, quickening now within them as the Science of God wings her omnipotent way from God around them to God within them.

The stirs and throes that the planet feels are the working of the words of the free Spirit of the Science of God proclaimed from the earnest hearts of the fearless and true as they sit in the silence helping on the salvation from doubt and discouragement and inequalities that have no right in this Kingdom now coming into our sight.

May 1st, 1892

Bible Lesson XLIII. Psalm 84:1-12. Truth Makes Free

The information held within the chalice of these texts has been as carelessly handled, as were the priceless manuscripts by the monks in the Nitrian monasteries of Egypt. Has anyone been preaching to believing audiences from these psalms that the curse of earning our bread by the sweat of our brow, by hiring out to our neighbors, may be entirely removed by the right word? Has anyone found himself glad to be told that reformatories and prisons are no use because they are founded on a belief that in God's house there is evil? In Truth there are no criminals. In Spirit there is no need of prisons and reformatories. Spirit and Truth are all. Shall we, then, close up our prisons and reformatories? Our first duty is to know the truth about them. "Ye shall know the Truth, and the Truth shall make you free." It is not for you to touch the externals. You are to know what is true. This is your whole business in life. Knowledge of Truth is its own demonstration. All things are coming to the world by its knowledge of Truth.

The Truth is, it is useless to study about heartbeats, nerve ganglia, bones, and blood, for there are no such things. They are but the shadows thrown down from the belief in matter. As matter is nothing at all, of course there is no use studying it.

Schools and schoolmasters are no use for they are founded on the belief in the absence of intelligence. Such a belief is utterly without foundation in Truth, for Intelligence is God never absent from any jot or tittle of His universe. God is not "the Great Absentee of the universe," as we have been believing heretofore. God is the only Presence. Any institution or performance founded upon any other proposition than that God is Omnipresence must fall to nothingness, because it is founded upon a lie.

All material things and all performances, workhouses, hospitals, sanitariums, are but the shadows cast down by believing in the absence of God from some spot or point or creature of His house. The belief is a false one, and as God is the only Mind in the universe of course the mind that believes in evil and matter is no mind at all. The knowledge of this mighty Truth will stop your career of effort at reforming your neighbors, because it will stop your thinking such lies about them. The instant you stop thinking lies you enter into the silence. Here, at the silence of thinking what is not true, is heaven. "And there was silence in heaven for the space of half an hour."

It is the silence of that half hour within your own mind that has left you to let your imagination run riot. Enter into the silence of heaven and the next speech that you speak will be from the Kingdom of Heaven within you. This psalm is about the House of God. It is the eighty- fourth psalm. It leads us to the most upsetting ideas - ideas that upset our most vital beliefs of the past. We are able to see that God is all, and that to know the Truth of God will open the gates of gold.

We find that we must have nothing to do in our minds with funerals or prisons or schools. If we do not allow our minds to think of such things they will never come into our sight. They will never come into anyone's sight who refuses to think of them, basing his cessation of thought on the knowledge that God being all, there is no room in Truth for evil or matter or death. Jesus taught this lesson by saying, "Let the dead bury their dead."

He meant, "Let those whose thoughts are running on such things handle the consequences of their own thoughts."

If a funeral or hospital or sickness comes into our sight it is prima facie evidence we have let our thoughts dwell on lies concerning God. It is considered a virtue by some people to build hospitals and schools for the carrying out of man's belief in the absence of God. It is no virtue. It is better to enter into the closet and be still to know God. God is Truth; Truth will redeem the nations from pain. Therefore speak Truth. Truth is peace. Therefore speak Truth.

This dwelling in the house of God, which is dwelling in freedom, is the redemption from two subtle lies that are hanging their curtains before the eyes of those who are estimated as being very pious and godly. One subtle lie is the doctrine of fatality, and the other subtle lie is the doctrine of limitation. There is no fate. There is absolute choice - absolute monarchy. They who know God are above destiny. They know that they never did or said or thought anything in the past, which could make "karma" or weave a net of consequences around them with any reality in it. God is their past. "I am Alpha." They look forward to no future of the consequences of thoughts or actions or words in Truth, for "I am Omega." They laugh at the stories written in their stars. They set auguries and omens to one side. They are not amenable to society or custom. They dictate to society and bring forth the customs of God to overthrow the customs of the world. They know that the idea contained in the teaching of fate is nonsense. God is our home. Do they believe in death? There is nothing to die. God cannot die. God is all. I do not believe that:

"On two days it steads not to run from thy grave;
The appointed and the un-appointed day.
On the first neither balm nor physician can save;
Nor thee on the second the universe slay."

It sounds well, but it is the sound of a dreamer who hides the silence of heaven, where there is no place to run from but God, and no place to run into but God. To know this lesson well is to bring the world to an end. What world? Why, the dream world, of course. As a dream when one awketh, so shall thy belief in old age fall off, thou son of Jehovah, equal in power, equal in possession, equal in knowledge with thy Father-Mother God.

Does God grow old?

As a dream when one awaketh, so shall poverty and want flee from thee, thou bride of the Maker of worlds. Thy Maker is thy husband. Shall God refuse to provide? Here is a teaching. For you to be greatest in the kingdom does not mean that you are greater than your fellow man, but that you are the greatest you can be. How great can you be? As great as you have courage to affirm. To be wisest in the Kingdom of Heaven does not mean that you are wiser than any others, but that you are the wisest you can be. How wise is that? As wise as you have courage to affirm.

To be richest in the Kingdom of Heaven does not mean that you are richer than your neighbors, but that you are the richest you can be. How rich is that? As rich as you have courage to affirm.

Riches are as Godlike as wisdom and power and health. "Oh, the depth and height of the riches of God." That is the reason the world in its dreaming scrambles so for riches. It remembers its home and its plenty. "Remember Me." To know this truth will keep you from thinking it a virtue to be earning your living by any service to your neighbors. To know this will keep you from speaking of knowledge less than your neighbors. To know this will keep you from thinking yourself poorer or richer than your neighbors. You will be quick to affirm at the gates of silence the highest Truth you can speak of yourself. And you will know enough to unite yourself in eternal unity with Omnipotent Spirit. You must unite by the statement of faith. - Faith is the uniting substance. "Faith is the substance." "I believe that my God is now working with me and in me to make me omnipresent, omnipotent, omniscient; I believe in Jesus Christ." Why do you say, "I believe in Jesus Christ?" Because "Jesus Christ" means demonstration of Truth. At the gateway of heaven stands Jesus Christ, "I am the door. Ye believe in God, believe also in Me."

"God (in Science) out of Jesus Christ is a consuming fire." That is, even the Science as we teach it chemicalizes with strange experiences, without the statement, "I believe in Jesus Christ." The denial of evil for instance, causes all manner of evil to come into your lot saying, "Do you mean that I am nothing? In me hunt your home. Can you prove me nothing now?" Here you are saved by meeting the results of your faith in demonstration. This is the mystery of Christ. It will not be clear until we have stood within its substance by faith. "I believe in God within me and without me. I believe in Jesus Christ." This faith is above limitations. "All things are possible to them that believe." "All power is given unto Me." And unto the Jesus Christ faith or the Jesus Christ man is given dominion over everything, so that he can say to the mountain, "Be thou removed," and it must be done. His word is enough. The man who believes in Jesus Christ, which is believing in the visibility of God, builds his church on a different foundation than the idea of saving souls. He knows that there is only one soul and that is God. Does God need saving? So he builds a church or temple within his mind "not made with hands." This temple is the lofty Truth concerning the universe and man. The loftiest idea he can name he does name. And the loftiest ideal he can form of God is that there is no one to save, for all are saved. This fills his heart with praise. This is the true temple. He builds his factories and shops on another foundation than the supposition that man must be clothed and fed and housed. He knows that there is but one man, and that is God. Does God need shoes and killed lambs? Does God need the labor of little children to beautify His home?

These things are the fruits of believing that there is someone beside God, and some place besides the Kingdom of God.

So in the mind the man of faith describes God as clothed in. the beauty of holiness. And his description of God being true, his thoughts go spreading over the universe like angels' fingers to lift the babies out of the factories and the lambs and calves out of the clutches of the butchers.

"He has his feet shod with the preparation of the gospel," this man does. This all transpires within his mind before the works are made manifest. This is the day when that angel sounds whose voice causes the elders to fall on their faces and the kingdoms of the world to become in visibility, as they are in Truth, the kingdoms of our Lord and His Christ.

The voices that speed through the air are from heaven. Listen to them, you who have eaten and drunk and been clothed with things, which your heart would ache to remember whence they came to you. Clothed with God, mantled with thoughts, fine and cheery with Truth. Fed with God. Living by the words that proceed from the Father. All this is the Truth. All else is but dreaming. These thoughts within your mind first are the finger of God writing on the walls of the universe the things that shall shortly come to pass. The looms must stop at the sound of the voice of this Truth. Do you hear the threats of the rebellious multitudes, with their red flags, their refusals to work, their strikes, their anger? They are the shadows cast by the beliefs of the dreamer who thinks thoughts that are not true.

They will not come to bloodshed. The angels of peace are speeding forth from the workshops of Truth in the mind and all that is good in them will be fed with a. new kind of food. All that is false in them will fall under the sword of the Spirit.

A new kind of loom is weaving today. A now kind of grist is grinding today. A new army has arisen today - the silent host of God. The old things fade and fail. "Hark the herald angels sing."

"Chanting the mighty evangel
That hastens the spirit to free.
'Tis liberty's beautiful angel
Coming straight from the Father to thee."

What a wonderful meaning this Psalm yields up. Did you ever think along with its Truth before? Notice how it spreads its wings of protection: "The Lord is a sun and a shield. He will give grace and glory. No good thing will He withhold."

We do not turn away from the visibility of this providing and protection of Jehovah. We believe in demonstration because we believe in Jesus Christ - the Truth and its practical application to the daily affairs and places of our lot. According to this the looms and the shops and the marts and the armies ought to stop. God hath ordained the end of things founded on imaginations. "But the gospel must be preached to all nations." It is first in all minds and then in all actions. Take your mind off material things. Fix it on Truth: Spiritual Science is Truth. May 8, 1892

Bible Lesson XLIV. Psalm 103:1-22. False Ideas of God

According to spiritual law it is found that it is good for the health to get hold of some principle and stand by it. If one is changeable, variable, unreliable in his ideas, one day believing one thing and another day believing another, he will be changeable, variable, unreliable in health. If he looks at principles or teachings to find what is true to his way of feeling, he will certainly be changing his ideas often because feelings are no criterion for basing judgment upon.

Feelings are dependent upon weather and victuals, upon finances and friendships. Then the writings of Schopenhauer or Emerson may strike the mood and one is a pessimist or an optimist according to the book that hit his feelings. Many a physical infirmity might be traced to the reading of a book full of brilliantly expressed falsities, like:

"There is no place where earthly sorrows are more felt than up in heaven; though it has pleased God to send upon me this great affliction of palsy."

Maybe the mind had been thinking of the kingdom of heaven as an abode of peace and rest. Maybe the mind had been believing that God is goodness, and has no substance in Himself out of which to make palsy; but here are these sentimentally expressed lies, and away go the ideas of God and heaven which would have been such a reliable tonic to the blood. This 103rd Psalm, selected for the International Course, has for its golden text, "Bless the Lord, O my soul, and forget not all His benefits."

It tells that it is possible to drop all our old notions, and thereby drop our old conditions any minute. It teaches that mistaken ideas are the cause of every bit of sickness, every bit of hunger, every bit of old age, every bit of cruelty, every bit of pain, every bit of misfortune. It reminds us it is easy to drop mistaken ideas and leave ourselves free from miseries of all kinds.

It teaches that to have the right idea of God is the first important state of mind to be conscious of. Whoever declares that he will not have anything at all to do in his mind with the idea of a God sending hardships of any kind has proclaimed a principle of thinking which will work wonders with him if he will not let appearances strike him down from his Principle.

Appearances and feelings must not count against your Principle. The Principle will lay the appearances low when you have held by it long enough to believe it in your heart.

The marvel about this Psalm is, that it lays out the appearances of old age that so many people have, and shows it up as just the result of believing in a God of limited generosities. It comes of believing in a stingy God. A stingy God is one who gives His children eyesight for a limited time and then shuts off on it. A stingy God gives vigor and intelligence up to a certain point and then begins in a tantalizing manner to withdraw them. This psalm is very explicit in declaring that if one has the true idea of God in his mind and won't be shaken off his basis for a moment that he shall "renew his youth like the eagle."

There is such a thing possible as getting the right idea of God and holding right to it until your youth returns, your strength renews, your beauty comes forth, your vigor rises, your health is perfect. Read over the psalm and then follow these ideas which it discloses to the bold mind of one who pays no attention to appearances, but fearlessly regards reasoning according to Jesus Christ as the right interpretation. The ministers that do the pleasure of God are those who accompιish His kind of works. "If I do not the works of the Father, believe me not." But if by reason of this Principle anyone brings to pass its works in even a slight degree we will take up the Principle and hold by it till we also do like works, or even greater works inasmuch as we may have some larger appearances and stronger feelings to meet than he seems to have. Any system of religion that lets its ministers get old and toothless, gray and tottering, spectacled and poverty-stricken, is not the Truth of God no matter if those ministers can reel off Sanskrit by the cargo to confirm their ideas. All these conditions have got to go away off the planets under the ministry of Truth.

The fourteenth, fifteenth, and sixteenth verses describe man as he seems to us while we are looking through the spectacles of believing that God made him a mortal and fleshly thing instead of out of His own immortal Substance. Looking at mankind through such a mistaken idea of

God's creative powers, we see all performances of mortality that are so deplorable.

Turning our minds off those people and telling the Truth about God's creations, we withdraw our belief from mankind, and away go all those appearances that made us feel so badly. Everything is glued together particle by particle by our believing. Withdraw the glue of our believing and they are gone.

Beliefs in lies rot. They fail as glue fails. There is nothing in a lie anyway. It seems to have quite a hearing for a while but it is nothing. The man of flesh seems to be something for quite a while but the first thing you know he is gone. All flesh is the appearance of a lie. There was a way of thinking about that man which would have glorified his presence till there could not have been any departure from him. All material or mortal and transitory appearances will vanish out of our sight when we do not believe that God ever made anything to die or be limited in power or wisdom or length of life.

Eternally increasing beauties and strengths and faculties stand forth upon our steadfast confidence in a truth.

Those who begin to name a truth that they wish to believe in and see come out in life often come to a stopping place because it seems as if their words about goodness did not work any better conditions for them; but, if anything, matters went worse than ever with them. This is the time to be firmer than ever. It comes to the whole planet full of people if you send them word that you do not believe there is any evil in them. It comes to your affairs if you send them word that you do not believe in failures. It comes to that sick man to whom you have given the bath of withdrawing the belief in his sickness. They all show up worse than ever. This is Satan let loose for a thousand years. Who is Satan and what are a thousand years?

Satan is the subconscious belief in evil, which you may be surprised to find you have kept hidden in your mind. The very hidden ideas of evil must stand out for you to withdraw your belief from. You must unglue every memory of evil from your mind. When all the nations are angry, just as it mentions in the book of Revelation, and Satan is let loose, it means that we have come face to face with all the smothering beliefs in evil which lie under our plausible conscious thinking about the goodness of God and His immortal and perfect creations. The most pious devotees have kept a mental reservation about the evils that might possibly come to them, even while they were singing praises of the goodness of God. That was their Satan in the hidden places. By and by, that reservation comes fronting us in whatever we have spoken about as good. It will last in our sight till we bring up from the deepest region of our mind the efficient idea, "I do not believe in evil at all. I believe in the good only."

While this final determination is ungluing even our unconscious belief in the possibility of evil in God's universe, it is our thousand years of struggle. The term "thousand years" simply means period of final struggle. "For the elect's sake those days shall be shortened." That is, we may be so determined to stand by our Principle that old errors give up their appearances at once. Determination is a terror to Satan. The words, "I do not believe in evil at all. I believe only in the Good," are the arrangement of a new base in mind and a new set of circumstances in life.

Every bit of the miracle working of Jesus Christ is easy to one who has established his base in Truth. Satan is to be bound and cast into the bottomless pit. That is, even our remotest reservations concerning the evils that might possibly come upon us are to be utterly annihilated. And not only ours but the beliefs in evil that the world has held, will be utterly annihilated. Everything has to be done in mind first, before crimes and pains and misfortunes perish from the seeming. Thus, the greatest ministry you can give forth is the ministry of your right thoughts. The greatest good you can do is to spread the gospel. You may fit out some missionaries to go telling this Principle. You may encourage some faithful minister of it whose bidding is to stand boldly out and give up his former ways of making a living for its sake. But believe it and preach it you must — some way, somehow. This will shorten the thousand years symbol, or your struggle with your present environment, after seeing the reasonableness of this Science.

It is reasonable, is it not, that if it will make your stomach strong enough to digest any sort of food if you will tell yourself that you are strong enough to do anything you please and material food cannot dictate to you, and if you can drink the strongest coffee and tea without their affecting you at all by the same assertion, that gin and rum and tobacco are as harmless as anything by the same line of reasoning? It is reasonable to you, is it not, that if schools are all founded on the idea of absence of intelligence, as soon as that idea of the absence of intelligence is withdrawn the schools will tumble down out of sight? Their foundations being taken out they must fall, mustn't they?

It is reasonable to you, is it not, that if the reformatories are built on the idea that the good is absent from some spots or creatures of its own creating, they must all fall into nothingness when we know the Truth that there is no absence of good? It is reasonable to you, is it not, that if Satan is the product of our belief that God has made an opposite to himself, there will be no Satan when we do not believe God made anything unlike Himself?

It is reasonable to you, is it not, that if God occupies all spaces and places, and as astral spooks and elementals are the product of our belief in spots of the universe where God is not the substance, these must all be seen as pure nothingness without any power to hurt, when we withdraw our belief of the absence of the Substance of God from some spots of His kingdom? It is reasonable to you, is it not, that if the mathematics of the schools are all founded on the supposition that five balls and five balls are ten balls, when there are no balls, the mathematics of the schools are all a farce? By studying the Science of God or Spirit we find that all numberings and calculations are but the symbols of eternal verities, and that we had better be studying the eternal verities than the symbols of them.

The geometry of God is the statement of an absolute truth as its starting point:

The straight line of an irresistible reasoning;

The triangle of the fulfillment of a word of good in the life;

The square of the daily proclamation that Truth preaches its own gospel, heals the sick, casts out demons, raises the dead;

The circle of the beautiful gift of clothes and food and shelter and home without working for them, either as rich slaves or poor servants;

The sphere of understanding how to breathe the airs of heaven and see and hear only the good;

The pyramid of triumphant forgetfulness of the former heaven and former earth, high over the memory of the dream of mortality with its beliefs in the wickedness and absence of God, with our name written in our foreheads. That Name which stands in Spirit for the special work set out for us to do in the kingdom from whence we came forth. To know our own name is the only knowledge that is worthwhile.

May 15, 1892

Bible Lesson XLV. Daniel 1:8-21. But Men Must Work

Does not the Bible tell us that man is to labor for his living, earning his bread by the sweat of his brow?

It tells us that man under the curse earns his living by the sweat of his brow, but under the Gospel, he is set free from that curse. He is under the Gospel to "labor not for the meat that perisheth." He is told that the seed of the woman shall bruise the curse. What is the seed of the woman? It is the teaching of Divine Science. The Science of Christ is figured by a "Woman" in John the Revelator's mind. When we are quoting Scripture, it will help us to know where ye stand and what we are talking about if we will explain whether, we are speaking of what goes on under the curse or under the Gospel.

Does it make any difference to our daily lot in life whether we are speaking of man under the curse or under the Gospel? Indeed it does. "As a man thinketh in his heart so is he." Many a man or woman could trace all their misfortunes to their continual harping on the Adam and Eve side of life, describing the dire effects of the fall and curse side. They might have been joyous and powerful if they had let their mind rejoice in the knowledge that words of Truth can annihilate the curse ideas as soon as they show themselves. What made the curse? The law of opposition. The idea of the opposite of the Jesus Christ man.

Is it not beneficial to study the ways of the opposite of Jesus Christ? Just as beneficial as to study the shadows of trees and rocks. Is it not reformatory to keep statistics of crime and records of horrors and tell them often to public audiences? Just as reformatory as it would be to study discords and not harmonies in music. We become like what we study. In this lesson on Daniel in the court of Babylon, are we not taught that poor food is more consistent with a righteous life than rich food? It teaches that there is just as much nourishment in one kind of food as another. Food is a symbol of religious thoughts. Daniel meant to intimate distinctly that he did not relish their religious ideas. At home in Jerusalem, he had eaten meat and drunk wine. There those foods symbolized the reviving words of Truth and the strong will of God. Here in Babylon they stood for the great idols, Bel, Merodach, and Nebo, to whom human sacrifices were offered. They intimated that man is governed by stars and suns and moons. They declared man is the victim as to happiness and health of blind forces. Indeed, material science was the god of Chaldea then, just about as material science is the god of civilization today.

In the fourth verse of this chapter of Daniel, you will see that Daniel, Hananiah, Mishael, and Azariah understood the Science of God or the Science of Spirit.

God is Spirit. Understanding this Science, they were able to symbolize their ideas of the difference between material science and Spiritual Science by eating a totally opposite kind of food from that eaten by their captors. They compelled pulse and water to signify the difference of their religion from the Babylonians. Was it necessary for them to signify their different ideas by different eating? No, but in those days everything was signified by symbols. Every idea had its outward action rigidly observed, as the Jews used the water of jealousy, the water of separation, water of feasts, etc., symbolically. Their teachers spoke in symbols. The first chapter of Genesis is symbolic. The second chapter of Genesis is symbolic. One stands for the Science of Spirit and the other for the science of matter. Whoever studies the first chapter will understand Substance, Truth; whoever studies the second chapter will understand nothing. Whoever thinks both chapters refer to man in reality will become much mixed. Whoever knows the first chapter well can handle the second one understandingly. Evidently Daniel understood the first chapter thoroughly, because he could make pulse and water do him as much service as meat and bread. Would he not have made a nobler demonstration of his spiritual understanding if he had gone three years without eating anything at all? Going without eating would have been to his mind a symbol of having no religion at all. It would have been the same symbol to his captors also.

Would it be a good plan for us nowadays to regard our eating and drinking as symbolizing the words and will of God? It is true that eating and drinking indicate the state of our mind religiously. If we feel hungry, we can be sure that there is some word concerning the will and purpose of our God which our mind longs for. If we eat even to gorging ourselves we shall wish we could keep on eating till the knowledge of that will comes to us. If we drink, we shall keep on drinking and wish we could drink more, even longing and thirsting for drink till we imbue drinks with strength to intoxicate, while the mind longs for some good news from Truth. Whoever is thirsty for strong drinks is wild for strong words of Truth. Where shall we get those strong words of Truth? We shall find them in Spiritual Science. At present Spiritual Science uses words just as much in the symbol as Daniel used eating and drinking, but there are certain signs now of Spiritual Science words bringing forth the full power of their substance right soon. All Spiritual Science words so far have been like alabaster boxes. They contain precious ointments but the alabaster boxes have not been broken. What do you mean by breaking open words as you would break open boxes?

I mean receiving the quality of their meanings. How can you tell when they are broken open and the words have poured out their Ointments? When the words concerning God as our health have made us every whit whole so that there is no blemish in us as there was no blemish in those four young Jews. When the words concerning God as our support have given us assurance of abundant provisions right in our sight and manageable with our fingers, just as all things were given to those four young Jews who lived by Spiritual Science in the midst of an age that lived by material science.

In this age of material science, the Spiritual Scientist should be defended by the supernal beings who fought for Elisha (that most perfect Spiritual Scientist of old). The Spiritual Scientist should be fed and clothed by the angels who ministered to Jesus Christ. When he breaks open the alabaster boxes of these mysterious words he is now using, he will find that the end of the world has come and the beginning of his life has sprung forth. Who were those supernal beings around Elisha? They were his thoughts personified. If he had seen demons and devils, they would have shown the quality of his thoughts. But as he had no such thoughts no such being appeared to him. The angels that ministered to Jesus were His supernal ideas. The more lofty our ideas the more defense and support there is in them.

How shall we break open these words we are now using? By speaking them fearlessly as the faith of our life. By writing them down carefully as the light of our judgment, by which we would be judged. By thinking them silently as the only thoughts worth thinking.

Ought a man sit down and fold his hands while his children go hungry that he may meditate on spiritual doctrines, seeing that all labor is the sign of living under the curse? No. He must keep swinging his hammer and balancing accounts till his knowledge of Truth takes those tasks out of his hands.

Spiritual knowledge itself does the turning and over-turning. It is very subtle in its workings. It is so secretive that the eyes and ears take no cognizance of it. But by and by its mission is visible. Knowledge of Truth is irresistible action.

At Kenilworth we saw, "on the ruins of solid masonry in one place the swelling root of a creeper had lifted one arch from its base, and the protruding branches of a chance spring tree had unseated the keystone of the next," wrote a traveler. Just so all these evidences of civilization shall be subtly undermined, even to the stoppage of steam cars and sewing machines, by the words of Jesus Christ concerning eating and drinking and shelter. Was not Jesus Christ poor so that He had not where to lay His head? No. He owned all the kingdoms of the world and the riches of them. When He wanted to fit out His disciples with purses and swords, He did not have to work and earn them, He simply had to speak the word and it was done.

What did He mean by saying that the foxes had holes and the birds of the air had nests but the Son of Man had not where to lay His head? He was speaking of that man who had imagined he wanted to follow His doctrine when he had not the faintest idea of what it was. The Son of Man is the word of God. The man had not let anything but the teachings of the schools and the business of the stores and factories rest in his mind. Not a single idea that there is a way of living untouchable by deal and barter, work and study, had ever rested in his mind.

Daniel and his three friends lived by a Principle that was their defense and support, and yet they did nothing like the Babylonians. This Principle of living is now being proclaimed. One after another of its adherents is being removed from the ways and works of the world. The end of material things has touched the hem of their garments. Will this doctrine hasten the end of the world? Yes. The end of looking to material things and being hurt by the world's forces comes with speaking Truth. Will there be terrible times upon the earth? The end of a shadow at high noon is peaceful; so the end of materiality as represented by civilization cometh as a thief in the night, softly. There is no shadow at high noon. There is no materiality under the reign of Spirit. At high noon you may speak some great affirmation, and you will never see any shadow to it. Twelve o'clock is high noon time. Exactly at twelve every day tell God what you would like to demonstrate better than anything else. Then affirm it as already done. In reality it is already done so you only speak a great truth when you affirm that a good thing is finished. To someone whose heart was depressed by misfortune these words were given as so bright that no misfortune could evermore lurk near her lot. She must keep them at twelve: "I am satisfied with my abundant prosperity, which from this date makes no delay in pleasing me."

To another whose heart was clogged with earthly cares the direction was given: "Write a letter to Jesus Christ and state your case exactly. Ask for help. Burn the letter and tell no one. You can focus all your mind and soul and heart into a letter. Writing is a great mystery. Jesus Christ wrote in the sand. Both these ideas come from the misty past of the mystics like Daniel and his friends. They disdained nothing and observed everything, even to interpreting dreams. They knew the law of high noon and morning and evening prayers. They did not need the second chapter of Genesis, which is the Babylonian side of the interpretation of symbols, which is judging man as on the down grade or curse side, a fallen creature under the curse of dependence upon skill and material things. No. They regarded all things as signs and symbols of our opportunities to step out of the shadow, away from Adam, out and away from the ways of materiality.

We will use nothing henceforth as signs of the needs of mortal and material man, but all things as signs of the opportunity of spiritual man to proclaim his exemption from matter and evil and the laws thereof.

This manner of looking at things will post you in languages without studying them. It will give you skill in mathematics without investigating them. It will give you the history of the sun and explain for you the times and seasons of constellations and comets.

Read this first chapter of Daniel with the knowledge that Chaldean science is all science of materiality, from astrals down to marble quarries. Take it home as a demonstrable verity that the understanding of Spirit gives easy mastery of all these things. If you do not catch this lesson, you will not rise up in your greatness, but plod along in your present appearance. Yet, there is a Spirit in you all, and the inspiration of Omnipotence giveth understanding of Spirit. May 22, 1892

Bible Lesson XLVI. Daniel 2:36-49. Artificial Helps

Confucius observed that there is a common faculty possessed by all men in equal shares, which if cultivated, makes the serf the peer of the prince, the un-booked the peer of the savant. A certain sea captain noticed that on the Island of Madagascar and among the natives on the coasts where his ship put in at Africa and Australia there was the use of another sense practiced besides the senses ordinarily exercised. By the use of this faculty or sense, they could foretell storms and calms, fair weather and foul with far greater accuracy than our weather bureaus are able to do.

Their system was quick and simple. It was as open as nature's sweet face. Ours seems to be stilted and complex. Ours seems like studying shadows. Theirs seems like converse with the substance that casts the shadows. There were other things the seers among the "heathen" could tell besides weather. They could foretell earthquakes and tidal waves. They could see the march of human events ahead. They could read the signals of the stars. There was one item in common with civilization, however, they could not prevent tidal waves, nor annul coming disasters. They rendered up a verdict exactly like Job's: "The thing I feared came upon me." This is civilization's proudest summing up: "Mankind is under the evangel of despair; we are all on a train bound for destruction. The most that we know is that we know nothing."

It was upon such times that Daniel appeared in the courts of Babylon. All the learning of the world was gathered under Chaldean skies. Their mathematics and music, their astronomy and surgery, business methods and commerce, were as dry and dehumanizing as ours of today. One of our profoundly learned physicists writes lamentingly, "There is a wide-spread want of an enlightened spiritual philosophy that shall counteract the materializing tendencies of the study of the natural sciences, which attribute faculties and functions to blind agents and give material forces and combinations the power to control life and destiny."

With his measure of the simple Judean spirit, unmixed with the stilted sciences of the highest civilization of that day, Daniel reproduced the dream of Nebuchadnezzar. In no way did Daniel suggest putting the coming kingdoms on their guard to strengthen themselves and prevent their demolition. He read their coming doom without the proposition of a remedy.

If he saw that the coming kingdom triumphant was to be the kingdom of spiritual morals he did not say so. If the king of material monarchies appreciated that the algebra and mathematics of ethical law should supersede the pride of worldly science he gave no sign.

Those figures stand out on the canvas full of information as sphinx's face.

In the realm of religion there are the golden, the silver, the brass, the iron and the clay periods. In the realm of science, the same characteristics are apparent. In the realm of political movements, from gold to clay is history.

It is the common conviction that the days we are now experiencing are the last of materiality. "The stone cut out without hands is smiting the image of all the ages" and breaking the religious systems, the scientific calculations, the governmental policies, in pieces.

"The kingdom on the earth, though not of it," is begun. The sound of its unseen hammer is the restlessness of nations, the conflict of capital and labor, the dragging forth into the sight of "the iron and clay mixed" science and religion and government, of the "Ishmaelites of Civilization" the rise of woman, the disgust of the observing of our school system, the general dissatisfaction at the existing order of things.

Whosoever preaches must preach that the old dispensation has closed. We will have none of it. He must preach that the new dispensation has begun. "Its will be done." This is the time when Michael and his angels fight against the dragon and his angels, and the dragon and his angels fight among themselves, but not against Michael and his angels, for they cannot see them.

The conflict of human dynasties is among themselves. The name Michael signifies there is only God. The angels with Michael are the teachings that belong to that proposition. The dragon is the belief of mankind that there is another power besides God, another substance besides God, other laws than God's laws. The angels with the dragon are the necessary ideas that go with such a great error of belief. These angels or ideas, with the people that represent them, get into a final fight among themselves. Each system blames the other for the universal restlessness, but no man blames his neighbor for the dissatisfaction that stirs his breast. Let him listen at the gates of silence. It is Michael and his angels moving down on the wings of the hour with the supreme truth — there is only God.

The conflict is first in the mind. Then it shows forth in the nations. Art, with its images of sense suggestions, falls down. Religion, with its proclamations of evil, crumbles. Science, with its artificial helps to life and health, falters and fades as the shadows of a ghost dance. Governments hang their heads and go out under the reign of demented, senile, or profligate rulers. They all are the outward formulations of the mental convictions of a power and a substance and a ruling besides God, the never absent good. However pious you have been, have you not believed in the necessity for evil, the reality of evil, the possibility of evil? That was your reserved opinion, was it not, while you were praising Jehovah and His Jesus Christ? Even at the golden height of your noblest consistency of conduct with belief, was such a reservation right? That reserved opinion has been the harboring of the dragon within your mind. If you have mixed it with the systems of church, or state or society of today, you are in at the "clay and iron age," and the blows of the silent doctrine cut out of the rock of Revelation are being felt by you in your restlessness and dread of coming evil.

The stone cut out of the universal rock is the bold word that there is only good intended for us all. Those two great doctrines in the mind have now come face to face. Those who recognize the reasonableness of the message of the archangel proclaim that "there shall no ill come nigh their dwelling." They smile at the host of Michael and answer back while the shakings of empires signal the end of all flesh, that "all things work together for good to them that love God," and they love the good God who sendeth only good.

With the acceptance of this proclamation that there is only good intended for us, there is no standing helpless at the sound of the earthquake. There is no expectation of death. Even the body knows that its mission is to transform and transfigure and not to be buried and fall into ashes.

The intellect hears the trump of love sounding in the crash of governments, and takes on the glance of Omnipotence when it receives the doctrine cut out of the rook without hands of mortality. This doctrine is that "God is all; there is only God." Nothing that opposes can stand under the fall of its hammers. No argument based on history or science, or experience, or appearances of any kind can do anything but rise like a baffled worm of nothingness to assert its vanity and die away in the shame of absence. When this trump sounds "they shall not judge after the sight of the eyes nor the hearing of the ears," for they shall know that all those things seen by eyes and heard by ears are the embodiment of the headstrong belief in mind that there is another presence besides God, another power besides God, another kingdom besides God's. They shall realize that any faculty that is exercised for the prognostication of evil in any fashion is still of the clay of imagination, whether it be the keen sense of the Madagascar child of nature or the stilted computations of civilized science. Though one should rise from the grave where you laid him in tenderness, and from the sphere of the cloudy substance of astrals should foretell doom, you would give him the lie, for you would know he was still of the clay of imagination, while the Truth is that God has only good for you and no evil or pain or fear forever.

All things that shake and tremble are founded on the belief of another power or presence or law besides God. They are an image of nothing ... an imagination without substance. They are the opposite of Truth. Side with them and evaporate like mist. Side with Truth and live in fullness of joy.

When you rise in the morning, are you afraid of the day? It is the dragon and his angels who fear. It is imagination that trembles. The trump of Gabriel, the hammer of the new kingdom, the war cry of Michael is calling you to make your choice of truth or error; of "God is with me" or "not with me." Every day sounds its tocsin: Choose! Every item of the day gives you the chance to proclaim what manner of faith you are of. Do you believe that God guides all your steps in safety and your affairs successfully, or do you not? When you purposed to bring to pass that particular result and each item thwarted you, as it seemed, did you see that that which was being thwarted was of the clay of imagination? Did you fret and be anxious, or rejoice in the sight of the workings of good?

In the stillness of your own chamber alone, do you appreciate that your millions are clay if one man can say, or one woman, or one child, that you overreached them? Do you know what that trembling signifies, which seizes your limbs sometimes, or gives you the blues? It is the dragon of imagination calling for his own destruction. It is the hammer of the Spirit striking its blows on your old ideas. Do not hesitate an instant. Proclaim, "I surrender my religion, my business policy, my possessions, to God."

Then there shall walk by you a high counselor, a noble comrade, a powerful friend. You will not then need to be careful and anxious lest someone get away from you what belongs to you. God is the pleader of your cause.

The light of His countenance shall shine on those with whom you have dealings, and they will be kind and true. Their Spirit shall respond to the Spirit that walketh by you and they cannot do you wrong. Every attempt at it will meet with defeat. "No weapon that is formed against thee shall prosper."

This is the second chapter of Daniel. It is the counterpart of the twelfth of Revelation, seventh and eighth verses. It is the proclamation of the highest Truth in all the brightness of its glory. It tells that though science and religion, and government have been as gold, at their best on this planet, their reign was imagination, for they have reasoned on the necessity for evil and the reality of material things. At their best, they have calculated on the basis of two, when there is only one. So religion has come to her clay and iron age, and at her best she cringes and flinches under the storms of this age, proclaiming with her latest breath that "God in His wisdom has suffered these things to be." It is a lie! God never permitted or ordained evil. It is all imagination. Let now the failure of the idea of two purposes in the mind that is God be our instruction. Science also has reached the formation of her understanding and looks helplessly upon the conflicts of poverty and riches, learning and ignorance. She has studied matter, when Spirit was her province. She sees no safety from cyclones, no help out of floods, no prevention of accidents. Governments have now struck the mire of their first imaginations, viz., that there are some who shall sit in judgment, and reign over their neighbors, when the Truth is, all are one. There is no one to govern. God is the only Being and needs no dominion over Him by any other creature. His word is: "There is none beside Me." All those things totter and fall. Founded on nothing their end is the end of a tale that is told. Even at the golden height of most honored consistency, they were founded on a wrong idea. There is a doctrine building out of a rock not seen by the eyes that have any power to see evil. It is binding all who accept it into one common knowledge, viz., the knowledge of good only.

There is a Science hewing out of the heart of Love, not studied mind believing in two substances. It is proclaiming Spirit unto Spirit that all do now know good and good only. The knowledge of Spirit only knowledge.

There is a government being wrought out of Omnipotent tenderness. Its proclamations cannot be heard by any who believe in the inferiority or superiority of one under or over another. Its pulsing strokes fall softly on the hills of anguish and in the valleys of despair "There is no government but self-government; which is the knowledge that God is the Omnipotence within and around every creature." Whoever believes that he has a right to govern or be governed by his neighbor, cannot hear the strokes of the hammer of the Almighty. Daniel and John saw our age in symbols. We feel it in the crashings of old dynasties, or the consciousness of a triumphant doctrine which defends and provides and holds us fast, fearless at peace on its bosom, — which? May 15, 1892

Bible Lesson XLVII. Daniel 3:13–25. Dwelling in Perfect Life

Napoleon said that when the reign of conscience should begin his reign would end. So he never let even a little glint of conscience get into his mortal kingdom till one day he felt a trifle sorry for his dealings with Josephine. This admission of the hint of a possibility that he could do anything that he could be sorry for opened a spot on the externals of his career where that quicksand rivulet of an idea for which he was famous could break out.

The rivulet was underground, like all the beginnings of quicksand streams. But like all quicksand streams, it broke out on the surface. Conscience made the basin.

The quicksand stream always running within his mind was the idea what he should do in case of defeat. It broke loose instantly when he made a soft spot by being sorry for one thing he had done.

It is not always a regret for what you have done that causes the quicksand idea in your mind to break out in failure or affliction. These lessons are adapted to every kind of mind and have purposed to show you that if you have a sneaking little notion that you are not quite master of your business or of your art, some unguarded word or action will give that little notion mastery over your affairs.

Even children should not get the idea that they are not yet perfect in their studies or in the art they have chosen. For, in Truth, their soul is the origin of the arts and sciences. "Their angels do always behold the face of their Father." Their inmost thoughts dwell in illuminated wisdom. To tell them this, is truer than to tell them they do not know. If you tell than that in Truth they are wise, they will find some way to express outwardly what they know at the soul.

If you were nagged with the idea that you did not know and must work to know, very likely you do not think very much of what intelligence you have. This poor idea of your intelligence or of your "learning" will break out on some great day in a failure of some kind which other people will say was owing to your foolish disregard of their opinions.

No such thing - it is the time for your own opinion of yourself to break out. There is no knowing what new idea opened up the chance for the old self-depreciation to show out. Maybe it was the idea that you never would have committed that secret sin the other day or a year ago if you had not been tempted more than you could resist.

In this lesson about the fiery furnace we see how surely every mind will have victory over disaster if it has had a habit of thinking that God will bring it out right. These three men had so ardently believed in God with them that when their belief in angry kings and their opposition to their religion broke out, their belief in God with them lifted them out alive and unhurt.

In the histories of martyrs, we often read of the flames and racks not hurting them at all. Some said that fair and wondrous beings came and stood by them, touching their wounds with fingers of ecstasy.

Napoleon thought it was a supreme necessity in battle to have heavy artillery. He was mistaken. The supreme necessity is a right idea of God. These three men did not think they needed any army to save them except their idea of God. They proved the righteousness of their idea by coming out of a very hot fire without even the smell of it on their garments.

They had for many years a sneaking little thought running under their general manner of thinking. That sneaking thought was that there was a great opposition to the true God in other people's minds. They should have faced that quicksand stream straight up just as soon as it came into their mind. For indeed there is no opposition to the true God in anyone's mind. They would never have been thrown into the furnace if they had met their early error with its noble truth.

By this lesson, we see that it is a greater demonstration of godliness never to get into afflictions of any kind, than to get out of great afflictions bravely. For we make our own afflictions without doubt.

Now you are thinking that the baby does not make its our afflictions, and therefore this idea is a fallacy.

In Truth, the baby does not suffer at all. You imagine that it suffers. Honestly take your thought that the baby is suffering off from it, and you will see it smile at once. The baby expresses one of your young thoughts that you have not been thinking very long. People who have great mental suffering by reason of thinking much that there is terrible opposition to their idea of good, see a great deal of suffering wherever they go, and they do not more than get in your house till the baby has pains and accidents to express their idea. They unite their strong belief in opposition to the good with your indifferent idea on that subject, and together you fix up the baby to scream and cry all night.

Let you both drop the idea and the baby will sleep just as its soul is resting. It will express its soul estate -- the real of itself. God is Rest. It will rest. Night is the signal that we should all express the Rest of God. God is as much Rest as He is Strength.

People who have to work nights are expressing their notion of much opposition to their idea of good. If they should once see the idea that God is Rest they would be taken up as by a strong hand and put down into some resting-place.

If they should go right back to their idea of there being opposition to the good and say, "There is no opposition anywhere, in all the universe, to my idea of good," they would never have any hard places to rest from. It is a high statement of Spiritual Science which Jesus Christ made, "My yoke is easy," "Ye shall find rest." You have been praising the martyrs, have you not? See to it that you praise their idea of the power of God to save. Do not get to thinking with them that suffering is a necessity to bring out the virtues of men. Do not get to thinking with them that the time of suffering is the time of manifestation of God's power.

Praise their idea that God will save, till by praising it you see clearly that there was nothing to be saved from except their notion that suffering is an ordinance of God. Then you will suddenly see how inspired Jeremiah was when he said that, "a man's word is his only burden."

This third chapter of Daniel shows that there is nothing to be saved from except our own ideas. It shows that one true idea held firmly will be a golden thread of light to bring us into the realm of all Truth. One true idea in your mind will take you through into all Truth, if you will look hard at it and never mind whether you know much or little, or whether your lot is hard or easy.

For instance one of these men, who came out of a hot furnace by holding an ecstatic state of mind, was named Azariah. This name signifies that he believed strongly in God as his defense in the day of affliction. It was a truth as far as it went and out of his hot affliction, he came safely.

Another of those men was entranced by the idea that all things are the free gift of God. It was the idea that:

"When earthly helpers fail and comforts flee,
God of the helpless, He remembers me."

This idea was just as capable of giving him the free gift of cool breaths in flames as Azariah's idea of defense. The other one was named Mishael. That name shows that he believed that his substance, the very substance of his body, was God. No one believes that fire can burn God. So whoever believes that the substance of his body is God will certainly never have anything hurt him.

The golden text of this lesson tells us that if we will hold any one of these ideas held by these three men, we will come off victorious over every trial. "When thou walkest through the fire thou shalt not be burned." Some things make up the fires through which one walks, and other things make up the fires through which others walk.

A true idea coming into mind will lift you out of your fire safely. A true idea in my mind will lift me out safely -- will lift anyone out who thinks it. One woman had a cancer on her nose, which was her fire of affliction. Someone sent her a true idea of God, and it rushed through her mind like a white stream of glory and washed that cancer out in one night. Another woman had a tumor, which was her hot furnace of trial. A true idea was printed in a little blue magazine in Chicago, and when she read it that idea rushed the tumor out of her body in less than twelve hours.

A man had a film on his eyes and it slipped off at the reading of an idea of God, which a friend wrote him in a letter.

To these three men, recorded by Daniel, the idea appeared as a man. To the great king Nebuchadnezzar, it looked like the "Son of God." Our ideas often stand out as beings who do not appear mortal and natural, like those we deal with in business.

This lesson suggests that we love the practice of the Presence of God. We love the marvelous. It tells us to go back to the first principle established in Universal Mind. That first principle is: "There is good for me." Everything says this unconsciously. When it says it consciously, the good begins to come toward it. When the mind says boldly of this good that it ought to have it, that good hurries to meet its owner.

The word good is a little waxy subject in the mind. We can "bring forth" out of it, or "make" out of this word whatever good thing we name as what we ought to have. Watch the word good for a while as you name it as what you ought to have. All things are made out of the word -- "And the Word was God." And God is Good.

There is a cord connecting your good with you. If you are anxious, your anxiety is a corrosive sublimate to eat off that cord. So you must not let anxiety rest in your mind. Jesus Christ said: "Take no thought." "Be not afraid." We can stop being anxious, and stop being anxious and stop being anxious, till everything we think we ought to have comes running swiftly to greet us.

"It shall come to pass that while they are yet speaking I will answer them." The idea of opposition to our ideas of good, which makes all the human hardships brought about by spreading this idea abroad, is called a "wilderness" by Ezekiel; "Lion's den" and "Fiery furnace" by Daniel. When Ezekiel was speaking of human experiences as a wilderness, he said it was the highest law to refuse the teachings of our fathers and mothers, our ministers and our schoolteachers. (Look into the deep meaning of Ezekiel, twentieth chapter, and eighteenth verse.) They all represent some ideas we have given great authority and prominence to in our mind. Every one of them had so much trouble that they represented to us more the idea of opposition to good than power of good. Whoever believes much in opposition to his idea of good, will get very blue and despondent. If he had an idea that it is his duty to work with all his might – "to widen the skirts of light and make the struggle with darkness narrower," he will be a philanthropist or reformer. Then we shall praise him. But his overpowering sorrow at the sufferings of this planet makes him a very lugubrious mentality to have around.

All the good the reformer does is by his idea that suffering can be ameliorated by his efforts seconded by his God.

That idea is very, very slim and tender by the side of his mournful idea of the power of the opposition to his God, however, and so he really fans the furnace of pain for those he would save. This lesson compels the conclusion -- Nebuchadnezzar hoping -- that God will save, and not the true thinker ignoring the flames. Shall the reformer and philanthropist look into the dens of crime and ignore them, according to metaphysics? He shall.

He shall not respect the sight of the eyes or the hearing of the ears, when they report pain. He shall not record the doings of misery. They are only his own long-held notions spread out in his sight. As he looks at these evidences of his own quicksand of past thoughts, taught by those who believed in opposition to good, he shall say "I do not judge after the sight of my eyes, nor after the hearing of my ears. I judge by my idea of the omnipresence and omnipotence of God. Let now God be manifest here."

He shall stand by that idea and that alone, till it is his vital faith. "According to thy faith be it unto thee." Shall a poor miner, a half-paid printer, a feeble sewing girl, a wounded heart, ignore the difference between their lot and the lot of a Vanderbilt or a Field? They shall. They shall look straight into the airs that are full of God and say to God alone: "Thou art my noble Comrade, my rich and powerful Champion."

They shall stand by that Truth until it is their vital faith. And they shall see God manifest, first by the unsought kindness of mankind, the unmasked comradeship of good people, the unbegged gifts of the rich and powerful. Then by the wonderful possessions of their own, whereby they are able to lift every burden off their neighbors with wisdom of action and without sorrow. It is written that David was a man after God's own heart, simply because he spoke so richly of God and ignored everything else. Every man is after God's own heart when he tells the Truth of God.

There is no opposition to God in Truth. Speak this out boldly and see it demonstrated. Tell the child God is with him as his High Counselor, and that there is no opposition to his God. Shout it to the beggars that God is their rich and powerful Champion, and nothing can withstand Him.

Tell it to the convicts that God is their noble Comrade, and nothing can oppose Him. Ezekiel saw in his fifteenth chapter that the very best old teachings would be burned up in the fires of Truth. There shall not be a pin left in the true teachings upon which to hang our miseries. This is Bible prophecy. The only pin we can tie to is the Truth concerning God, which is first thought of as a righteous principle. It then shows as a helper out of the troubles we are now in, and then shows as the only Presence knowing nothing of trouble any more at all. June 5, 1892

Bible Lesson XLVIII. Daniel 6:16-28. Which Streak Shall Rule

Every mind has a religious streak. Every mind has a business streak. Every mind has a political streak. There is a streak of every department of human endeavor in every mind. Each one of us lets one streak or the other dominate. We can choose which streak shall rule.

Some streaks have much admiration bestowed upon them when they are prominent. Some streaks receive a great deal of censure.

When Bunyan saw a drunken thief, he said: "But for the grace of God, there goes John Bunyan."

Oliver Goldsmith was very stupid at school. The streak of love of letters was not uncovered in him till something happened that uncovered that streak and we have his inimitable books.

Something happened to you once, which uncovered the streak of mechanical tendency and you became a printer, or a stenographer, or a sewing machine operator, or maybe you are an inventor.

If you admire scholasticism, why did you not uncover that learning. You have without doubt (according to metaphysics, which is mental science, as taught by Jesus Christ) as much ability to become a world-famed scholar as President Eliot and President Harper.

If you admire statesmanship, why did you not uncover that streak in your reservoir? You might just as well have uncovered the streak you love and admire as the line of hiring out to your neighbors at a dollar and a half or so a day, which you know very well makes you "mad" when you think of it.

When the religious streak is uncovered, it passes through three stages if we give it freedom to be natural. If we let our religious tendency come to the surface freely, and let it spring forth from our center without hindrance of prejudice or bias, we shall get into the genius of it swiftly.

But whether we nag and cuff our religious ideas or not, they run through three stages before they, as one stream from our mind, strike the sunlit heights of miracle working.

To be doubting ourselves, and speaking ill of ourselves, is nagging and cuffing our genius, and has the effect of prolonging our time of travel up the mount of enchantment.

The three stages up to the point of availability to turn water into wine, make bread out of nothing, coin gold out of bones, heal sickness, raise dead people into happy life, stop pain everywhere, are hope, faith, love.

It is not till love gleams and transfigures on the heights of our religious teachings, that we are capable of working miracles without ever a failure.

Whoever fails once in his attempt to perform a cure or carry on a ministry is tarrying at the threshold of faith or hope. He has not reached love.

Was Daniel at the court of Darius the Mede in the city of faith or of love as to his own mental state? Love is understanding. It is specially written of Daniel that he had understanding. But the name Darius means restrainer, and Daniel was his prisoner. So we know by this that Daniel was at the gateway of understanding, just ready to enter in, at 80 years of age, when Darius threw him into the den of lions. (This lesson is Daniel chapter 6).

Another way we may know that Daniel had not entered into the third stage of his religious aspiration is by the fact of his being in a den of lions and having such a pack of enemies.

Whoever has enemies does not understand God; has not struck the third round of religious ascent. Whoever gets into great trials has not entered into the delectable country of love.

Whoever has hope only will get into troubles. If he has faith he will get out of them. If he has love, he will have an enchanted life, free from sorrows.

This simple division will tell you how far you have given your religious streak its liberty. For the liberty of a faculty is necessary to its perfection.

The same is true of every faculty that is true of the religious one. But the Bible lessons are intended to show that the religious streak is the one that is capable of quickening all the others if it is allowed to leap and spring like a fountain, forth from our center.

Columbus had uncovered his idea of the sphericity of the earth. Every child ever born on the planet knew it before him, but paid no attention to his knowledge. Then there came a time when Columbus had faith.

After his discovery, he had hoped that the world would rejoice in the new country. But people did not want Columbus to have so much glory and treasure, so they persecuted him. He had enemies undermining his reputation and efforts in the most subtle fashions. One night he heard a voice saying out of the darkness, "Fear not, I will provide for thee." Then his faith quickened.

In every line of endeavor, there is the genius of success. The instant one strikes the round of love, or understanding of his art, he is no longer hounded, but honored.

Each faculty can call on its spirit of success to hasten it on to victory. If you are in a line you have chosen, call on the god of that art to give you victory. It is sometimes quite necessary to call the god of battles to make him triumphant, instead of on God as a principle. For a close issue, a necessity for quick action, demands the close, quick action of God. This might make it seem as if there were many gods, instead of one God. No, God is one, but God acts through your line for you and through your neighbor's line for him.

There is a God of business transactions ready to lift you into prosperity the instant you specify that it is along that line you would like Him to act.

God always works for prosperity, bounty, beauty, and peace. But you might put the abstract principle to working for the dematerialization of your body before you wished to disappear, if you should spend much time praying, even in a scientific fashion, unto God, as God in the abstract.

We are all getting this moment exactly what we have prayed for. We get into our daily lot exactly what we have described God to be.

A man had a habit of going before light every morning into a mountain and praising the wisdom and knowledge of God. It was not long before he was noted for his wisdom and drew many wise people around him.

Another man praised God as the spirit of union-unity. He declared himself married to the Spirit of God. He described God as his Provider, his Merciful Protector, his High Counselor. Thus, he was miraculously provided for, carefully guided away from every danger, wise in counsel.

This was the exact opposite of the Guyon and Fenelon type of union with God. They called upon the God of safe transit through suffering. Jesus Christ taught the God of safe transit over suffering.

Bravery because of hope in God, or faith that God will save, is not high religion.

Absolute safety is the only religion worthwhile. The teachings of men that bravery in battle or boldness in a cause, are God-like, are humbug. In high truth there is no one to fear, for nothing has any power to hurt and no one warts to hurt.

In high truth, we dwell at the center in safety and greatness with God. Why not tell the truth about this country through which we are walking? The whole truth instead of stopping short would astonish you.

The truth is there are no lions and no den. The truth is that God is the God of Heaven, the God of safety, the God of prosperity. Try telling this story to yourself for a while. Daniel was well enough as far as he went, but lion's dens have no charm for you. You love the stories of the mansions of goodness with harmony around you better. So does everyone.

According to the uncovered spring of the fountain of God leaping toward the sunlit heights of the companionship of Jesus, I rejoice that my high counselor, Truth, has told me that it is a low kind of religion which teaches that God afflicts or permits afflictions and then takes us out of them that we may be thankful enough to satisfy His greed for praise.

"As I live, saith my God, I know the thoughts that I think towards you — thoughts of peace and not evil, to bring you an expected end."

See that? The expected end is always triumphant prosperity.

Knowing this awakens love. Knowing this takes away all fear. Keeping on in this knowledge is mastery over every circumstance, not by desperate struggling either as man with man to see who will beat, or with God to see if we cannot win Him over, but by easy praise.

The love of God in the heart through knowing His character causes us to praise all things. They will do exactly as we want them to if we praise them with the wisdom that our high religion teaches. See how the earth pours forth grains and fruits, foliage and vegetables because the ministers in their pulpits praise the goodness of God in her.

Then see how some people lie down and starve, while millions of beggars put up their wan faces in all countries, just because the ministers have taught that God is better pleased with sackcloth and ashes, hard bread and fasting, than with beautiful clothing and plenty to eat.

They have seen now the fruits of their words in full measure.

Of course scientifically, they were in the stage of hope, where the mind tries every expedient to see which will demonstrate redemption from evil. They have felt afar off that there was something wrong about our clothing and food. This was the hint of the spirit that clothing should not be made with material hands, of material substance, nor food produced by such processes. According to the high truth, all clothing should fall upon us from the Beauty of Holiness, and all food should come to us from the word of God.

But neither by splendor of silks, nor by squalor of sackcloth, is the road to the raiment and food, which is ours by divine right. Only by the pathway of Truth are provision and defense.

Daniel was enough inside the gateway of love so that his mind praised the lions for their obedience to him. The least little shining of love will make even the chairs in the house move around at your bidding. The mountains would move into the salt sea of the west, and lift up their rocks of protection at the command of the least little glint of the love which tips the heights of religion.

This love manifests itself in praise. You would be found praising even your debts for their goodness and tenderness and loving-kindness to you. Debts are heavy burdens in the mind that has not entered the portal of love, where you can praise them till they walk away to spots where God has laid by your treasures. They really are your safe guides into prosperity.

Did you ever try praising your affairs? No? Then try telling them how you love them for their goodness. Praise them that they hold for you the secret of good.

You have been hating your lot, have you not? Your lot is your lion's den. Now that you have got into it, praise the lions. Poor dumb affairs. They are not to blame. Lovingly speak to them. No matter how dry the den is, how frightened and trembling you feel. Do not play the Darius, hoping something will turn up. Be Daniel. You need not try to be brave. Just practice the words of loving-kindness. Talk to your affairs as you would to a frightened child.

The cross mother frightens the child still more. The loving mother quiets it and sets it to play or to work again.

A timid little woman always most afraid of dogs or anything was always beset by dogs. (Of course she was. Whatever you fear most, will come sailing up to you by and by). She learned this law of praise, and when once a savage dog broke his chain and sprang toward her, she touched the gateway of love just a bit and spoke to him as a masterful lover of dogs would speak, and he shrunk away to his kennel.

Daniel struck the gatepost of heaven when the lions faced him, and looked upon them in love. "God is love." "My God hath sent His angel and hath shut up the lion's mouth."

The angel that God sent to Daniel was the one that the same God has sent to you to read this lesson. That angel is named Praise. Praise your hardships. Speak tenderly to them. Take them close. The lions were friendly to Daniel. Your hardships are friendly to you.

Daniel believed in his God. "God is love." Love sends an angel to every trial. Always the angel is Praise. Not praise of a Great Being sitting on a throne, but praise of the trial.

Such a friendly lion as that one is that faces you up little mother. Tell it you do not hate it. Such a friendly lion as comes looking into your eyes, brave, hard-working father. Tell it you understand it. Such a great dumb friend is that lion, whose eyes look into yours, lonely, unprotected heart. Look him straight in the eyes. Tell him God's angel of praise walks beside you.

In Spiritual Science, we do not think it a sign of much knowledge of God to have troubles come upon us, but we know there is always a sure and swift and merciful way out, if we have got into them.

Here you perceive living troubles are called lions. Last Sunday, diseases and sicknesses were meant by fires. You have heard many a woman and man say that living troubles are the worst of all troubles, have you not? Well, there is where some living people have got you in their power in some way-seemingly-remember, there is no reality in trouble, though while it seems real it is just as hard to bear. People have you in their power if they have any power to hurt you, if they have any hold on your lot to wound you by what they do.

This lesson is for such conditions. It teaches that you face the condition square up: the debt itself, not the one you owe. The grief itself, not the one who grieves you. The shame itself, not the one who shames you. Those who do you wrong are Darius. The feeling that faces you, or the thing they do, is the lion. What you say to the situation will fix the situation. Then, when the situation yields, "They have no power to hold you or hurt you forevermore."

"The love of God constraineth me." "How can I keep from singing about the angel abiding with me, closing all the lions' mouths, into whose den I have been so foolish as to fall?" This is the way you feel long before your friends, who have yielded to the temptation to hurt you, feel sorry like Darius that they failed you just when you needed them most.

We are not called to martyrdom of any kind, but being in it, let us take the Daniel way out

We must take a good stand regarding our religious streak. It seems that Jesus Christ was positive that we get all the graces, if that streak dominates. Daniel was sure of it. Moses was sure of it. Moses and Daniel could not help getting into trouble. Jesus said He took our troubles voluntarily to show the highest way out of every sort and kind thereof

By His methods He tacitly praised both Daniel and Moses, but by His tears at the grave of Lazarus, He showed that Martha and Mary and Lazarus would have given higher evidence of understanding Him, if they had kept alive and well, instead of getting sick and dying.

To let the scholastic streak loose in us is to become pedantic, lean, dry as dust, and rheumaticky. The highest honors of men will be awarded to us. But what are they worth?

To let the philosophic and speculative streak loose is to become cold and critical, intellectual and unmerciful. We shall get the praises of our own generation and the reverence of posterity. But what are those worth?

To let the management of finances loose is to have thousands of men and women and children by the throats, and to be cowered before by our neighbors, whose labor we are buying. We shall found, mayhap, some great institution, which believes in the absence of God, and a great monument may crumble in some noble city to mark our resting-place. But what is that worth?

Jesus Christ said, "The fashion of this world passeth away...My words are Life...I am the Truth."

Come back here to the foundation whence the living waters flow. It is not too late to begin all over again, uncovering the living stream of the religious faculty which wells in every mind.

And then, if we but let the stream flow freely, untrammeled by the ideas of even the martyrs, hope will quickly clasp hands with faith, and love will chant victory over sin, death, and the grave.

On the white wings of Truth fly, soul of man! June 12, 1892

Bible Lesson XLIX. Review. See Things As They Are

Astronomers tell us that we see points of light in the skies which we name stars, that are the lights of globes long vanished from the heavens. It takes light so long to travel that we have only just received the radiance they sent forth ages ago.

Metaphysicians tell us that we are just now seeing people in the light or shade of ways we used to think. We may have ceased to believe the imaginations of our youth, but the beliefs of that time often proceed forth from us and cover some person or circumstance with our imagination of them, which they ought not to be judged by.

It is the province of the knowledge of Absolute Truth to cause us to see things as they are; not through our predilections. It may happen to one who has carried a heavy grief for twenty years that some idea enters the mind which takes out the core of the grief, and yet the mind will sometimes feel mournful on the shades of the memory of how the heart used to grieve. One often loves or fears on the shadow of what he used to feel positively.

Religionists tell us that the world lay in the night of deep darkness till Jesus, the Sun of Righteousness, arose and broke the night with the glory of His life. And now, all the ignorance and misfortune we experience are but the broken memories of a night long since erased.

Material things and human experiences are all the symbols of thoughts. The thought that there is a mixture of goodness and evil in the universe may have been reasoned out of our mind, and yet what we used to think about good and evil being sadly mixed may now cover the ways of our neighbors or the state of the world with what seems to us to be a very bad state of affairs. If so we must get rid of the "shades of the departed." In Truth there is a way to be rid of them.

All belief in astrals is the remnant of darkness of mind. All coverings of people with our past ideas are astrals. Let us be rid of astrals. Let us look back upon Alpha and. forward to Omega. God, the Lover and Friend; God, the Keeper and Protector; God, the Provider and Inspiration is behind us and before us. This is Truth.

There are some ideas that come into the mind and stay there as embedded as slivers in the flesh or bullets shot into undeliverable places. An instance of how stories will penetrate and shed abroad their effects is here in point:

A young lady was reading in a Spiritual Science lesson of a man who had kept saying "The Lord is your keeper," till the words had saved a child from the hurt of an accident. The accident took place minus its hurt. The beautiful text, 'The Lord is your keeper," found a lodgment in her mind. There it lay ready to spring forth when an opening should be made for it. The opening came when the train on which she was riding ran off an embankment. Suddenly like a living creature the text sprang from her mind and caught the baggage car in such a position that the coaches were saved. No one was hurt.

"Thy words are Life to them that find then."
"Truth is a shield and buckler."
"The Truth shall make you free."

It was mentioned in a recent magazine that for the last fifteen years, drunkenness, and crime had been terribly on the increase. The whole plan was then made plain, whereby the innocent holders of horrible stories are the shedders abroad of temptation.

For just about fifteen years the eloquent crusaders against vice have transfixed impressionable audiences with stories of wickedness, which they have unconsciously projected, as the beautiful words, 'The Lord is your keeper," flew on its mission.

What kind of stories do you fix into the minds of the people you meet? Ideas are living things. They are caged lions of prowess. They are projectiles from small bore-rifles or heavy caliber guns.

The Bible lessons for the last quarter have been loaded with ideas whose purpose and sure results are to cause those who have read them under the light of Truth, to be workers for the redemption of mankind from its imaginations of evil. You, who have carried one single idea around with you, whose reasonableness and grandeur have captured, have stopped some lie on someone's lips before it was uttered - have caused some hand about to strike to fall down - have taken the sting out of some cup - have withdrawn the drowsiness from some brain.

Which of them has appealed to you most out of the last quarter's mine of golden texts?

This being a review, let us name them. They are the radiance of stars in the firmament of Jehovah, and of their glory, there is no end. The stars of the night may fall from their bright places, and the suns of the invisible heights may be darkened ere their first beams strike our planet. But the words of Eternal Truth shall go on and the hearts that love them shall rise on their wings of light out of the reach of sin, death and pain.

The first one was April the third (this quarter). Its point was that you attract people who represent your thoughts; as Socrates said that grief would attract sickness, waste of property and death.

A young metaphysician suddenly discovered that by being with one who was a reliable healer of sickness, he caught a state of mind quite different from what he had been holding. It was efficient to cure without his making any effort. He said he just left his mind free to take on the strong lights and shades of other people's minds, and knowing just how to drop their errors he could keep their virtues. He noticed that being prosperous is entirely a state of mind. He is now practicing being near prosperous people so that he may minister the quality of mentality that draws prosperity when he walks among the wretched. He means to get so strong in the idea of the providing bounty of the Almighty, that stories of poverty cannot stick in his mind, no matter how real they may seem to others, not even if some great preacher describes them.

While training to be strong on the side of power, health and loving kindness, do not tell anyone your experiences. Self-feed and self-increase with Truth. Truth told before you are positive as the archangel may be so argued down that you feel as weak in spirit as a rag of nothingness. Jesus Christ said: "See thou tell no man."

Remember that methods count for nothing. If you are in the proper state of mind, you might as well sell warming pans in the torrid zone, like Lord Timothy Dexter, as to sell lace at $100 per yard, like Steward or Field.

You certainly must have noticed how some people are lucky, anyhow. That is because they have a mind that attracts luck. This Science teaches one how to attract good into his life. It is a good doctrine to preach to the disconsolate. God is the feeder and healer and companion, according to this doctrine, and nothing is too small a situation or state of affairs for His goodness to pay close attention to. If you stop to think of it, no one is so prosperous and wise as Jehovah. That is why we are advised to talk with Him much. Misfortune and ignorance cannot stay in His presence. Stop often and commune with the Owner of the Worlds.

The next was that all kinds of divorce came from the dark belief once started that God is without, and not within. It dropped its shades down over men till they thought other people could get the advantage over them, so they fell to fighting them. This was warfare on the battlefield and in the home. Did you ever think that many a martial hero got his prowess from the brave fight his mother made with that fate which she believed had given her husband the advantage against her?

Why did she not rise and proclaim that God is both within and without, since God is everywhere? The Jehovah within the feeblest little woman is the Jehovah without in the husband she fears or the legislation against her. Who shall prevail against the Omnipresent God?

Now, the idea that God is within us, not without us, is just as divorcing as the other that He is without, not within. For it gets us to feeling able to get ourselves healthy, but gets us into tangles with the outside world. It withdraws us from our fellow men and makes hermits of us. We get to thinking that people do not understand us. We get a multitude of feelings, which separate us from people.

The third lesson was the injunction not to feel responsible for anything - to let God take the responsibility. "At destruction and famine thou shalt laugh." They tell you that the cars have run off the track and killed a hundred. According to God, it is no such thing. The whole thing is the shadow of an idea, which never was true. So laugh in your soul and silently tell your High Counselor you do not believe He ever let such an event happen in His beautiful kingdom. Then you will do and say to the messenger the right thing. Many will be suddenly helped into healing and life. Turn to your Comrade, Jehovah, when they report evil concerning your home, your prospects, your friends. Tell Him, "I know Thy goodness towards me. How Thou dost glorify me continually."

The fourth tells us to practice every night, and very early in the morning, telling the Spirit of God that we never made any mistakes. Because God being our mind and our life, mistakes in that mind and life are impossible. Then, through the day, act from the standpoint of having done very wisely always. Take it for granted that methods do not count. Nothing counts except our relation with God. If one has "wasted his substance in riotous living," and feels downhearted, he is to tell the Spirit that there cannot be any waste in Truth, because all comes from God and goes to God.

"Omnipresence none can flee,

Flight from God to God must be."

One who had formerly been too economical for any use got up from table and burned a plate of doughnuts, saying, "I praise you for your increasing substance, food from the table of God. Wherever the airs blow this smoke there someone will kindly feed a neighbor."

To her hearers it sounded like superstition. They thought she had gone daft. No, she was spreading the healing word. Her stinginess was broken down. She had to do something exactly opposite to her stinginess. "My ways are not your ways, saith the Lord."

The fifth tells us that we must learn to get our living in some other way, than earning it by the sweat of our brow by hiring out to our neighbors.

The result of that idea that got embedded into mind ages ago that man must labor in a material fashion is that now it is almost impossible for the laboring classes to rest a moment without suffering for it. The average wages for an adult are $1.02 per day (1892). He pays rent at the rate of four or five times what the same home would have been a few years ago. And the poor man's taxes are out of all proportion to the capitalist's taxes.

It is the result of the curse or lie concerning labor. Jesus said, "Labor not for the meat that perisheth." He advised looking to God for clothing and food. All the shiftlessness of mankind, all the weariness of them, all the discouragement, are from ceasing to expect the Almighty to provide. Therefore, this lesson advised all the world to put up its hands and receive from the invisible Hand, of our Everlasting Parent, all its provisions.

Every single morning at some particular hour, tell the Spirit that you do not look to any enterprise or to any human being for your provisions, but to the Spirit only. Then go on as usual about your daily tasks, till the Hand of Love stretches down and changes your lot. There is a change of affairs belonging to every child on this planet.

"Let's take by faith while living
Our freehold by thanksgiving."

The only labor enjoined according to Jesus Christ is thanksgiving to the Omnipotent God. "My yoke is easy," He said. Here we find that it will soon be made utterly impossible for one to get more goods than his neighbor. The truth concerning our God as our Provider will equalize all things. Caste will be abolished - not by anarchy, but by prayer. Labor and capital will soon be erased - not by fighting, but by thanksgiving to God. The morning that dawned on Galilee's waters is just falling on my lot and on your lot. God is here.

The sixth tells about Satan. It shows that all the satan there is or ever was is our subconscious thought that after all maybe God intends for us to be afflicted somehow. While the preacher is praising God for being so good to him, he is secretly thinking how often, God has seen fit to afflict him or his family, "in His inscrutable providence." All subconscious or secret thoughts come to the surface in home, business, friendships, and positions among mankind.

Many a poor minister or half-starved pietist may lay his decrepitude and misery to his own reserved opinion concerning God. Each one must face up this satan of thinking, "What if evil should be my portion whether I call upon God or not?" Meet Satan promptly. Jesus Christ is the antidote to Satan. Look your vague terror in the face with the name Jesus Christ. That Name means the visibility of God.

The seventh shows that if you know what is true according to the Life of the Spirit, your knowing is like a river set flowing. One does not have to strive to carry out his Truth by stopping his factory when he hears that all clothing should be made out of the Word of Truth. He does not have to close up the schoolhouse when he learns that all schools are founded on the lie concerning the absence of intelligence. No, he sees that his knowledge is all the power he needs to exercise. He need not stop eating to show how long his God will keep him alive without food. His knowledge will regulate his actions. No man should give up any thing by force of human will. All should be accomplished by the irresistible action of the Principle. The action of Spirit is as positive with us when we hear it as it was when it struck Saul to the earth.

The Supreme Truth that is now being believed by so many people is flowing through the bodies, and homes and affairs of men like a river. Away over the horizons, into the abysses of a forgotten dream, are all the former ways being washed.

"And the former heaven and the former earth shall be forgotten; neither shall they come into mind any more."

The eighth shows that the science of mathematics, of stars, of stones, of chemistry, is as helpless to provide against earthquakes, tidal waves, lightning, plagues, cyclones, as the simple Indian's sure prognostications that these things are coming. Only the Science of Spirit annuls calamity. This lesson shows that our boasted civilization

is the mixed iron and clay age spoken of by Daniel. We have had our golden height of sincerity that man is ruled over by his brother man by

right of inheritance from God. This has descended into the scramble for power on every hand. We have had the golden head of conviction that some men are given more judgment from Jehovah than others. This has descended into the systems of cramming with masses of teachings that are foolishness with God.

We have had our golden height of sincere believing that the church was instituted for the salvation of souls, which has now descended into the flinching and cringing of the preachers in the face of death and disease, as powerless to hush as the schools.

The scramble of the religious for salaries and honors in common with the believers in material methods is the mixture of clay and iron.

And all the time the hammers of the true kingdom are sounding on the ears of those who know that the Spirit of God is in every man equally as in his neighbor, so that there is no need of any government, save the knowledge of Spirit. This age closes the reign of intellect and matter.

The sciences of the schools shall not count us in hand for this kingdom only so far as they wear down the intellect to acknowledging that the most it knows is that it knows nothing. To study the sciences of the schools chafes the brain into inflammation and softness. The study of the Science of Spirit quickens the intelligence to know what was and is and shall be.

The ears can hear the sound of the voices of the workmen hewing out the mansions for those who do not mix their knowledge that there is no soul to save, for God is the only Soul, with the former idea of salvation.

The ninth and tenth show that we never need to face up people who have done us injuries, but we are to look the injuries straight in the face and get right with them, after which it will be easy enough to get on with our fellow men and women. Paul and Peter and James saw this, but not so plainly as these lessons bring out.

Tell those troublesome affairs that they are your kind and loving friends with ability to go right to the treasure house where your rightful inheritance is, and bring you your rights at once. Love them and praise them. The other side of them is delight. They will fly to the places whence your help can come easily. The first thing you do after praising them is right. You were not intended to be burdened, or sick, or ignorant, or unfortunate, or abused. These states of situations need praising, and loving and directing, not hating, and repelling and striking. They are angels of goodness in disguise. Talk to them wisely. Never mind people. Keep your world under your feet, not on your back nor in your arms.

The last is all about keeping your own counsel. If the Spirit tells you to go and heal a dying case, do not tell of it. Go and do as you are bidden and come again bringing your triumphs. If the Spirit bids you rest, obey and ask no odds of any man. If you are given to spreading your spoken words concerning your secret with God you will be saved so as by fire. That which is true of the world at large, preach boldly. What the Spirit gives you alone keep as the secret of the Lord. The Spirit intends for you to cure everyone and raise everyone to Life when it whispers to you. It does not come to take you by the hand through tribulations, but out of the reach of them.

There is a particular way for you to get out of that difficulty you are now in. Keep counsel with no one save the powerful Champion, the Lord God of Sabaoth. "Thou shalt hear a voice behind thee saying: This is the way; walk ye in it."

June 19th, 1892

Bible Lesson L. Psalms 72:1-19. Value Of Early Beliefs

"With those elect,
Who seem not to compete or strive,
Yet with the foremost still arrive,
Prevailing still.
Spirits with whom the stars connive
To work their will."

There are some people, who are bound to be foremost. "There's a destiny that shapes their ends, rough hew them how they will." They do not answer when they are accused. They do not need to. They do not try to have their names enrolled on the scrolls of earth's great ones. They do not have to try. It is written in their foreheads that the nations shall call them blessed while they smile as little babies in their cradles. They are the answers to the prayers of the saints. Their minds are docile, simple, innocent, confiding, always.

All children expect to be good. They look only for goodness when they stretch up their fingers and open their eyes for the first time in our arms. They expect justice. They take Providence for granted. And some little ones are left so free that they keep to the last that open expectation of the universe always doing the right thing by them. These are enrolled on the annals of fame.

For the universe purposes only good to us all. We keep our windows and doors open and in it all rushes. Such minds are the right kind of vacuum. The gods love them, and come in and sup with them freely. And this is all there is to greatness — taking the best for granted.

Everything you ever accomplished you have accomplished because you have from childhood kept one childish trait of taking for granted. Maybe you dragged along the weight of supposing you would have to scramble and struggle to carry it out, but that was a notion that did not frighten you out of your childish expectation of some one thing.

To be supremely good one must be supremely childlike, taking no notion of having to try to be anything along with his expectation of all things. It is the children, who enter the kingdom of God.

This lesson is a wonderful reminder that it is never too late to be little children all over again. We may become again, as we were when we were first born — knowing neither good nor evil, docile to the will of destiny.

"Conduct me, Zeus, and thou, O Destiny, where'er thou wilt."

Solomon took many, many goods for granted. He took not the idea of enduring chastity. So in this psalm 72, where his own expectation of righteousness left off, he saw by prophecy that one would come who, by reason of expecting all things, holiness included, should, no matter what happened, be King of Kings and Lord of Lords.

When Jeremiah is forbidden to call himself a child, it is meant that he should not be after the order of one who cringes and trembles with fears of evil. This is not the child, who is Son of God — equal with God — but the shadow of him.

Solomon says that this type of character shall be a judge, a savior, a king, a peacemaker, a bountiful provider, a counselor, a friend, an instructor. He shall teach mankind how to have all things without scrambling and struggling.

Jesus Christ taught this. He promised a hundred-fold more human goods by His principle of expectation than by all the methods of action now in use. He said that the bounty of the Spirit of the universe would fall wonderfully over those who would take things for granted. And in the next sphere of experience we would be sure to drop the notion of death: "An hundred-fold more in this life, and in the world to come everlasting life."

In noticing the expectations of good, which have characterized the great, we mark that they all took death for granted. This is not laid up against them, but it is promised that they shall not take that into the next sphere of experience.

Here it is remembered that the mind of the profound thinker, who has received the gift of seer-ship, has ever declared that for the most of us on the earth, there are seven spheres of experience through which we must walk. This earth is one of them.

Those who hasten their experiences here may pass the others, which have pain and sorrow, swiftly, hardly touching them with the wings of light, which our life here in righteousness has furnished us.

Jesus Christ intimates that most of the people passing the next sphere still expect death as the portal through which to step on into the next beyond. But those who understand Him will not take that belief along, and will fly the spheres on wings of deathless life.

As no one has yet entirely practiced His principle of expecting provisions of all kinds straight from the Spirit of righteousness, we have an entirely new field of Science before us.

Solomon sees that it will be natural for gold and silver to flow to that kind of scientist. And gold and silver shall be nothing to him any more than the applause of people or the air he breathes. He shall see that all things are provided by the Spirit. He shall see that all things are done by the Spirit. It shall never occur to him to say that he wrote his books by hard work. He shall not think that he conquered his enemies by kindness. He shall see that the Spirit wrote his books and the Spirit furnished him his friends.

Dickens told the people that he had only one genius, and that was the genius for hard work. The pugilist thinks his strength is his muscle, but there is nothing of intelligence or strength but God. It is acknowledging that it is God, who causes the work to bless the world with its light.

Every child heard its name called when it was young. Some listened and knew that the Spirit meant something for themselves alone. Others forgot. You heard your name called. Do you remember the day? Go back in memory, and sit down into that state of mind again for a moment. So lovely is this Spirit that broods overhead that all the intervening days may be blotted out, and you may be a child again, hearing your name called and feeling the open, docile mind again.

It is our privilege to begin over again today. From this time on we will take things for granted. This state of mind "shall deliver the needy, and him that hath no helper," says this psalm. It goes on to tell how easy all the honors of the world are to get. Things come. It is "not by might, nor by power, but by my Spirit, saith the Lord."

It was taught by Jesus Christ to be a terrible thing for any of us to teach children to expect anything else but the best to come to them. He did not praise civilization. He called civilization the knowledge of His doctrine without the practicing of it: that is, knowing the ways to be well, and happy and provided for, but doing the ways that make for starvation and caste and blood poisoning.

This hearing the doctrine preached and closing up the ears against it till the hands and brains are obliged to use other methods, brings great sorrows and pains. It makes a solid substance for the devil to feed on.

The hearing mind that is easily blessed along some one line never is hurt or frightened along that line. If you have kept the childhood expectation of being always fed and clothed, you are never stung with misery lest you come to want.

The devil of the world — which is the belief in evil — might come again and again, tempting you with tales of disaster and famine. But he would find no food in you to feed on, and so you would feel no torment of that kind. The feeling of torment along any line is the sign that the devil is feeding on you and enjoying himself immensely. Now the devil cometh to Jesus and findeth nothing in Him.

If you are very sensitive to blame or censure, why, you have a solid bar of eatable food for the belief in evil, which is called the devil, to feed on. You certainly will get a great deal of torment from the intentional slights and censures of people, and likewise from their unintentional woundings. Now the devil cometh to Jesus along this line and findeth nothing in Him.

If you care a great deal for your reputation and have fought like a hero for your good name, you have a solid lump of human feeling for scandalizing tongues to bite you in the back and hurt you. But if you never closed up the open window of that childhood's expectation that all people would be kind and just to you, the scandal of a million would only make you smile indulgently. For you see that the devil cometh to Jesus and findeth nothing in Him of feeling to torment. Sensitiveness to praise and blame, or jealousy of friendships, is most excellent food for the devil to feed on.

Is there a devil going to and fro, seeking whom he may devour? No, that is only our own belief in or fear of evil of some kind. That fear is the bar of flesh with which we closed up the window into which was streaming one line of our goods.

The Messiah's reign described by this psalm is simply the description of a state of mind into which Tarshish and Seba, Sheba and the isles, all flow and shimmer their blessings.

Tarshish is a figure of speech meaning riches. Take riches for granted. Do not hustle and bustle and feel so anxious about riches. Really, you were born to riches. You do not have to shout, drive a sharp bargain, nor hold your own in a deal. The devil must not find any food of such idea in you.

Seba is a figure of speech for greatness of character and position. You do not have to try to be great. You were born to greatness. If you think for a moment, that someone is going to get the position over you, then indeed you must take down the shutter of that notion. It is a bar of "bringing up," or cultivated characteristic of such a solid flesh substance that the devil eateth a good morsel by keeping you in an inferior position when you feel fitted to a higher one. Take your greatness for granted. Do not fight and connive. You need not pay someone to help you into your seat. Do you not see how you are taught that it shall come to you with this state of mind?

Sheba is a figure of speech for noble reputation. You came forth into this sphere with the expectation of the perfume of a reputation for virtue and wisdom. If you laid across the open window the fear of misrepresentation or injustice, what torments you would feel from the bitings of report. Jesus kept that bar of human feeling away. It was a flesh spot, the devil found not in Him at all. He was so silent at calumny that the Shekinah comes strolling over the ages from the temple halls of His presence on Calvary.

Sheba always stands for the perfume of Holiness. Of Sheba, Herodotus says that the land exhaled an odor of marvelous sweetness. Diodorous tells that the wondrous perfume thereof extended far out to sea.

Strabo said that this perfume of the spices of Sheba made them so valuable that Sheba was the wealthiest spot on earth. The people made their furniture of gold. This riches of Sheba signifies that to expect people to speak well of you is a sure state of mind to be supported by. It is a forerunner of poverty if one is afraid someone is talking against him. Loss of some goods will follow on that idea.

"The isles" is a figurative expression for believers in your doctrine — converts. Never think for an instant that people will not believe in your highest teachings. You were born to inspire confidence. Never think you must trim your sails to curry favor. "Speak the word boldly that is given you to utter." Put no bar on your lips. "But," says one, "suppose one feels like preaching communism, free love, etc." He does not feel like preaching anything that defrauds a single creature of a thing if he is of the Messiah's mind.

This psalm gives the description of how the mind with which you came forth expecting all people to believe in your words was the mind to help the needy and helpless, not to rob them. The Messiah spends no time robbing, nor preaching of such.

The highest truth is the highest defense, support, strength, and peace. Better not put the idea of getting away from your neighbor that which you want, across your childhood expectation of good. That is an idea that makes the torment of anger and resentment, very excellent eating for that devil of impotent rage which tried Jesus and went away as hungry as a shad of the seas of nowhere.

On the top of the mountain there is a handful of corn that can shake the earth with plenty, writes Solomon. The top of the mountain is the highest doctrine of Self. The Self is the I. The only I there is, is the one God. "I am God, and there is none beside."

Some day you will find the central intelligence of your being proclaiming His name within you. This will be after you have become as expectant of good as an infant. There will be no bars of flesh — no human dreads. "Truth is not cumbered by matter." This is the handful of corn that shall drop its increase till the whole earth shall be filled with the knowledge of God as the waters fill the seas.

When that Name speaks within you, at the summit of your being, you will do great works easily. The Name shall speak a doctrine forth, to which every knee shall bow. At this moment it is proclaiming in a voice the ears of flesh tell you they do not hear: "I can preach the truth through you. I can heal the sick for you. I can cast down evil by your presence. I can raise the dead where you walk."

The glory of God from whom the child came forth need not have any coverings of flesh suitable for the devil to eat. There need be no imagination of evil to torment: the earth. With this knowledge the imagination of evil is put away. The knowledge of truth is the only knowledge worthwhile. See what experience your ideas of evil have brought you. Watch what experiences your knowledge of truth will bring you.

Your first estate was God. You may drop what you have heard unlike God and be a child again seeing God. Expecting good from every direction, you shine forth glory over all your world. You are of "those elect…with whom the stars connive to work their will." June 26, 1892

Bible Lesson LI. Acts 1:1-12. The Measure of a Master

Emerson tells us that the measure of a master is his success in bringing all men round to his opinion twenty years later on. We all understand the term "twenty years" to mean any length of time the master happens to take for establishing his principles. The old masters had to wait many times twenty years for bringing men round to their opinions.

"For prejudice, that spider shrewd,
Did o'er them weave, in wicked mood,
Her cobwebs through the halls of fame,
From threads of slander, threads of shame,
Till death, with bosom bluff and strong,
From groins and rafters where they throng,
Swept clear away the unclean array."

The master's opinion must be truth or his opinion will not be made of stuff strong enough to bear the wear and tear of time and ignominy. The seven crusades are now judged as sentimental folly. Gamaliel's idea is known to be wiser. "Refrain from these men and let them alone, for if this counsel or this work be of men, it will come to naught." (Acts 5:38) This lesson (Acts 1) brings to thought the teaching of mental science that there is a particular and special characteristic exercised consciously or unconsciously by each one of us when we meet one another.

One very beautiful and enchanting mind could not be happy except when people were adoring it, so it sought among the ways of winning praise and found that all people have some one touch of vanity in them. With an instinct quickened by a hunger as sharpening as physical starvation, this mind would run the gamut of your human foibles, till your weakest vanity was discovered. Then with the precision of a Guido Reni it would make that the keynote of all your conversations thereafter, flattering that one love of flattery in you till you joined the ranks of adorers. But time always cheapened the flattery, and by and by that skillful player on human foibles could not bring any more grist to your mill. Being carnal and temporal, not divine and infinite, the supply of stimulants gave out.

Another character loved to be praised for keen quick-wittedness. So whenever it was making preparation to meet "the Count" or "the Duke" or "my Lord" or "the distinguished Mr. or Mrs. So and So," there was always an imaginary conversation prepared coming by instinct wondrously close to what did take place, in which this seeker for praise of repartee was figured as quick and sharp indeed. The right retorts and responses were written down and learned beforehand. Everyone did praise this marvelous quickness of brilliant response. But by and by people grew afraid to associate with this mind because there was no parrying its thrusts. It was like the mechanical gambling machine, which no human player can win anything from. So great and small avoided it.

It is found by physiological psychology that we are all given to touching some vanity of intellect or sentiment in our fellow beings, which, if we be too indulgent of its practice, surely bringeth us to grief.

There is only one chord in our brethren we can wake to eternal delight, and that is the one Luke touches, namely the Theophilus chord. This chord is the love of God strung fine and strong across the soul of every creature from the archangel to the human dwarf. Whoever loves to strike this nature, never absent, always in tune, always responsive, will win deathless friendships, eternal comradeship, and wholesome encomiums.

Luke was the healing mind, the artist, the musician. This healing mind is in us all. At its highest it is quick to run the gamut of men's tastes and virtues. It calls your attention to your own possibilities it puts so glowingly before you. It tenderly sweeps the heartstrings of love and tells you how you are beloved by one whose love cannot fail you, whose treasures of wisdom and joy are awaiting your acceptance.

To read the writings of Luke is to awaken in ourselves the skill akin to his. For to read an author is as though we associated with his character. Do not be surprised if the admirer of Shakespeare is a panderer to human foibles; or if the admirer of an egotistic poet is egotistic.

The true physician diagnoses your case as an easy one to cure. He has one remedy only. He always uses it. The more of it you take, the healthier you get. He sees that you are heartsick, and tells you that you have had only the "John Baptism," which is simply the promise of something good to come to you in the future, and that indeed no heart was ever made to feed on promises – it must have present satisfaction. He then tells you that no matter if you are an organ-grinder, or a shoemaker, you really have the possibilities of a Beethoven and of a John of Patmos. He says that all you need is to have your soul's secret keys played on by a Master Hand.

This is the truth. The strings of the soul harp quiver under His fingers. "Ah, God my Maker, I love Thee!" you respond. The hot tears flow. The hardness is melted. No one has told you who you were till Luke came into your neighborhood. The hardest enemy of the God who has seemed to let him have a lot inferior to his neighbors, finds that as soon as the true God is described, and His real dealings with every creature are proclaimed, he loves Him with all his mind, and strength, and heart, and soul.

Luke (the Christian who represents you as a being of God-like genius) gets martyred by the preachers who preached the worm-of-the dust doctrine till they got you down to beggary and your neighbor into luxury. But Luke's teachings live, and the preachers themselves are converted to his teachings if they ever listen to him an instant.

He always preaches Jesus Christ risen, alive, at hand, ready to manifest any instant. Jesus Christ is this power of the knowledge of God, which quickens into abiding demonstration. By which is meant that the knowledge of Truth is the Jesus Christ power. This knowledge of truth being kept in mind – held onto as true – by and by becomes so real that it is outwardly demonstrated. The outward demonstration is the Holy Ghost power of Jesus Christ.

This Holy Ghost power of Jesus Christ is possible to every one of us, on every plane of living. Suppose on the commonest scale of this principle you are knowing to the fact that the one you are working for is not paying you as good wages as you earn, and as you know that he can afford to give you – this knowledge of right, this knowledge of justice– is your Jesus Christ power. Hold on to this knowledge, and it will quicken by and by into the conscience of the meanest employer on record. Something will take place without any intervention on your part, which will either set you into a field that will more than make up for what you have seemed to lose, or turn his heart and purse inside out to make restitution.

People have the most practical doctrine in the Jesus Christ teaching as set forth by Luke. Commentators and Bible historians have searched all around for a historic Theophilus, but they could not find one. Luke was speaking to the Theophilus chord in the soul of the peasant, and that of the king. That string that vibrates with hope and faith in God and wakes the airs with loving cadence, when it is touched in gentle mother, or ruthless pirate.

Luke is so very personal that he is divinely impersonal, for Luke is the artist of God and the health of "my people Israel." No matter what plane you live on, this Luke will heal you by waking the love-of-God chord in you. He does not scorn you if you are a farmhand, or a brakeman on the train. He says, "What do you really want?" Then he tells you that always the God within you is able to lay hold on just what you think you ought to have. He then tells you that after you have gotten that desired object well into hand, then you will be on another plane, and will be naming something else as your aspiration. He shows you that on having attained that object – your God within – which pushes your knowledge of what you ought to have, forward and still forward, quickens your knowledge with the white glory of the Holy Ghost, and from that instant all things are done for you.

Luke says the knowing power within is Jesus Christ, the owner of the kingdom of the world and the riches of them, who will restore unto you your lost Israel or the beautiful home and happiness you had years ago.

There is a broad hint in the eleventh verse that people ought not to be looking into the skies for their Jesus Christ power. They have a right to think of it as here and now working with them tangibly and helpfully.

According to this idea it is as unscientific to found an orphans' home and trust to prayers to bring skimmed milk and burnt porridge enough for each day, as it was for the ragged monks of the thirteenth and fourteenth centuries to go begging crusts from door to door. Any kind of living, which an unprovided-for Christian calls trust, is as removed from the demonstration of Jesus Christ unto the power of the Holy Ghost, as the dumb hope of the vagabond dervish that Allah will send him a money price for exhibiting the hooks through his eyelids.

Jesus Christ and the Holy Ghost are visible, tangible helps to our getting on in abundance of possessions – so abundant that we do not speak of them as remarkable and unusual signs of our uncommon piety.

Jesus Christ and the Holy Ghost are visible, tangible helps to our wise words, so that we are not set over or under our fellowmen, but realize that there is no respect of persons with God.

Jesus Christ and the Holy Ghost are visible, tangible aids to our perfect health, so that we do not need to fear disease, pain, old age, accidents, and deformities. All these things will disappear with the knowledge of truth. The truth is that to know a principle, and to hold on to your knowledge of it, will win your cause as sure as you live. Right here we are called to notice that so far all our great teachers have thought sorrowfully of the extreme length of time that it has taken for great truths to win their way. Why should this be so when the disciples were only ten days turning from disciples (learners) into apostles (teachers)? Because people have believed in time and heaven to come. They have looked afar off. "According to thy faith be it unto thee." (Matthew 9:29) If God is within and without every creature, only waiting for the right words to be spoken to do exceeding abundantly above all that we have asked, we will take down the veil of belief in time and lay hold of our fullness of joy now.

Knowing that all things are ours now by right of being in God and having God within, is a power of itself. It brings the Holy Ghost demonstration. He is a mental tramp who has no idea where the support of his household is coming from each day and for all time. He may call his vagabondism pious trust if he wants to, but it is ignorance of ways and means, which Jesus Christ never practiced and never recommended. The world's way is for one never to know the day the banks may fail, the business collapse, the strikes ruin him. It is the Jesus Christ way to know a truth that shall make us free from even the idea that we have to trust blindly in God for our living, for He knew a sure working principle close up to each one of us. What we know to be true is now working for us. Holding on to it brings it into sight. "And this is life, to know." Whatever we know ought to be done, we may be sure is hastening to be done. To know that it ought to be done now is to take off the veil of time from out sight. Seeing good times come to us now is the Holy Ghost.

The instant the knowledge of the NOW strikes us we have the power of the Holy Ghost. After the idea of time falls off and the now is in us, we can stop the supposition that money and book learning, or position and fame, are worth striving for or speaking of. These ideas are all the result of having people touch the human strings, which weave the veil before the soul. Their cheapness is already striking the earth with terror, so the loving physician of this hour comes to our discouraged hearts and wakes the soul chords by telling us the story of the power of truth. He paints our own powers in living science before our eyes. He calls it Spiritual Science, which means knowledge of truth. He tells the story over and over. Every time he tells us that our own knowing of truth is as full of energy as the knowing of Paul, or John, or Stephen, we lift up our heads with new hope.

And now he tells us there is a quickening energy belonging to us which we had better use. It is the knowledge of what right thing ought to be done now. The news is the thrilling delight of the Holy Ghost. The Holy Ghost is the ability this day to fit out our people with purse and script and sword, exactly such as the best people in the world have, without being spoilt by such possessions or boastful of our great piety, for these things are but outward symbols of our knowing what is true and what ought to be done now.

The knowing exactly what ought to be done is Jesus Christ. The actual presence of the finished work is the Holy Ghost power of Jesus Christ.

If you are troubled by the unequal distribution of property in the world, are you sure that all of the Hottentots and states' prison convicts ought this day to have exact shares of all property by violent seizure of the lands and personal goods of the property owners? If you think all men ought to be taught how to use property before such a seizure, then you really are thinking that knowledge is the thing worth while. Why do you not say so, then? And if you would be very particular what kind of knowledge you would have brought to the inhabitants of this planet, seeing that knowledge of mechanics and languages has not brought the right state of affairs to pass, why do you not state explicitly and definitely what kind of knowledge you want them to have?

One has to know exactly what he wants to have done, and know that it ought to be done, to be indeed waking the true and omnipotent chord of mankind. That which you would have them know is that God is within all creatures equally, without respect of persons when they speak the truth of God.

If you are in doubt about its being a knowledge of God you would have people possessed of, since the preachers of God have seemed to be as weak and unprovided for as the rest of the world, then be exceeding particular to define what kind of God you would have the world think of, for people always get into their own lot and put into other people's lot the highest ideas they can conceive of. Their highest influence is that which they think to be true.

If your highest conception of God was got from the theology, which represents Him as partial in the distribution of powers, faculties, and virtues, either by inheritance, or by environment, then your knowing is not the knowing of truth. Luke, the physician, has not spoken to you. The love chord is not wakened in you. You need healing of this. It is no wonder you are worried about many things.

Can you not change your mind to think that the spirit of God was breathed into Pilate as fully as into Jesus? This is the truth. Herein is the truth of God, so good. He who can hold on to this knowledge will see his knowledge break forth as the morning in the smiling faith of a planet. This is the truth. It is Spiritual Science. There is no respect of persons with God.

"There is one God above you all and through you all and in you all." (Ephesians 46) He never sent any evil upon any creature. This is truth. And in your heart you think this ought to be true, do you not? You know it ought to be true. And this knowing which you now admit is touching the wings of the Holy Ghost with the winds of your thoughts. Let the winds of positive knowledge of what ought to be true blow on till the white fire of knowing that it already is true flames hot on the earth!

We do not believe that this need take any time. We do not believe that Jesus Christ thought of time as necessary to bringing to pass perfect health, perfect wisdom, and joyous prosperity for every creature. All the time it has taken to come face to face with the golden age of peace on earth has been the masters' belief in time. Indeed, they have all accused Jesus Christ of being 1900 years coming among us again. We have no human foible for such masters to quicken to belief in that teaching. The love of God is quickened by the healing knowledge that "Now is the accepted time." (II Corinthians 6:2) July 3, 1892.

Bible Lesson LII. Acts 2:1-12. Chief Ideas Rule People

In metaphysics, we have ultimate conclusions, and steady reasonings. Two ultimate conclusions, have lately been thrown before the students of metaphysics, which have affected them differently according as their caliber and quality varied. These two statements are: "I am God," and "There is no God."

The steady reasonings that would lead up to these two statements are those reasonings, which the schools of theology ignore. They are strictly Christian, however. Jesus Christ told us to keep His word. He meant us to repeat them as our own. If "I and the Father are One," (John 10:30) I am that One. "If I am meek and lowly of heart," (Matthew 11:29) then I can never get meek and lowly enough to satisfy the words, till I am no-thing. So each "I" must have its highest and its lowest swings of obedience to wisdom.

There are a great many half-conscious ideas floating around in everyone's mind. If one of these swift reasonings is choked off or ignored, it retreats like a lion to its lair; but it will come up again quite as alive as before, not quite so unconscious, and if you put it down it will not go into its cage quite so willingly as at first.

All these interpretations of Scripture, which honesty compels the illuminated mind to make, have run around in the metaphysical minds of men and women for ages. Eckhart, a pious monk, said he could not rise to his highest wisdom, till he first got rid of his idea of God. Telling such an idea aloud would have astounded him when it first walked around his mental planet. But by dropping his idea of God purposely, he rose to the LIBER BENEDICTIONUM. For his idea of God, which was wrong indeed, so filled his mind that he was almost good for nothing.

Some people feel better to admit there is no such god as they used to believe in. Evidently, they fear something or someone. Others do not hesitate to speak the word boldly because it seems to set them absolutely free for the True God to deal with them. The True God cannot be moved from His lofty place by the rejection of all ideas of Him previously held. The True God is not a being to fear. Nothing that anyone says moves Him to anger, revenge, or reward. I am "the same yesterday, today, forever."

The "I am God and there is none beside me" (Isaiah 46:9) is not a word that the mortal speaks. The intellect at its highest pinnacle cannot speak it. Only the free Spirit proclaims it. When the intellect repeats the high statement, it gives its strongest characteristic absolute sway. One has a streak of jealousy in his composition, which with all his ability and seeming virtue, does act as prime mover of his words and works. Maybe unconsciously to himself, maybe consciously, but his jealousy rules him. His steady reasonings bring him to the conviction that indeed the true "I" of every man is God. So he repeats the affirmation. Which dominant note in his composition do you think springs to the front? Which trait of disposition comes up in delighted freedom? Jealousy! So he does and says the most ridiculously jealous things. He makes a complete idiot of himself before people who never suspected he had even the shadow of a shade of the slimy creature.

This is why the prophet said: "There is a destruction in the city when the people say I am God." He meant it was not safe as a general rule for the thoughts of men to rise up and let the strongest one on the outer plane proclaim the name of Jehovah as its own. That should be taking the name of God in vain. Moses took this name and it was temper, that appropriated it. So he came to destruction along the line of his greatest ambition. It is always noticeable that those who say, "I am God," letting their governing trait have the word in common with their other traits, get worsted on the very line of their ambitions.

If you are supremely generous and speak this affirmation lightly or vehemently, by and by you will get to giving away everything that you possess. If you read it from Moses or David or Isaiah or Jeremiah as a part of your Bible lesson, very likely you read it lightly, so your last dollar and last piece of goods and last comrade probably will not disappear speedily. If you speak it vehemently, as the high reasoners speak it, you will rush to the ends of your goods with the legs of Ahimaaz. "His word runneth very swiftly." (Psalm 147:15) "By thy words thou art justified and by thy words thou art condemned." (Matthew 12:27)

But there is a thought which may say, "I am, and there is none beside me!" What is it? Is it, "I, Victory, am God?" Oh no! Because the pride of intellect may take up that word and make you a supreme example of pride. Pride holding the reins of victory brings destruction. Solomon said, "Pride goeth before destruction." (Proverbs 16:18) It cannot be, "I, Success"; it cannot be, "I, Health"; for a very ugly trait like enjoying other people's misfortunes might "flourish like a green bay-tree." (Psalm 37:35)

Is it, "I, Jesus Christ, am God?" Some of the profound students of the law of words spoken silently and audibly by us, tell us that it just as surely as we live, gets us into the exact tribulations experienced by Jesus Christ, if we made the Jesus Christ idea the God idea of our mind and speech. They never use the name as the dominant name of their mind because they fear His afflictions. They are afraid of His "cup".

And this takes us straight to another idea of the profound metaphysicians. They got so afraid of the "I am's" that they thought maybe David meant the word "Thou" when he said "Lead me to the rock that is higher than I." (Psalm 61:2) So they tried the words, "Thou only." Watching their experiences, they perceived that the situation of Job became theirs: "The thing I feared has come upon me." (Job 3:25) For what one is most afraid of is his ruler; and a ruler a god. So when one fills his mind with the words, "Thou only," he hurries the things he is afraid of toward him. What mind is there, that does not let some fear overmaster everything – by spells?

If it is adoration of something that masters you, as, for instance, adoration of gold, why, how afraid are you that you will not get gold? The two ideas will stand out in bold prominence and fight each other for mastery over you. Fear generally wins.

"So shall thy poverty come as one that traveleth, and thy want as an armed man." (Proverbs 6:11) The church of today is a bold example of the clinch of its two ideas in mortal combat. Some branches thereof are lean with want, and some are fat with surplus of gold. A secular paper says: "The undue deference paid to money by the churches is disintegrating church influence among the masses." You see they have said, "Thou only," for ages.

Softly and indifferently sometimes, vehemently sometimes. Here is the summing up: "The Christian Union management is utterly amazed to find that the masses do not attend church."

And all this is why certain thinkers took the Eckhart idea of denying that there is any God at all. They reasoned that there could not be any destruction of the true God, because a God who could be destroyed could not be worth mentioning, and the gods who might get their heads demolished were only too welcome to be utterly absent.

Would words of denial and words of affirmation so surely affect human destiny as all this describes? Yes, this is what metaphysicians are convinced of. They watch people and see how they are all the product of their chief ideas. They see that the ideas held by people are hurrying them to old age, disease, failing sight, loss of friends, and death. "One event happeneth to them all" (Ecclesiastes 2:14)

Do the metaphysicians think these conditions are avertible? They do. They see that common ideas make common events. They would break up some of the race ideas entirely. Can they do so? If a few fishermen stopped the clock of time and set it to measuring itself from their idea; if unlettered devotees dictated what should constitute the civilization of the nations, – other apostles of a right conviction may not flinch at the task set before them.

What is their task? It is to change the mind of the race from believing in sickness, old age, death, poverty, and inferiority, to knowing that just the opposites belong to every creature that walks.

This lesson is concerning the special characteristics of the body of men who had followed the teachings of a very persistent and authoritative man named Jesus, who called Himself the Christ. All these men had had cowardly and jealous traits of character which, with all their religious notions, they had not eradicated after three years of listening to the highest moral precepts, and watching the noblest of living examples. All of a sudden, their mean, and wicked and untruthful traits are transformed into lofty, upright, and righteous ones. They have held some idea in mind till by force of its own nature it has bloomed into glory. It has taken cowardice, jealousy, and quibbling by the vitals and tinged them with its own splendid fires. The tongue of the learned drops the "soft language of the Latin" on enchanted ears. The tongue of the eloquent touches to entrancing melody the speech of wild Araby. The tongue of healing falls tenderly on the bruised hopes of dying Egypt.

Here is the transformation of a few gathered in an upper chamber, such as the revival of their ideas must bring to pass upon a whole globe of people according to promise.

"When He, the Spirit of Truth, is come, He will guide you into all Truth." (John 16:13) The lesson may be found in Acts Chapter 2. Here we see that though for three years, certain very religiously inclined men had held one Name in mind with thoughts of doubt, fear, pride, and jealousy, and many other mixtures foremost, yet it conquered them all, according to their wisdom, healing power, and mastery of nature.

They had held the Name Jesus Christ without any knowledge gained from former lives. They had held it in timid wonder. They had held it in half doubt. They mixed with it the thought of the scorn of their neighbors. They put it into the alembic with their memory of the seeming defeats of Him who personified it. But according to orders, they held it.

Every word contains its own potentiality. Kept in the heart – it will germinate, quicken, and spring forth. There is one word that is King of Kings and Lord of Lords. It will act as leaven in the measure of mental meal. Whoever keeps it will see his ambition to rule among men come to defeat. He will see that he cannot do it. Yet this Name will lift him out of shame and regret. It will take off the edge of humiliation and pain, as an anaesthetic dulls the anguish of amputation.

Whoever keeps this Name in his mind will see his money and friends leave him. Yet the sorrow and poverty that he experiences will not hurt him so sorely but that "bread shall be given him," (Isaiah 33:16) and new friends will make up for the failure of the old ones. That money and those friends first came into manifestation by other ideas quite unlike the meaning of that Name.

Whoever keeps that Name past such crucifixions, regarding them as signs of the swifter coming of true honors, true riches, and true friends, will some unexpected moment feel the rush of the white wings of the Spirit. Thereafter he knows what duties were laid out for him to do from the ancient days. He knows just how to do them perfectly. They are no hardship. There is no laborious effort to bring something to pass. He knows where his clothes and food are to come from all the rest of his days. He knows who are his friends. He never speaks folly. He knows all Truth.

And His presence is a quickening fire to all who meet Him. Like cowardly Peter transformed into the intrepid speaker who converted three thousand in a day, so the world will be converted by those who hold this Name in their hearts. The Name Jesus Christ shall take me over the stormy waters of passive human experiences as Jesus walked on stormy Galilee.

The star that shone over Calvary's mountain shall shine over me. The Life all protected that folded the sinners who held on to the Name till it called the ears of the nations to their ideas, shall fold us today amid the clashings of teachings wholly unlike His, though claiming His Name.

It is no wonder at all that it has taken ages to bring us to this moment when the holy winds are about to fill the world. For the Name has had but slight hold in the mind of man. One may set his face like a flint in his will to hold out in his own ways with the Name only read from a prayer book, or spoken to the vague imaginary god or the mind, and it will not be this side of the grave that it will boom with the splendor of transfiguration.

He who holds the Name lightly shall hardly be kept from the full consequences of his own special characteristics, though he speak the high phrases of Science.

Each civilized country stands today reaping the consequences of its formal holding of the Name which has within its own potentiality the quickening energy to feed and clothe and educate every child of earth.

The fulfillment of every longing of man and angel lies with the blowing of the winds of "the Holy Ghost whom the Father will send in my Name." (John 14:26)

There is one nation, that has proclaimed great faith in this Name. Yet, it has prayed unto a god of a strange nature called bravery in danger. To please this idea of a god pleased with bravery in danger, they court dangers. They set up schools of fighting with swords to prove how like their god they can be. Now, there is never any knowing how a god of the imagination ruling over a body of men, or one man alone, will turn on his worshippers, even though they have repeated the formal words, "In His Name." Their women and dogs stay at home and do the work, while the men and horses parade before nobles. So there is much want and little hope. And it is boldly written of those brave knights that they would not dare face public opinion by refusing to gash one another's face with swords if there was a call to do so, – not a bit like Jesus Christ in this kind of ministry.

Another nation holds in mind an imaginary god who is pleased with dominion. They reap conquests over small peoples to show how their idea of God acts with them. At the last, they take pride in hunting down helpless foxes and innocent rabbits. Instead of their God taking them from glory to glory of efficiency in dominion over poverty and squalid disease, they count the victims to these foes by the millions, and helplessly bow before such captors as the Name Jesus Christ should have led captive ages ago.

What do the cries of the starving, the half paid, the discouraged today mean? They mean that there has not been the right teaching concerning

Jesus Christ. The bishopric is now being taken away from those who might have taught that it is not a superstitious manner of teaching which tells us to hold the Name of Jesus Christ in mind as the chief theme of our thought, till it quickens into the feeding, clothing, and housing power of the motherhood of God, which is the Holy Ghost Power here described.

Daniel looked in upon this day, which sees the fulfillment of the time of keeping the sufferings of a man of history, instead of His Name, in mind. "The wise shall understand," (Daniel 12:10) said the angel who showed him how we should be wondering about these strange times.

And the wise do see that with all their keeping of the words of Jesus Christ as we have them translated, there is no descent of Power over the races to put foolishness and sickness and poverty away (however unreal, the highest metaphysics may name them), till the mind of today shall obey orders like those fishermen of the Far East and kindle to living fires, with the simple holding in mind, day and night, of the Name filled with the demonstration of God among us.

Many a student of life's laws waits the very powers of wisdom he longs for, till he obeys orders, like Peter and Stephen. Many a laggard in healing efficiency and providing energies waits these signs till he obeys orders like a soldier in the ranks and fills his mind with that mysterious Name. Do you suppose it means a man of history, whose human blood was shed for us, and whom by acknowledging as the crucified Son of God we fulfill His commands? No. The Name means transformation of human traits into divine glories. It means the triumph of Spirit over matter. It means the sudden awakening of all who speak it into absolutely new conditions right here and now. It means that what is taken away is restored a hundred-fold. Whoever has the courage to hold it is hurried past the scenes of human destiny into the upper chamber of peace, where the winds of a wonderful Power shall seize him, and he can work miracles.

He that would save himself the hasty passage shall wait the miracle-working fires.

The cloven tongues, to be sure, are denial of evil and affirmation of good. But they cannot speak the language they were intended to speak, so that the multitudes can come into their rights, unless they have for their substance a Name whose body is fuel to warm a universe. The wise understand this doctrine.

July 10, 1892

Bible Lesson LIII. Acts 2:37-47. New Ideas about Healing

There is a story of the war that in a certain prison men were dying of thirst and they all fell to praying the Spirit of God for water. Directly, a living spring of water sprang up in a spot where no sign of a water fountain had ever been seen, and their thirst was quenched.

There is a story told of two missionary women, who though they had petitioned in vain to many rich men in favor of a worthy cause. They got no assistance till they knelt and prayed the Spirit of God for the direct bounty of His storehouse. The next morning they had a gift of several thousand dollars.

It is said that the Monitor could not have come sailing up to rout the Merrimac had she not been filled with the winds of prayer.

When Spiritual Science first came forth as a distinct religion, its disciples were thought to be too devoted to phenomena in their religious ideas, because they took the Bible teachings concerning healing as really meaning that people might be cured by Christ now.

Bodily healing was laid great stress upon, and it went against those teachings considerably, because the Scientists seemed to be devoting spiritual ideas to physical uses. It was a marvel that they held their own, because there were a great many of those ardent disciples themselves who had unhealed infirmities, and they often failed to demonstrate the cures their religion proclaimed itself capable of making.

It is not anything against arithmetic that a boy with a non-mathematical head cannot prove the principles proclaimed in its pages. It is all against the boy. It seemed to be against the religion itself, however, if a failure on the part of a student of Spiritual Science occurred. The practitioner and his religion were classed together as nonsense. The reason it has lived and counts its converts by thousands is because it is Truth. "The eternal years of God are here."

Healing of bodily ailments, still continues to be part of its ministry. It will form a still more marked part of its ministry when there is more stress laid upon the impartiality of the Omnipotent Spirit in dealing with mankind. If we will often assert the mighty truth that the Spirit is as liable to convert and illuminate a prizefighter as a Sunday-school superintendent, we shall see more demonstrations of the power of the Spirit. "With God is no respect of persons." (Romans 2:11)

The instant one yields his human will to its native nothingness and lets the Divine Will sift its Light through him, he is likely to have illumination of Truth which the ages will bask in. What he has been in the past counts nothing. "Though your sins were as scarlet, they shall be white as wool." (Isaiah 1:18)

He who preaches much this one special Truth of God will feel many fences being taken down. He will feel a larger humanity. He will not have any time to spend thinking his neighbor on the right is in no favor with God, while his neighbor on the left is in all favor. He will never dare say anyone did his healing by any other power than by the Spirit of God. He will be found telling that all good works have for their substance the one Spirit, as there is only one Spirit.

As we go on studying the Science of Spirit, we find that every part of our life is included in the ministry of Science. Not only bodily health, but also our support, and defense.

The result of the study is very comforting. We found that really it is as good as an army to have faith in God in a time of danger. It is as good as a bank account and a storehouse of provisions to believe that God is a Fatherly Provider.

"The Almighty shall be thy defense and thou shalt have plenty of silver." (Job 23:25)

Heretofore these Bible teachings have been considered very beautiful rhetoric but not in the least safe to follow out literally. "Trust in God and keep your powder dry," a verse from the "Ballads of Ireland," has been considered a much safer religion to follow literally. At the moment, when as students of Truth, we catch the idea that we do not have to keep our powder dry, for "the Almighty is sufficient," the Bible texts are no longer vague poetry but strong bulwarks. There is now growing swiftly a feeling that we must make great principles practical. If an Emerson tells us that "all evils are the mis-creations of the human mind," he must realize that he is telling a Truth with power in it great enough to heal him of softening brain.

What the children are taught in the classroom, they must find their teachers living forth in the church sociable. Two young men were seen kicking a little pony the other day. A lady who had always been answered insolently whenever defending animals from abuse before, said to them that it must be they knew that kindness was better than cruelty to manage animals with. They hung their heads and actually went to caressing the pony. They have evidently heard their teachers say so at school, but upon getting among men, they had found them kicking and lashing. Example is better than precept to young folk. All they needed was the sight of a wild pony tamed by gentleness, to tame their little terrified horse with the gentleness they had stored up in such a large measure within themselves. They really have as full measure of kind feeling as Jesus Christ. Schoolroom teachings bring the ideas forward. The sight of those tremendous welts on the cart-horses hide the practicality of the idea. They think men do not do the way of the moral law.

This Bible lesson (Acts Chapter 2) is an object lesson. It tells the practical result of actually accepting the gospel of Jesus Christ.

The apostles got an immense number of people to be baptized in the Name of Jesus Christ. Then the Name filled them with a mysterious intelligence. They lost all fear of coming to want, even under the reign of Tiberius Caesar, who, you remember, is historically referred to as "one of the most infamous tyrants that ever scourged the Empire of Rome." They lost all fear of sickness, all fear of pain, all fear of man or beast or instrument of death. Not only that, but they could do things. They healed multitudes – they fed thousands – they comforted everyone.

In a small way, they lived in times exactly like ours. That which was true of their bondage to Rome is true of the whole world's bondage to an Emperor who rules the whole earth now (speaking from the standpoint of appearance). This Emperor's name is Material Science.

Daniel figures this ruler as "a king of fierce countenance and understanding dark sentences." (Daniel 8:23) He takes the capitalists by the neck, and causes them to employ little children to help them get rich. He takes the laborers by the neck and combines them to do violence against those who have not his mark in their foreheads. He takes scholars by the neck and runs them into vivisection. He takes churches by the neck, and causes them to reason that the sorrows and wrongs of the poor are sent by the Omnipotent wisdom, to teach the rich generosity and compassion. And that the overbearing, and withholding of the rich are to teach the poor submission and long suffering. They thereby make the Almighty a doer of evil that good may come.

Daniel said that in this day all transgressors should come to the full. They should be brought to their full by the hastening power of Material Science. He said that this king would not reign by his own power at all, but simply by people's belief in him. But, "under his policy all manner of craft should wonderfully prosper" (Daniel 8:25) And indeed, so it has.

And indeed, how the universal belief that there is a science of war, a science of medication, a science of employing our neighbors, a science of dress manufactures, and education by material methods, has seized the race mind. But there is in reality no such science. It is only a belief.

So Daniel saw that when it should reach its fullness of dominion it should "suddenly be destroyed, and that without hand." (Daniel 8:25) For the true Science is the Science of Spirit. This Science is silently stretching forth its unseen fingers, and over the porches of every house, temple, and factory is writing, "Weighed in the balance and found wanting." (Daniel 5:27)

It is under the reign of Material Science that there are such multitudes of hungry and unemployed people while earth is teaming with productions, and the storehouses, barns, and warehouses groan with over-abundance.

The Science of Spirit operates quite differently. People shall "have all things in common." They shall "eat their bread with gladness and singleness of heart." They shall "have favor with all people." They shall not fear anything. They shall "work signs and wonders." (Daniel 6:27)

Under the reign of this doctrine, those practical signs will accompany every single man, woman, and child, which the right prayers of a few now and then bring to pass today. The state of mind that brought forth the answers for a few shall be held by a whole earth-full.

The age of Tiberius Claudius Nero took in the manhood of Christ and the Acts of the Apostles of Christ, as Material Science has been reigning since Spiritual Science was first proclaimed, and has been dealing with the disciples thereof ever since. The end of it is to be exactly like the end of Tiberius. He was murdered by suffocation by unrecognized hands. That is only a symbol of the unseen hands that will shut off the faith of the people in church, state, and educational policies. Suddenly the rich man's gold will not be worth anything, for people will not use gold in exchange. The manufacturer's warehouses will not be worth anything to him, for the people will not use that kind of goods. The scholar's Latin will be no use to him, for no one will study it any more. The chemist's compounds will evaporate unmissed, because they are no longer thought of as anything but memories of an empty dream.

The Science of Spirit takes up the same ideas the apostles held whom Luke and which the Acts tell about. It shows that all outward things are symbols of ideas held in mind. It tells us that if we live with our ideas, our worldly and physical matters will take good care of themselves. This is not true, however, if we live with false ideas.

If you are holding the idea that men ought to travel from point to point by balloons, and you sit and meditate on balloons all day long, year in and year out, there will be no signs in your affairs of true ideas holding you in their grasp – for your business and clothes will get thin like the gas and gas bags you are meditating on. If you are thinking all the time that there is but one mind in the universe, and therefore whatever that mind knows you know, and whatever you know all men know, there will come such mysterious helps to your affairs and to your possessions that you will be ready to exclaim, "Wisdom is better than riches." (Proverbs 8:11)

For it is true that there is but one mind in the universe, and it fills your mind and all minds alike. This is a healthy idea to hold to. Strong bones and vigorous limbs will grow within you. Your idea builds them. The idea ought to get such a hold on your mind that you could know all things going on everywhere every moment. It ought to get so real to you that you could hear it speak. Nothing could be lost from you. Nothing could be hidden from you. The ancients advised us to let our heads fall slightly forward, relax all our muscles, drop caring about anything, and thus give free way for a sweep of wisdom to flow through. "The spirit hath a voice to teach thee." The words that came to one mind, which had not been exhibiting wisdom, were so gracious and willing that they demonstrated in noble judgment through hard places. It was the Spirit that said: "Let divine wisdom now be demonstrated by the excellent judgment with which I administer upon affairs."

The idea that we are made entirely of Spirit is a good one to live with. It will cure a sprained ankle to think that Spirit could not be sprained. But if we were holding the idea that we were made entirely of Spirit before the chance to get sprained came about, there could not be any sprain take place. Cicero said, "For thou art not the being that this figure shows. Thou art a Divine being, since it is the Deity in thee which moves, feels, remembers, foresees, rules."

To hold the idea that we are made in reality of Spirit, and then suddenly to think of our bodies as ugly old things, or wish we could die, would certainly cause an accident of some kind. The fall of the mental barometer would be sudden, and the outward symbol would be sudden.

This keeping their mind steadfast to the "Apostle's doctrine" was what made the people that Luke tells us about so successful. It is here said that "fear came upon every soul." This "fear" is just what stirs the mind when it is aware of the importance of its thoughts. It is simply unwillingness to change the ideas from lofty to ridiculous or untrue. Following a rule in mathematics is the evidence of the same kind of fear. If we work against the rule, the answer will not come right.

To regard everything as a "sign and wonder" (Daniel 6:27) of some Spiritual idea is to get the handling of everything. According to Truth, the left arm stands for hope and the right arm stands for faith. If the left arm is injured or feeble, then, we know that we have not really hoped for some good that we ought to have taken for granted. That left arm or hand will never get well till we honestly expect that good to come to us which we will not let ourselves expect. It does not make any difference if it is the coming back of some great blessing we have lost, which seems impossible. If it is on its way to us it will be hidden by our not expecting it, and our arm will not be well.

If our right arm is hurt or feeble, it is faith we have chilled. Faith and hope ought to work together so strongly in our mind that they work out for us a sight of things as we want them. Expect everything. Have faith in its belonging to you. Then your eyes will surely see it. The sight of the eyes is the symbol of a satisfied delight of mind. If anything has been ailing your eyes you have been restless and unsatisfied, you have longed for something, and it has not come. You have not let hope and faith work actively in your mind. Studying all the principles of Spiritual Science stirs the faith and quickens the hope. Studying physical eyeballs and the nature of bones and nerves would not make the arms and eyes well.

Ideas of Spiritual things knock over the old material ideas and we do not believe at all as we used to, after a little study. Old people find out that Spirit never grows old. This idea quickens their mind and over falls the notion that they are too old to learn the noblest Science there is, in its perfection. They find that, holding steadfastly by this new idea, sets them back a few years. Holding it still more tenaciously strengthens them in their reviving. Suddenly some bad news comes. If they remember that there is no bad news in Spirit, nor to Spirit, they will rise buoyantly up, and sail like a ship over the billow. If they do not remember this part of the true Science they suddenly look as old as they ever did.

Some people are not honestly interested in the Science of Spirit for a long time. Their thoughts are all wound and twisted around material things. They only think of the Spiritual teachings in the hope to get material gains of some kind. Now, for a long time the most extraordinary blessings attend them. Their eyes are healed. Their backs are strengthened. Their families are healthy. But there is one thing that still seems to refuse to yield to all their thoughts about Spirit. They were so filled with hope at first that they rather ignored that one unchanged condition. But by and by it is thrust uppermost in their mind and they actually feel cross at the Science for not fixing up that one point.

This unmanageable condition stands for the human will. That human will is still set to material issues. It is cross-grained to Spirit. Here is an affair that never will go the way you want it. Your want must be changed; for the want is simply your ugly will. At this point Jesus Christ said we ought to take our mind entirely away from caring whether it were brought to pass or not. The dissolution of the human will is demanded. It has been an ugly clog in the passageway where some wonderful idea was meant to flow through.

The question of the bounty of God has been ignored by many spiritually minded people, for at first they were so thankful for bodily curing. But after a while they do not feel thankful for that, they are so anxious about ways and means. The Spirit has no anxiety about provisions. These "apostles" had no anxiety about provisions. Therefore, they had everything in bountiful measure. They had given up the idea of having any ugly set will about anything. "They continued praising God." While anyone is snarling and clutching after some material issue, which only the yielding of the will can put into its right place, nothing of the spiritual teaching really interests them. It drops like rain on a tin roof.

The swan praised the airs, the tinkling waters, the sunny groves, the tender grasses of another clime to the heron. "Are there any snails there?" snapped the heron. "The grace of God fills you, Divine Wisdom guides you, all is being managed in love by love itself for you," whispers the Science to one whose one sore subject is uppermost. "But if that is true why do I not have this thing?" or "why is not that event demonstrated?" snaps the unyielded listener.

All things stand for ideas. Therefore get the ideas right. Get away back to the protoplasm of a will absolutely yielded. Start an amoeba to living strength by rising up with some noble idea, which you pledge yourself to live by. Protoplasm is the life stuff that is shaken into amoebas by warmth and moisture. The degree of heat and the character of the moisture determine whether an Aristotle or a tree shall spring forth. So the submerged will is the Divine Life stuff out of which the word of what shall be done springs forth. All things are possible to them that speak their word from this last formless substance, a will lost in willingness.

The pietists of the past thought they were yielding to the rod held by Divine Love. The Scientist knows he is yielding his will, which is the only rod there can be held over him. When this is melted, the substance of his mind is the shining Substance of the God-mind. At this point the Divine fiat is spoken. Out of this he shall be fed, clothed, and housed. When a whole world takes the Science of Spirit as the word of God, it will be cured of certain ails. When it "continues in the doctrine" it will be cured of other ails. When it yields its will to bring things to pass by the science of matter, it will be found expecting all things to be furnished directly by Spirit. It is far more satisfactory to have even a little knowledge of Spirit than a large brain full of knowledge of matter. All answered prayers represent a moment of yielding to Spirit. This is the apostles' doctrine. July 17, 1892

Bible Lesson LIV. Acts 3:1-16. Heaven, A State of Mind

We do not look for a good translation of Cicero's De Senectute from a poor Latin scholar, and we should not look for a good translation of Jesus Christ's gospels from a materialist, even though he might occupy a high seat in the world's estimation.

The materialist usually makes heaven a place of abode, while the spiritual Jesus evidently meant a state of mind. The materialist does not teach that there is a state mind, possible right now, capable of healing all manner of sickness. But Jesus Christ certainly taught that there is. The materialist right in the pulpit proclaims that material methods for healing and material methods for getting a living are expected of the followers of Jesus Christ's teachings. But Jesus Christ healed by His spoken words and silent thoughts. He got His money and bread by speaking words out of whose fabric or substance He formed all He used. He told all the world to go and do likewise. He would not admit that if a man said, "I do not believe this," he was an obedient follower of His. For He would say, "Why do you not believe this when you claim to believe My words?" He most certainly would tell us that there would be more genuine education in the laws of healing by studying the meaning of His name, and by learning how to have faith in His name, than by all other studies put together.

Here are two men in Acts Chapter 3, who once knew nothing about healing the sick or addressing a multitude, but after about three years of studying spiritual teachings they have beaten the materialists of the most noted schools of pharmacy, and can address an audience so eloquently that the orators of those times are jealous of them. They have demonstrated the third strength, which John the Revelator calls the strength of the beast with the face of a man. This is the strength of doing — the strength of works.

All this world is in love with works. But nobody can work the works of God unless he has demonstrated the two strengths, which precede works. The strength to endure and the strength to dare, go before the strength of works. The strength to endure is called a lion by John. The strength to dare is called a calf. This animal always stands for youth, so John here means the daring of youth. The third strength is the strength of doing. The face of a man is his evidence, prima facie, of what he can do, what he has done, and what he is going to do. So the lame man looked on the face of Peter, the daring, and saw strength so alive and contagious that he caught strength clear down to his feet and ankle bones.

David said, "In Thy light shall we see light." (Psalm 3 6:9) Whatever quality there is about a face, which we see and appreciate – that we ourselves will be like, by looking steadfastly at it. Even the beauty of a face will transform us into beauty, if it is delightful to us.

We accomplish that which the steadfast light of our countenance shows. None can hinder or interfere with the result of our face. This face transformed from thoughts of material things to thoughts of spiritual has the healing strength of the Son of God. Paul said that in Jesus Christ we could see the light of the knowledge of the glory of God. Looking steadfastly upon this face we also shall know the glory of God.

The apostles had seen the risen Christ. They had gazed steadfastly upon Him. Thus, they were risen above the bondage of material hardships into the freedom of Spirit. The lame man caught the idea of freedom from their strong light of freedom. Seneca wrote: "We should will to be free, to snatch ourselves from the bondage of fear. You must free yourself from the fear of poverty."

The memory of a pure face in the mind, just at a moment of temptation has wrought many a miracle of resistance to temptation. In the midst of tribulation, if one can remember how the face of the vision of Jesus Christ looked, when He came that once to the view – there will a great strength to endure, and a strength to be silent come charging the fainting heart. Whenever in the vision of the night a face of wondrous light or kindness comes to one, he should keep that face ever in mind. He should obey the idea of Peter, "Look on us." Its whole meaning will come clear. Its quality will be communicated.

Do not look at the faces of people who strike you as wholly ugly. Do not remember the sinister countenance of an enemy. Their hatred for you, or against their victims, will come to be your hatred of them. "Hatred shall not cease by hatred. Always 'tis by love that hatred ceases."

This lame man had got his lameness from the face of his mother. Her face when she looked at him in her mind, before he was born, was full of some idea of a bondage. The face of a slave to even an idea is sure to communicate slavery. There is no knowing where the bondage will show forth. In this child's case, it showed forth in his feet and in his possessions. He was a slave to lameness and to poverty.

Whoever thinks that afflictions are dispensations of God, is the slave of a lie. Do not look much at him, because there is no knowing where his chains will fall on you. You do not like afflictions even in your ankle bones. And you certainly do not want your possessions to have a chain hitched around them and dragged out of your reach. Many a great orator has looked bravely out from behind the prison bars of his idea that rum is a great curse. His enlargement of nothing has strengthened the chain of your small opinion of yourself, until your small opinion of yourself has demeaned your countenance, so that people now think less of you than ever.

For why should a man think that if Jesus Christ is here there is any curse here? Is not God omnipresent? Of whose face shall he report that his thoughts have dwelt on if he would set you free? On the face of a curse which is nothing, or the face of a Christ that is all? "Who shall save us from our curse save He who seeth no curse in us?" "Who shall save us from our sin save He that seeth no sin in us?"

Mind is all. Everything and every condition is reducible to an idea. A false idea may be looked out of countenance, as this lame man's idea was dissipated. But a true idea cannot be looked out of its strength, as Peter and John held their own even while the eyes of a crowd were seeing with positiveness that they could not cure by the strength of their spirit. This is the strength of endurance. They endured or held on and held out, recognizing no power in opposition. They won the case. The man lame from birth leaped and walked, praising God. What a principle that was which they understood! We will not look on the face of one who says we may not understand the same principle now; for principle is one and eternal. Understanding is one in all men. Whoever believes differently from this carries a look of blindness to truth. He might give us blindness of eyesight. We will rather look on the face of free Jesus Christ, who said, "Go and do likewise." (Judges 7:17) "And these signs shall follow them that believe." (Mark 16:17)

These two apostles, Peter and John, exhibited the strength to hold their own without recognizing the power of opposition, because they had taken off one bandage from before their eyes. The world's idea had put it on, but the Jesus Christ idea had taken it off. That bandage over anybody's eyes always gives a countenance of weakness. It hides the "lion of the tribe of Judah." (Revelation 5:5) The weakness that comes from accusing the living creatures of the world of impure appetites is the hiding of the first strength of revelation. "My strength is as the strength of ten, because my heart is pure." "To the pure all things are pure." He who beholds all things in purity without the accusation of impurity sets free the strength of the power to endure, symbolized by the first beast in the fourth chapter of Revelation– "the lion of the tribe of Judah." (Revelation 5:5)

The strength to endure all things without being intimidated by numbers of opponents or moved by the speech of a world set against one, is uncovered by taking off the bandage of belief in the presence of evil. It is a hiding of the second strength of the face to believe that people are deceitful. They cannot deceive us by telling of the hordes of astral vampires invisible to the eyes of flesh, nor by reports of the wickedness and poverty of the living creatures on earth. There is no deception. There is no power in evil. There is no bondage to matter. This is the strength of daring, which is the strength of youth and beauty, untaught in the ways of the world, and with no example before it of the results of a truth.

One has to refuse to accuse the world of having even an appearance of the dominion of Satan. Though the voice of one who seems wise tells of the power of evil, reject his words. Injustice has no power over justice. Vice has no hold on virtue. Gold cannot buy honor. Appetite cannot decoy goodness. It will keep you young and bold forever to believe always in the goodness of people; to deny the reports against your husband, your brother, your father, your friend. To refuse to believe that people that seem good are hiding evil will make the strength of the young behemoth, whose vigor none can daunt and whose goings none can hinder. The fire and fervor of the calf of behemoth are the eternal youth of one who cannot be deceived into thinking that there is any evil where good is proclaimed. They believe in the goodness of their neighbors though a thousand tongues denounce them. They are the strong in youth and beauty. The first wrinkle sets in the face and the first darkening of the skin comes with the belief in a scandal against a friend. The young behemoth is the strongest of champions; the strength of the beauty and daring of youth is the championship of the accused.

Take off the shackles of belief in the presence of evil. "Be not deceived," (I Corinthians 15:33) said Jesus Christ. He could not see evil. Peter and John here saw only soundness and wholeness. In this bold strength of daring to see good where a world saw evil, they rose to the power of the Son of God.

The ability to accomplish great things comes forth from its hiding place under the covering of flesh with the breaking of the third wall of error built around the thoughts of the heart. "There is no condemnation to them that walk not after the flesh but after the spirit." (Romans 8:1) Take down the condemnation of mankind, from before your face. "Henceforth know we no man after the flesh but only after the Spirit." (II Corinthians 5:16) Permit the mind to speak of mankind, from the standpoint of the Spirit, not from the standpoint of flesh. As flesh, "man is as prone to err as the sparks to fly upwards." (Job 5:7) but as Spirit, "in him is no guile." (Psalm 32:2)

If what the mind dwells upon is exhibited in the face, "Who shall save us from our sins save He that seeth no sin in us?" And who shall see no sin in us save He who seeth us as Spirit, and not as flesh? It is not in the face of one who mourns over the sins of the world that we are to see the strength of salvation from sin, with healing clear down to our ankle bones. No! it is in the face of one who never speaks or thinks of the sins of the world. He has taken down the curtain of condemnation from before his strength. In the face of such a divine thinker, I see the face of Jesus Christ. In Peter and John, strong with the freedom from condemnation, strong with the sight of the "Holy One of God," the men of that day read the way to do right. The lame man felt sound and whole. He earned his own money by testimony concerning the goodness of God. Possessions flowed in upon him.

In the fearless, strong countenance of Jesus Christ, whose name was their only idea, Peter and John saw all men in one.

"I shall be satisfied when I awake in Thy likeness,"(Psalm 17:15) by seeing Thy face in all faces. July 24, 1892

Bible Lesson LV. Acts 4:1-18. About Mesmeric Powers

It is a noticeable fact that all who believe that people are exercising mesmeric powers instead of spiritual powers are reputed to be old and well stricken with years. Whenever anyone accepts the fundamental principle of Christian metaphysics, he thereby announces that he does not believe in two powers ruling the universe. He believes in one power only. Then if he talks about a second power he is talking and thinking of nothing at all. He is exercising his mind on pure nothingness. He might as well be fighting windmills in fever so far as any use to himself or anyone else is the outcome.

There are not two powers at war with each other in the universe. There is just one. That is God. The mind that imagines another power, and tries to inspire itself with zeal to fight and defeat it, is a will-o'-the-wisp mind, and must get aged and die quickly, because will–o'–the–wisps are temporal. The effect of imagining that a lover of God is exercising psychological influences is very withering. One who thus accuses his brother always has aging skin, darkening cuticle, wrinkling epidermis. Also he has the reputation of being aged, often of being dead.

To be seized with an ardor to go out and reform the world is to be seized with a sudden enlargement of the accusing instinct. How do you know that the world needs reforming? Maybe it is only yourself that needs reforming. If there is only one presence in the universe, and that is the Omnipotent God, who is it you are going to reform?

Just as soon as you sit down in Jerusalem (the self), and take yourself and all your own thoughts in hand, you will find more changed of heart and newly converted people appearing in your presence, than ever you supposed were possible. What you have thought in the closet is thus noised on the housetops. According to metaphysics, the converted, so-called, are simply showing forth their real nature. Their real nature is spotless Soul. When you think well in the temple of your own mind, they will go forth to represent your own thoughts. They could not show you their real nature while you were thinking of them as under condemnation and needing redemption.

To take the idea that there is nothing to hate is to enjoy life better. The imagination that there is something to hate is very shriveling. The knowledge that there is nothing to hate is very reviving. One can reach the point where "every prospect pleases" by thinking there is nothing to hate.

One can reach the point where he actually thrives in a house where people are speaking words of animosity. They will not seem like animosity to him. And so he will smile them out of sight. Either they will become very gentle and gracious or be taken altogether out of his way, "and the place that knew them once shall know them no more forever."

On this principle of there being nothing to hate, you can see that you ought to think that if anyone is sending what is called evil thoughts toward you, you ought to be a great deal stronger, a great deal happier than if they sent no thoughts at all, for when their ideas come near you they seem so lovely to you that you smile on them and back they return to their sender all sweet with healing praise. Who wins the case—you from your standpoint or the sender from his?

To be seized with the idea that a man needs healing is to be seized with an accusation against him. He does not need healing. You need to drop an imagination. You need to stop accusing the son of God of being unwholesome. As God pronounced the man good there must be something ailing your ideas if you do not see him as God sees him. The whole secret of mental cure is to see no disease in anyone because God sees none. Who shall save us from our disease save Him that seeth no disease in us?

There is a man in Boston who has the reputation of imagining just how a perfect human being ought to look and keeping his mind's eye on that image he has set up within his mind. Then whenever a sickly or deformed person comes into his physical sight he instantly closes his eyes and looks at the perfect image in his own mind. He then proceeds to speak mentally to that image somewhat in this fashion: "I see you, Arthur Brown, as a perfect being. There is no blemish or disease of any kind in your wonderful body. I see you perfect from your head to your feet. You are animated and vigorous, strong and healthy. I see you as every whit whole. In the name of God I pronounce you alive and strong and healthy through and through."

Of course he is more explicit sometimes and spends some time praising the parts of the beautiful image he sees within his mind which Arthur Brown has taken pains to complain of. This practitioner of healing minds his own business, and heals thousands of people by this method. There is great deal of scorn lavished on him by some who think it is more Christian to use the same kind of formula without having a mental image set up to look at while the mind is thinking of the perfect child of the living God.

Whatever way the metaphysician proceeds to "treat the case" you must know that he is the most successful who sees the least imperfection. According to this principle, you can see that it is not the reformer tearing his hair at the "appalling increase or crime," but the cool denier that there is any crime who will effect most cures of crime. There are two standpoints from which to view all the people in the world. One is from the appearance standpoint and the other is from the reality standpoint. We always see things and feel things from the standpoint from which we speak of them.

To believe that anyone can steal anything from us is exactly as bad as if we had stolen something. For, looking at life from the reality standpoint is looking at it and seeing that in Truth there is only God; so as God cannot steal anything from Himself no one is here to steal anything from anyone.

Doubtless this seems like very idealistic reasoning to people who "judge by appearances," but if it has more effect on humanity in the way of changing them to be more like God to reason this way, why not try this way?

To think that by holding the name Jesus Christ in mind we are likely to have exactly His experiences as reported by the evangelists is to suppose what is not true. To hold the two words Jesus Christ in mind is to have your own experiences hurry along and get under your feet in a very short time, instead of dragging through a haggling period of three-score and ten years.

There is a victory –just victory in the character and office of that principle called Jesus Christ. The two words mean the visibility of good. If you want to make good visible keep that name in mind. Do not neglect the twelve lessons of Science by any means, but that name in mind will hurry up the demonstration of those twelve propositions.

If you are quiet and have nothing special to attend to, then it is the time that the mind should be taking hold of some great truths of Science. "Have your feet shod with the preparation of the gospel." (Ephesians 6:15) If you are on board a steamer, look abroad over the wide waters and send the noblest thought you can think toward the land where the multitudes hide the white soul of God. Talk to the spirit of mankind concerning its perfection. This will cause the ways of the mortal to fall off like mantles for the ways of the immortal to come into sight.

If you do not sleep at night remember that it is "the Lord holdeth thine eyelids waking," (Psalms 77:4) for the purpose of uncovering your Spirit of those thoughts that make your life not pleasant. If you believe there is an evil destiny written in your stars, give orders to the stars of destiny to stand back for your victorious Spirit to walk unhindered through life.

All material things are but shades of the thoughts men have thought. They have no reality in them. All astral shapes are but the shades of thoughts men have thought. There is no reality in them. All miseries are but the shades of the thoughts men have thought. There is no reality in them. All the thoughts that made the shades are no-thing — no-thing at all.

This is no new doctrine. That all the sensible, material world is phantasm has been taught for ages. That only the good has any reality is the oldest doctrine known to man. That healing from sin is seeing no sin is gospel teaching. That curing of disease by seeing no disease is the quickest curing, is the oldest practice on the globe.

Jesus Christ had no new doctrine. The apostles who stand here in this fourth chapter of Acts do not claim that they have anything original. They do not think that Jesus Christ made a great discovery. They simply think He lived His principle, and so are they living His principle.

To see all around a question is to decide upon it very differently from what we would decide if we saw half way around it. The Sanhedrin sat in a semicircle and judged concerning the merits of the Christian doctrine from a half–way–round standpoint. They knew enough to know that these healers of disease had cured by using a Name in which they believed. They had heard of such things before. This made them very learned judges on the subject of healing by names. But here again they saw only from a semicircular standpoint (also sitting point, which is all the more typical of their mental viewing of spiritual principles). They did not know that the Name that stands for the Omnipotent Jehovah is the only name that can take unlettered fishermen and make them the peers of the Sanhedrin; and more than their peers. They do not see that it is the power of a Name that discomfits them in the presence of two wandering Jews. All they see is that by the use of a Name a lame man has been healed.

They are grieved because 5,000 people have been converted to confidence in the truthfulness and divinity of one who lived a principle. Annas, Caiaphas, John and Alexander sit in adverse judgment on the Name that can work miracles, on the men who work miracles by the Name, and on the working of miracles in general.

This is not only historic. It is what is transpiring within your own mind this minute against your two-miracle-working powers. You have a Peter and John pair of faculties in your mind. The Peter faculty is bold and reckless in trusting to the Spirit to support you, defend you, and heal you. The John quality does not see the evils, does not feel the material conditions. The Peter sees the material situations, but denies them recklessly. Putting these two faculties forward when you see a cripple will heal him. The two faculties, or ideas, are sure to come forward if the Jesus Christ principle is once accepted by your mind. The more closely you occupy your mind with the Name of Jesus Christ while the twelve laws of Science are being worked, the more boldly will the Peter and John stand out and the closer they will stand together. They are a sure cure for deformity.

They are the denial and affirmations of Science actually speaking aloud to the public audience of all the thoughts you ever thought. Now up comes your religious and worldly Sanhedrin.

The "Annas" impression within your own mind is that you are ambitious. The "Caiaphas" impression says you are deceived into thinking that a mere personal influence or will power or thought transference is a true healing. This will invariably fill your boldness with the Holy Ghost power. You will know you are right to be bold in the cause of Spirit, and right to stand steadfast to the point or reality utterly oblivious to appearances.

But the Sanhedrin of your judgment cannot tolerate the reputation of a John utterly abstracted from appearance and a Peter defying them. You fear that people will fear that you have lost your good judgment. You forget that Jesus Christ teaches that people are the expressions of your own thoughts. The John of the Sanhedrin is the forgetfulness of your primal principle. John is always abstracted. He is either utterly oblivious of both principle and personality, as John in the Sanhedrin, or utterly oblivious of materiality as John the apostle.

Here you will perceive that you are afraid of losing your prestige. Fear is a monster. But what are we afraid of? The principle idea of the Jesus Christ teaching is that there is nothing to fear. The greatest promise of Principle is that He leads captivity itself captive.

Here is the time to be quiet and watch principle removing all fear. The Sanhedrin of past ways of thinking should be kept utterly silent within your mind when you feel like trusting the Spirit, and also when you recognize what it is to see from the spiritual standpoint. You should not argue a word with your Peter and John. If you do you will command yourself to be silent with respect to your doctrine instead of with respect to your accusations.

The greatest accusation you make against your miracle-working energies is that they do not know anything. "They do not realize what they are about." You reflect that there has never been anyone living on the face of the earth who holds on to the spiritual doctrine against the power and learning of the world. Peter says, "I don't care if there hasn't." John says, "Eye hath not seen nor ear heard, but to us it is given to know what is in God." All the memories within you remind you that Jesus was crucified, the apostles were murdered, the converts were martyred. None of them lived against a learned church, which looked coldly on miracles. Your own mind accuses your own energies of not knowing what they are about. You accuse your own highest powers of foolishness and ignorance. You accuse all the people of the world of foolishness and ignorance who permit themselves to speak boldly against the reality of every material thing and every thought of materiality. You accuse all the people of the world of foolishness and ignorance who speak steadfastly from the absolute standpoint. The absolute standpoint is the standpoint of Absolute Spirit, where even the ideas of carnal mind are forgotten. But you fear that since no one has lived through the ordeal no one can.

These are the days prophesied when the Spirit shall be poured out on all men, and there shall be but one Lord mentioned, and His name One. "They shall not hurt or kill in all my holy mountain." (Isaiah 65:25) You may keep still and not accuse. You may be silent and not remember about the demonstrations of the past thinkers. One thing is expected of all the people of this age, viz., that they will "forget the things that are behind and press on to the things that lie before." (Philippians 3:13) One always begins anew by ignoring the past. You can keep silence with respect to all things. Most certainly, the Sanhedrin of the past, which is your church and school, has no such quickly working principle as these two ideas (denial and affirmation according to Jesus Christ) demonstrate. Therefore, the old judgment ought to keep still.

Stop the accusation of foolishness and ignorance. Stop thinking anyone has to be taught anything, exactly as you would stop thinking anyone has to be converted or redeemed. The whole secret of inspiration through your whole mind lies in dropping the idea of there being any foolishness or ignorance in anyone or anything.

The Sanhedrin should have kept silent in its accusation that the two men who wrought the miracle were foolish fanatics. They should have kept silent in their belief that these two ideas would steal any prestige from them.

Prestige is of the Spirit. "The Spirit bloweth where it listeth." (John 3:8) Their belief that they could be stolen from caused them to be thieves, though they stole nothing. They attempted to steal the liberties and reputation of two men, but as there cannot be any stealing, they stole nothing. Their fear of being stolen from acted like Job's fear upon them, for even their names are forgotten, while posterity is ashamed of their memory as posing for wisdom. If they had been silent, they would have received the fourth strength of the Spirit, which is the strength of inspiration, the strength of wisdom.

Let the judgment council ever sitting in its semi–circle of only half appreciating the situation you are now placed in, keep absolutely still. Silence will be the opportunity for divine inspiration to thrill you. Isaiah says that the strength of Zion is to sit still. He says that your strength is to be demonstrated through quietness and confidence. The inspiration of Omniscience will quicken your mind by keeping still when the great ideas of Science come into your mind. You do not accuse those who speak them of not demonstrating. This is the speech of those who complain of Jesus for not coming down from the cross, and snarling against the martyrs for not stepping forth out of the flames and the racks.

John the Revelator saw how the fires of a sudden and wonderful inspiration should kindle in the face of one who should not accuse the high doctrine as folly. He pictured it forth as the eagle, which if it light on the earth, knows now the bondage of earth, because its pinions are swift and strong. It builds its nest on the unscalable mountains. Its eye gathers its strength of sight from the blazing sun of the noontide. All the flying things fall back before it. The earth is nothing to it only to do its bidding. The waters are nothing to it only to obey its behests. The airs clear the way for its flying. The sun is its strength.

This lesson is one. It has many suggestions. It brings to mind all the doctrines of Jesus, but its point is one, viz., when you would feel not to know which way to turn – when it seems as if your good name would be lost if you did not defend yourself – when you reflect that you have never seen the spiritual doctrine hold its disciples victorious during their lifetime – when you would accuse yourself of having made a blunder (as the Sanhedrin), keep still and watch the majestic operation of the name Jesus Christ – the inspiring wisdom of the Spirit.

In you, there is the Holy Ghost, which inspired Peter and pressed for the silence of that council and for the setting free of Peter and John. In you it whispers: "By your silence as to doctrines of men, I, the Spirit within you, am able to light my candle of inspiration at the shining fires of

Omniscience. By your silence I am able to fly the boundaries of the senses and live the ideal life free thought can find. I will build your house of honor in the watch–towers of Omnipotence. I will fix the glory of Jehovah on your patient face. The fourth strength of God shall be yours. This is the strength of inspiration. The shades of the dead shall not be in the earth or on the waters or airs where you fly. You shall be fearless and free, wise, buoyant, and honored. Gird on the armor of silence under the accusation of folly, and Christ shall give thee light."

He, "when He was reviled, reviled not again, and as a sheep before her shearers is dumb, so He opened not His mouth."

Now is the great time for silence among the thoughts of the mind. The time of the Spirit is ripe. That which was nineteen hundred years ago is now and there is nothing new. "Endure as seeing Him who is invisible." (Hebrews 11:27) "Fear nothing." (Mark 16:6) "Look unto Me and be ye saved." (Isaiah 45:22) The strength of Zion is silence. The inspiration of silence is now wisdom. July 31, 1892

Bible Lesson LVI. Acts 4:19-31. Points in the Mosaic Law

Sitting in a semicircle, the Sanhedrin saw only half way round the question of right. So they commanded Peter and John not to speak and teach in a certain Name. This was because it would surely seem as if they must have been in the wrong in their idea of religion if the apostles were right. For by the religion of the apostles great signs were given, while with their religion there was only discussion of nice points of Mosaic law.

At first when great spiritual truths are presented only a few can see them. Those few are always fired by those truths with boldness to speak them, which is wonderful. Truth is a fire that burns by itself. The only fuel it needs is words. Keep on speaking or thinking as we are led and the fire keeps on burning. One has to tell the strongest and fiercest ideas he has in his mind in order to get wholly on fire. There are some fierce truths under the cover of these simple texts of Acts 4:19-31, which will kindle a wonderful flame of immortal light and beauty within us if we will read them.

The first is that no one ever needed to be taught anything. The highest doctrine of the archangels is known to the roughest human mind. They are closed pages or open ones, according as he expresses what he knows or keeps still.

To open a class with the knowledge that everyone knows exactly as much as the teacher will help the teacher to express himself more powerfully. Peter and John spoke out the folded judgment of the Sanhedrin. It is only clasping the covers down on a wonderful book when people talk about colds and coughs, and cheating. These things not being true will not kindle that wonderful fire which such words as eternal health, immortal safety, everlasting increase, will kindle.

The Sanhedrin knew exactly what was right. They did not express it. The apostles did express it, and at once, the Sanhedrin let them go. Even a horse will not hurt you if you tell him what is right. A lady was telling of how she spoke to a runaway horse about obeying God and not fear, and her idea stopped him at once. Another was telling of speaking to a tramp who has seized her, about the God of right not letting him do any harm, whereupon he suddenly let her go and ran away. Both those ladies thought the ideas silently within their own minds. It was appealing to what the beast and the man both knew in common. Even the stones know what is right and will give us our freedom if we speak to them. The intelligence of right is everywhere and in everything. Intelligence is Omnipresent. What shall we do to make the beasts and the stones do the right they already know? Speak to them. "Without the word nothing is made" manifest.

And when once we begin to speak what is right and true, there is no stopping our utterance. It keeps getting fiercer and hotter till the houses are shaken where we are speaking. The earth that seems so immovable shall itself "reel to and fro like a drunker man," saith the Scripture, when everyone speaks forth what he has kept silent about so long.

The Indian whispers to his pony and he speeds like the wind. What does he tell him? He speaks to that intelligence that is more fleet than light and it lifts the willing limbs to fly to the rocks of protection. The jockey in the Country Fair has unwittingly given the secret of making the prize horse. He told him that he must win, for the family needed the money with which to get out of debt. The love in the horse is God. Is anything too hard for love? Intelligence is love.

The apostles only spoke just Truth enough to set themselves free. They might have spoken enough to set the Sanhedrin free. Why did they not speak so much? Just as Jesus Christ said, "I have many things to say unto you, but ye cannot bear them now."

Intelligence as to what is exactly right always blunts the intelligence of what is wrong. Have you never been surprised when acting innocently and in good faith to see how many ideas people would hunt up to devise against you? "Lying in wait for the righteous to condemn them for a word." But when their judgment is appealed to be your knowing exactly what is right they cannot think of another thing, and what they have said of evil falls into nothingness, is forgotten. Lies are nothing. Evil devices are nothing. They fall of their own weight if you hold fast to your knowledge of what is right.

"Right is right as God is good,
And right the day will win;
To doubt would be disloyalty,
To falter would be sin."

Because the apostles knew in their hearts, and the Sanhedrin knew in their hearts, and it was spoken very definitely, the Sanhedrin could not think of a single other thing to do by which to hurt the apostles. So they let them go.

There will come a time when your enemies cannot think of another thing against you. And what they have already devised will not count against you. It will be something for them to work out of themselves. History records that this Sanhedrin and the Roman emperors and high officers who persecuted the Christians all met most horrible fates. What was such a sequel the sign of? Simply of not expressing what was right. What is this law of hardship and suffering which causes the silence as to what mankind knows to be right? It is the law of shadows. As the darkness gets darker when the sun is hidden by the earth, so the hardship gets harder when the expression of what we know is hidden. We must either speak boldly or think loudly what we know is right.

You will notice that the apostles never took any credit to themselves for having cured a man over forty years old of a congenital deformity. They took it as much for granted that the name Jesus Christ would work through them to heal as that the man Jesus Christ had worked healing. They had easy faith for healing. They had not such easy faith for their own defense, however, and were utterly astonished that their appeal to the judgment of the Sanhedrin had set them free. Just as soon as they arrived at a place in mind where they would expect to be kept as free from danger as they were to be full of healing power, they would get easily out of every kind of danger and would absolutely escape martyrdom.

Evidently, the apostles never had the confidence in their doctrine to defend them that they had to support and heal them. That they were finally martyred is evidence that they had no great faith in God as absolute safety.

Here they convened together to give thanks unto God for all that had been done and to ask for still further help. We cannot ask too greatly of the Spirit of God. The only fault is that we do not ask enough. We often say: "All I ask is for just enough to do this or that." That sort of an idea is worse than not asking anything. It carries the idea of limitation. It is an intimation that God is so stingy that He will be pleased at our asking so much less than

He expected we would draw upon Him for. Whoever has made such an expression had very economical, miserly people around him when he was young. He is "about forty years old" in ankle twisting, like this man Peter and John healed.

The apostles here asked for the most stupendous gifts. They asked that wonderful signs might be given them that the whole earth might know they were right.

Before they stated exactly what they wanted, they described the character, and nature and works of their God. This was fuel to the fire of their spirit. We can see by this principle of describing in such glowing and extravagant language the nature and office of their spirit, that the same principle operates when we describe evil. There is but one principle. Principle means unvarying and logical sequence. The unvarying logical sequence of describing the power of God in the very highest and most majestic language the mind can bring forth, is to set fire more and more to our spirit within us until it makes outside things obey us exactly. Hezekiah won a mighty battle by first describing his God mightily. The reformers have increased pauperism and crime by describing these things as "terrible," "enormous," "fearful," "increasing." This talk feeds their belief and outside things have to act it out. The same principle holds good in everything. There is but one principle. The same principle operates with the prizefighter as with the preacher of righteousness. One thinks highly of his strength and the other thinks powerfully of Satan one moment and of God the next. Each meets in life what he describes.

There is your son; you look at him with a miserable regret that those bad boys have such a hold on him. They come into your mind as terrible. When you speak of them, you tell how strong their influence is. This way of thinking and speaking has to show out. Do you hear that voice near you saying, "Look unto Me"? (Isaiah 45-22) Turn and describe Jesus Christ as having all the power in creation. Tell what a mighty influence the Jesus Christ this moment is exercising over and in and through your boy. Rise higher and higher in your magnifying. These words will have a sequence; that sequence, still another. On with the praise of the Omnipotent Jesus! The very house may shake when you are talking to that Presence.

Now, where is the power of two, or four or nine boys over your boy? Nowhere. And those boys, are they bad as you thought? No, by no means! They suddenly take new turns – take to study, to trades, to thinking. You were utterly responsible for all they seemed to do before by not describing them as Jesus Christ saw them. Swedenborg says the angels looking at us see only our virtues — our faults are blank to them.

"But," you say, "the boys were bad before I saw them as bad." Because you saw what someone else had thought, you caught a memory that had followed them around from somewhere or someone. Why did you not have stamina enough to think for yourself instead of picking up other people's notions?

The fifth affirmation of Science would be a good one for you to hold often: "I am governed by the law of God, and cannot sin, cannot suffer for sin, nor fear sin, sickness or death."

This principle is God. It rules everything. Describe yourself, keep on describing yourself, and you will become externally just what you describe. Many people are poorly thought of by their neighbors because they once used to describe themselves as less thought of than someone else – or less successful than someone else. Other people feel their self–description. For one to say, "I am prosperous and powerful and strong and great," is to give every thought in his mind a chance to enlarge itself. The slumbering malice of his nature may rise right up and appropriate that, "I am powerful and strong," and all his virtues may stand back in amazement. So do his neighbors when his malice gets to acting out. Here is when the name Jesus Christ is the Savior. Malice cannot get any hearing at all – it is converted into love by the name Jesus Christ. These apostles described their God nobly as Creator and Governor and Keeper, but they said that all their noble description applied to God as the Jesus Christ of man, the meek and mighty lover of all people, seeing in them all nothing to condemn.

This trait lies very low, very deep, very hidden in mankind. It must be warmed out of its hiding place in us by the most brilliant and glorious description we can make. To the Jesus Christ in the world, to the Jesus Christ in each mind — hidden but living — SPEAK!

This is "Jesus Christ in you the hope of Glory." (Colossians 1:27)

Not till after many of these wonderful descriptions of Spirit did the mighty signs follow the apostles. They increased in power, and strength and wisdom daily. They became – filled and blazing with spiritual power. They became the increasing successes of the world. They would not have been known as anyone, and today would have been as unknown as were their cousins and grandfathers, had it not been for their describing God as Jesus Christ.

Emerson tells us that largeness of influence, and largeness of power, is demonstrated only by the healthy constitution. Eric is capable of reaching Newfoundland because he has just such a store of energy and health, of mind and body; but Biorn and Thorfin will – sail farther and reach Labrador and New England because their store of power is greater. Without the doctrine of Jesus Christ in you might be a Boswell; with it you might be a Shakespeare of originality and grandeur. Without this character within you warmed into shining appearance, you might be a whining invalid. With the description of this hidden glory within you, wooed forth into the splendor of its highest demonstration, you are King of kings and Lord of lords.

Elisha described God mildly and sweetly. He went about his prayers as modestly as a simple girl. His healing power, his comforting force, ceased with his martyrdom. But Jesus — "I am the Light of the world," (John 8:12) "I am with you always" (Jeremiah 42:11) — the Life of the ages. The dead of the misty past shall rise and walk in his Life. The living and the dead of the momentous present may be healed and rise triumphant now into glorified Life; future nations and armies are destined to live and transfigure in the light of His Name.

And all who know only the Jesus Christ power and purpose within themselves shall be Jesus Christ. For we are that which we know and we do that which we are. Therefore, knowing only Jesus Christ, we are that character, and being that character we do His works.

He, to whom the principle of meekness and majesty, non-condemnation and nonresistance, exhibited by Jesus Christ seems far off and almost impossible because of education or personal traits, must call himself into the circle out of his half-exposed powers of trust to the Name without reasoning why, till the power of it breaks forth some day.

"The Holy Ghost, whom the Father will send in My Name," (John 14:26) is the final victory for which the soul longs, and presses to demonstrate. All the earth was made to be under our feet — not by strife and competition, but by the easy faith of the soul in its right to dominion. No other way ever marked out has the soul's acquiescence save that which is herein taught by this chapter. Knowing this will win – who shall hesitate to undertake to cast himself into that trust in it, which the apostles showed forth? Who will hesitate to cast himself into an infinite trust in it, far out of the reach of that trust of the apostles? Who is afraid to trust his life, his talents, his powers, his time, his money, his reputation, to this Spirit of Love and Power and Light, knowing no other name, no other object, no other friend or foe, time or circumstances, save it alone?

In the last days of confidence in material things the Angel or Spirit shall stand in the sun proclaiming to mankind that all things have the spirit of wisdom lying deep waiting our praises to spring forth into loving obedience.

The Sanhedrin forbids us to teach that all things are filled with intelligence, and can understand our speech. The hard Sanhedrin itself yielding to speech is demonstration against its beliefs. If that fossilized body could dissolve from its sternest purpose by an appeal to its judgment, even the hardest of stones may melt into milk for our refreshment.

Disease, age, death, and poverty — these will yield up their treasures. Buddha, the wise, caught a hint of this doctrine: "I now will seek a noble law unlike the worldly methods known to man. I will oppose disease, and age and death, and strive against the mischief wrought by these on men.

It is a fierce truth to tell, but it is fuel to the fires of power when we say that there is as much intelligence in the rock as in the brain of man – in the fly as in the archangel – for intelligence is Omnipresent, Omnipotent God – absent from nothing in majesty, love, and responding kindness.

The two are dropping great secrets to them that believe in their wisdom. The stars are letting fall the words, men have waited for ages to hear. They promise, and teach and foretell. The commonest things are not what they seem. They are God in their substance, God in their wisdom, God in their love. There is no place, where there is more God than another. "If I make my bed in hell, Thou art there." (Psalms 138:8) Believest thou this? To believe it is life and the power of the Holy Ghost. There is nothing so joyous to believe as that all is God. August 7, 1892.

Bible Lesson LVII. Acts 5:1-11. Napoleon's Ambition

Victor Hugo wrote of Napoleon at Waterloo: "Awaiting the throne of the world, St. Helena became visible."

In this lesson of Acts, fifth chapter, first to eleventh verses, two people are awaiting the honors of a company of noble-minded people, and the tomb of disgrace becomes visible.

Paul wrote to the Galatians: "Whatsoever a man soweth, that shall he also reap." (Galatians 6:7) Napoleon sowed ambition and reaped St. Helena. These two sowed ambition and reaped their St. Helena — apples of Sodom.

It is written of every human being that he has four A's to overcome in his nature, born with him, leering along by his side and sifting their flavor through all his thoughts. The four A's stand for Approbativeness, Amativeness, Ambition, and Acquisitiveness.

They are all purely mortal characteristics, and show forth in their order, most apparent in the four quarters or seasons of human life, namely, childhood, youth, middle age, and old age. Some people take all four of the A's along through the whole passage from so-called birth to so-called death; these have the strange marks in their faces which make them called "disgusting". That is the way approbativeness indulged in, finally rewards its victims. Awaiting the smiles of empires, we meet the common disgust.

Each of the four A's permitted to get lodgment serves its recipient with the same fate. Here it is ambition and approbativeness united. In Napoleon, it was ambition, pure and simple. He cared for no favor of God, man, or Satan, so he carried his point. These two cared, beyond all things for praise, but were bent on carrying out their own purposes also.

"A house divided against itself cannot stand." (Matthew 12:25)

Ambition and approbativeness in the same head, work cross-purposes. Sudden death at the sudden crossing of their swords is very common.

Peter himself had been a great liar. This is what makes him so horrified at these two poor little liars. A coward is always greatly disgusted at the cowardice of another. We all make a great show of disgust at the very things we most tend to ourselves. This is the law of mortality.

Ananias means, "grace of the Lord" and Sapphira "beautiful". On the spiritual side of the nature there are four A's. They are the substance of which the other four A's are the shadow, namely: Artlessness, Attractiveness, Aspiration, and Ascendancy.

He who talks much or believes much on the side of evil cannot help showing one or the other of the first four A's in a marked fashion. He who talks much on the side of the good and will not admit that there can be any evil in a universe occupied by goodness, cannot help showing forth all of the last four A's sooner or later.

Ananias and Sapphira had permitted themselves to discuss the question of poverty. It is a poor question to discuss. Plenty of people have shut off their time among us by reason of having discussed the idea of poverty. It is a discussion of nothing, a discussion of absence, a discussion of vacancy. Whatever we discuss comes to pass upon us. Discuss nothing and come to nothing. We may discuss within our own mind, all alone by ourselves, a vacancy or lack, till the place that knew us once, shall know us no more forever.

These two people had two themes, which their names signified on the spiritual side, which they ought to have discussed continually. These two themes were the grace of God, and the beauty of comeliness. In speaking of the grace of God, Ananias would have come up high into the mountains of the truth that God is such an abundant Provider that wherever the word is spoken that "God is my support and the support of the universe," it shall be proved by some marvelous benefaction or unexpected success.

It was intended by his spiritual nature that he teach those who were destitute. He was intended by his spiritual nature to teach those destitute disciples the law by which Jesus made up purses for His twelve missionaries to pay their way without having to beg, borrow, or work for their money. Talking on that side and meditating on that idea, would have made Ananias a teacher of the law of self–increasement. But you see he talked and thought on the nothing or absence side. So he "died".

Death is nothing but a hiding. It always comes as a result of thinking about nothing. Nothing else ever brought on death in the world but talking of nothing. The absence of riches means no riches. "No riches" is but another expression for "nothing." Very likely he had said, "Poor Peter; too bad he has no money; nice man; strange this law of healing will not work in supporting its followers without calling on us. I declare! Now wife, we have worked carefully to save our money, and it seems pretty hard on us to give it up to these poor fisher folk, who never had anything before and very likely will not know what to do with it. Your father would feel pretty bad if he could rise from his grave and see us throwing away his hard–earned dollars this way."

Thus they talked on the vacancy and absence and nothing side till it actually "killed them". Killing is only thinking on the nothing or absence or vacancy side, till it suddenly demonstrates. All "sudden deaths," or being "murdered," as the mortal expressions run, come to those only who have had a perpetual discussion on the absence or vacancy of something or other. Talk of nothing and come to nothing. Put this down as an axiom in metaphysics.

Do not give pennies to so–called beggars with the idea of their being "poor things." If you do, you will come short exactly as much as you gave. How should you give them their pennies? Exactly as you would "carry coals to Newcastle" or give a lace handkerchief to Mrs. Vanderbilt. The bounty of Jehovah Jireh is pouring down its sluice — ways forever to man. There is no exception. How can we see it? By talking about it, thinking about it, and rejoicing in it.

Approbativeness, amativeness, ambition, and acquisitiveness, are all on the nothing side. They are on the vacancy side. They are words, which mean absence. They will hide anyone who will let them get a hearing. Artlessness, attractiveness, aspiration, and ascendancy, are words on the substance side. Whoever thinks or talks upon the ideas which these words bring up, will show out great beauty and power of character. Talk about the defense of innocence, the comfort of the spirit, the enchantment of inspiration, the grandeur of goodness, all the time, and there cannot any death ever occur.

Death of anything is only hiding it. Nothing need be hidden. Life need not be hidden; beauty need not be hidden; riches need not be hidden. Nothing hid beauty but talk and thought on the absence and vacancy side. Remember death is only hiding. To speak of riches as hidden means the same as calling people poor. It is death of their riches. Death is only a hiding. Nothing need be hidden. "There is nothing hidden that shall not be revealed." (Matthew 10:26)

Are you in the habit of speaking of your business slightingly? It will soon be hidden. You are talking of the absence side. Do you pay your servers less than they earn, on the plea that you cannot afford more? Something will hide from you. Maybe someone will hide. Many a toothless, homely old woman commenced to hide her beauty when she "made believe" to someone that she had not in her possession something which she had.

There is never any telling where "the make believe" will strike. Love is sometimes hidden by "making believe" that we do not know something that we do know. Children are often hidden by our making believe we believe something, which we do not. The other name for "making believe" is either approbativeness or ambition. Either one will strike something out of sight. You cannot tell how the idea that four plus one makes seven will work out your problem in arithmetic or trigonometry; so I cannot tell you just how your present "A" will strike your affairs.

Jesus just stood and cried at the grave of Lazarus because Lazarus and his two sisters had talked about His absence till it had made them so sick in heart and head that one of them had "died" (became hidden). The fact is, and was and ever shall be, that Jesus Christ is in us, and near us and with us. He had been with them all the time in Spirit. (If they had not talked of His absence in Spirit, He could never have seemed to be absent).

What was the weeping of Jesus? Was it not grief at their thought of absence? But if He grieved at their idea of absence, was it not just as bad as for them to believe in absence? Yes. What we complain of in another is what we are thinking about. He did not truly grieve. He did not truly recognize their talk of absence. That was the way He seemed to them to be doing. When the Spirit descended upon Him and said with a loud voice, "This is my Beloved Son, in whom I am well pleased," (Matthew 3:17) they said it thundered. When He hung on the cross and cried with a loud voice, "How Thou hast glorified Me!" the people said He cried, "My God, why hast Thou forsaken me?" (Matthew 27:47)

In the same way, while He was giving thanks in great ecstasy of gratitude to the presence of life, they said He was mourning at death. Then He spoke His silent thanks aloud, and explained that He only spoke aloud because of the people thinking He was mourning.

It was the habit of the people constantly to misrepresent His words. Therefore, He spoke in object lessons. He promised to become visible again among all people as a pure, spiritual doctrine, without any parables. That time is now.

There are a few words He is speaking on the spiritual side, which make those who hear them very happy. There is inspiration in them. To hear them is to breathe them in. To breathe them in is to understand them. Understanding is the right word to use for aspiration. Aspiration in its true sense is the breathing in of the Spirit. It is a good treatment to think silently in the mind that we are now breathing Spirit. The air is Spirit. The air is God. Breathe deeply and be pleased to be breathing God. Some people have been cured by doing this.

One word, Jesus Christ is now speaking, is that there is nothing to overcome and there was never anything to overcome. Another word is that there is no defeat possible to the one who is in the right. He cannot even seem to be defeated, if he will hold himself from talking or thinking on the defeat side. Defeat is absence of victory. Absence is vacancy. It is the law that to talk on the defeat side is to talk on the nothing side, and to hide the victory side. This victory is not the overcoming of something, but the bringing to light of something.

Wherever did the church get the idea that the Christian life is a warfare? Not from Jesus, most certainly, for He was very explicit in proclaiming His doctrine as an easy one. "I will give you rest." (Exodus 33:14)

Emerson tells of "Benedict," who though not quoting Jesus Christ for saying that, "My words are life," (John 6:63) yet kept himself alive and came off conqueror by talking and thinking on the "word–of–life" side. Hear him: "I am never beaten. I meet powerful, brutal people to whom I have no skill to reply. They think they have defeated me. It is so published in society, in the journals; I am defeated in this fashion, in all men's sight, perhaps on a dozen different lines. My ledger may show I am in debt, cannot yet make my ends meet, and vanquish the enemy so. My race may not be prospering; we are sick, ugly, obscure, unpopular. My children may be worsted. I seem to fail in my friends and my clients, too. That is to say, in all the encounters that have yet chanced I have not been weaponed for that particular occasion, and have been historically beaten. And yet I know all the time that I have never been beaten, have never yet fought, shall certainly fight when my hour comes, and shall beat."

Dante tells us that on the planet Mars we will find the saints of earth, who fought and bled in great bravery for the cause of Christ. But Spiritual Science teaches us that those who "fought the good fight" and died as brave martyrs now know that they did not need to believe in the possibility of martyrdom. There was nothing to fight for, nothing to resist, for the doctrine of Jesus was safety enough. "My words are Life." (John 6:63)

They did not need to hold out bravely against opposition. There was nothing to oppose. "My words are peace." They are entirely careful now to be found speaking on the peace and freedom and easy side. They understand this teaching about not hiding anything, by talking of its presence, instead of its absence. They know that the four A's all belong to the vacancy side, and to be admitting that we have any one of them is to be hurrying to look upon our sandy St. Helena, or our sandy sepulchre. They hear the voice of their victorious comrade, Isaiah, in its truest word, that the strength of Zion is to sit still – not to compete in the lists with mankind.

Take up this song of the Spirit: My strength is in my peaceableness. My strength is in my meekness. I compete with none. Thereby I am now victorious. My strength is in that I neither strive nor cry nor try.

There shall not a bone of my world be broken. Because with Jesus Christ, who ran not in the lists for the favors or possessions of men, I also run not, but am at home in my house of content. There was never any power risen against me or my doctrine. And I am not and never was a power risen against any doctrine. High over the memories of my words, which made my walk upon earth with the banner of truth over my head, a warfare, rises my spirit, buoyant, unchallenged, unhindered, knowing no warfare and nothing to win, for this is the rest of Jesus. On the earth, this rest is mine for the taking. There is no death to their hopes for them that speak of the Spirit.

Hereby we are sowing the seeds of immortal life to reap Jesus Christ, our King.

August 14, 1892

Bible Lesson LVIII. Acts 5:25-41. A River Within the Heart

It is said that pure water if it were set running over the earth would dissolve the rocks, the sands, the woods, the lead pipes, the iron pipes; nothing could withstand it.

There is a river within the deeps of the heart clear as crystal which, if it were set flowing, would dissolve the flesh, dissolve the intellect, dissolve the sorrows, the pain, the poverty of the world. It is the clear water of a pure motive, a noble purpose. A purpose is that which one has resolved to be and to do. Sometimes the God — implanted purpose is not let to run forth at all. It is not thought out in the mind. It is not spoken by the lips. If one has let the deep crystal purpose of God in his heart be thought out by his mind, he has made a channel for the dissolving motive to flow outward over his world, and it is written of him that he is good and great.

Newton said, "Let physics beware of metaphysics." The prophet when feeling the Spirit inspire him, said, "The earth is clean dissolved before me." The pure motive in the heart says, "I dissolve slanders; I melt false reports; I disintegrate oppositions."

People talk of the seven millions of incurable invalids in the civilized world. People talk of the immorality of the globe. They inform me that the rich are becoming richer and the poor poorer by the mistaken legislations of the nations. But the scriptures tell that this is nothing, nothing at all, in the truth of a principle believed in. The scriptures tell me that if a few, a very few, people would mean exactly what they say when they are praying, their meaning would dissolve the sickness, melt the wrongs, make straight through the deserts of poverty, a highway for the bounty of God to flow down, and put away forever the legislation of councils all over the earth.

We find that the best of men do not let the crystal spring of their God — implanted motive really express itself even in their thinking. The Buddhist or Brahmin saint abjects himself down the act of burying himself in the sands for weeks that he may show how absorbed into the universal oneness of Brahma he may get himself, but there is a rock laid across the fount of his spirit which keeps him from accomplishing his wishes. That rock, he never attempts to dissolve by stirring to action the deep crystal sea at the root of his soul. At his lowest point of abjection, he never means to give forth the truth that the soul of the woman is God as the soul of the man is God. So he works at the problem of how to be well, how to be prosperous, how to be happy, and lies down with the question unsolved.

The minister of the civilized religions of earth prostrates himself into humblest devotion, but there is a rock laid across the dissolving waters in the deeps of his soul which he never attempts to touch by stirring into action the marvelous truth that there is no necessity for evil in God's universe. He tells of the One Presence all God. He tells just as sternly of the necessity for evil in that One Presence. Or if as the mystic, he forgets to think it in consciousness, as the object of his devotions, it is an unsolved creed in his mind unconscious.

At the most dazzling heights of priestly devoutness does the praying man leave across the springs of his soul an ugly blockade of expectation to depend on the money of men to support him? Then he does not mean what he says when he tells the Most High that He is the support of the widow, the provider of all men. The crystal waters of dissolution of want, the melting of need, are not let to flow. He must still work at his question of life with the expectation that men will provide, while his lips praise his God for providing.

"This people honoreth Me with their lips, but their heart is far from Me." (Mark 7:6)

In metaphysics, we affirm that expectation is nine–tenths of the cure. That which we expect is that which we mean. While we are expecting anything or any action unlike the perfect health, the perfect success, or the fullness of joy, we have a rock laid across the expectation of the crystal fount in the soul.

How to honestly, truly expect the most marvelous cures, the most brilliant achievements, and the most heavenly delights, here and now, is the principle teaching we look for. He who can teach the minister how to honestly, truly expect to see in his life what he prays for, has made him a minister indeed.

To expect the full measure of all we bespeak is the first stir of the waters of that dissolving sea, at the root of the tree of our life. And to honestly expect is to mean what we say. To mean what we say is to have a nameless Presence over–ruling our hurts, liquefying our hardships, melting our troubles, so that we walk in a pathway of peace.

In this Acts 5:25-41, we see first that it is only in one sphere of belief where troubles are known and felt. That is the sphere of belief in the necessity for evil that good may come. It is the last thin layer of belief in the necessity for evil laid across the fount of the statement of God in the mind, when we are told that the saints must be tried by afflictions to purify their natures. This is not true. Afflictions and humiliations are not necessary to perfect saints or the sinners so–called. God made them all His own perfect

Substance. As the Substance of God does not need trying by the fires of misery to test its fineness, so the nature of no man needs to be tried by humiliations to make it shine as the light.

Millions of trials wait for the dissolving waters of this crystal fountain to break forth. From the majestic prophets down through the cycles to the aureoled saints of our century, that rubbish of the thought that God tries the good, has held back the fulfillment of hopes, has dammed up the answers to prayers.

Bunyan was shut up twelve years in prison for preaching of God. He had humbly accepted the error that it is the way of the good to lay hurts in the path of the just. It is believed now that he did more good to the world by being shut into prison than he would have done by being left free in the prime of his strength. He wrote the "Pilgrim's Progress" because he had time to write as a prisoner. But Christ sets the captive free. Who shall honestly lay to the charge of the Lord of Hosts that His works are best wrought out through bondage or trials? Say, rather, that it was because Bunyan did not absolutely mean what he said when he preached that the truth is freedom; that Christ sets the captives free and leads captivity itself captive.

Who could shut up the Spirit of God? Who could imprison the purpose of God? Nothing can stop the waters of purity from dissolving the globe when once they are generated and set into action. Nothing can hinder the word of protection when once it is generated by the honest faith of a soul. The teachers of Bunyan need never have taught him that trials and hardships are good for the Spirit. Is it true that Bunyan's book had a wider influence than his preaching to crowds would have wrought? Who can say that he would not have written a nobler book, if he had not let the barrier of a belief in the necessity for trials lie across the word of truth when he preached it?

To have preached to multitudes believing he was not then in prison, but kept free from it by the grace of God, though worthy of death, would have been one power of Good. To be the writer of a book filled with beautiful ideas of the chastening life of the martyrs of Christ, held tightly under the bars of a practical experience of slavery, was another power of good.

But what of the good of a life free as God from bondage? What of a life stepped forth out of pain by its words of pure truth honestly felt? What of a life that can stand out from the poverty, the shame, the trials of a human lot through giving free course to a gospel of absolute safety, absolute peace, absolute provision, and absolute health? Has anyone tried that doctrine?

After thousands of years of practice of the statements of God's goodness to man, caged in by the beliefs of His miserable love of afflicting His people, let us forego the old lies, and rise like a bird from the snares of the fowlers, free faith, free spirit, free life, free God, from the soul! The only good the worn-out accusations against God has done is to make us sharp to see at this time that such teachings would keep the generations of men purifying and cleaning and refining through tortures world without end.

Tortures begone! It is a principle, no mind with a spark of high purpose, noble resolution, lofty love of the right, will cower under for a moment. It is not necessary that evil should transpire for good to be done! Is there any belief left in the heart of man that a noble character, a lofty purpose, a pure truth, is its own defense? Then let the loftiest idea you can conceive of rise up as your principle of faith — your untrammeled confidence.

The noblest conception of the power of God to come, charging the nations with glory in this hour of our anguish as a betrayed goal of beggars and dying, is that all the pain and poverty and despair shall fall out of sight in an instant. As a world, we repudiate the principle that it is through mistakes that we learn wisdom, or through afflictions that we become good. Across the fountain deep in our hearts where the living waters flow, we allow no ideas of the Apostles, or martyrs, or saints, or divinity students to lie as planks in our creed.

This chapter teaches that good does indeed come forth from a pitiful knuckling to errors in mixture with true ideas of God's purpose with man, but "terrible as an army with banners" is the glorious thought it flings forth like an arrow of light from an infinite sea of pure crystal, that the children of God are free-born and free-sandaled to run on the highways of peace.

All good for the untrammeled faith; all peace for the unhampered judgment; all health and all delight for the unhindered knowledge of the way of a pure purpose set going on earth. The purest purpose is truest. The truest purpose works quickest. The truest purpose is that nothing shall hinder the touch of the doctrine – that there is no necessity for the world to be in trouble or pain, and no God ever ordained it.

This is the doctrine which shall "suddenly destroy, and that without hand," (Job 34-20) the armies of sorrow, the nations of trouble. It shall suddenly destroy the imprisoning legislation of capital and politics, the ugly diseases and sorrows of papal decrees and prophetic impositions, for a whole earth full of apostles of the rejection of the necessity for evil, as it did destroy the prison bolts of the Sanhedrin for a handful of apostles, as recorded in this chapter.

It shall melt all the machinations of all the enemies to one man alone, if he abide by the knowledge of the dissolving potency of a pure principle purposed in the heart. There shall ever be heard a Gamaliel at the courts where the cause of them that purpose the gospel of free God is tried. The rocks will cry out, the chains will unclasp. There is freedom for the idea now preached that we need not crouch behind the bars of the Fenelon, Guyon, Protestant Emersonian idea, that we are perfected by trials, or brought forth into greatness by shame.

Why did the man Theudas fail in his enterprise? He crouched under the pious falsehood that the way of the righteous is martyrdom. Why did Judas of Galilee droop and perish in baffled endeavor? Only because he shrank back to the cage of the religion of his fore–fathers, that the life of the just is a pathway of thorns, and the death of the righteous is torture. Why did the Russian lovers of freedom from despotic rule go in weeping exile to the Siberian wastes? Because they did not rise from the chains of the ideas their fathers laid on them that, there is hardship and torture for him who strikes for freedom. They had no idea of the practical application of the text from the wells of inspiration. "Stand and see the salvation."(Exodus 14:13)

Why did these apostles here mentioned get free from the prisons, free from the captors, free from the laws of their land? Because they let their confidence loose on the bolts and the motives of despots in a stream fine and small, but sufficient to dissolve iron bars, stone laws, and steel motives. Why did they all suffer martyrdom, after this beautiful demonstration of the setting–free power of expectation of good? Because as this lesson unblushingly utters, they "rejoice that they were counted worthy to suffer shame for the Name of Christ." They had not suffered shame, they had demonstrated the setting–free power of the gospel.

To suffer shame is no sign of the Christ. That Name is freedom from shame. It is honor and glory. That Name is not the synonym for suffering and sorrow. It is the Name for stepping forth from prisons, from councils, from despots, from armies of capital, from legislation of men bent on defrauding the poor of their rights, from slanders, from pain, from hunger, and from sickness.

That Name is not the prophecy of ages of waiting for just dues, as these apostles have waited, because they refused the mighty doctrine of Jesus that "now is the accepted time." (II Corinthians) You need not wait for your rights. You need not believe in its being good for your soul or your life to have trouble. You need not think it is good for your neighbors to be shut up in prison or hurt by the law of cause and effect. Nothing is good but good. Be not deceived. You need not pray for submission to evil. You need not ask to bear pain. You need not court tribulations by thinking of them as the ways of God with those whom He loves. They are not His ways with His people. Fenelon and La Compte taught that we yield ourselves as victims to the persecutions of men, because God wills it. This is not Truth. There is no salvation from sin, sickness, and death in such doctrine. Emerson teaches that the gods overload with humiliation those, whose name shall shine on the scrolls of fame. But these gods are not God. They are the imaginations of men. A purer, truer stream flows forth this moment. It is the river, whose purpose is to make glad the city. It is the Science of Good. Whoever is one with its purpose is free. August 21, 1892.

Bible Lesson LIX. Acts 7:54–60. Acts 8:1-4. The Answering of Prayer

There is an invisible aura about the heads of very pious people, which makes their prayers very slow in being answered. It acts with their fulfillment exactly as the atmospheric ether acts with the earth, viz., as a defense from outer attacks and falling debris. Not long ago an imaginative astronomer explained that, the reason the inhabitants of Mars cannot communicate with earth's people, is because of the mental resistance which surrounds earthly heads and is symbolized by the resisting atmosphere. So for a long time they have been beaming upon us a mental treatment to yield our stiff-necked notions, especially our religious ones, and to receive the ideas they have for our advantage. The non–resisting attitude of mind which the yielding of our religious prejudices would inspire, would open a clearer means of communication between the inhabitants of the two planets.

The imaginative men in the realm of great scientific researches having given us all our discoveries, directly or indirectly, we as a race listen to them better than we used to. A prominent Boston paper declares that Professor Holden will never be a discoverer because he looks too much to the pictures in his telescope for his ideas. He imagines nothing. Newton imagined that the earth had an attractive quality, then went to work to prove his imagination. Columbus imagined a new continent and set out to prove his theory. Franklin imagined that lightning and electricity were identical and experimented to prove it. Lavoisier imagined the metallic bases of the earth and set about proving them.

The power or faculty of imagination is from God. It is far above the manifestations of the senses. The senses obey the theories of the mind like slaves. Men who imagine microbes in the human body put their microscopes to work to find them. The docile microscopes say yes, and the eyes wink assent.

This exactly agrees with the Buddhist bible, which declares that the world is what we make it by our thought, it moves by our thought, it changes at our word. Schiller, in a moment of mental keenness said, "What the Spirit promises, nature will perform." Every aspiration of the mind will be fulfilled. It will not be fulfilled, however, till the mind has struck some one moment when, instead of hoping the event may come to pass, it suddenly feels "It is — it is!"

The faculty of image–ing is the creative gift. He who uses this beautiful gift skillfully may companion himself with princes of wisdom and daughters of beauty. He uses his mind with as delicate exactness as a watchmaker handles hair–springs, and jewels.

Now, if the saint has set his mind to the idea that his God is one who always puts very good and holy people into very hard places and often tells them that they must wait and wait and wait to see their hopes fulfilled; the saint who so imagines will manufacture an aureole about his head to keep himself from seeing that the things he is praying for are right there at his elbow. This atmosphere, caused by his imagination against God, is sometimes visible to the naked eye of those who think very much as he does. They all think that it is a mark of great superiority. They do not see that it is really such a setting of the will against God, that even little children suddenly feel themselves liable to be naughty, and almost afraid to move lest they do something to offend these very pious heads.

The aura of imagination that God's will must be done to hurt and torment is a mental will exercised over all people who come near. They mentally compel young and old to step around as they say. Thus, even if their will is set to morality, and young and old act better when they are around, it is no credit to them, for it is by will power and not by Principle that they govern.

If people do not do right because they act from Principle, their notions are mechanical. There is no life in them. If rich men do not give generously to a worthy institution till a strong will is put to manipulating their minds, their giving is chaff. It will soon be forgotten that they gave. Indeed, their subservience will become the jest of the shrewd public press.

This aura of imagination against God's intentions keeps blessings outside its tough ether, exactly as meteoric showers are kept outside the aura of earth. It has been supposed to be a great protection to the earth. As a supposition governs the conditions and not the conditions the supposition, it had verily seemed that we needed to be protected as an earth from some terrible droppings from Perseus. Not so! The passing heavens have new ideas to drop. We will open our mind to receive them. Their openness of mind will disintegrate the atmospheres and a new heaven and a new earth will dawn upon our ecstatic vision, as it has been proclaimed that Stephen's gaze caught them in free delight.

If we imagine that falling lights from Perseus are dangerous to our earth, we proudly proclaim that our atmosphere protects us from them. So the atmosphere toughens in obedient power. If now, we boldly proclaim that there are some great advantages to be derived from a rarer atmosphere through which the feathery metals of dissolved systems may come sifting, soon we will rarify our atmosphere. Those with keen vision of coming actions tell us that soon our airs will be too rare to breathe except for those who understand managing their bodies by their minds.

If one astronomic mind has faith in his imagination strong enough to set to work to prove it, he will teach men to think less admiringly of the so called saints, and their tough wills must soon fall from our mind circles to give us a chance to think all is good, rather than part is bad and part is good. This will hasten to change the enveloping ethers.

We will take the first real practical step toward overcoming evil with good. This will open our windows to Mars.

Highly rarified minds tell us that God is truly above goodness and virtue. Dante got clear enough from former ideas to see this for a moment.

Thus, it would really come to a pass where practically we would overcome goodness with God. This would open our skies to the truths of the suns. A truly inspired metaphysician caught a moment like this of Stephen's as here related. (Acts 7th and 8th chapters). He said: "I am convinced that man must drop his concept of evil; for each man's good has been his God, till he has set it against his neighbor's concept of good, which was his God, and all the wars of religion have resulted. They were simply the pitting of ideas of good against each other."

An occult book tells us of a pious preacher who promised another pious preacher to come back and tell him of his experience after death. As preachers are great on proclaiming death instead of life, of course he went through that process. Both of them had made intense pictures of a place of hot torment for all sinners after death. Both of them had pronounced themselves unworthy sinners. The logical outcome of such imagination would, of course land both of these "unworthy sinners" into the place they had built for sinners. So, when that one died and came back to tell his experience (as people have done) he said to his friend: "I am in hell fire, and am put there justly, too." He tried to tell more but he could not. He did not like the place he had prepared for himself at all. Yet the justice of the law that reads: "He createth the fruit of the lips," (Isaiah 57:19) was soon perceived by him. He without doubt went immediately to work and denied that he was a sinner, refused to create, or permit to exist any longer, a hell, and soon floated to some such happy opposite as Stephen's mind had prepared for himself.

The microscope reveals what the mind declares. The telescope shall show forth tiny moons, swinging in happy nearness to the loving face of Mars, if Swift and Voltaire imagine them till they see them with their naked eyes.

"What the Spirit promises nature will perform."

We have a marvelous mechanism called mind. With skilful handling thereof, we may companion ourselves with high causes and noble comrades. We do not use this mind for ignoble imaginings when we find how obediently it manufactures all things we please. The successful man or woman is the one who uses his mental mechanism to make lofty concepts and holds it steady to them. The successful physician is the one who does not use his mental instrument to brook over "cases of sickness," but is more engaged in ideas of cure. The successful mental practitioner or metaphysician is one who purposely clears his mind machine of the clogging dust of the names and the looks of diseases. While people are describing them, he is forgetting them. That practitioner will surely see what he manufactured by concepts.

One metaphysician was given to clogging her mind with the ideas of how sick people look. She learned how to let fall such ideas, but then she had nothing in mind to take their place. So she bought the most beautiful picture yet conceived of Jesus Christ to hold in her mind to see while men patients were talking of different diseases; also a lovely picture of the Madonna to keep in her mind's eye while women patients were detailing their long lists of miseries. No need to tell that she is a brilliant success at healing.

People are bound to look to us as we insist. Stars are bound to tell us what we determine. Bugs and stones will say yes to everything we tell them to be and show forth.

By this Principle you are able to see that Stephen had a highly beautiful concept of the place such people as he should come into if they would fix their mind's eye on it right in the midst of all sorts of daily experiences. He held this idea clear on through his old ideas of how meanly humanity serves its kindest friends.

There was one important point Stephen was not clear upon. That was how to direct his mental machine in such a way that his treatments would strike exactly where he wanted them to. Here you perceive he treated the rabble to go free from the consequence of their vicious ideas. He did not want the poor things who were seeking their good by the mistaken line of stoning him to go through the siege of the destruction of Jerusalem, which was to be the logical outcome of the intense ideas shot forth by them before they hurled the stones. But Stephen's treatment for the law of cause and effect to cease for their sakes shot over their heads and struck Saul with all its force.

What the highly–wrought treatment for an unlettered multitude intended, learned Saul got all the benefit of. It struck him to the earth like a cannon ball. Many Spiritual Science healers have the same experience now. They treat powerfully without apparent results. Their treatments fly entirely over the heads of their patients. The treatments are not lost, however, and all over the earth men and women of great power and learning are struck blind with astonishment to think they never before saw how falsely the God of heaven has been talked about and how the law of thought proceeds to fruitage.

So the rabble went into the terrors of Jerusalem, but Paul rose from the astonishment of Saul.

Stephen's senses were all trained to obey his mental images. He did not feel the stones at all. He did not see the rabble at all. He did not hear their shouts. He saw their mental concept that it was for their good to kill him. He tried to erase the concept but did not accomplish it.

He was probably more than satisfied to be told that Saul was to accept the divinity of Jesus Christ, and that it took all the force of his own mind to hurl Saul's mistaken notion of his good. When Saul's idea of good was eliminated, the purity of his mind from both good and evil caused the actual character of Jesus Christ to be so near and clear to him that he understood Truth above the very heavens of Stephen's gaze.

This is the way the ideas of Spiritual Scientists are now acting. The demonstrations of their splendid thought shall rise from every city on the round earth. Men and women with living glory shall prove that higher is Truth than the heavens of the faithful Scientists of today, with their traditions of the past still clinging to their ideas so what they feel each other wrong when they are right; seeing their good opposed to their neighbor's good, even willing to see sin in the motive and purpose of those who are acting from religious instincts as set as their own. There is a clearer atmosphere possible to me if I drop my idea that your good is my evil. There is still a clearer atmosphere if I drop my idea that my good is your good. I have lifted myself out of the traditions of even my own idea of good when I let God overcome all my own notions of what is good.

God is above goodness. God is above knowledge. As birds clear their feet from the snares of the fowlers, so the coming Pauls shall clear their names of our Stephen–like ideas of what is good. A Science, too pure to set his neighbor down as in error, shall rise from the science now preached and shall be lived. There will then be no earth atmosphere left.

August 28, 1892

Bible Lesson LX. Acts 8:5-25. Word Spoken By The Mind

Words, which the mind speaks intensely, may go through the air straight to some human being and "lasso" him to bring forth whatever they command. This is thought transference. It is all in the realm of the human or mortal, even if the mind at the end of the line is stirred so healthfully that its body is healed of neuralgia or heart disease.

Then again words spoken intensely by the mind may go up into the skies, and break open like clouds and rain down their results in ways unexpected. This is answering of prayers. It is more satisfactory by far than the practice of what is called "treatment" of a mind on the plane of thought transference.

Sometimes a man can "talk another man into giving" a large donation to a church or school. He might "think him into doing" the same thing. Some people can talk an invalid into health. Some people can think him into health. Either of these ways is "treating" by thought transference.

Some people throw up their words into the mental airs by a course of reasoning, in which they tell what they would like to have done. They speak so earnestly and hotly that the words go into the right stratum of feeling and drop down on exactly the right heads to carry out the plans proposed. This is answering prayers. Abraham Lincoln practiced this way. His words went high up and touched the right upper mental stratum to break open and drop down on the head of the captain of the "Monitor".

This seems a very cool explanation of the science of praying. It is the true explanation, however. The principle of it is exactly as demonstrable as the principle governing any other mechanical operation. All principle is God. We have to understand how words work with as accurate certainty as we would have to understand how a cook-stove works — or to "hit or miss" works.

It has always been the custom of those who brought forth the answers to their prayers by excited throwing of their words up into the airs (to that mental stratum called their God), to speak very scornfully of those who "lassoed" people into doing what they wanted them to do by thinking directly at them. To think straight at a Vanderbilt or a Mackey to endow a new college has not ever been regarded as so honorable a use of words as to openly talk him into so doing. And of all ways to make words work, none is in such favor as tossing them high up in an ecstatic frame of mind against another state of Mind called God. For a high up state of Mind is intelligence. Pure intelligence chooses, according to judgment, just the right one to help us when we need help.

To keep your mind always throwing beautiful words into the heavens is to be in a constant state of prayer. Your works will be exactly like what you are describing. If you speak the words "pure intelligence," they will fall down as a new perception of some principle upon some head, perhaps away off in Australia. The new perception may come to yourself later on. Every new perception of any principle makes some kind of new demonstration. If you suddenly catch sight of the principle which governs praying, why, even before you use words for the purpose of bringing something to pass, that perception has wrought a miracle somewhere.

This perception of a principle is God. The God within you touches the God without you. The veil or "middle wall of partition," which is ignorance, is suddenly parted. The instant you thrill with pleasure because you see what is true, you have wrought some kind of miracle somewhere. If you are clear enough in understanding of the law and gospel of mind to make your words do exactly what you wish, and for whomsoever your heart shall choose, you are Peter and John of this eighth chapter of Acts. If you are able to convince people that this is a demonstrable principle, and by keeping your mind sending up ecstatic words, can have them constantly dropping healing potencies on yourself, you are Philip at Samaria.

The power of Philip is the working efficiency of prayer. His arrows of thought go straight up and come straight down on himself. No prayer is lost. Ministers are often blamed for not curing the sick and working instantaneous reformation of character, when it is only because their ideas do not go straight up to fall straight down with power of the healing and reforming sort on their own selves. Paracelsus would not undertake to cure clergymen, because he was indignant against them for not curing themselves by their own prayers. As well might we be indignant against Philip, who could cure the sick and cast out devils by his prayers, but could not thrill his hearers with the hot perception of Truth, which Peter and John could do so beautifully.

And way down in the scale of methods for accomplishments, was Simon, who "treated" people mentally, till he lassoed them to his will. His idea of what was good was Peter's idea of what was evil. So Peter's idea of what was good was the scholar's idea of what was evil. Peter scolded Simon for not throwing his words and will straight up just as he did. And the Sanhedrin scolded Peter for not talking to people about material things in the usual fashion; also, for not using material methods of healing just as they did.

Samaria is an important figure of speech in explaining mental processes. It means, "watch-post." It means, "turning-point." It marks the beginning of another era. If you have been sending high and unmixed truth into the heavens without getting any special returns upon your own mind, there will suddenly come a time when your power of healing will break forth. Other powers will come besides the mere power of healing physical bodies. Some of your arrows of Truth will have hit the mark and opened a channel directly over your own head. The rest of them have gone aslant and brought their help to others.

After this baptism of power, your mind feels differently altogether from what it did before, and your face is entirely different to look upon. There is a certainty about it, a look of confidence.

If you have had this healing power for some time without the evidence of the Holy Ghost, and have felt that you would like the quickening glory of one whose mind and body are on fire all the time from an incessant descent of radiance from above, you will certainly come to some wonderful day when so many of your words have penetrated the heavens straight over your head, that you are on fire enough to kindle a new quickening of earnestness in others.

This will give you a new look in the face and still another kind of confidence in the principle you are advocating.

This Samaria sign–post of prayers just answered, takes place whether we are thinking of Jesus Christ as a Son of God nailed on a tree and calling upon us to believe in His divinity, or as a living demonstration of the One Principle at the root of all actions, from the logical sequence of mathematical propositions to the kindling power of right words. There is just as much fire of the Holy Ghost called into demonstrations at a gathering of metaphysicians as at a Methodist camp meeting. And the staying glory of their baptism is as dependent upon their constancy in prayer as is the Methodists'.

Peter had the Holy Ghost baptism even to a great shower thereof. It was his privilege to have it so that he could keep himself alive to this very day in our sight. But he was much occupied with denunciation of other people, and also he spent a great deal of time, along with other professed Christians, boasting how much shame and disgrace and misery he had had to suffer for Christ's sake and the Gospel's. You can see if right words are sure to bring gladness, health, life, new power, and real safety, such talk was more an evidence of not having a right state of mind, than a virtue to boast of.

This power of the Holy Ghost cannot, as Peter indignantly informed Simon, be bought with money. Each one must put up his own words, and each one must perceive the principle for himself. Sometimes a sharp way of speaking will suddenly crack the crust of a man's old ideas of things, and he will not be satisfied to work along the old ways. Peter practiced cracking the crusts of old ways by sharp words. Sometimes Jesus rebuked severely. He did it wisely, as a sculptor would skillfully strike off a piece of marble to make an open brow on the statue's face.

We are sculptors of our own character. We are the architects of our own powers. Bayard Taylor wrote at twenty-three, "I will become the sculptor of my own mind's statue. We sculpture out nobility of character by never answering when we are accused. We preserve the original whiteness of our character by never accusing. We glorify our character by saying often, "Thou Holy Presence! I am folded around with Thy glory." The instant any one of these powers is felt by us as now working, we have marked a new light on our face. We have touched our Samaria.

You perceive that Samaria for Philip as one thing; for Simon another; for the converts another; for Peter and John another. Each one marked his life with the ideas he had been holding. Some had held their ideas for only a few days; some had theirs for three years; some had been thinking for years along their lines and suddenly snapped away from them to begin a new train.

Along the line of Jesus Christ there is sure to be given a power to heal the sick, cast out devils, raise the dead. Along the line of Jesus Christ there is sure to come the Holy Ghost baptism. He understood every one of the ways of working used by the people of His time. He so filled Himself with Holy Fire that if He touched common clay it passed the healing fire through itself and cured blindness.

This healing fire is an actual burning which seizes even our bodies after we have been dealing with Jesus Christ doctrine of the law of mind and the gospel of Spirit for a sufficient length of time. You will remember that Jesus spoke of kindling a fire. The ancient mystics speak often of a flaming fire, which burns within us without consuming us, but which burns away all the dross of folly and ignorance of mind and the impurities of our flesh at the same moment.

Many people are now feeling this flame within different parts of their bodies. It is the same burning which they felt within their hearts on the way to Emmaus, after talking with the Risen Christ. It is often set into flame by repeating the Name Jesus Christ for days and nights at a time without stopping to think what the Name means. It is often set to burning, by thinking over the majestic lessons of Spiritual Science. It is the descent of flames, which some word of a divine meaning can bring down for us when we send it up.

It is the kind of fire, which is to burn the world when the day of Samaria touches it. That day will spring forth when a teaching utterly devoid of remembrance of our former ways of thinking is continually put up from our hearts into the heavens. Its words of ecstatic praise will penetrate the heavens of pure love to drop down new feelings into far away people. "Then all the proud, yea, and they that do wickedly, shall be burned." (I Samuel 12:25)

All the people are to be burned alive with this enchanting Fire of the Holy Ghost, which is now already burning the pride and unkindness out of many, and flaming through their lungs and hearts to burn away the dross. Lungs stand for wisdom. So when the mystic fires are felt in that region of the body, we know that some old nonsensical ideas are being consumed. The heart stands for love. So when the marvelous fire which His doctrine kindles is felt in the heart, we may know that some old prejudices are burning away. If those who have felt the fire of the Holy Ghost of their own thoughts in different parts of their bodies will consider that all the errors which that part hints at are being burned away, they will understand how the whole world is to be burned. The fires of Jesus Christ in Truth are now kindled. If you have been long speaking up into the bosom of the free Spirit your beautiful praises of God, your radiance is nearer and nearer its enchanting descent.

The world will love these fires. We hasten to bathe in them. They are the peace fires of the new heart the Jesus Christ doctrine is kindling today. Its power to heal and quicken will not slip away from the new church.

September 4, 1892

Bible Lesson LXI. Acts 8:26-40. Just What It Teaches Us

Swing your mind to the supremest statement: of praise of your Spiritual nature you can possibly make. This is affirmation. Drop your mind to the lowliest statement of your human nature you can make. This is denial. At the point of mental experience between the two orders of expression is your power of demonstration over the undesirable conditions that beset your pathway.

In Spirit, you cannot speak too nobly of yourself. In the mortal, you cannot speak too lowly of yourself. Spirit is the Omnipotent God. Mortality is powerless dust. Jesus taught this law of demonstration. He said, "All power is given unto Me in heaven and in earth." (Matthew 28:18) "I AM that I AM." (Exodus 3:14; 6:14) This was affirmation of His Spirit. He then said, "Of myself I can do nothing." (John 8:28) "The son can do nothing" (John 5:19) This was denial suited to mortality. From these two kinds of speaking, He composed His miracle-working mind.

There were two Philips. Both were very efficient at healing the sick. Therefore, they had both taken, either consciously or unconsciously, high affirmations and lowly denials also. One sometimes takes these two states by strong feelings without words. He strikes the two notes of his mental scale at the sounds of a preacher's words. He feels the power of his exalted Spirit; he feels the nothingness of his personal human. The exact poise between the two feelings is healing power.

You can come at this point, or polarity, by exalted praise of your spiritual "I" followed immediately by denials exactly correlative, or by beatific feelings followed by corresponding self-abasement.

Jonah kept his mental eye fixed on the temple while he was physically in the opposite place. There is a way of pulling yourself out of very humiliating circumstances by keeping the mind's eye fixed on some sweet memory. At the gateway between the affliction and the sweet memory is freedom.

Paul told the disciples whose powers of demonstration were marvelous, to call to remembrance how that after they were illuminated they endured afflictions. He was catching a hint of the science of demonstration by mental attitudes. He was tacitly enjoining them to keep their mind's eye on their glorified moments, while stones and prisons and fires were trying their hardest to call their attention.

Did you ever dream of an angelic being looking into your face? If now, while some hurting trial is near you, you will keep steadfastly remembering that face, you also will touch the poising point in your nature where what you do not like must fall out of your life, and what you do like must begin. But before ever any hardship comes into your human experience avoid its coming by making the lofty proposition, "I Am Omnipotent Spirit. I am meekness itself." These down and up springs of the wings of your mind, will take you over the hardships of earth as a bird's wings lift it high away from the guns of the hunters. That hardship or affliction that touched your neighbor, but did not touch you, was put out of your way by some sweet vision that once occupied your memory, while some hateful prognostication was being uttered. While they prophesy cholera, let the optimist keep up his sunny trust in the best. At the poise between the optimist's hope of happy safety, and the pessimist's miserable fears, is "the health of My people Israel."

This lesson is all about the lovely swing of the mind and the demonstration that never fails to follow that dip of the pendulum called meekness. Philip made a convert of a princely scholar, a nobleman of the retinue of a queen. This was demonstration. Had Philip not been mighty in Spirit, he never could have been obedient to its voice and run after a great scholar with confidence in his mission. It was a ridiculous thing to do, so it would have seemed to a rabbi, but to docile Philip there was only one law, and that was obedience.

The measure of your pride is the measure of your abasement. And between the two states of shame and vanity is your troubled existence. This is not in the realm of the Spiritual, but it works itself out in close imitation of the omnipotent heights of the Truth and the meek docility of the Philip who lists to its call.

This lesson, which touches the downward dip of the truthful mind and its happy power of demonstration, begins at the twenty-sixth verse of the eighth chapter of Acts. "Go down unto Gaza, which is desert," said the voice. So down towards the desert went Philip. Four words express the desert place of the mind, which has once proclaimed "I am Omnipotent Spirit." At its Gaza spot it speaks, "I am obedient, meek, docile, teachable." No great affirmation but has its lowly opposite. No lowly denial but has its majestic "I AM." The meekness of Philip touches the right chord of the scholar. It is not the powerful intellect, the dominating will, which appeals to the school-bred man; it is the innocent unpretentious Philip, obedient to the extent of running whithersoever the Spirit pushes him, hearing no voice but its call.

There is no call for you to be learned in order to be great in the power of the Spirit. No; be so meek that, as in the thirty-second and thirty-third verses, which tell how the Lord of Life and Glory was shamed you are a fool in docile gladness for Christ.

There is no need for you to be talented, or accomplished, or rich, or of noble family in order to do mighty service as a minister of the Spirit. Nothing but docility is called for — teachableness, and obedience.

Philip was all this. Therefore, he could teach the splendid glory of the humiliated Jesus. Why should we not be struck with the profound words, "I am of judgment," while knowing our judgment as God, if it is so of Jesus of Nazareth, who knew himself as Jehovah, but let his judgment be called in question?

Have you not heard many great thinkers, noble philanthropists, or grave scholars, speak of how much better it would have been had Jesus Christ lived to this day, slipping away from jailors, the cross, and the tomb, and appearing again and again in their midst till the whole world was redeemed? Thus was His humiliation complete. What the most kind-hearted would call the best judgment, He is secretly thought not to have had. "I have no judgment. My judgment is God." At the poise between these words, the Teacher of man, the wise expounder of doctrine, opens His lips and the grave scholars listen with rapt earnestness. In the closet of silent prayer, you may touch the glistening mountains of illumination and the shaded valleys of meekness so spiritually set free that your thoughts run unseen to the princes of learning. By their side you will stand in the holy sweetness of power to drop into their wondering hearts the beautiful doctrine that if they will leave off their study of matter and follow you down to the waters of Spirit, their light shall break forth as the morning and they shall know all things without having learned.

They may be called away with the swift horses of Candace into a gladness of mind to be free from hunting among the dry dust of materiality for the knowledge that ages of study could never give. How easy to be taught of the Spirit! How quick to know all things, the Spirit!

A majestic friendship sprang up between the prince of scholars and the spiritual Philip, which was a sweet halo of healing through the lifetime of the eunuch. Friendship is a healing principle. Steadfastness in friendship is a steadfast healing power. Unreliable friends are unhealthy companions. Many a recovery from sickness has dated from the loving remembrance of some eternally steadfast friend.

"There is a friend that sticketh closer than a brother." (Proverbs 18:24) Keep your mind facing that Friend, till you are drawn away from that place where you now are into the home where the heart can sing. You may be found at Azotus, your stronghold, your castle. From this home, where none can molest you, into which none dare enter who have enmity to you or your doctrine, you may shed abroad the fame of your teachings even unto Cesarea, chief city of the Romans, or the very high towers of pride, of riches, and worldly conceit.

This lesson teaches that obedience, meekness, docility, and teachableness are the preludes to power. From these stones in the deep places of right thoughts, we step into the easy demonstrations of what people have been working so violently to accomplish. From these easy demonstrations, which we never struggled to make, we step swiftly into our stronghold, our castle, into which no enemy comes. God fills it with friends for our sakes. From the strong castle of defense, we shed abroad still further radiance of our light. Cesarea gets our ministry. We did not try to be great. We accept our inheritance from Spirit. We did not try to do works. We are obedient natures for works to flow through.

Philip was obedient to Spirit, not unto pride. It was no impulse of hope to get something from association with a great personage. He was simply obedient to a spiritual prompting. It was the quick docility of a man in love with spiritual teachings, satisfied utterly with keeping his mind on them, not moved with the ideas of fear or of favor. He was not obedient to the clutch of an impulse, but yielded to the Spirit. He never went into Azotus, his citadel, till he had explained the humiliation of Jesus Christ. Then he preached denial, for he took the prince of eunuchs down to the water and baptized him, which is the symbol of mental cleansing from old ideas. It is the teaching of the lowliest state of mind as necessary to the quick ear of a right scholar. It is the skilful teacher of denial, who feels the freedom of fearlessness. There is no terror in the meek mind lest we get to be fanatical, or go too far on the run of our reasonings. It is the skilful teacher of absolute denial who is taken up into the citadel, wherefrom his ministry spreads into all the cities. He is taken into his stronghold. He does not strike and struggle to get there. An arm stronger than all the soldiers of Candace lifts the sweet teachable teacher into Azotus.

The teacher of supreme denials by lines of pure reason never is caught in the fingers of grief or anger. He is not obedient unto these. He denies the power of these mortal claims. Thus, he becomes a vacuum into which all the miseries of earth strive to rush. The people who bring their miseries to his presence are bathed in the placid waters of his purified mind. It is good for them to come near him. But he does not feel them. He knows not their miserable thoughts. Then when he has cleansed them by his persistent meekness, as well as himself of all knowledge of them, he is taken up, up and away into his own house of safety.

God teaches you the mighty principle of meekness. It is the first sign of the nearness of your power of demonstration. It is a communicable quality. It opens your eyes and ears to the ways of Spirit.

Meekness unto grief is not meekness; obedience to the impulse of sorrow or pride is a denial or ignoring of Spirit. This vacuum from Spirit causes poverty, death, or unkindness, to come close and cling to your life. They find their own and stay near it. They are not cleansed and purged away forever by touching the sphere of your thoughts. Socrates explained how subtly grief in the mind, though hidden by smiles and pleasant manners, will draw like a vortex. Notice how even the servants will change to pertness if you are secretly grieving. Notice how people take to chiding you for imagined offenses. See how quickly they strike you with suspicions of your guiltiness of something they tried to devise in their hearts. See how the trades go against you; the sales of your own store are smaller; the ships cast their cargoes into the deep waters but half insured. This is the steady pursuit you will feel while you are obedient to grief in the heart.

Grief is to be denied. It is Spirit with its buoyant winds of denial of all human passions and proclamations of unlimited, unassailable gladness unto whose voice you are to be obedient.

So this lesson teaches that it is by fearlessness of the world and its utmost stretch to the deeps of the denials of Science that the right state of mind to do great works is attained. Works must not be the results of hard effort. They must be all done by the Spirit. The strong house, the citadel of mind, the high tower of defense, from which you are to diffuse your message abroad shall not come by your efforts. It shall come by your persistent lowly denials, obeying Jesus in teachable meekness. "Deny thyself." (Luke 9:23) You shall rest on the watch tower of your safe retreat, your castle, your home, your Azotus, by the fearless praises of the Jesus Christ nature within you, waiting your obedient, ungrudging "I AM IT." "I am nothing save as I am Spirit."

He who omits the denials of Science never rises by the bold action of Spirit into "Azotus." It is the meek teacher of denials, who is castled in unassailable security. He it is whose teachings shed abroad to the cities of the world. He it is whom the Spirit "catches away'" to an impregnable stronghold.

"My soul on wings of glory
Mounts up to happy skies
Here none can pursue us,
Here none can undo us,
God is our Home."

September 11, 1892

Bible Lesson LXII. Review. The Healing Principle

There is always some man or some woman near us, who is capable of thinking about us in exactly the right way to bring us our healing. The right idea to hold of healing, is not only concerning bodily cure, misfortune, or inefficiency. The healing principle is every moment operating through some special man or woman near us, but whose motive and character we are probably misunderstanding. That one, by our having a right feeling toward him or her, is our mascot. But we must first get the right attitude toward that person. If you would learn who it is, that can put you in line with your prosperity, put yourself through a process of mental statements called denials. They will act as purifying waters to wash the dust off your understanding of what is your wisest course to pursue. They will clear your vision to see whose powers are efficient to work a blessed demonstration for you. They will make you perceptive and docile to welcome your fulfillment. It does not make any difference whether you are a newsboy or a college president, you cannot truly get at that blessing that is nearest your heart till you have taken in the proper attitude of mind. You may get around every other circumstance of your lot easily, but you cannot approach the particular blessing, till you have gone through the gate of the denials of Science. Then, further than this, some of you must practice on the denials, till your mind is as meek and humble as the mind of the man who had lain thirty-eight years at the edge of the pool of Bethesda.

The Bethesda pool was typical of the cleansing waters of meekness. The angel who troubled the waters was the symbol of the perfect Word. Many people use the perfect words of denial for a long time before they get meek and listening enough to hear the voice of Jesus Christ in the right man to cure them. Only the humblest and poorest and lowliest one among them all near the pool knew that the One who was called a malefactor, a glutton, a Sabbath–breaker, was the living power of healing in their very midst.

There were many Jews nearby, but they were positive, opinionated, churchmen. When they looked upon Jesus Christ they were looking into the placid clearness of His pure mind, so like the clear waters of Bethesda, and they could not see His mind at all. They just saw themselves reflected in Him, as you would not see the water if you looked into a clear lake, but only see your own image. So they condemned Him at once, though He was not condemning them at all. His clear innocent mind acted exactly like conscience to them. He assured them that He was not accusing them, but that made no difference, they kept seeing themselves in the placid waters of His mental presence, and scolded themselves hard, thinking all the time it was Jesus, the malefactor, they were accusing.

They had the very One in their midst who could have cured them of their longing for help. If they had not put their own notions forward, but had stopped and listened to His loving doctrine, lo, their bruised hearts would have been lifted up.

In metaphysics we find that Jesus Christ is always speaking through someone for our special help, but we also are putting our notions of things forward and do not get the messages. There are certain denials, which will take down the rocks and fences from before our mental understanding, and show us our helper, whom God in love hath already furnished, who now talks with us every day, who maybe is the one whom we dislike and ostracize.

Denials are found in the second lesson of Spiritual Science. They have a beautiful effect upon the mind to make it listening, obedient, and easily cured.

The Christians of the world are all waiting and wondering why the strife, and poverty, and sorrow of mankind, are not cured by their preaching and praying and printing. These things are their own images thrown forward into the clear placid purity of the Omnipresent Mind, whose name is Jesus Christ. They cannot be cured except by ceasing to project their ideas. If the Christians find it a great task to stop projecting such ideas into this Mind in our midst, let them learn the seven denials of Science. If they do not know what these denials are, let them get some metaphysical teacher to teach them. Certainly, they cannot see Jesus Christ until they have used them. That is, they cannot find their demonstration of the world in peace and happy prosperity, till they have used them.

Jesus Christ is not already here in this earth in the sight of any, except the exceedingly meek. Such have nothing left to be cured of. They are satisfied. They have received in understanding and without controversy all the lessons of the Scriptures.

There are eleven points to be remembered in the review lesson of today. The first you will find in Acts 1 (Lesson 51). It shows how Luke treated the whole world by writing down all that he knew of the acts of people under direct spiritual illumination. He calls to that region of mind in all mankind, called "Theophilus." He does not recognize our unbelief or our opposition nature; he is like a practitioner of mental therapeutics who keeps telling the sickest looking man or woman silently that they are perfectly whole. He writes his treatments, Luke does. Some people nowadays write to their patients and read their written treatments over and over. Sometimes they sing the treatments which they have written –they do not send their written words by mail to their patients, but sing and sing them all by themselves at home hundreds of miles from their patients. Many a doctor of medicine has learned this little secret of metaphysical practice and sends through the mental stratum, which leads to the heart of his patient a healing message.

Luke is not entirely given over to curing human bodies. He is taking the whole world and speaking to it as though it were one man, for other purposes than bodily healing. The whole world has a cord in its bosom, which is the love of God. Luke harps on this cord. When it is wakened in you, you will be bodily cured, mentally comforted, and spiritually alive. Luke is a wonderful physician. He finds that the spiritual nature quickened has power to set all visible nature, all society, all government, all educational and laboring interests to rights. Hufeland, a Prussian physician, found that he himself could quicken this nature in certain ones among his patients and cure them.

Luke takes the whole world and calls us "Theophilus." He strikes and strikes on that cord common to all men till he feels it become the dominant tone in us all even to the cure of poverty, ignorance, sordidness, and quarreling.

Truly, the sum and substance of his treatment is the sixth message to the world, which the orderly metaphysician speaks. To the whole world the orderly thinker says, entirely ignoring in his mind all appearances to the contrary, "You are the perfect creation of the living God spiritual, harmonious, free, flawless. From every direction everywhere come the words of Truth making you to know that you are wise, glad, and at peace. Your Life is God. Your Substance is God. Your Intelligence is God. You are now the living manifestation of Jesus Christ." While you are being told of how crime, and suicide and poverty are increasing, keep this Luke song singing within your silent mind. It will make you a Spiritual physician like Luke.

The second point was that all the power the Christian church has demonstrated so far, is by reason of its actual mention of the Name of Jesus Christ, for the doctrine He preached, has slipped away from the fingers of the religion of today. It is the mixed-clay-and-iron age of ignoring the actual doctrine taught by Jesus. We cannot revive it except by the continual repetition of the two words Jesus Christ. The power of the Holy Ghost is to burst over and through the life of him who continually speaks that Name while speaking the orderly arrangement of the doctrine He taught. There is no power of the Holy Ghost in the science out of Christ any more than there is in the church which still believes that God sends afflictions, keeps us in hades, tells men to earn their wages of each other, and makes one of us to be abler or wiser or richer than our neighbors.

The third point was the explanation that the perfect doctrine is brought out by dropping our belief in evil first and our belief in virtue second. Our virtues stand as much in our own light as our vices. For instance, we think it is wrong to steal. We believe that we could not steal because it would be so wicked, even if we were in great need. This seems to us very honorable. It is nothing of the kind — it is pure nonsense. There truly is no such thing as stealing. God is all. Can God steal from God? This knowledge is the dropping of our will against our neighbors. We feel really benefitted, when they take our goods away. We say the goods have gone into the fingers of God.

We do not notice if people take away our reputation: we say God is using our name in love and wisdom. We take the mental attitude that all mankind holds all things in common. We hold this idea so steadfastly that soon we begin to even up in our possessions with our neighbors. They become very generous with us and we are very generous with them. We see that brotherhood and sharing all things in common are sure to stand out in easy fulfillment when a few minds drop their ideas of their own virtues. If we believe in virtue we are sure to believe in vice, so we drop that miserable amoeba from our minds, for there is no telling which way it will swing its tough little body, whether to thinking our neighbors are better than we are or we are better than our neighbors.

The lesson on Acts 3 (Lesson 54) conveyed this idea, namely, that we make gods of our beliefs. We must not think our belief is good, no matter what we believe, for then that belief will deal with us. Peter and John stood in mind for a moment above believing that the lame man was either lame or not lame. They were in the meaning of the Name Jesus Christ. There is a super-intelligence, which the mind opens to in high doctrine. This lights the face with strength of Spirit. Whoever catches sight of the face just at the moment is healed. The lame man caught strength in the faces of Peter and John. Strength being what he needed, he was healed.

The Name Jesus Christ often gives moments of a keen intelligence, which very soon demonstrates in the affairs around us. This is the kind of knowing which is the true power. We neither believe nor disbelieve–we know. Nothing deals with us in these moments — we are! It is for the people who believe in something external to themselves that the law of belief operates. Then it is for people who believe in their beliefs that the law is still operating. Jesus Christ believed nothing — He knew. His knowing was Himself.

The next lesson is about two characteristics we each of us have. One is the John – the other is the Peter quality. If we have the John characteristic in error, we shall think that the doctrine of silence means that we are to keep silent as to our principles, our doctrine. This is John of the Sanhedrin. If we have the John quality in Truth, we shall know that the teaching of silence is meant for our not retorting when we are misused. We are to bide the time of pure Spirit. We must speak from the Absolute standpoint always.

The Peter characteristic, held in error, gives us a continual self-deprecatory feeling. We think it good for ourselves to mouse and prowl around into our faults and call ourselves bad names. It is often a great comfort to do so, but it is not scientific. The Peter characteristic in Truth gives us forgetfulness of our faults and sudden gleams of the underlying intelligence of our own mind at the exact point where all the momentum of our actions and words starts. We are impetuous, but spiritually powerful.

The next point is, that whatever we know to be right we must speak out boldly. We must not be afraid of making enemies, we must not mind going into Coventry for awhile when we know what we are doing is right. There is a force and a defense in pure right, which is better than an army with banners. It is perfectly true that describing a murder to a public audience will cause the most innocent audience to make every man, woman or child they meet who has the least leaning toward crime to go straight and do exactly what the lecturer has imbedded into the minds of his hearers. It is according to mental law that Stead's pictures of London's rich men's wickedness left such vivid impressions on his readers' minds, that they sent many a man to practicing the same crimes. It is the sure action of mentality that the eloquent descriptions of drunken homes have pushed the plastic wills of the masses to hurry and carry out more pictures like them. The Sanhedrin forbade the Apostles to preach that things and events yield to a Name held in mind. But the Name held in mind, together with the sayings of the Man who demonstrated what the Name means, will do more to drop the mantle of pain and trouble off the planet than any other process. His sayings form a demonstrable Science. His Name makes us the living demonstrations. It is a mystery how just speaking the Name over and over works us up and over — but it does.

The lesson on Acts 5: 1-11 (Lesson 57) showed how it is best for us to stop sometimes and not seem to be running in the lists with other people of the world to see who will win. We must not compete with anyone or anything. We must just do our simple duties of each day, expecting no rewards, fearing no failures. We have no world of temptations to overcome. We are expected to be brave. Nothing is expected of us. We may absolve ourselves from all responsibility of our past words and actions by saying, "The words that I spoke in the past, it was not I that spoke them, but the wise God speaking through me." We may rest free today by saying, "The words that I speak this day, it is not I that speak them, but the wise God speaking through me." We may go fearlessly toward our future by saying, "The thoughts and words of my future, it is not I that speak and think them, but the wise God speaking and thinking through me."

The next lesson shows that it would keep the world forever on the rock of cleansing and purifying itself by sufferings to believe that God sends afflictions to purify us with. He once made us perfect and was pleased with us. We have never fallen from that estate. We have only one nature with any reality whatsoever in it — that is our perfect Spirit fresh from the creator's heart. Job was perfectly right. "Thou knowest that I am not wicked... Thy hands fashioned me." (Job 10: 7-8)

The next point was that our perfect thoughts often speed away off to some heart, which catches their import more perfectly than we ourselves caught it. Paul got Stephen's treatment and had a more perfect idea of Jesus Christ's Presence and office than Stephen himself had. Every new set or Spiritual Scientists stands out a vast improvement on the old ones who are still hunting out heresies in their neighbors. The young ones have gotten a whiff of the notion "I am holier than thou." (Isaiah 65-5) They are so beautiful and strong, and shine so with the super-intelligence of their understanding, that:

"We feel the airs blow o'er us,
And the glory shine before us,
Of what mankind shall be,
All pure and kind and free."

The next lesson tells that when you step into a higher mental sphere it is as though you had "died" to your friends who do not step along with you. They will torment themselves by scolding your ways, but you can do only one thing, and that is, FORWARD!

The last of our lesson is that the Philip quality of your mind, held in error is the idea that Christian submission means submission to grief, or poverty, or misfortunes. The Philip quality in Truth is the rejection of these and meekest yielding to Spirit. All three things are nothing. Spirit is all. We often speak sentences of nothingness of misfortune and trial, and of the presence of peace and delight, which go and stand in the chariots of learning and work new understandings in faraway minds. All is Mind and there is no opposition to Truth.

September 18, 1892

Bible Lesson LXIII. I Cor. 11:23-34. The Science of Christ

D'Albert treated with coldness a brilliant young man who had solved a difficult problem in mathematics, because he told him he had worked it out to earn a seat in the French Academy. "You will never get on with that motive in your mind," said D'Albert. Looking over the busy students in a normal school, I metaphysically perceived a certain number of them, working up their notes with the sole idea of making their living by and by as capable expounders of the propositions under consideration. I did not feel on the purposely sensitized plate of my mind any reflection of actual interest in the subject they were treating.

A sharp and fearless critic of human motives said to a band of reformers that "if all the saloons, etc., were closed up in a night the reformers would be the maddest lot of people in the world," because "Othello's occupation would be gone." Some people have gone so far as to believe that the doctors would be a very disappointed set if all the people in the world were to be made perfectly well in an instant.

The Science of Christ teaches that we live on our motives. If our motives are to get bread, and clothes and good repute in the world, we may get these things, but there will still be left a hunger, a nakedness, a loneliness, which externals cannot satisfy. D'Albert meant to inform the young man, that the real honors of the Academy were won only by those who loved mathematical principles for their own sake. There is an initiation by motive, which is the esoteric doctrine open to all peoples of all tongues who love the doctrine for its own sake. It takes only a few words for the "initiated" to perceive their own kind in a speaker. A brilliant list of accomplishments is not the entrance ticket to the ranks of the truly esoteric.

When accomplishments by which you make your external living have failed you, if then you have felt the love of the Jesus Christ principles for their own sake, that love will attend to your living. If you can at once drop the idea of depending at all upon any external performance, but kindly engage in each duty as not essential to your support, or defense, or life, or health, or peace, your "seat in the Academy" will be given you at once. Your house external will be shown you. The idea of "making your living" will not be in your mind.

Riding on the train, you pay for your fare because the conductor has faced you with "Ticket, please!" while you were trying to avoid having to pay your fare. The payment of the fifty cents has nothing to do with the case a year from that time when you lose a hundred dollars; for you are living by your motives, not by the outer transactions. Some are faced up soon with their motives, some late, but there is a harvest from motives ahead of us all.

Science is science, and whether it is the Jesus Christ Principle of Life we are working out, or the mathematical principles of abstruse equations, we are "initiated" by love of principle and not by a trick of computations.

The golden text of today's lesson contains this same idea. It makes mention of the outer performance of right actions with which the outer church is satisfied, and the inner performance with ideas with which Principle, the true church, is satisfied. The text reads, "Let a man examine himself, and so let him eat of that Bread and drink of that Cup." The lesson is found in I Cor. 11:23-34. It tells of breaking the body of Jesus Christ. There is a very visible meaning to breaking the body, and a very deep or esoteric meaning. The visible meaning is that the body of Christ is His doctrine. Whoever believes His doctrine in his heart eats His body.

The esoteric sense describes the effect of believing His doctrine. It coincides with the "Bhagavad Gita" teachings of "attachments." The mind gets "attached" to ideas. The mind gets glued to notions. According to these attachments, our "body" or quality of character is made up. The Jesus Christ doctrine eaten till it is bone of our bone and flesh of our flesh causes us to be "broken up" over and over.

The Jesus Christ doctrine does not let us get crystallized to anything. We cannot remember the past with either joy or sorrow. "Leave the things that are behind." It will not let us form the habit of anticipating the future. If we get to looking forward we get "attached" to the future. This looking forward is sure to result in a timid apprehensiveness or dread as we put forward our thoughts into it. The Jesus Christ doctrine, or body, breaks us up often when we eat it. It is itself broken into omnipresent ideas for omni-eating. It touches the tiniest event of each day to quicken it with life. It vivifies the dreams of our nights with omniscience. It takes away our memories of past events and people. It astonishes us with knowledge of present meanings of actions small and great. It gives us sight of the harvest of motives. It satisfies us with the outcome of ideas.

Through not eating the doctrine of Jesus Christ, but trying to impress the history of a personality upon itself, Paul says that the church is "weak, sickly, and asleep." He lays stress upon the principle of not judging of our neighbor's actions because our own actions cannot be judged by them. The people who spend much time memorizing external facts about things suddenly find their minds broken up and they remember nothing. If they have not identified themselves with the principles for which those external facts stand, they get the reputation of being old, or brain-cracked, or crazy.

It was an unworthy eating and drinking of life events that they indulged in. They missed the meanings, and must be counted in with the gluttons and wine-bibbers of scripture, as much as if they had spent their minds thinking of old and new wines, different kinds of roasts, and delicate fries.

There is but one subject with which the mind can be legitimately employed. That is pure Principle. "What principle is involved?" we must ask. The principle being true, we proceed to think it. We become it by thinking it. Now, Principle never gets old or cracks. So we, being Principle by thinking it, never get old or cracked.

If any sage or saint has the reputation of being aged, or having lost his mind, we may know at once that he occupied his mind with ideas of externals. He must have said a great deal about what it was religious to eat and not to eat. He must have tried to explain whether people should wear long or short hair, red or black dresses. He very likely trimmed his sails to keep in with people who knew about art, literature, and finance, not drinking the knowledge that the principle we are occupying our mind with takes care of our comrades for us, and finds our proper seats in the right places.

One who lately drank the blood of pure doctrine (using Paul's figure) found his family afraid to buy certain articles for fear they might fail to pay a coming note. He told them to buy what was needed for the house and let the future obligation take care of itself. He felt that by laying up for the future they fastened themselves into it to the discomfort of the present, which would certainly have the effect upon his family that it has had upon the church, so glued to its hopes of a future-appearing Jesus Christ-viz., "Weakness, sickness, sleep" (or loss of miracle-working energy). He saw that the doctrine of Jesus broke up his old "attachment" to laying up for a future.

The true doctrine breaks up all our old notions, but leaves us stronger and stauncher for the breaking. Facts about Pericles, Plutarch, Phidias, and Philo, statistics of drunkards, or records of cholera ravages, are very husky eating. They have no blood in them. They too, break us up, but they leave us blanks; we have to put out groping fingers after something we know not what. "Infants crying for the light, and with no language but a cry."

Pure doctrine eaten and drunk by us breaks up our notions and rolls them as debris down the stream of our principles. We find that if we suddenly see into a principle, everything that occurs immediately after that insight is the effect of that insight. For instance, you suddenly perceive that the reason why we have strikes is because the church has taught that man is under the curse, but sometime he will be free, instead of proclaiming that this day is every man free. You see the contracting effect of belief in the fall of man, so that some of us have fallen below each other in the scales and are subject one to another. You see how ideas go over the world, crossing and re-crossing each other in the minds of people who cannot imagine how they came by them, till the Jesus Christ doctrine of all being born of God from the beginning cuts some of the cords of the prevailing ideas and makes men feel that they have as good a right to peace and freedom as their neighbors. You see how working along on the externals by establishing charity houses and handcuffing criminals will never work the amelioration and reforms hoped for. You realize how definitely some strong mind must now set going the clear-cut statements of the Absolute Truth.

Well, the clear realization of all this, by one bold mental stroke, will knock off a dozen of your friends, tear up some of your estates by the roots, grind some of your fairest hopes to powder. But this pure knowledge of pure Principle, which will roll so much debris about your head, will also roll to you along its vitalizing stream some comrades whom winds cannot shake, some fortunes which come straight from lovers of your ideas, some new prospects for your family with unassailable strength in their excellence.

He that would save himself from the action of Principle had better not enter upon the study thereof. He had better play around among externals holding his goods by the skittish tenure of materiality. This is what Paul means by saying that we should not be judged with the world. The same sloughing off, of existing conditions takes place with people who deal with externals, because it is the nature of externals to change. The difference between the ups and downs of things under the law of materiality trusted, and pure Principle understood, is that the substance of things is more clearly felt and seen by those who get everything broken up by the stream of their true ideas, while they who trust in material ways see nothing except their losses.

We cannot judge by appearances, and the mere effort to do so is "eating and drinking to damnation, not discerning the Lord's body." A minister of the strict sort declared that he was so opposed to spiritual healing that he would rather his own beloved parents should "die" than be treated by such a practice. Not long after one of his parents suddenly "sickened and died." Had he known how arable, how fertile the soil of an intense or excited state of mind is to carry out suggestions, he would not have said that.

The one who believes in Christ as a principle of healing ever present among us is eating of the Lord's body. He who does not so believe is "eating damnation," so Paul says. He means that his words come to pass upon himself and his affairs exactly the same as do the words of those who speak

Truth, but that one goes out in nothingness, while the other lives. He tells us that if we hunger we had better eat at home. The deeper meaning of this idea is that before we get out among people we had better rouse our minds to the most perfect conclusions we can decide upon, which we would wish to see come to pass, and then speak some strong words to bring them to pass in our lot.

If we wait to speak Absolute Principles when occasions arise among our neighbors we may eat too greedily to "condemnation" — that is, we may speak what we will wish we had not when our neighbors arouse our feelings. It is not a good manner of "eating" to speak forth that it "seemed as if we should die", when we relate some anecdote or describe our sensations, for that speech will bring up an occasion when it will verily seem as if we would die. If the minister had thought it all over carefully before he committed himself to eating such words he would not have spoken them into the soil of a hothouse to bring down his father so soon.

According to Jesus Christ there is no reality whatsoever in the fruits of false or foolish words, but they seem very real indeed, and as there is a scientific way of averting the shades of error, we are here advised to take it. A lad took the positive word, one day, in the company of some grown friends that he would always be lucky. Immediately afterwards a piece of good fortune came to him, seemingly by reason of his wise exertions. A metaphysician told him it was because he spoke so sturdily while he was in company with others. He could not see how it was because of what he had spoken a month before when it was, as it seemed to him, wholly due to his "hustling at the right moment." "Your hustling would have come to nothing if you had called yourself unlucky when you were in the presence of other minds," insisted the metaphysician. "Your words are always going before you and lighting on your opportunities."

This is exactly what the thirty-fourth verse of this lesson means, whether Paul got so deeply into its meaning or not. Jesus told them to enter the closet and get it settled in their minds what they wanted to have brought to pass before they got out among men. Then, when excited, they would fill the rich moment with rich seeds. Higher than the flights of the archangels sings the meaning of every Scripture text. Down among the brooms and spades of the peasant's cottage rustle the wings of the angels of comfort these texts send forth. There is no moment when the white mercy of God is not touching each feeling, each word, with opportunity to make life a manifest garden of peace.

This lesson is called a temperance lesson. It is a perfect temperance lesson, because it insists upon our eating and drinking right ideas at home so that when we get among people we shall eat and drink with great results. You will notice that Paul does not tell them not to meet together to eat because he knows that words spoken in moments of excitement in the presence of others count so powerfully. He simply tells us to get our minds settled on the ideas, which we would like to see carried out, and then we shall not be off guard when we get talking in company.

Another thing about eating at home first is that the ideas, which we have thought profoundly, have a more enduring demonstration when they come to pass. If the boy had thought out that idea that he must always be fortunate on the principle that he knew God as the provider, and that God could not fail, his speech to his friends would fasten to an enduring demonstration of success, having an everlasting reason for the hope that was in him — not transient prosperity, like a hothouse rose that blooms to fade quickly.

In explaining Bible texts, do not stop at their outer meaning. Push them to metaphysical or esoteric meanings. Compel them to explain your commonest emotions. Find how they teach your mind to conceive its own law of easy mastery over your lot. You do not need to be always grubbing, and toiling and moiling while your neighbors lie in hammocks at the seaside, if you will understand the Bible. You do not need to have that dark cloud hanging over your life which makes your riches such a mockery. You do not need to dread forever something, you cannot tell what. You do not need to be glued to any of these things. They will loose from your life, with your understanding of the esoterics of the Scripture.

With this principle in your mind, this principle of the flowing torrents of pure understanding, which roll down and away the environments and possessions of men, you can see it is time someone spoke over the crossing and chaotic ideas of mankind, the absolute statements of Truth and stopped describing the heterogeneous state of affairs formulated by foolish words spoken in hot moments. If in volatile France, Voltaire's impetuous thoughts have been suddenly cut off by the statement that "Voltaire had no soul," so in plastic America your heartfelt pronunciamento, hot from the splendor of Truth, may cause to dawn this day the fulfillment of prophecy, which stops the slaying of animals for our clothing or food — stops the pain, the misery, which our preachers call the mystery of living — sets in order the Divine law of protection, providing, and delighting, by the same quick demonstrations of understanding that Jesus Christ made. As atheism practically received its deathblow by a statement, so misery shall lie down in forgetfulness under your omnipotent word. What is misery but the fruit of a mistake figured out on the boards of life? If Truth is a river of cleansing, shall not the mistakes be clean washed off the world's life very easily? Does this seem reasonable to you? If it does, you have prepared the way for some demonstration of a new sort of good to come into your affairs. Just perceiving the reasonableness of Truth is all you have to do about it. Perception is demonstration. Hold steadily to your perception of the reasonableness of this doctrine whether you see it work out or not. It does its own work. It will work in unforeseen ways for your happiness. It will go speeding on to happify the lot of others.

The glory of this doctrine is that the instant you do truly perceive it you love it. You do not love it while you are studying the rules for thinking which lead up to the perception of it, but the clear light of the gospel is not possible to them that are not obedient unto the law. And the God, who is neither law nor gospel, but is the Principle running through them, is not in you and visibly round you till you perceive reasonableness. The perception of reasonableness is God. So much Principle as you see the reasonableness of, so much God do you demonstrate, either immediately around you, or remotely from you, hastening now toward you. September 25, 1892

Bible Lesson LXIV. Acts 9:1-31. On The Healing of Saul

Swedenborg taught that the physical body is capable of being recuperated and cured of maladies by material means up to a certain point; beyond that point it must have spiritual food for renewal, and spiritual treatment for its cure, or fall under the death process.

Zoroaster (1200 BC) said, "One may heal with holiness, one may heal with law, one may heal with the knife, one may heal with herbs, one may heal with the Holy Word. Amongst all remedies, this is the healing one that heals with the Holy Word; this one is the best that will drive away sickness from the body of the faithful, for this one is the best healing of all remedies."

There are a great many invalids and sick people wandering up and down the earth for healing who will never be healed till they open their minds as docile little children to the Healing Word Zoroaster refers to.

Poor Saul of Tarsus needed healing of too much schooling, too much hearsay learning. He had swallowed every idea of God, which his schoolmasters had given him, just as he had swallowed the Mishna and Gemara, unquestioningly. So he wandered up and down seeking heretics to persecute, thinking to get his healing that way; but we know that it was the Truth, the Holy Word, he needed to restore his mind to the right state, just as we now know that people who have descended from chasers of heretics now need both bodily and mental healing by the right word.

"A right word, how good it is!" "Who can measure the force of a right word?" "He sent forth His Word and healed them."

There are millions of Sauls belonging to Brahmanism, Buddhism, heathenism, and Christianism who, from hunting out heresies in their neighboring denominations, have now a great deal of trouble with their eyes, because such stupendous truths are now being proclaimed that their antique ideas fall flat when they esoterically meet them.

People who feel confident that what their parents and teachers told them about God's "mysterious" delighting in Jesus is true, have their confidence in a reed so brittle that when the wind of a Stephen's treatment strikes it they drop to the ground with eye troubles, rheumatic joints, quaking nerves. The only reason they do not know that it is their mental error meeting the spiritual truth of some illuminated mind is because they are not as good timber as Saul. He was hardier, bolder, abler by nature, than they, and hence had not been so enervated by his "much learning" as they are by theirs. He had more presence of mind to understand his emotions.

Oliver Wendell Holmes says that, "the world's great men have not commonly been great scholars, nor its great scholars great men. The active mind feels itself above any and all human books." It is said of Whittier that if he had been a great scholar he would have enervated his genius. Not many minds are rugged enough in their natural genius to take too much ipse dixit. Saul, however, was one who had not been enfeebled by schooling; he had only become religiously knock-kneed, consequently he made a powerful opposition to the voice of the Absolute Truth when it struck his mind. He became totally blind.

At the present time, there are wonderful truths coming and going through the mental atmospheres, which act as treatments to the scholastic minds. If scholastic minds make powerful resistance, they have powerful ailments. If they make pusillanimous objections, shying around the questions that arise, they have half-blind, half-deaf, half-enfeebled bodily states. All the ailments of intellectual people are due to their evading spiritual teachings.

There are prophecies in the earth that about this time many people shall suddenly fall by the wayside of human life; "The places that knew them once, shall know them no more forever." They shall disappear like shadows.

If spiritual truth is the substance, and intellect and flesh are shadows, when spiritual truth shines hot overhead, why indeed should not the representatives of intellect and flesh disappear? Do not shadows always disappear at high noon? Saul could not be cured till a spiritually awakened member of the despised religious sect touched his blind eyes. Saul then became Paul the Apostle. Whoever yields to the irresistible truths of Spiritual Science becomes well aware that the spiritual intelligence of an Ananias is more capable than a Gamaliel to cure him of mental infirmity and physical disorder.

If according to astrology, it was written that about this time you would die, you could not die in the old way if the living truth of Jesus Christ had appealed to your judgment. But you must make some change of mind and action as totally unlike your old self as if you had died. You do not disappear from the sight and sound of your former companions, maybe; and maybe you do; but you will make as definite a change of life and mind as Saul made by turning into Paul. The acceptance of a new line of reasoning changes your mind and life. You are dead to the former mind and life. If you have always been thinking that strong, bold, vigorous, active warfare against evil and wrong is the way to erase them from the human lot, and suddenly the illuminating text of the "Bhagavad Gita" concerning the futility of active opposition to wrong, and showing the more excellent way of Spirit, comes clear to you, those with whom you have worked will know you no more among them. They have not seen the truth with you.

The full acceptance of the perfect truth would take us entirely out of the reach of our old methods. And it is the full acceptance of the Absolute Truth now, by those who see that it is the Lord's second coming unto full salvation, which is putting as many as do receive it out of the reach of the old experiences and old methods.

To those who are afflicted with the disease of poverty, the perfect truth with respect to Jesus Christ comes with healing of poverty. If any of the agitators of these times think they are doing the Lord service by persecuting anyone or anything, they must be told that they are mistaken. If their methods are carried out, it would be only changing the money from a Rockefeller's hands to their hands, and we have abundant evidence that they do not understand finance. No, there is an acceptance of some spiritual propositions, which would externalize as practically for the healing of poverty as Saul's blindness was healed.

It is the acceptance of some unwonted propositions, which has healed thousands of men and women in later years of bodily infirmities. Half the time they did not know which proposition cured them. They cannot tell which proposition by their "not accepting" makes them continue miserable in certain other ways.

One has to accept certain truths for the cure of lameness, and other truths for the cure of shaking palsy. So one has to take certain ideas for the cure of timidity, and certain others for the cure of poverty, just as practically as the kitchen girl would use chalk for cleaning the silver and sand for the floor.

There was one who would not be healed of a particular kind of bodily sickness till she accepted the idea that Joshua caused the sun to seem to stand still, that Elisha multiplied the widow's oil, raised the Shunammite child to life, etc. Her belief in the limited action of Spirit was like a fence to hold in her malady.

Whatever the reason that makes you a machinist, with not wages enough to take care of your family, you may be sure it is not because you are not as capable as the neighbor, who throws away more daily than you earn weekly, but because there is some one thing that you do not believe which you ought to believe. The instant you believe it, whatever it is, you will have some unexpected help from somewhere. Remember that any limitation is a disease. And take notice that poverty is a limitation as much as blindness or palsy.

The most cures of bodily disease have been made by calling them nothing but dreams snubbing them as delusions. Poverty has usually declined to leave the premises by such a simple process as calling it a dream, snubbing it as nothing but a delusion. That disease has required some more metaphysical doctrines, as for instance, that there is no God ruling over the world or over us — that all the God there is, is our own Spirit. We may be utterly astonished, and as "struck down" as Saul, when we first hear the idea. But if "Ananias" gives us the touch of his efficient explanations (or laying on of hands, as the ninth chapter of Acts calls it), we shall feel new power, new strength, new knowledge. It will be seen by us as a reasonable doctrine.

Some people have to believe in symbols before they can be cured of the disease of ignorance. Symbols, and signs, and dreams, and astrological foretelling, are all perfectly accurate. They are not to be despised. See how much more Saul and Ananias knew after they had praised, and believed in signs and dreams.

Do the stars then govern our destiny, according to Spiritual Science? No! We govern the stars and our destiny. The stars and the dreams are only innocent handwritings of our present status and our native possibilities. They are as truly nothing as the symbols of algebra. "The invisible things of God are clearly seen by the things that are made." And these "made" things touch us for good at every turn. Generally, we do not believe that dreams and stars tell us entirely of good. We believe they stand for evil, for dangers ahead, for deaths, for losses; but they forever prophesy of good only.

All the signals now thrown out concerning the speedy dissolution of this world and all things in it, are signals of the great wave of spiritual understanding, which shall touch the mind of man, now so diseased with mistaken statements of God, as Ananias touched Saul's eyes. There is a touching of the scales on the eyes of the world's theology, which will make the end of Saul and give us Paul throughout all the earth. There is a touching of the scales on your mind, which will snap or dissolve the filmy ideas, which make you cringe before anyone or any situation in all the world, and show you wise as Socrates, Plato, or Jesus. Perhaps you must say with vehemence, "It is not scholastic lore I need, it is to let my free Spirit speak its 'I AM' in me and through me and by me."

Perhaps you are to speak forth the statement of pure metaphysics that, "It is not money I need, but to let the free Spirit within me claim its independence of matter, its independence of people, its independence of all things. The Spirit within is the Substance within. God is the only Substance. Shall God depend upon money, upon people, upon suitable circumstances, to have all things, know all things, and do all things? Neither then shall I depend upon any thing, or circumstance, for the "I Am of me — the only I Am — is God".

Now this reasoning requires no exercise of the will. It simply requires your expression. The Physical Research Society, quite independent of the doctrine of Jesus, discovered that there is no need to exercise any will with our reasoning with people at a distance, in order to make them respond, nor indeed with people near at hand. The reasonings accomplish their own meanings, as the words of Jesus Christ to the mind of Saul carried their own weight.

The Buddhists teach that four classes of people accomplish results with "righteous working" — which means right reasoning — viz., the afflicted, the searchers for truth, the poverty-stricken, and the wise.

The afflicted are sure to be relieved of their afflictions by talking to the inner nature, which rests, so peaceful, within all bosoms forever. The restless wanderers of the earth, who are wondering always what is true among the multitudinous religions and philosophies, (which amount to nothing as far as practical help goes), are sure to get convinced of what is true without a shade of doubt, if they address with praiseful words, the wise inner nature, forever resting so calm in their bosoms. The poverty-stricken come into their rightful inheritance if they speak to the all-holding Owner of worlds, forever resting so royally free within their own bosoms. The wise accomplish all things by describing face to face the Omniscience, that sits as Omnipotent Principle, forever within their own bosoms.

"Why, then, did the Buddhists not reap the fruits of such beautiful doctrine?" Because they never spoke truth to their own inner nature. They never practiced what they preached. Do you practice praising through the night watches while you are restlessly tossing with inability to sleep — praising and praising the Supreme Spirit resting within your own bosom? It was no more incumbent upon them, to practice what they had heard of truth, than it is upon you to do so.

Simple proclamations to the nature and place of the Spirit will cause the proclaimed results to come forth. Absolute Truth will bring absolute victory. Hear the Buddhists praising the Spirit within them for establishing caste, for distinguishing against women, for making certain animals more sacred than even their own children. Is that absolute truth of the impartial, responding God?

Hear the Buddhists at their praises of the Spirit that dwells in their bosoms, telling it that it responds in their lives with exactly what they proclaim that it does, thus making themselves the arbiters of their own lot in life. Hear the Christian at his devotions calling his God a mystery. Hear him beg of a hard task-master to lessen the poverty, the suffering of his lot, fearing his God will not lessen it more than he believes that He will. Is that telling the Absolute Truth to the inner nature that waits in calm majesty the touch of your right words? Your own inner wisdom will not spring forth if you beg it to come. It will only stand out on the affairs of your life, on the health of your body, on the wisdom of your mind, by your describing it just as it is. Zoroaster called the proclamation the Holy Word, the whole Truth. Of what do you need healing? Of the idea that you have had a hard life? Look now, to the smiling majesty enthroned within you, and tell it of its eternal peace. Do you need healing of sickness? Look now at the gracious Self — dwelling in everlasting security within your own bosom, and tell it of its beautiful health.

Do you need healing of poverty, or of sorrow at the poverty of the world? Within your own bosom sits the Maker and Owner of all the universe. Is He poor? Is He in want? Is He mournful? Describe the greatness of that Center within you. As the sun breaks forth from the night, as he rides free on the highways of ether, so shall the sun of your world rise, so shall the scales of your night fall, so shall your mind ride free on the highways of the mistaken ideas of the world, and no man, no woman, no animal shall ever again cry under the dark doctrine of pain, of want, of ignorance, of loneliness, or of bondage. Some of you cannot be absolutely healed till you hear the response, "I am God. There is no God." All is God. God is now free. For this Being within hath a loud voice to touch you. Its Word is the holy healing of your world. October 2, 1892

Bible Lesson LXV. Acts 9:32-43. The Power of the Mind Explained

Anaxagoras, 500 B. C., finds the force which shapes the world, not in the nature of matter, nor in impersonal forces, but in a world-ordering Mind. This supreme Mind is distinguished from matter by simplicity, independence, knowledge, and supreme power.

Peter cured a "paralytic" and raised a "dead body" to life. It is evident he was not exercising the magnetic or mesmeric forces, for he explained that it was by the action of Jesus Christ the miracles were wrought, by the training potency of the words which represent the demonstrations of health and life. There has come up a revival of the idea of mental training by repeating words, which concentrate many meanings in them. By repeating "Om" in various fashions the Brahmins said man would become God, for man would gradually appropriate an understanding of "Om" and understanding is God. With this understanding, he should govern his world. And man is not truly appropriating of "Om" or Understanding, any more than he can demonstrate. This is the same as the saying of Jesus, "If I do not the works of the Father, believe me not."

Spiritually we take from Spirit only what we are willing to give forth. The prayer, "Forgive us our debts as we forgive our debtors," means that we cannot take any more forgiveness than we can give forth. The same with mercy. The same with friendship. The same with all good. No one is realizing or enjoying a moiety more than he is bestowing.

There is but one lake on the surface of the globe that has no outlet, and that is the Dead Sea. All of us belong in mental geography to some material country or sea, which is more typical of us than any other country or sea. Those who are choosing not to give forth of their mental riches belong to the Dead Sea type. To give forth our mental riches is to be speaking and thinking what the Spirit is doing; not mentioning what the flesh is doing. "The flesh profiteth nothing."

Dorcas had been thinking of the kindness of God till her hands had wrought many great deeds. Peter had been thinking of the Life of God till his voice could raise the dead. Aeneas had been thinking of the unexpected actions of God in miracles till be sprang up from palsy, because another, who also believed in miracles, spoke suddenly to him. Two people together visiting at our house, both strong in confidence that our prayers will be answered will quicken our spiritual faculties to lay hold of the blessings we are seeking. On the same principle two visitors, strongly intellectual believers that we are very foolish to trust so much to aid from miraculous sources, will chill the atmosphere and discourage us mentally till we begin ourselves to doubt. This will make a delay in the answers to our prayers. What kind of people are near you those of simple confidence in miracles, or those who consider all expectations of incalculable interposition in your behalf folly? You may compute your depressions or exalted hopes from the mental radius of such people as are your companions.

Peter was an uplifting visitor wherever he went. All believers in the power of Mind welcomed him with delight. He meditated so much on the visibility of God through repeating the Name Jesus Christ that miracles always accompanied him. Something always transpires wherever we go which is of the nature of our persistent feelings before we arrive there. Peter cured Aeneas and aroused Dorcas according to this lesson. He had taken his mind off the external persecutions of the young church so long that he was in an exalted state of mind just suited to heal. People, who are thinking of how badly they are used, or how badly someone is acting, do not carry enlivening atmospheres with them. The persecutions of the church were suspended about long enough before Peter went down to Lydda to give his buoyant mind time to quicken with extra ozone through breathing and eating and drinking two glorifying words. He told Aeneas that those two words were the healing force working instantaneously with him. "And Peter said unto him, Aeneas, Jesus Christ maketh thee whole: arise, and make thy bed. And he arose immediately." The two words always come to fruitage exactly the moment our type of mind gives forth its confidence, its love, its expectation to them.

Aeneas believed in miracles, but he did not believe it was quite time he himself received one, did not think himself quite ready for one to take place for his own benefit. Peter was the very opposite. With Peter everything was NOW. His belief in the "now" of the miracle struck down the "by and by" of the paralytic's mind, and up he stood whole. The entire battle of mind, one the "by and by" kind and the other the "now" kind, showed forth. All battles are in the mental before the externals figure them out. One idea in everyone always yields to some idea in every other mind that it meets. Some outside movement will indicate it. You believed James was in the wrong till you met Thomas and talked with him about the Presidential campaign. You never mentioned James, but you go home in certainty that James is right. This is because Thomas understands the truth of the case. Your idea is eliminated, beaten out, by Thomas's understanding. No words spoken aloud, no special thoughts on the subject are necessary. Every change of sentiment, every new manner of looking at a question, results from someone's understanding the true inwardness of the question. If you are a procrastinator like Aeneas, get somewhere near impetuous people who never can wait a moment for anything. If they believe in miracles, you will find yourself dispatching your work with miraculous speed.

Similarly, if you are one who belongs to the multitude of those who tell what good works used to be done, either by the apostles or in the early day of the faith cures of Spiritual Science, you need to have a Peter type of mind come visiting you at "Joppa." It is death, or old age, to talk of what used to be so much better than is now. Peter, the impetuous "Now," puts every idea of the past out of your house and makes his own prompt action startle your shrinking wish into exhibition. Peter himself is no more eager for great miracles of cure than procrastinators and backward lookers are, but he believes in expedition. Peter was the idea of instantaneousness which Jesus left to walk visibly when He thought it expedient that He go away. The idea still remains, though Peter, its representative, himself has gone away. We find this idea of the dead being raised to life, as Tabitha was in this ninth chapter of Acts, and of Aeneas being healed, instantly, always exhibited by the effect of certain people's mental presence among us. If they are utterly given up to the idea they do strong works promptly. If they take the idea faintly they do not do mighty things promptly, but simple works, like cheering people quickly, or giving excellent judgments without waiting to think. Only intense confidence wakes a man out of paralysis and a woman out of death.

The mind that raises the dead to life with a few words, and quickens palsied limbs with a sentence is the one that is all given up to what already is. It does not talk to you about "growth" and "evolution." Those words get utterly routed when the true Peter-mind saying, "There is no time in Spirit, no growth or progress in Spirit all is now," comes near.

Aeneas represents one who thinks of what great things are going to be done. This is palsy. Dorcas and her friends represent those who rehearse what great things have already been done. This is death. Peter represents one who sees life and accomplishments as neither past nor future, but now.

The body is not the only thing that gets palsy by looking forward. Knowledge, ability along any chosen line, stops, paralyzed with the idea that some time we will attempt the work we see ought to be done. Be bold to believe that today is the day meant for your healing, or for stirring prosperity along some line.

"Boldness hath genius, power, and magic in it.

What you can do or dream you can, begin it!"

The body is not the only thing that acts out deadness by looking backward over what used to be done. The enterprises you ought to be engaged in this moment, which were intended for your quickening delight and unalloyed success, will have nothing interesting or stirring in them when you think of them if you talk much of the past. It is as bad for the mind to contemplate the past as it is to anticipate the future even worse, if this lesson is taken literally. All is mind. You will see plenty of charm in enterprises if you never remember the good old times nor hope for better times. Refuse to meditate an instant on what has been or what shall be. Just this minute is the minute everything is alive, healthy, strong, and successful with you in Spirit. You can demonstrate as much "present" as you appropriate the idea of — as you let of Peter into your "house" — into "Joppa." They could not do anything with only a part of Peter in their cities — that is, with descriptions of him. That means we have to have the idea of "now" get complete possession of our premises.

How shall we do this? Peter did it by repeating the Name Jesus Christ over and over. Those two words usually hurry a man or woman over a whole lifetime of experiences within a short time.

The speaking of the word "now" has prompt efficiency with some people. It is not superstition; it is as sensible for mind to hold, by repeating over and over certain words, as it is for the outward body to eat oatmeal. One feeds the mind and the other symbolizes feeding the mind. Aeneas had mental starvation. A few words refreshed him. Dorcas had mental exhaustion. A few words revived her.

Peter was so pleased with the natural result of keeping the idea that Jesus Christ is now working, healing, and encouraging among us, that he concluded to stay in that state of mind, so he abode many days in it. This indicates that if you have an exalted certainty of the healing and quickening power this instant you may keep it intensifying with happiness as long as you please. That gleam of glad recognition of your own spiritual nature will be your constant home of bright rest by your saying, "I will abide here forever."

People should not say that "they were at one time in just the right state of mind to do great works, but do not feel equal to them now." The name of the Good is "I am." It is the Freemasons, who have changed the statement of Being from "I am that I am" to "I was, but am no more." If they had kept the teachings of Moses, while letting his mighty inner voice proclaim itself, they might have had every sign of the presence and working of good among us which we are asking for. The new Freemasons, now reviving the Spirit of Christ, do not say that they "were" strong, they "were" wise, they "were" rich, they "were" happy. They know very well that to be telling of the past is cold death. Notice how cold and dead Dorcas was to those who thought of what activities she used to exhibit; so even the most inviting prospect in our affairs will seem to have no life, no substance, no goodness in it for you who keep talking of "I was, but now am not as strong as I would like to be or as well, as wise, as satisfied."

To look forward is paralysis. To look backward is death. The name of the good in us ready to demonstrate with the world of affairs is I Am.

After we have settled the question of "now," we may say, "I was." Being confident of today, we may speak of "I will be." The Good lies back of us — "I am Alpha." The Good lies ahead of us — "I am Omega." The Good is now here.

Peter showed forth another important principle, that is, we are not to be mindful of praise or blame if we would do our most enlivening works. Peter was indifferent to blame, Dorcas was dead to praise. This combination wrought a miracle. We are not to swerve to the right for blame, nor to the left for praise. Keep your mind's eye on your own business and have as little as possible to do with the opinions of people.

Still another fact comes to light in the ethics of life from Peter's conduct as set forth in this lesson, namely, do not attempt to fight for your reputation or character. Be above reputation, above concern therefore. If Peter had failed to bring Tabitha into manifest life, he would have had the reputation of proclaiming a science he could not demonstrate. It would seem as if he were filled with vanity to even attempt to do the works of Jesus — to even say they ought to be done. He did not care what he might seem to be; his whole concern was with the duty that lay before him. He practiced his Science on every situation, regardless of appearances.

Lastly, we see by this lesson, that Peter had the solution to the ancient question of "how to animate the particular from the universal." Every "particular," which means every single manifested thing, can receive unlimited renewal, infinite reanimation, from the universal, by the absorption of the kind of living fire which gets kindled by independence of mind in regard to spiritual matters. If you perceive that "Simon the Tanner" is a spiritually awakening companion, commune with him often, be comrade with him much, though the church and your social acquaintances object. To be in the right and know it, with "Simon the Tanner," is better than to be pampered by opposing princes. Be comrades with the spiritually minded that you may be a better minister to the unspiritual.

October 9, 1892

Bible Lesson LXVI. Acts 10:1-20. Faith in Good to Come

Cornelius and Peter magnified every sign, and vision and dream that came to them as signifying some new power for good. Abraham was noted for believing every symbol to be the intention of some great good for him. Believing so innocently in the good, sure enough, each prognostication turned to their advantage eventually, no matter through what seas and winds of trial it steered its way to reach them. Cornelius gave "much alms and prayed God always." Peter had regular hours of each day set apart to prayer.

The true prayer is affirmation. The true almsgiving is denial. We hear of thousands upon thousands of worthy people asking assistance from rich church members, but not getting it, because the good, kind church people do not realize the difference between where and where not to bestow their bounty. They hide discernment — they show no judgement.

A systematic course of affirmation and denial, or speaking truth from both positive and negative, such as is mentioned in our present lesson, the tenth chapter of Acts, would uncover their judgment and quicken their discernment. The power of discernment and strength of right judgment belong to all men and all women and all living creatures in exactly the same quantity and quality.

Every man is as divine as Jesus Christ. The only possible distinction between any man, no matter what is his calling or seeming character, and Jesus, is that Jesus Christ told of His divinity and yielded Himself to His words, while the rest of mankind, even if they proclaim their divinity, do not yield to their words.

The measure of casting one's self into one's words is the measure of that person's demonstration of divinity. Abraham kept to the saying that was constantly in his mouth — 'The Word of the Lord." Everything that came to pass with him, or came near him he was sure was the "Word of the Lord." No matter through what seas of experience we pass after having an uplifted sense of the action of an unusual phenomenon in our lives, we are to see by faith some great good to come. It is sure to arrive. A right practice of keeping to this speaking of our divinity and casting ourselves into our words would make us demonstrate all of our divinity as Jesus demonstrated all of His. Then, like Cornelius, we would bestow our alms wisely and our prayers would be availing.

Outward wise almsgiving is the symbol of right denial. The right denial for want, hunger, need, beggary, is, "There is no want, no hunger, no need, no beggary." This is speaking Truth from the negative. Then the hands will make haste to act in such a fashion that those words will be proven all around in our world. There will be shown to be no want, no beggary, no lack. What the mouth speaks, the world shall make visible. A metaphysician, who had come into the knowledge of the necessity for putting his idea on the negative side, or denial side, instead of the positive, or affirmative side, had to change his thoughts from running on the words, "I am satisfied with the bounty of God," to "There is no need of the bounty of God." His first way of putting it had suggested the opposite to his peculiarly sensitive mind. The words, "I am satisfied," could not make his mind work with his affairs till he had said, "There is no lack." Cornelius was evidently one who used both forms of mental speech, for here it speaks of his prayers and almsgiving.

Peter was on the positive side. He had experienced one great denial and mentally thereafter, he had to come at the mechanism of his mind on the positive side only. Today it is the same old law of using the wheels of our mind by positive turns of expression or negative modes, or both.

People who are always feeling that they make mistakes but would like to do the right thing must pattern after Cornelius and use both ways of thinking. The "I" of us all stands back and uses its thoughts as the hands use pens or needles. The "I," the "ego," understands the Substance, which keeps it renewing the re-enforcing itself continually. It knows what thoughts to use to make it seem to be an erring mortal mind making mistakes, and what thoughts to use to expose its irresistible perfection.

Giving up all actions and all thoughts, leaving our destiny and character in the keeping of the "Ego" that understands all things, as a regular, daily practice, we shall have unerring visions like Cornelius, and instructive dreams like Peter. They gave themselves regularly to praying.

In the course of these lessons, there has been a constant repetition of the idea of speaking and thinking in an orderly, truthful fashion. Now it has come to where we must make mention of that high form of prayer which is without words, without thoughts, leaving the true "Ego," the "I," that is above thoughts, above words, to deal with us. We are to set apart a certain portion of each day to this speechless, thoughtless "letting be what is." The "is" which we by thus ceasing from thinking can let manifest, is not by any manner of means the material criss-cross appearance of physical phenomena. These are not that which is. That which really "is" we shall be absolutely glad to know. That which is "not" often changes its manner of dealing with us, from unpleasant to entrancing. That which "is" is changeless, eternal joy.

There is an intimation given by this lesson of the occult teaching that we are to stand aside and let the Warrior that dwells within us fight our battles for us, yet we are to act as though we did the fighting. It teaches that forever this Warrior within is indeed fighting our battles for us, but we do not stand aside. With all Peter's habit of positive confidence in the dealings of Spirit with him, he stopped to dispute its making known by him how practical we must make his religion. Many of us have spoken against the common sense of some little signal thrown out by the Spirit for our guidance because it did not appear under the circumstances we should have chosen. The meanest things, the homely things of daily turmoil, are not mean or homely when seen from the spiritual standpoint.

There is no voice truly speaking to us except our own Spiritual voice, whether the sound of it seems to reach us from within or without. The ancient secret doctrine taught that the Light of the world is within us all, and if we cannot perceive the Light within ourselves, we cannot perceive it anywhere. The voice that spoke to Moses was his own interior voice. It sometimes reflected itself upon the external atmosphere, but it was his own Spiritual voice. Our voice of the Spirit may seem to speak from without, but forever it is the Warrior within, the Light within, the Voice within, escaping forth when we know what is true, or when we see a vision with a warning, or hear a voice with a message.

Thus if we stop to argue against it we make a conflict within ourselves which is as sure to show forth in outward events as Peter's arguments against his own Spiritual judgment showed forth in the opposition of his Christian colleagues. Peter finally yielded to the spiritual voice that broke forth from his mind and reflected itself on the airs around him; so also finally, the Christians who opposed him yielded to his judgment. No argument worth giving voice to can be brought up when a spiritual principle is announced.

What possible worth is there in an argument for the reality of crime. Is it an argument for its reality that we claim to see it with our eyes and hear it with our ears? What use is there in such an argument as that, when every identical thing we see with our eyes, hear with our ears, feel with our sentiments, is the formulation of a belief?

Why do we need to believe in such things as if they were real when our belief is entirely within our control? Shall we not believe what we please? And shall we not please to believe what stands to reason? From time to time there have been strong, wise reasoners trying to show that all external things are dependent utterly on man's ideas. Aristotle, Descartes, Berkeley, Collier — read over their writings, and see what brave struggles they made to disentangle the mind of man from the network of belief in outward and seeing phenomena as having any controlling efficiency further than mind itself has given them.

One moment Peter showed confidence in the voice of his Spirit, the next he reverted to his old prejudices. "A house divided against itself cannot stand." Have we not all believed one way one moment and another way the next? Have we not, therefore, tangled and mixed environments? How do we know what sort of affairs would surround us if we were to believe one way constantly?

In our lesson, it speaks of the ninth hour and the sixth hour. The ninth hour is three o'clock in the afternoon, and the sixth hour is twelve o'clock in the morning. In mental training, they are important hours in the day. One is for withdrawing accusations from the world and from ourselves, and the other is for making the affirmation we would see soonest demonstrated. At three o'clock, Cornelius felt his prayers and alms taking effect before his very eyes. There are times when Spiritual ideas, that have been held in mind, are seen plainly to be coming into manifestation. He heard a voice announcing that what he had been thinking, and speaking, had come up as flowers in the sunshine of the Presence of God. He teaches us patience, persistence, and presence of mind. When it comes to a time when all things respond to our ideas we do not dictate to them, we listen to them.

There is a law by which things work exactly according to our ideas, as there is a law by which roses bloom according to their climate. Ideas in your home make a climate in which things and affairs spring up. A family always denying that they can afford this and that will fix their business affairs so that it will some time be very apparent that they cannot have anything. A family always fearing for the children's health will fix one of them to be a chronic invalid early or late in life. Yet the invalidism and the lack will not be real; they will simply represent the ideas of those who worried so much. This principle being known, we see how great a practice it would be for us to stop, like Cornelius, from having any ideas at all for a while every day. It would give us a great rest, and as ideas fall down at once into the sands at our feet when we let go of them, we shall thus leave our Spiritual "self" free to see and hear things from its own standpoint. There will be no more puzzling over books on language, no more worrying over mathematical computations of how to make both ends meet, no more scrambling and struggling for place and power, no more competition. The divine "Ego," being uncovered of the ideas that we must go through these things, will calmly tell the universe, as the maker of languages, the origin of numbers, the owner of its world, that it was only the illusion of the "what might be if it were not free," which has circles around mankind.

ius loved the fruits of his ideas. People who complain are only \[complainin\]g because they do not like the fruits of their ideas. As it is good \[for gr\]ound to lie untilled for a space, so it is good for our world if we do not forevermore plow it with our ideas, harrow it with our notions, enrich it with our erudition concerning the nature of evil, the origin of religion, the history of Rome, the marbles of Phidias, the statistics of crime; nor sow it with seeds of new science, new policy, new inventions, all relating to total unrealities. Peter did not love and he did love, all in a minute, the fruits of his past ideas. He should have kept silent when he was faced by the net full of creeping and crawling creatures. We will not think anything. Then they will fall away, leaving only the sight of spiritual kindness, giving us freely the sound of love at every turn, feeding us, prophesying for us.

Peter had no cause to dispute that what was spread for him to eat was good, only such cause as he had learned independent of spiritual judgment. We have no cause to see evil in our world, only such cause as we have chosen to believe exists unlike supreme goodness. It will be a great rest for us to cease believing contrary to what is true. It will spread our table with bread and milk and honey to cease from thinking at all, while the living Spirit is working out our provisions, our wisdom, and our actions for us. It may seem to the world that we are thinking and working, but indeed Spirit is responsible when we choose to cease from imaginations. "The Father that dwelleth within us doeth the work." October 16, 1892

Bible Lesson LXVII. Acts 10:30-48. Emerson's Great Task

Emerson teaches that the gods always overload with disadvantages those whom they have appointed to great tasks. Homer must be blind; Virgil must have asthma; Epictetus must be a deformed field slave. As Emerson had been appointed by the gods to a greater task than any he had in mind, he was more overloaded than any, for it comes unto a man that what he really believes, what he really covenants with as a principle, will work out with him.

Peter had been really preaching that God is no respecter of persons, so he was faced up with the compulsory companionship of people with whom it was an "unlawful thing," according to Jewish creed, to "keep company," no matter how good they might be. Had Peter refused to stand by his preaching when this demand for a demonstration met him he would have been defeated in his later conferences with the Christianized Jews. Many of us can attribute our misfortunes and failures to our once having refused to stand up to our ideas when they confronted us with their situations. As Peter stood to the practicalization of his religion, he won by his arguments when the Christians got to quarreling. Moses taught this idea to Esdras by a figure of speech, "Let the waters bring forth." Surely, the conscious words and thoughts we speak do bring forth. And there is no principle we can fellowship with which hurries us into its situations like a high and lofty religious sentiment.

The greatest miracles on record have been wrought by highly religious people. Religious principle acts like a hot sunshine over the waters or flowing ideas of our minds, and warms and vitalizes them so that they bleed with life at every point where we cut them. Our words are alive.

Any principle held as the light or guide of our life will by and by, vitalize our words with its purport. Klopstock was waited upon by some musicians from Goettingen, who travelled to Hamburg to ask what he meant by a certain passage in "The Messiah."

"I do not this moment recollect what I did mean," he said, "but it would pay you, gentlemen, to devote your life to finding out what I meant." He had such living, practical confidence in his principle that, being one with it, he knew that what it said through him was right.

Hannibal "swore eternal hate to Rome" as a boy, and lived and taught that hate principle so constantly that the sound of his voice was a terror to his foes. Hannibal is at the gates,, was the synonym for "destruction is nigh".

When a high religious proposition strikes the mind and becomes its daily theme for years all the words brought forth in relation to it live and act. If you were to set up an imagination of a perfect human body in your mind and describe that continually you would make healthy bodies appear near you for a long time, but as it would be an imagination of a form or symbol it would fail you sometime. The enduring and increasing power is our religious reasoning.

The twelve propositions of Spiritual Science are the highest religious reasoning. They have perfectly shining meanings lying just back of the outer wordings of them. It has been found that whoever penetrates these outer wordings and sees, hears, smells, tastes, feels, and knows the splendid intentions of them, finds his outer eyesight his hearing and knowing faculties sharpened and quickened. It has also been found that it is a stubborn stopping short of penetrating into the meanings of things, which causes a loss of the faculties in so many people.

If we do not want our religious ideas to work freely with us we have to throw up hard barriers of refusals. If you are wondering why your high religious ideas do not carry you more safely over the trials of your lot, you will find it is simply because you let your mind descend from its lofty reasoning to describe material performances.

Michael Angelo would not allow himself to discuss the faults of other artists. He shut himself alone with his own lofty ideals, and so kept his mind in a high altitude all the time. This caused itself to express what belonged to it perfectly. If you have a leaning to some special kind of art, increase and improve your ideals of it. Do not discuss the opposition of it at all. The belt of your planet is small — very small — if you stop from talking ideals to discuss imperfect works. A critic always has a small belt to his sphere. A critic is always a small mind. For one who is in the daylight of his art while he is thinking ideals, is in the nighttime while he is thinking of poor works. So if he turns from the perfect to the imperfect quickly his planet must turn quickly on its axis. Look out for the highest along your own line.

"One science only will one genius fit,
So vast is art, so narrow human wit."

Keep your mind on ideals. This continual flow of the river of thought will bring forth fruits at every turn. Let it do so. Peter here preached Jesus Christ so eloquently to the audience of people he once would have shrunk from, that it has become a living and active Christian idea that there are no high, nor low in Christ. All are equally endowed; all have the same opportunities to perfect themselves in their art, whatever it may be, by keeping the highest ideals in mind, by making idealism their religion. And the highest idealism is religion, no matter what you are studying. Its highest swing is Jesus Christ, or the expression of soul. In the practice of Christian healing we do not set up an image within our mind, and we do not imagine how a perfect man or woman would look; we keep reasoning onward along the lines of what God thinks. Like Kepler we say often, "O, God! I think Thy thoughts after Thee." At every turn, this way of thinking breaks forth into demonstration.

If we descend from our upper stratum of reasoning to discuss the faults and foibles of human beings, we are astonished to see how chilled we get with the disappointments of people not being cured, helped, or comforted by our high line of thought. We are apt to think the high lines of thought are not demonstrable.

John the Revelator speaks of four themes, which cause the mind's descent so that high demonstrations do not appear. Jesus speaks of our never discussing certain subjects if we would keep the mind swinging on the axis of eternal day. We must not talk about what is healthy or unhealthy, expensive or cheap to eat; nor discuss what we ought or ought not to wear;

nor confer with each other about what is safe or unsafe, good or wicked to drink. We may speak of the doctrine that heals, cleanses, quickens, and comforts. Doctrine is the only safe theme.

John the Revelator says that if we do not bring out the perfection of health, wisdom, and peace, in everyone we meet, it is because we have stopped to talk about, or think about, one of four things. One of these things that the mind must forever be above is thinking that we ourselves, or any other living creature, have appetites or passions lower than the breathings of the Holy Ghost. He who preaches Jesus Christ must hold forever that no man of flesh is our father. God alone brought us forth. Do not descent to talk of heredity of appetites or associations with temptations if you would make your words vascular at every point where the demonstration of purity is called for.

Another topic that the mind is not to descend into thinking or the voice into speaking about is that there is anything against anyone or anything. Whoever says opium is dangerous, or distillations of cereals or compositions of minerals are offensive, is descending from the ideal reasoning of God, who pronounced all things good. No one shall speak against the climate, the draughts, or the actions of earth's creatures, for he who would see them good must think along the thoughts of God. We shall not permit the lowering of the mind's holy reasoning into the thought of the talk of sin in the world or in ourselves. Sin is not a theme we can give any thought to. Many a good reasoner in Science wonders why his thoughts do not live and thrive at the harbors of demonstration where he halted them. He may remember that yesterday or last week he descended into the idea of the selfishness of Mary, or the jealousy of James or his own temper gave him regret. A fall of the barometer of reasoning must chill the delicate process of demonstration.

Peter here keeps up his majestic thoughts of the wisdom of God as pouring through all mankind, and permits not his mind to linger in the suggestion of how differently he had formerly believed. This stately march of thought suddenly breaks forth in the audience. "The Holy Ghost fell on all those which had the word." By this uplifted sweep of the Science shall the Holy Ghost fall upon this whole world.

The African Princes shall lift up their hands from slaughter, for there is a reasoning driving over the planet from the mind of the changeless God. Asia shall feel the shadow of her long belief in a karma folded around her ignorance, flee away into the infinite day of pure knowledge as God thinks of His people. Europe shall let go her clutch on the masses, through keeping them in poverty, for a high tide of Spiritual feeling is being driven over her shores by the sunlight of a pure and undefiled doctrine, away out of the jurisdiction of the church that has stopped on the line of her march of teaching the everlasting protection of God, to teach that He also calls some to misery. America shall cease from her mad scrambles for gold, for her mind shall catch the secret gleam of a Light that is shining from a people as inspired as Peter, with the certainty that undefiled Science will feed and clothe and heal without traffic or competition of man with man.

"The Lord shall suddenly come to His temple." The God whom ye have covenanted with shall write upon the bells of the horses, "Holiness," and upon the hearts of the world, "Peace." If ye have covenanted with hate, ye shall have a name that shall strike terror like Hannibal. If ye have covenanted with love, ye shall have the healed world for the signal of your chosen principle. If ye have covenanted with the principle of the absolute equality of all men in rights of possessions, happiness, and wisdom, like Peter, be sure that "the messenger of the covenant, whom ye delight in, shall come suddenly," and the gift of the unstinted Presence of God shall be demonstrated in the happy and wise earth, which prophecy has prepared for this age. In Spiritual Science there is no covenant with hate. The love of God is her only theme. Make your covenant now with love.

October 23, 1892

Bible Lesson LXVIII. Acts 11:19-30. The Teaching of Freedom

As lions crouch on their haunches and rally with mighty skill all the living forces concealed within them to spring far and hard, so the Christian Jews rehearsed the prophesies of the Messiah to come. They preached that Jesus had fulfilled them till their confidence was generated to the point of irresistible oratory.

Emerson tells us it is the man, drunk with conviction, who convinces. The early Christian apostles were drunk with conviction. They rallied their conviction by constant repetition of their reasons for believing that Jesus was Christ. For a long time they as a body of Jew Christians, rehearsed their reasoning among themselves. Then the fires of their religion broke out and they told the twelve points of Christian doctrine to the outside world. As the trained ranger over Texan plains lassoes the wild steer, so the trained Christian thinkers added a multitude of believers to their incontrovertible principles.

Every separate statement of Bible history is the "Rosetta stone" to the solution of an individual problem, a national situation, or a church state of affairs. As the masterly reasoning and transcendent religious sentiments of prehistoric Egypt lay like a sealed book under moonless night to the early Greek scholar, the Roman priest, the Oriental traveler, the German, French, and English savant, till Champollion, threw the light of wise interpretation over the hieroglyphics of the "Rosetta stone," so have the Acts of the Apostles lain under the cloudy materialism of modern interpretation, till Spiritual Science threw the ray of her twelve-pointed star of revelation over them. Hereby we learn to interpret what made the Christians of Apostolic times so efficient in converting to accord with their ideas. Hereby we learn how by constant thought upon the oneness of man with God in Substance, Wisdom, and Power, the young Jesus of Nazareth suddenly broke loose from His human nature, which works no miracles, and became in demonstration divine nature which works miracles.

At Cana of Galilee Jesus made the silent proclamation of His marriage with God and transformed the six stone water pots to tankards of red reviving wines. Under the light of the morning star of the science of Christ, we read that so His doctrine milled in the heart shall transform the six homely circumstances of every human lot into the red wine of beautiful associations. In the desert place, Jesus increased five loaves and two fishes to abundant provision for five thousand men, besides women and children, by blessing and praising the meager supply. The new radiance of the revival of His thoughts in pure metaphysics tells us that, we also in the seeming desert of our cheerless life, may take the few little possessions we do have, whose meagerness has so long offended us, and praise and bless them till they multiply into new treasures straight from the bounty of the ever-willing law of praise.

At the grave of Lazarus He thanked the Life-force that it had a law whereby if He spoke boldly forth the command of His soul, His command would be obeyed by the breaking forth of the Life-force in the dead and buried Lazarus. By the light of His love, I read my story as it lies here at my feet. I see, as the glory of His intention strikes my understanding, that when grief or resentment holds my whole being in its intense throes, that then is the supreme moment for me to decree a thing and it shall be established unto me, "Come forth, divine healing power!"

In this eleventh chapter of Acts, beginning at verse nineteen, we see that there shall spring a moment over the entire earth when all the people shall see that the light in all mankind is One. The prophecy of the great white rose of spiritual blooming shall be fulfilled. "And in the days of these kings shall the God of Heaven set up a Kingdom which shall never be destroyed; and the Kingdom shall be left to other people, but it shall break in pieces and consume all the other kingdoms, and it shall stand forever."

This everlasting Kingdom is the teaching of Spirit that there is no need to teach children not to tell lies, for if they know what the Spirit in them is speaking they cannot lie. There is no need to teach men not to overreach, for with the spoken words of the Apostles of Jesus the Light that now lights every man shall flame forth with the Holy Ghost of love and mercy. As the early Apostles showed how the carpenter's Son, by speaking forth to the world His inner knowledge, shone with Christ, so the apostles of today declare that by speaking forth the same Mind that was in Jesus, all men can shine with Christ.

This Kingdom is the teaching of freedom. There is a transcendent freedom awaiting the people. The Apostles threw off the yoke of caste ideas and breathed the breath of the knowledge that there is no man, no woman, and no child less than Christ. This free air gave them new healing powers, new providing energies. They were able to send food in the days of famine to far-off people. But they still held themselves under the yoke of expectation of martyrdom; they still held themselves under the fear that some of their members might speak too freely of the freedom of God.

Martin Luther rose up from the slippery staircase of belief that good works will open the spiritual nature to heavenly powers, to the more upright position that "the just shall live by faith." He breathed the air of a new freedom. But he still held the idea that no one could be saved into spiritual airs except by obeying his dogma. When the still freer doctrine that man is greater than his dogmas was offered him, he closed down on the opening rose of his opportunity and refused the loving Melanchthon's eternal friendship, because he had not yet accepted his ideas. He had not been staunch to confidence in his ideas as right. He had made himself free by them; but man's freedom for himself to worship God after the light of his own mind may take the swing that others must see as he does or die.

The great Chrysostom could answer like the free Christ that they could not exile him, for God was his home. They could not defraud him, for his treasures were in heaven. They could not defame him, for his witness was in heaven and his record was on high. But he chained himself from a new freedom by being among those early church fathers who believed in the subjection of women and abject obedience to the rod for little children.

See the wondrous glory that shone over the multitude at the free utterance of these preachers at Antioch! Their voices stirred the proud city to name them by the most Divine Name that the planet ever quivered under. See them close down on the opening rose of opportunity after opportunity to show themselves in full fellowship with the absolutely free Jesus. Why did they expect martyrdom and imprisonment? Though Agabus prophesied famine, should they meekly agree with him, with the example of the blasting of the fig tree still pictured in memory? Had they not heard that Christ opened prison doors to set captives free, not to receive them? Had they not heard that Christ is Truth? Could they not gather from the coming and going of the risen Christ that they need not die to reach heaven, that they need not preach regulations about eating or clothing, for the Spirit should clothe and feed wisely?

When they spoke of "being transformed by the renewing of the Mind, having the same Mind in them which was in Christ Jesus," need they have refused the next teaching of the over-beaming sunshine of truth, that all Spirit is God — powerful to close down on the schools, the churches, the kingdoms which tell that some are inferior, some superior, some clothed and some needing clothes?

To this day their idea of waiting to go through the tomb to be in Heaven has held the church from the bloom of life. But the Truth is not that we wait for our life of immunity from pain and trouble. The Truth is that we as Spirit are above the necessity for time. As Spirit, we do not stop amid the clashing ways of mortality. We rise out of them now. Their idea to which they were chained has come down over the centuries to us and held us as a Christianized people in its folds, that we must send missionaries and alms to the benighted and hungry part of God's Presence. The Science of Christ understood, tells that abiding at home, the Spirit of man may speak to the Spirit of man and there shall be food and raiment come folding the people with gladness.

Does such a message from the Spirit within us, speaking that which is true of Spirit, stop the sending of ships to the Blacks of the islands and books to the heathen of India? It will work out to the sight of the mind a new consciousness, an understanding why the far races beg us to send truth and not run to their shores.

We have no right to speak of the darkness of mind of races stepping on the planet of God. "The Light that lighteth every man," lighteth them also. We have no right to speak of the hunger and sadness of children walking over the plains of the earth of our God.

As sickness cannot be found when we proclaim from the Spirit that it is absent, so ignorance cannot be found on the globe when you sail around her God-protected belts. Go with the gospel that man is all-wise with the wisdom of God and you will not find a Black man eating his neighbor or hurting his children.

"Seek Me and ye shall find Me." Go seek God in the wilds of Africa and see Jesus Christ smiling with infinite beauty, and unlimited wisdom, from every face you meet

"Is this practical," you ask, "with the reports of the Livingstones and Stanleys of civilization explaining the darkness and sadness of Africa?" Just as you have now received the doctrine that sickness and bodily pain are not here, but only an imaging forth of what we have supposed, so there is no need of missionaries, no need of books, for ignorance, savagery, and race distinctions are only the mirage of our supposition. Seek wisdom on the islands and find wisdom. Seek the splendor of judgment and the knowledge of all the ages focused into all living creatures, and find them.

This is the kingdom that shall come to the earth in the days of the kingship of scholarship which believes in ignorance — of government which believes in inferior and superior — of church which believes in imperfection. Enlarge the bounds of your ministry. Open the expectation of your mind. As true as there is no sickness, so true is it there is no poverty, nor ignorance.

Shall there be an end of such a doctrine as this? Is it not what God says of His Kingdom? Shall I dare tell what God does not tell? This doctrine is Jesus come waking us up in our home. It shall stand forever.

October 30, 1892

Bible Lesson LXIX. Acts 12:1-17. Seek And Ye Shall Find

People seem to be all seeking something. They take a multitude of ways to arrive at the object of their restless search. It is written: "Seek and ye shall find." So the good or satisfaction people are seeking they will come at without doubt. Some things people get right away on this plane of existence, called mortal. Other things people wait for the astral plane to fulfill.

Herod loved to "please" the majority vote. So he beheaded everyone that those in power of public opinion wanted him to. Peter loved to do things, which he thought would please one man. So he kept courting martyrdom and imprisonment. They had very rough ideas of ways and methods for bringing about a satisfied state of mind, but hardly more rough than the ideas people nowadays have, who imagine that it pleases Jesus Christ for them to tell that the Christian walk is one of hardship and suffering.

It is related of a soldier in the East Indies that his comrades threw a basin of hot soup into his bosom to test his patience after his conversion to

Christianity. He had been a prizefighter, and they hoped he would fight at this insult. He, however, looked up calmly and said, "This is what I must expect if I become a Christian." Well, who taught him to "seek and find" such things as that? Was he not rather bending like a reed under the wind of a popular opinion of the Christian walk than standing straight up like a pillar of faith with the early proclamation, "I do not believe in violence and hardship?" "They that seek Me early shall find Me." Who is this "Me" the soldier might have found? "The Prince of Peace." He had a right to the peace of God. Does God suffer? Then remember it is not God-like to suffer. Those who are most like God suffer least.

People imagine it is very pleasing to God for them to tell how ignorant they are. Is God ignorant? Did He have an ignorant mind out of which to form part of His children? Is He not our Father? Did not His hand fashion us? Out of His own Substance created He not us? Is not that a rough idea of what is pleasing to the Infinite Wisdom who "fashioned all hearts alike?" Some imagine that it pleases God for them to be sick, lame, or poverty-stricken. Did God have a portion of His Being sick, lame, or poverty-stricken, out of which to make these people?

Even with a few of these notions lugging along in your mind, it is amazing how grandly one little ray of truth given forth will work. Pastor Harms, of the Hanover Mission, did not believe in begging. He did believe in getting money by the Spirit of God. So he told the Spirit daily how good It was to him, and let such a warm stream of gratitude run free over the universe that it attracted to him $14,781 in one year. No one had bent him to the notion that a Christian ought to go half naked and hungry, but he did yield to a point on the "barely enough" idea, for he felt it was a "skin of the teeth" getting through, that after all his prayers he had only $15 over his expenses. He would not let the full doctrine of "abundance" flow through him.

Peter, in this twelfth chapter of Acts, had evidently let the protecting idea flow freely enough" — so that it was only reined in by his seeking a crucifixion later on. "Not yet", was his constant idea concerning his own cross. Some of us hold the "not yet" for our benefits. We are all seeking our good. According to the law, we shall find it. As it is meant for us, let us put out our hands and take it as Peter took the angel's word and got out of prison. We have great wisdom belonging to us particularly; by putting out our hands — right ideas — we shall show forth this wisdom. We must put the right ideas to it unceasingly, as it is written the Church did for Peter that he might be set free. To the radiance of your own wisdom, speak truly how strong it is, how efficient it is, how beautiful it is. You will get out of this prison house of your imagination that to shut wisdom back is pleasing to the Divine Wisdom, makes you more companionable to your friends, or is of any present of future advantage to yourself.

You have a hidden Peter, a hidden healing power. Be a Church praying without ceasing for the freedom of that healing power. Tell it how quick it is in action, how sure it is to touch the right case, how willing to speed with strength every instant. Our lesson tells that as soon as the angel had wrought the miracle of delivering Peter out of prison he "departed." Of course, if one believes that the power of God comes and goes, leaving him when he has had some signs of it, he will experience accordingly. Tell your healing power how its strength and quickness abide with you, increasing daily. Your talks to the hidden energies of your being are either putting soldiers around them who will guard them from appearing outside, or they are setting the guards at naught.

What is your habit of speaking to your healing power? How do you speak of it? Some have put four quaternions of soldiers to guarding their healing powers and it is only by several nights spent in unceasing description of the healing Spirit that it comes forth freely to heal one case. The complaining, and mourning, and wondering, and lamenting because the healing power does not work through them quickly are quaternions of soldiers and stone prison walls to the healing energy.

How do you speak of your power of loving? How do you think of it? That loving power God gave you is eternal in its ministry. It need not be killed with the sword of persecution as James was by Herod. Do you think your love will cease because it is scorned? Do you think it is too weak to endure the desertion of those unto whom you sent its ministry? Tell the bright stream of your power of living that it is warm and strong enough to melt all the hate of a world. Tell it nothing can withstand it. Tell it how wise it is in dealing with all people. It speaks a word here and keeps silent there. It defends a child here and supports a whole family there. Each energy has all the potency of all the ministry in its nature. Each energy is strong in wisdom, quick in healing, wise in speaking, able in supporting and defending.

Is it your habit to tell the twelve energies with which you are endowed how perfect they are? If not, spend as long time as this church did telling of Peter's free goodness. Then a maiden will report to you that Peter is come out of prison. That is, some credulous person will believe you have great healing power, great wisdom, strong powers of some kind, as Rhoda, the maiden, first heard the voice of the liberated Peter.

You will not believe that credulous character. You would rather a bank president or a city mayor told you that you had such liberated powers.

Then, if you do not really feel satisfied that there is Omnipotence in your healing power so that it can melt down every obstacle from your path, why you may hide it under another set of ideas, as they did Peter for new fear of Herod.

But the mighty doctrine still remains that the angel of the Lord forever encampeth, the power of the Spirit is able for all things, and they shall not hurt or kill the Spirit set free at our will. Peter will continue knocking. Wisdom knocks without ceasing for approval. So we will without ceasing, tell of its strength and quickness. We will exercise it on every little event of our life and on every stupendous occasion. Shall the insect under the buttercup have less attention to the paintings of its little back than Orion's belt in its splendor? Shall the minutest bit of good I would have brought to me have less of the strength of my wisdom or love than my destiny in the sum total of my life's happiness? As my purpose is utter consecration to untrammeled Truth, so is my purpose to make the daily lot of the newsboy and my boy one and the same in strength of beauty, freedom of wisdom, and power in making the imprisoning notions of past teachings nothing — nothing at all.

What these two ranks of seekers go forth to seek they will find. It is not their good to win popular favor by shutting their wisdom and spiritual energies into the hidden places where they have been taught they are now kept only to be won forth by the terrible battle with ignorance. They shall hear the noble doctrine of Jesus that there is no danger in the pathway of Spirit, no failure in the judgment of the Divinity pressing for utterance at the gateway of every pore of their being.

The black man on the Saharan oasis shall not be sought for his rescue from evil. God shall be sought in his face and in his life. For what we go forth to find, we shall find and how we proceed is according to what it is we proclaim we are seeking. What we do is the energy we liberate. We liberate what we choose. We are transcendent beings, using or not using our energies according as we choose.

The prison and cross for them that seek them. The glory of Jesus in quick demonstration for them that seek Him in all events. Ignorance and sin if you seek them — the goodness of God if you please. "Seek and ye shall find."

November 6, 1892

Bible Lesson LXX. Acts 13:1-13. The Ministry of the Holy Mother

The people have always used two ways of bringing to pass life, health, strength, support, and defense. Either by material performances or by spiritual exercises great miracles and mighty improvements have resulted, or failed to result. When life was to be saved in great multitudes, soldiers with sabers and guns have slain other multitudes to save it. If starvation stared a city in the face its strong men tore down and pillaged other cities to get bread for that city, or cultivated patiently the seeds and soils to bring enough to the families. This is materiality and its processes, sometimes peaceful, sometimes violent.

By spiritual of metaphysical processes the same results have been reached without any such exertions of muscles or patient delving as the material or physical ways demanded. Instances by the million are reported through the ages, of how, by a metaphysical operation called prayer, miraculous things have been brought to pass. Elisha, a gentle prophet of Israel, a thousand years before Christ, came to the rescue of a besieged city, and by praying caused a great abundance of provisions to be suddenly spread before the host of starving people. The king with his strong and willing army had utterly failed to bring the needed assistance.

Elisha could do great things and small things by the exercise of a metaphysical process called prayer. Nothing was too small and insignificant for him to pay loving and majestic attention to, and nothing was too great for the mighty sweep of his spiritually enlightened faculties. He was very like the Supreme Spirit, whose cooperation his prayers invoked, in the respectful tenderness with which he touched the tiny wants of little homes and the immense wants of kings and kingdoms.

The Supreme Spirit lights the flaming points of distant Arcturus with glory and reddens the wings of the insect under the grasses. The great God delights to wheel in heavenly splendor the sunlit worlds of Canis Major at the foot of Orion, and to move in speechless happiness the microscopic infusona swimming in speed around each other in the tumbler on your table. So Elisha raised up with tender kindness the Shunammitish baby, and drew the ax head from the bottom of the Jordan for the simple-hearted laborers, exactly as readily as he opened the dropping globules of ether to disclose the heavenly hosts that loved him.

After Elisha, Hezekiah, a king in whom the knowledge of the ways of that metaphysical presence men have called God was quickened, lifted up his voice, and spoke words whose import unlocked the gates of assistance where no material or physical power was available, and swept the fields of a host determined against him. Not a sign of harm was visible when the spiritual exercise of Hezekiah had wrought its mission.

"The king is not saved by the multitude of an host, neither the strong man by his valor," according to the spiritual doctrine of processes for demonstrating life, health, strength, support, and defense. No gathering multitudes, no mechanics of civilization or barbarism, can match the sweep of a prayer which has let loose the floodgates of energy stored in the circumambient ethers around the heads of nations.

The company of Scotch Covenanters, whose enemies chased close, stopped at the sound of the voice of prayer of Saunders. "Spread the cloak over us puir things," rose his childlike petition, and the messengers of mercy dropped their soft robes down close, till with a fog of hiding the pitiful band were covered and the discomfited enemy turned back defeated. They called it a fog, but it was the hem of the mantel of a protection, whose white kindness touches the pillow where your head rests, ready any moment to be stronger than sorrow, more terrible than an army with banners, if you will but touch its sweet chords with the words of your heart. Nothing material can reach it, nothing unjust, or angry can stir it, though it is as willing as the mother who bent over your cradle, and as capable as your highest hopes could ask.

Choose people, resting, walking, studying, or competing, whether it is better worth while to become at one with the Spirit brooding ever over and near and through all the earth — or to go on in the ways of the flesh — whose competitions and strivings wear the heart sore, and strike the hopes back, till the skin is withered and the eyes have lost their light.

Ever and anon the lovers of the spiritual ways have spoken, but the noise of the world has been too great for the sound of their teachings to touch that inner ear which must respond before the mind is willing to cease using the hands and brain of physical existence to bring to pass its assistance, its life, health, strength, support, and defense. The noise of the world has even drowned to their own ears the sound of the teachings of those who have struggled to free themselves from the harrowing ways of materiality that they might be united with the peaceful successes of Spirit.

Ages ago the Zoroastrian prophets taught a lesson of how to live by the Spirit out of the reach of the fret and turmoil of matter. Taking the wings of the words of faith, we rise into the airs out of the reach of pain, away from the lashings of fate, free from disappointments of trying to win our way in a world gathered to defeat our every purpose, they said. But a sound of the world's beliefs rose high on their bewildered ears, and they stopped to parley about what evil things the Spirit saw in different kinds of foods and the marriage of castes. So they drew the gates against the Spirit with bars as strong against its beautiful ministry as if they had been stone walls clinched with steel bolts. For the Spirit is only wooed by praises. She only moves down on the hosts embattled against us when we unlock the filmy gates between us by the keys the truth in our hearts tells. The Spirit cannot look upon evil. She sees none in her life. She touches none in her pathway. When talk of evil begins, when scolding or descriptions of troubles or wickedness begin, a gateway is closed against the glory-shod feet of the Holy Mother of mercy and love.

The Brahmins spoke of her white robes of healing and she let them fall over the bruised spots of their lives ages and ages ago. Then they refused that those born in lowliness, and those born as women, should feel the touch of her seamless robe of healing, and closed the invisible gates against her streaming balsams of cure for all evils. For God the maker of worlds, God the Father, is careful of God the Spirit, the Holy Spirit, the Mother, that she shall go down only where the gates of hiding are opened by Truth. Praise without blame, kind words without tincture of censure, the Holy Motherhood of God may slip down through, and with the soft fingers of divine tenderness smooth the brow of anguish or give the help that is needed.

The ministry of God is the Spirit of God, the Mother. The Mother is fair, and kind and untouched by the name of sin, sickness, or death. He who would live must open the gates for the Mother of Life by thoughts that eschew death. So Paul closed the gates against the Mother Spirit, the Bride of God the Father, and down fell the sight of poor Elymas (Acts 13:8-12). Tender words, gentle words of healing life, balming, forgiving words, would have opened the gates for the Bride to walk through, that the perfume of her holiness might have seized the heart of Elymas to speak forth in raptures of the power of the Spirit of God as greater than all the acts of his legerdemain. He might have seen how sweetly mysterious, how strongly miraculous God as a Spirit can be, ministering unto the sons and daughters who constitute the sonship of God in their divine nature. But Paul caught a sight of the blackness of sorcery and called Elymas such names, as the ears of the Mother are never permitted to hear. The protecting Father hath a law that the mother ministry of the Spirit shall never pass through the walls where hard words are spoken.

Make smooth the grasses,

Cover the pathway with leaves,

My bride's feet are sandalled for peace.

The early Church forgot this law of God the Father concerning the ministry of God, the Spirit Mother, and closed against her mercies, her kindness, again and again, till the healing of her seamless dress touching the bedsides of pain and disease was by and by lost sight of, and miracles have been so few that men have even doubted if the Spirit ever wrought any.

There have been twelve messages, which the metaphysicians of the ages have given, which have had the opening of the closed gates in their strength and wisdom. The Spirit has stepped forth through them. John the Revelator called them foundation stones to the beautiful temple. He called them gates of pearl. Paul had been right in saying that we are the gates of God. He had spoken some of the messages with the unlocking skill in their meanings. The Spirit of God has always stepped into sight with miracles of healing, and uplifting, and comforting wherever they have been spoken. All the world which has had freedom from speaking the words the Healing Mother must not hear has agreed in the messages or statements which make straight and smooth her pathway over the needs of mankind. We now call them the twelve lessons of Divine Science. The early wise men called them the twelve genii of power — the twelve labors of strength — the twelve energies of being. Here at the center we dwell. There at the gates dwelleth She. It is ours to open the gates. It is Hers to enter in through the gates. "Go through — go through all the gates to make way for the people," cried the prophet. Letting Paul's closing down of the Spirit aside, seeing the opening of the gates of the loving deputy's mind, we will mention the true ways of Jesus. We will touch the hinges of pearl that from this moment we may not hide the ministry of the Motherhood of God.

Did you ever notice how careful the noblest and tenderest husbands are that their beautiful wives shall hear nothing hard or pain-giving. They are the living symbols of the carefulness of God the Father that the Spirit, the Holy Spirit, shall not be found where censure, criticism, scolding, maligning, or crying, are going on. The filmy walls between her merciful ears and our harshness are as thick as the stones of the ancient prison walls so far as her hearing is concerned. Yet she is near, close, ready, all-powerful, all-capable, empowered with the signet ring of God, the Omnipotent Father, to hear all our prayers. Open the gateway to her ministry of a new life by telling what her blessed ears may hear about life. So she will stream into your soul with a new life-quickening, and forth from your soul will go to the dying a stream of that ministry called raising the dead, which Jesus, whose ever-present Mother she was, brought to pass so often.

We may let her in by telling things to her about health, which the Protecting Father would willingly let her listening ears hear. Do you know the second message of Science concerning health? It is the only one by which she may enter into your soul and by which she may go forth where your heart chooses to heal and cure the hurts of the world.

There is a third message. It is about strength. If you are ready to speak as the Father permits the spiritual strength to hear, she will revive your energies, and up will spring the strength of those for whom you would have strength transform out of weakness.

The fourth message is what she is ready to do about supporting you without your struggling against any odds. The Spirit would have you as satisfied as she is with home, bread, and wine, and milk and honey. But she may only hear the fourth message of Science concerning support. You may rest back of the gateway of plenty, till you give her the open sesame the Father will let her come in by.

She will shelter you and the world if you will let her in by the fifth message of Science. She may go before like a wing of defense where the danger is lurking, and no ill shall befall where you speak the safe words for her to hear concerning defense.

The sixth message will give you the character presence which high thoughts on majestic themes can give. She will show you how to think so as to be the Sardius stone, shining as one whose soul converses with the immortals.

The seventh message she has consecrated to the spoken word. She will speak with a voice, and speak through your voice, so that the ears of the people will sharpen and their hearts shall leap at your words. The sound of your voice may be full of healing, full of uplifting. She will touch your pen with the fire of inspiration if you are bold enough to tell her those words about writing things of great purport which the Father gives her permission to hear. She will touch your throat with songs of the cherubim and seraphin, chanting great symphonies around the seas at the foot of the mountains of Paradise, if you tell her what God is giving her ears to hear, about the voice that enchants with melodies that cause the hills to drop down their odors of healing and apples of bliss.

She can make your fingers supple and skillful if you know the words about skill, when she, bending low by your pillow, may hear. She can make you so beautiful that the beggars will forget to be hungry. Her smile may light on your face with its own love-lit glory, if you know the eleventh message the great God calls the opening of the gateway to the sight of her face.

She will teach you how to love so that all hate shall be melted where you speak and where your face is seen. The genius for loving so that anger is smiled into peace, the genius for loving so that sorrow shall rest into gladness, she can enter into your soul with that love and pass over the world with it. You must make her hear by the twelfth message of Science, which is the only one the great love of God permits to hear.

She was bending close over Paul, but he would not open the door by the key, which his heart held in a secret recess. If he had given the Holy Mother the twelfth message of Science, Elymas would not have been struck blind. No, he would have loved Paul with the love of a brother, and gone with him over the cities where he knew their secrets, showing him all things in patience and sweetness. The Scriptures are given for warnings. This lesson is a warning. Do not think the mother tenderness of the Omnipotent God as spirit of miracle working ever hurts. It is when words are spoken which her ears are protected from hearing that blindness and pain and disappointment fall to the lot of the world. God is good. The Spirit is love. The miracles of Spirit are for joyous fulfillment of hopes. Whisper the words to the ears of the Mother. Let down the bars between her everpresence and thee. She will enter in and go forth clad with the miracles of Jesus.

Let him that heareth come! Let him that is athirst come! None is so lowly, none is so wicked, but she will bend and hear, if he will not use the words the Father never permits her to hear. She is wooed by praises; she hears great praises of God the Father. She loves the descriptions of His majesty, His mercy, His watch-care, His omnipotent love. Do you know the words the Father openeth the ears of the Spirit to hear? November 13, 1892.

Bible Lesson LXXI. Acts 13:26-43. The Power of Lofty Ideas

If a person is in great trouble and affliction, he should make the highest and most Spiritual affirmation that has ever struck his mind as a beautiful truth of God. He should keep on repeating that idea in his mind till affliction is left behind. He will then be delighted to find that he is stronger, more buoyant, wiser than he ever was in his life before. The trouble has not left him the worse for wear, because it has not touched him. His lofty idea only has touched him. Keep it as a rule of mind in the time of great persecution by circumstances or people, no matter how they come to pass with you. Touch not the earth; touch God. Here Paul tells of how, by the high arm of God, the Israelites were brought out of Egypt. They took their highest ideals of Spiritual power and held to them while they were in sore distress. Our highest ideals are the strong arm of God leading out of whatever bondage we seem to be in.

Paul immediately goes on to say that God destroyed seven nations in the land of Canaan. God never destroys anything. If, while we are looking straight into this Spiritual Presence, full of goodness and peace, we keep speaking of God's making men so constituted that they cheat, hate, fight, then those words come back upon us in a crowd of people who misuse us. We do not need to say God ordained it or made our lifelines to run in misery. We must be free from our ideas if we would run on smooth lifelines. Some of the finest minds through the ages have discovered the marked and immediate connection between ideas and events; they have left out one proposition, which now we use — change ideas and events change; drop ideas and events cease.

Paul here says that God suffered their manners forty years in the wilderness. God suffers nothing. He endures nothing. The Israelites in the wilderness simply spoke halfway and compromising texts concerning delivery from bondage, therefore they took extra time to get out of desponding conditions. Hope and faith must unite in the mind to bring strong, quick deliverance from your hardships.

Notice that children have just as much faith that miracles of help will be wrought as the parents' hope will let them have. A child's confidence runs up to the express expectation or hope of the mother. "God will hear us when we have scraped the bottom of the meal barrel, Mamma" "I hope so." If the mother had taught the child that there is no such thing as the bottom to a meal barrel, his confidence would have run up to that teaching. That family would always be provided with abundance of meal. Let the mother's teaching run buoyantly, and hopefully up to the idea that there is nothing on the earth but what they can have in full, rich, bountiful abundance, and up the child's confidence will run to meet and mingle with the teaching till the earth with her bounty comes hurrying to fulfill the faith of the child.

Has God changed toward the mother and the child? Did God suffer because the meal barrel was empty, or rejoice because it was full? Does the mathematical principle you are dealing with suffer when you say you have got your problem all wrong because you said if X squared is 64, then X must be 77? No, X will always equal 8, if its square is 64 — no matter what you say. You need not lay your misery to the Principle we know as God if you will tell how God made your happiness less or more. You shall lay your misery to your ideas of God, not to God.

Paul often rose to stupendous metaphysics, as when he said, "We can do nothing against the Truth, but only for the Truth." The Truth shines the clearer to us when we see how unalterable and how un-cajoleable it is. If the Israelites complain about Truth because it did not hurry them out of trouble, they never touched Truth, which is supremely free from trouble. If nations fell back when they appeared, then nations fell back because they had confidence in the hopes of their leaders. They believed as high as their teachers taught them they might. They were free as far as they heard and had confidence in Truth. If a doctor goes into the sick room and tells his patient with buoyant cheerfulness that he is sure to get well, the patient will get well if the doctor's hope strikes the faith cord of the patient. If the doctor has such buoyant cheer right straight along and never lets his mind get nipped by that hidden fear of evil, which his mind keeps in his cellar, the patient's faith will get hot enough to take him into splendid health. Thus, two of them together work the cure right through the sickness. Hope, and Truth, and faith in Truth are quick freedom from evil.

The whole of faith and the whole of hope ought to be united in every mind. The Jews of old had covenanted with God for a Messiah to come in the process of time. They also covenanted that the Jews should refuse him when he did come. So it all came to pass. But the everlasting Truth still remained that the Messiah was then with them and able to save them from trouble and hunger any moment.

Paul refers to the time when the Jews had been so self-willed that they would have a personal king. He then shows how David, the shepherd boy, came up as a fruit of their strong will, which sometimes drooped into sweet meekness. If this strong will is in one mind, it will drive its life environment all askew. If you have a strong will, you must be exceedingly meek to listen to the word of those people who get on in the world by high principles. The strong will, bending to hear a great principle suddenly strikes fire, and the clear and beautiful judgment rises. Martin Luther was not nearly so brilliant and able by scholarship or native talent as Melanchthon, but he was more meek to his religious teachers, consequently there came a moment when his judgment stood upright on its feet. He had come to the fruiting time of will crossing with docility. There is great strength always born with good judgment. He was strong to proclaim his new confidence that it is not by works that we get spiritual but by faith.

The commonest intellect, with the poorest sort of education, will be enabled by the union of will and meekness to sit in council halls as wise and sound in judgment. Without docility, such a character is obstinate and stupid. Always there is one idea to gather ourselves to and rise within — on the union of it with our strongest trait — into freedom, peace, and wisdom. The genius along any line should speak out and think out the science of the art he is the master of. Gasner, the matchless healer, could not explain, on scientific principles, the process by which he healed the multitudes. Consequently, the science of his healing was as invisible after his brilliant cures as before he touched Germany with the comfort of his presence. It is exactly as if the mathematical genius should be able to tell mankind about the coming conjunctions and transits of heavenly bodies by lightning — like calculations from first principles, but could not explain how he did it to his admiring fellowmen.

Every brilliant cure has its perfect explanation. He who shall arise with a good explanation of how he brings to pass instantaneous bodily cures will be the Jesus Christ of the age unto which he comes. His own body must be perfect. It must vibrate to the touch of his Science as blissfully as Paganini's violin lifted and enchanted his audience when his fingers of fire from immortal altars quickened its fibers.

It is by the twelve lessons in law and twelve lessons in gospel, united in one mind, that success is best manifest. One by one, the conditions of our human lot are transformed, as we go on from mountaintop, to mountaintop of thought about God. We learn that we do not need to tie to even the loftiest Truth we have so far realized. The Jews did not need to fulfill the prophecies of their fathers. They did not need to pin to a tradition that they should hang on a tree the Lord of all the earth when He came. We do not need to pin ourselves to the doctrine that the just shall live by faith if we have found that life is forever in us, whether we believe it or not.

Martin Luther held himself pinned to the fourth mountaintop of Science, till he wrought out the freedom of a planet from the idea of living by works. But when the gentle Zwingli offered him the hand of love and friendship, independent of doctrinal differences, he had the offer of his lifetime to spring to the heights of a principle more glorified than his mind had touched, namely, "He who loves me transcends me." Doctrine to the winds when friendship lights the hilltops! Was not true friendship, love in the heart, able to cause difference of opinion to be nothing? It would not have hurt his doctrine, but would have untied him from a post to which he was gathering himself if he had accepted the loving friend ship of Zwingli. He who ties to an idea is as struck with death as he who ties to a tree in the wilderness.

There is always something dead in the body of him who tries to tie others to his ideas, for the chain around the ankle of the slave is clasped around the neck of the captor. If you do not believe in tobacco, that is no reason why your mind should tie your neighbor to your idea of tobacco. Mentally take your clutch off him, and, being free from the chain of your censure, he will rise up to a clearer sight of what it is his soul seeks. He will be more healthy. You will suddenly be free from a burden of your life. You have been tied to your own opinions and have tried to tie others to them. From the time you take the yoke of your opinions off your sons and your neighbors' sons, so dead sure you are right and they wrong, they will breathe the air or goodness and you will rise free from that physical disease or pain that represents death through being tied to ideas.

Paul agrees in this, Acts 13, like a person in a nightmare, with the idea that the prophecies of evil must be fulfilled. He agrees like a person half-waking with the promise, "God shall raise him from the dead". This is true. This moment dead hopes will arise if you let go your ideas of what people ought not to do and what they have done that you do not think is right. In all the universe, there is only yourself and God to describe. Yourself as rejoicing in the peace and love of God, and God as all that is good. Paul should rise to the Absolute of the promises. He should get clear from traditions. No corruption for any man more than for Christ, for God is freedom. No death when we speak truths, for God is freedom from death. No burdens, for God is freedom. No pain, for God is freedom. No prophecies, for God is freedom from prophecies. No waiting, for God is NOW freedom. Mind is free to be as wise, as great, as powerful, as it has courage to let go its past ideas. God has no ideas of the past. God is freedom of ideas, past or future. Therefore unhitched from opinions, we are free as God. Paul refused his freedom. We receive ours. November 20, 1892.

Bible Lesson LXXII. Acts 13:44-52. Acts 14:1-7. Sure Recipe For Old Age

There is in the spiritual pharmacopoeia a sure recipe for old age. You will remember that Thoreau speaks of the young man as a demigod, because his thoughts are only half in sympathy with the earth; the other half is still clinging to the glory that he had with the Father before the world was. It is by letting go his hold on the expectation that Divinity will prevail and the hosts of God will miraculously interpose in his behalf that he gets way-wised to earth and uses the world's methods with greater or lesser success. Then, instead of stepping from the prime of manhood into the glorious beauty and power ordained for him from the foundations of being, he gets watery eyeballs, brittling limbs, and grisly cuticle. This is called old age. But no man would ever have stepped from the aspirations of youth with its way-winning beauty into the estate of old age if he had chosen at the flood-tide of opportunity to let go the world's ideas rather than to let go expecting the Spirit of Glory to do all things.

The little child's thoughts do always behold the face of pure goodness. Youth and early manhood have not yielded quite their ears and eyes to the voices and sights telling things of evil. And if only the things of Spirit should ever be told them there would never be any sign of decrepitude, and mortality's mold creeping over them. Who told the child that danger lurked in his pathway? Did you? Was not the Spirit within him strong with the safety of the Spirit without him, stronger than all the dangers you could imagine, till he listened to you and let go his own inheritance of safety eternal?

Is it not Satan tempting the innocent over again every time we prognosticate hurt? Would it not be more like taking a draught from the walls of the Spirit of youth for us to see as the child sees, speak as he speaks, expect as he expects, than to be his so-called wise guardians, careful instructors, grave fore-warners of evil?

To the church, this mighty doctrine of eternal youth was entrusted. She has struck the rim of her own old age by describing the pitfalls that lie in the pathway of youth, and the mold of the lack of honest confidence in her goodness has begun to wizen her pulpits. So to the Gentiles, those who could not believe that if God is good and occupies all space and all place He could call a Son to die, or a world into hardship, is now given the doctrine of Jesus, that whoever tells Truth does not fail or die — he becomes transfigured in the sight of the nations. At the floodtide of his letting go of the religions that urge him to beware of evil, he finds himself absolved from the world, free as the Elohim on the joyous streets of the city of God.

Transfiguration is the birthright of man. "Where I am there ye may be also." He who rejects everything except the real meanings of the teachings of Jesus ascends into His glory. "Understanding is a wellspring of Life." As the body thrives in appearance by assimilating right food, so the mind quickens and gleams by eating of the doctrine as Jesus did truly give it to man. Every time the mind understands a principle of good, it increases in stature.

If you see that it is perfectly safe to tell children their nature is God, and their pathway is absolute safety, that seeing is a new quickening of your mind. If you do not see it your mind must have some other idea ministered unto it. If you see that it is as if you had loaded yourself with barrels of stones to have listened to ideas of defeat, disaster, or injustice, as part of the intention of God for your life to meet — when that was never the plan of the Divine Goodness with you — you will breathe freely and rise with new buoyancy upon agreement with Truth.

In this thirteenth chapter of Acts, from the forty-fourth verse, we see the process of perfect doctrine as it has risen for the religions of the world to accept. They turn from its light, but the so-called irreligious, or Gentiles, receive it gladly. This lesson is an object lesson. We are the people meant. If we have understanding that all is mind, not materiality, nor persons, we will see that the light that shines now among us is the speech of un-resisted Truth. Whoever lets Truth be expressed in un-resisted freedom through him rises as on wings out of the reach of his daily encounters with the world. There is nothing he fears. Sickness drops off. Misfortune glides out of his reach. Fears that his children or good name will fail do not come nigh him. As he thus gets freer and freer he is not aware of himself as a "demigod", but God.

The glory of the church of the Jews was that by the preaching of the Presence of God, that Presence came visibly into their midst. The receptivity of the Gentiles was the spread of the manifest God. As it is written, "Light to lighten the Gentiles and the glory of my people Israel."

So it is today. It is the glory of the church that she has preached the goodness of God and the second coming of His Presence, till now the idea of His goodness permits no mixture of accusation against Him as laying schemes in our pathway to test our quality, nor slaying a son to evidence His loving kindness; till now we understand the second coming to be the un-resisted proclamation of the absolute Good.

The power of the Holy Ghost is on them and in them that let it be known that the life-inspiring Spirit is now moving in un-threatened splendor from mind to mind over the earth.

The healing Spirit is running with unassailable purity from life to life the round planet over.

The strengthening Spirit goes forth with irresistible vigor from heart to heart.

The sustaining and supporting Spirit blows aside the mantle of poverty and despair, and those with their hands on the products of nature cannot hold even a loaf from a child, so overpowering is the breath of the Name of Him who stands now in the earth.

The defending Spirit tenderly smoothes out the pathway of man so that today there can be no ill come nigh the dwelling of him who knows that he was never meant to believe the teachings of a God who needed propitiating. He whose face is set to the doctrine now come, sees that every hurt, every accident, every disaster, has come from the doctrine of propitiation for sins. Whoever lets fall that idea is free to walk boldly through these days which have come as the fruition of that age-old idea of a Creator who needed to be bought off from His anger. Strikes, and embezzlements, and hospitals full of groaning — all stand forth as the fruitage of holding the youth of the world to such teachings concerning the dealings of the God of Heaven with man, as drag them in mind to think that a friend instead of the Divinity woos in their bosoms. So the weary old age of the earth now lies down defeated. "The earth waxes old as a garment."

But the mind that is God is set free to think through all who do not play the part of the Jews in this lesson. They shine and glow and invigorate with a life not of the earth. A new mind rises — a new mind sends over the world thoughts that take them that think into the mountains of safety. The speaking forth of the Mind of God is the trumpet that sounds in these days as Paul and Barnabas sounded in their day. At the sound of the word of Truth, a whole disease melts away into the mists of nowhere. At the sound of a spoken word the diseased earth shall melt with fervent heat and the skies roll away like a scroll. They are all, as they stand out, formulated of the teachings given to the children concerning the Maker of heaven and earth.

The recording Spirit is given un-resisted freedom to write on the stones and in the sands that that which is true must reign now from henceforth; not what is false.

The joyous Spirit sings of what has already come to pass — now that the doctrine of Jesus is preached.

The skill-inspiring Spirit is not hindered as it touches the fingers of youth with eternal genius of an order needing no schools, or ships, or apprenticeship, to teach how to handle the white Substance that waits in the airs for the fingers that are moved by the Mind of God to make those new clothes and new houses to live in, foretold by the prophets for this age to fulfill. The judgment and beauty of Truth are set free. There is none to resist the beauty of judgment and the judgment of beauty, which is Jesus Christ, named in the mind.

The love-inspiring Spirit is moving with un-resisted freedom, declaring that to them that see her lifting the veil of the false thought of ages there is now liberty and delight, with no bondage to hurt or fear.

Here it tells how the multitude of the city was divided, part holding with the Jews and part holding with the Apostles. Now, they who still hold to the doctrine of worthiness, shedding of blood for sins, the cross, the necessity for evil, may turn over into the worldly signals of senility, while they who hear the Spiritual winds sifting through the noisy sounds of materiality may go from city to city preaching the immortal beauty that wakes to never glory in him who keeps hold of his birthright. November 27, 1892.

Bible Lesson LXXIII. Acts 14:8-22. The Healing Principle

In the year 1814, a young Japanese by the name of Kurozumi Sakyo, lay in what his doctors pronounced to be the last stages of consumption. It was his pious daily custom to worship the sun and his ancestors, also the celestial and terrestrial kami. One day he resolved that when, after his death, he himself should become a kami (deified spirit) he would devote all his time to healing the diseases of mankind. His devotions were always marked by a peculiar gratefulness of feeling towards the sun and the kami of his parents. He did not beg for favors like most devotees. His prayers were not petitions; they were loving thanksgivings.

One day it occurred to him that he ought to bless and give thanks to heaven for every tiniest event and object. As everything he possessed, great, or small, had come from above, it must all in turn be remembered in his loving thanksgivings. By thus resolving upon a still further exercise of his mind and feelings, he began to experience a new cheerfulness. Certain Japanese believe that continual cheerfulness invokes a positive spirit — Yoki. They believe that all disease has its rise in someone's yielding to the spirit of gloom — Inki.

Kurozumi did not look to be healed of consumption. He had not asked to be healed. But while he was at the very ebb-tide of his malady, with his heart entirely absorbed in thanking the sun for its marvelous goodness in giving him so many friends and such a good home, he rose suddenly, strong and renewed. He was in perfect health. A miracle had been wrought. He began to be so ecstatically grateful to his god that a still further miracle was wrought upon him. He breathed in the positive Yoki or cheerful spirit so intensely that his breath became vivified. He found that it would heal every sort and kind of disease and soothe the sharpest pains. He thus began while yet in life, to breathe upon sick and diseased mankind that healing principle he had supposed he must wait till after death to exercise.

From that time on his grateful patients and their families regarded him as a living Kami. He had spent three years in honest expressions of gratitude for what other people considered only the commonest procession of favors from heaven, when the cheerful spirit, Yoki, took absolute control of his life, even unto the healing power. It became an elixir vital, a renewal of vitality, to his wasted body.

We see by this true event, that the descriptions of the goodness of deity, which the very devoted have ever given us, are those which have in their nature a potency that will operate if they are continued as mental exercises, prompted by the will to do right for its own sake.

If the young Japanese had been three years practicing giving thanks as a species of Spiritual gymnastics, whereby he hoped to attain health, he might not have felt very grateful even then, while his racking cough and feeble limbs reminded him that there was something he did not feel just right about. He looked into the face of the spirit of the sun and told it of its own goodness without any purpose of any sort in his heart. Yet, health came as a natural outcome of the daily elation of all his thoughts by the words he had spoken. His words generated a warm feeling. The feeling and words generated an elixir, which formulated a healthy body.

There is something in the being of deity, which calls for our delight in it, whether it is filling every vacant spot in our sphere of life or not. We can look beyond our ideas of our own lot in life, and away from all that we have experienced, into the great fact of a good beyond good, and there will be a nameless pleasure in this sight that will open our lips to speak praises we cannot help feeling.

Often people who are greatly irritated by their environments can look beyond their feelings and thoughts into the great fact of their being something too great and too calm to be like their affairs, and that sight, if only for one second's space, is a rest of soul for which they are grateful. To prolong the sight is to feel the elevation of soul that is its still further rest. And still deeper pleasure compels newer words of thanksgiving.

Some do go through all the items of their human possessions with honest praise of their Giver, up into sudden moments of facing that great fact of being, and down from that sight of the Presence which is not moved by the excitements of pleasures or pains they come buoyant and transformed.

This going by the pathway of praises was the method of Kurozumi.

Looking beyond all things and beyond all ideas, into the nameless Presence, beyond the God described by mankind, Mary, the Mother of Jesus, watched the stir-less Being of true Deity, and that immaculate sight brought forth a Messiah. All the highest words of her most devout descriptions of God now formulated into her sight.

The doctrine of Jesus is a way of bringing to pass all the affairs and events of life by a way that is easy, a burden that is light. It is this doctrine of looking away from the ideas we think, and the emotions we feel, into this Presence which has never been described in words, but which, when Kurozumi stepped into sight of it, brought forth his healing. And which, when Mary saw by that inner sight we are all capable of exercising, brought forth the long-expected Messiah.

"Rest in the Lord and He shall bring it to pass." Kurozumi passed into speechless and thoughtless ecstasy by words of brightness. We need not go by words or thoughts into sight of this changeless, move-less Principle we call God; we may recognize its vicinity and wait for effects. Its effects are the sweetest fulfillment of mighty miracles.

"I will make a new covenant with you." "Cast all your care on God, for He careth for you." Under this direction let now your covenant with the omnipotent Spirit be that you will do nothing either to benefit or prolong your life. The Mighty God, ever present, shall care entirely for your life. You will not do anything either to benefit or perfect your health or strength. The Mighty God, waiting in eternal majesty near you, shall do all that needs doing for your health and your strength. Neither for support nor defense will you lift your efforts, the sustaining and upholding Spirit of good shall support and defend your life.

The deep thought and quickening speech of Omnipotence shall do your thinking and speaking. The words that you write, and the praises you sing, shall come from your sight of the ever-abiding Principle, that asks nothing of you, but covenants with you to do all works for you. Principle whose immaculate sight, un-smirched by intentions to struggle and strive, has caught the elixir which falls into the soul of him whose faith rests for the Lord to bring to pass.

The genius for action is born of a speechless sight of the action-less Being of God, as Jesus was born of Mary's speechless conception of the Presence of God. Covenant with the Presence un-nameable, the Everlasting Spirit we speak of as God, for your beauty. Let it inspire you with the genius for loving, and being loved, as Mary let it inspire her with the genius for bringing forth the only Lover the world ever knew.

Look into this 14th chapter of Acts, and find the verses where Paul, who had praised Jesus Christ till the electric fires of the mighty Name had made his eyes and voice alive with the healing principle, faced the Spirit, and waited to bring forth the cure of the cripple of Lystra. After steadfastly beholding," his voice commanded with power. Then, exactly as the people tried to make out that Kurozumi was a superior being come among them, so did the Gentiles offer to worship Paul and Barnabas. But Kurozumi of Japan, with his praise of the sun, stepping into ecstatic vision of God — Paul and Barnabas stepping by praises of Jesus into glorified sight of the Presence of Spirit — many walking in maidenly whiteness over the silver stones of beautiful prayers — none of these was a being superior to those they walked among. "I said ye are gods." "Ye are all sons of the Most High." Ye are beings, all, of transcendent powers. The grandeur of supernal Presence enshrouds you all and waits for you to let go your clutch on the vanities of old ways of doing.

The Gentiles, who offered oxen and garlands, and would have done sacrifice unto Paul and Barnabas, are only ourselves, when we are offering our efforts and strivings, willing to sacrifice ourselves for the reformation and redemption of a world God finished in beauty and love, and waits for us to see as He sees it.

The perfect creation waits ever near us. Looking into its changeless, move-less splendor, Mary brought into our sight Jesus, one of the glorified inhabitants of the City of God.

We, looking into this country its stretches of fields elysian, and hilltops of light we call air en-swathing us, may catch a vision true enough to bring to the sight of our race other inhabitants of the golden-walled temples of heaven.

Here it tells that we shall enter this kingdom of heaven only by much tribulation. (Verse 22). But this is because we believe in doing and clutching, and striving, and working to do our duty toward enlightening, redeeming, and civilizing the world. Paul and Barnabas believed in struggling and striving to convert the people. It was as if many had struggled and striven to bring forth Jesus Christ. It took the silent sight of the abyss of Deity, deep of soul calling unto deep of soul, for Jesus, the inhabitant of the Heavenly City, to come stepping into the manger of Bethlehem. It takes the enraptured silence of our yielded life for the heavenly hosts of God to come walking down as on highways into the midst of this age.

But it is here. "Hark the herald angels sing." We do not try to improve or redeem the race. We stop here to see the race as God sees it. And over the highways of our immaculate silence troops of Elohim come nearer and nearer. Here in the workshop of the mystery of mind we find that secret of God, which is the revealment of good. That which Mary did by making a pathway of effortless silence, over which walked our beloved King, we may do for all the inhabitants of descending Jerusalem.

With one foot on the sea and one on the land, the angel proclaims that time shall be no more with the acceptance of this, the doctrine of Jesus. "He careth for you." On the swift thoughts which are the flowing seas, let the angel put one foot to indicate the subjection of thought. On the old doctrines in which we have settled beliefs, let the angel put one foot to proclaim that we surrender our creeds and our doctrines of salvation, redemption, and reformation, of everything to the silence of the great, perfect world of God, which was in the beginning, is now, and ever shall be, "very good," as God sees it forever.

Kurozumi breathed the electric elixirs of a swift sight of the great fact of a nameless Presence here on earth. We will gather to the deeps of our being the elixirs of long, speechless knowledge that God is here. As He healed the sick, as Paul and Barnabas healed and called multitudes to hear their words, because of swift, speechless sights of God, so we, by abiding in the knowledge that healing comes from sight of God, and not effort to find God, or please Him, will hear the voices of the myriad hosts chanting great songs of gladness that we have made holy highways for them to walk over into our midst. December 4, 1892.

Bible Lesson LXXIV. Acts 15:12-29. Washington's Vision

There is always something or someone near every one of us telling us the wisest course to pursue. If we learn to be observing and to have our minds made up to an issue, we shall have clear sight and hearing to receive right directions. The Oriental metaphysicians found out that to cease from thinking is a clarifying process for the mind; so they practiced ceasing from thoughts. They wondered greatly why the nameless satisfaction they were seeking did not result to them by the clarifying process of non-thinking. They never found out formerly, and have not yet been told, that if the mind is positively set upon any conviction it is locked in the prison of that conviction. Stopping thoughts only shuts the few portholes and windows of the prison; it does not break down the walls of a mighty conviction. There was not an Eastern mystic who was not convinced clear to the roots of his mind that God ordained castes and sex inferiority. Six thousand years of cessation of thought would not molder the walls of that gloomy conviction.

The Occidental metaphysician now practices cessation from thinking because he has been told that it is wonderfully clarifying to the mind to stop thinking. He also is surprised to find how far away the glory of the satisfaction he hopes for still remains. He stopped thinking, while his mind was set as the everlasting hills into the determination to be recognized by his fellow beings as of some consequence, or as a mighty character. He hopes for the plaudit, "Well done." This also is a prison house with walls unmeltable by silence at the roots of mind.

When one is very sincere, he is very opened. He may not be as able as his fellow-men as regards talents or education, but he will have such open ears for the counsels that lie around him that his wisdom will be the marvel of his age.

George Washington was a genuine lover of his cause. The preservation of the independence of his country was to him his God-called mission. Recognizing the hand of the free God in the strike of America for liberty, he flung his life to the winds of the principle the strike represented.

The following narrative was related by Anthony Sherman, an octogenarian, who heard the account from Washington's own lips:

The darkest period of our Republic was the year 1777, when Washington, after experiencing many reverses, went into winter quarters at Valley Forge. Often I observed tears course down the cheeks of our beloved Commander when he was considering the sufferings of his brave soldiers.

Washington was in the habit of praying in secret and calling upon God for assistance, and it was only by the help of God we passed safely through those days of adversity.

One day Washington spent the whole afternoon in his room alone. When he came out, I observed that he was much paler than usual, when he related to me the following:

"Whilst I was sitting at my table this afternoon engaged in writing and my mind heavy with sorrow, I suddenly observed directly opposite to me a most beautiful female.

"I was so much surprised, for I had given strict orders not to be disturbed, that I could not find words at the moment to inquire the object of this unexpected visit. Two, three, and even four times I repeated the question without receiving an answer, the only effect being that she raised her eyes a little, I now experienced a most curious sensation spread over my whole body. I wished to rise from my seat, but the steady gaze of my mysterious visitor kept me spellbound. I again tried to speak to her, but my tongue was tied. An unknown, mysterious irresistible power had taken me prisoner. I could do nothing else but steadily gaze at the apparition. Gradually the room filled with light, and the form grew more clear and bright. My feelings were those of a dying man; I could neither think nor act. My steady gaze at the figure was all I was aware of.

"I now heard a voice, which said: 'Son of the Republic, behold and learn!' At the same time the figure stretched out its arm and pointed with its finger towards the east. Light clouds arose in the distance, which dispersed and revealed to my eyes a most astonishing picture. Before me, all the countries of the earth were spread out, Europe, Asia, Africa, and America. Between Europe and America, I saw the waves of the Atlantic

Ocean toss backward and forward, and between America and Asia the waves of the Pacific Ocean.

"Again, I heard the voice: 'Son of the Republic, behold and learn!' Immediately a dark form like that of an angel appeared over the ocean between Europe and America. It then dipped water from the ocean with both hands, and with its right sprinkled it over America and with its left over Europe. Immediately dark clouds arose from both of these countries, which met in the middle of the ocean; here they remained stationery for awhile, then moved westward, and wrapped America in darkness. Lightning flashed through the dark clouds, and I heard the groaning and shrieking of the American people. Again the angel dipped water from the ocean and sprinkled it as before. The black clouds withdrew and sank into the sea.

"For the third time, I heard the voice: 'Son of the Republic, behold and learn!' I looked towards America and saw populous villages and cities from the Atlantic Coast to the Pacific Ocean. Again, I heard the mysterious voice: 'Son of the Republic, the end of the century is near at hand. Behold and learn!' The dark form of the angel then turned toward the south, and coming from Africa, I observed a horrible phantom making its way to our country. It floated slowly and heavily over our towns and the country; the inhabitants arose to make war on each other and formed in battle array. As I looked at this scene, I observed an angel surrounded with light; on his head he wore a beautiful crown on which was inscribed the word 'Union.' In his hand, he held the American flag. This he planted between the contending armies, crying out: 'Remember you are brothers.' Immediately the nations threw away their arms, became friends again, and gathered around the flag.

"Again I heard the mysterious voice: 'Son of the Republic, the second danger is past; behold and learn!' And I saw the villages and cities steadily increase in size and number, until the whole country was covered with them — the whole extent, from the Atlantic to the Pacific, and the nation had multiplied in as countless numbers as the stars in heaven, or the sands on the seashore. Again, I heard the voice: 'Son of the Republic, the end of the century is at hand; behold and learn!' The dark angel then put a trumpet to his mouth, blew it three times, then dipped out some water from the sea with his hand over Europe, Asia, and Africa. My eyes now beheld a most terrible scene. From each of these countries dark heavy clouds arose and united in one mass; through this mass, dark red lightning played. I saw troops of armed men advancing, and then sail across the sea to America, which was immediately covered by the black cloud.

"And I saw how these immense armies desolated the land and laid towns and villages in ashes. I heard the roar of cannon, the clashing of swords, the cry of the victorious and vanquished millions engaged in deadly strife, when again I heard the mysterious voice proclaim: 'Son of the Republic, behold and learn!' The dark angel then again took up the trumpet and gave one long and terrible blow. Suddenly a light burst forth and drove away the dark cloud hovering over America. At the same time I saw the angel with the beautiful crown, on which was inscribed the word 'Union,' descend from heaven, holding in one hand the star-spangled banner and in the other a sword, and accompanied by legions of heavenly spirits. These united with the American people when the latter were almost overpowered, who took fresh courage and formed in battle array. Again, amid the horrible noise of war, I heard the mysterious voice: 'Son of the Republic, behold and learn!'

"After this voice the dark angel dipped out water for the last time from the sea and sprinkled it over America, and immediately the dark cloud retreated with its armies, which it had brought along, leaving the victory to the Americans.

"I then again saw towns and villages rise in the same places where they had stood before, while the heavenly angel planted the star spangled banner among the people with a loud voice: 'As long as the stars are in heaven and as long as the dews descend from heaven to earth, so long shall this Republic exist.'

"At the same time he took the beautiful crown from his head, on which was inscribed the word 'Union,' placed it on the star-spangled banner, and, kneeling down, cried out, 'Amen.' The apparition then began to dissolve, and at last the mysterious female was all that remained before me in my room, and again I heard the voice: 'Son of the Republic, what you have seen is explained as follows:

" 'Three dangers will come over this Republic. The second is most to be dreaded. When this one is past the whole world cannot conquer her. Let every child of the Republic learn to serve his God, his country and the Union.'

"With these words the form vanished. I arose from my chair with the conviction that the birth, progress, and fate of the United States of America had been revealed to me."

These words, said Mr. Sherman, he heard from General Washington's own lips.

We know that the first two sections of the vision have been fulfilled. The last is now upon us. The reason for so vivid a picturing of the future of his country before him was because he needed a strong reassurance from some quarter. He had come to where he could not be pacified with the ordinary helps of his mind's reasoning or his religious convictions.

We, who are genuinely in earnest with respect to our lofty purposes, can be as plainly reassured of victorious freedom from whatever bondage we experience as the lover of the Republic was. Keep on knowing that you are a transcendent being with transcendent powers. This is honoring the handiwork of the Omnipotent Mind that sent you forth. It is a principle as worthy of espousing as the principle of liberty for a people whose property and labors are owned by a foreign nation.

The principle you espouse who take the Name of Jesus Christ as the synonym for Truth, Life, and Freedom, is that "all power is given unto Me in heaven and earth." You know that it is not only Jesus Christ, who is this all-powerful Being, but it is yourself as handiwork of an impartial God. Everything rises up near you to testify to your spreading righteousness. The golden text of this lesson, Acts 15: 12-29, tells the story of mental liberty from foreign notions as the free republic tells of freedom from former yokes. "Through the grace of the Lord Jesus Christ we shall be saved, even as they." (Verse 11)

It is as great a principle to proclaim that we are free from former religious and hindering beliefs as to proclaim that we will not be taxed without representation or permit a black man to be chased in the Everglades. If we think we have the perfect doctrine and the denominations are wrong, we are imprisoned into a mental belief — which is mental stealing. For we certainly are mentally withholding from others their right to our idea that as Sons of the same Father with us they know what is right as well as we do. We will hand them back the idea we have tried to steal away from them. We will give them our free knowledge that they are wise with the free wisdom of God.

We will probe the thought wells of our minds to still deeper teachings. If I thank God that He has given me my perfect hearing while I believe that He has made you to be deaf, I am taking away something from you with my mind. I am believing in a God who bestows and withholds. I am mentally stealing your rights. It is not praise of God I am giving when I look upon Him as any such being.

This mental giving up of former suppositions is taught by the ancient metaphysicians as the final freedom from stealing. It is a wonderful treatment to send over the ethers into the hearts of this age. The dark cloud that hangs over the planet through the mental unrest of mankind's feeling its bondage to something it knows not what — is the cloud that Washington saw. The teachings of Spiritual science will go to each heart and take out the wish to slay and torture from even the roughest and angriest, as the wise James poured oil on the Jews of this lesson. Peace will steal into their violent feelings by the free kindness of our beautiful teachings of the rights of all men to their transcendent wisdom and goodness. We do not need to speak aloud to the world concerning their rights any more than the good mental healer needs to speak aloud to the prisoner of paralysis. Thoughts go stealing like ointment into the clogged hopes of the world and mind is set free by the angels of light.

Now more than ever, each event and each man tells you of your own freedom and the triumph of your own cause. Believe nothing that you may be free to believe all things. Think nothing that you may think as the omniscient Mind of God.

With the abstaining from those things we have felt were our virtues, whereby we took from the free-handed Truth our realty by being grateful for blessing withheld from others, we are obeying the injunction of James in the twenty-ninth verse, "Abstain from things strangled." We have to be true to our principle of liberty for all men, even in the depth of our hearts. "For the Lord looketh on the heart." We do not think it is a virtue to give thanks to God for our home, our friends, and our table, while we secretly steal from that same God the honor of believing that He has provided all creation with exactly the same blessings we have.

We let go our secret hold on the rights of the nations and silently shed abroad the final treatment of a closing age. If we let go our strangling ideas, all the multitudes will lift up their heads with freedom, and long before Christmas, Christ, the Providing Jehovah, will be here, and there shall be no more pain or poverty, for the former earth is passed away.

December 11, 1892

Bible Lesson LXXV. Review of the Twelve Lessons. (LXIII through LXXIV)

Claudius, the fourth Emperor of Rome, was in the habit of exclaiming: "What! do you take me for a fool?" The consequence was he lost his memory, and became so absent-minded that he did indeed appear like a fool to everyone. Suetonius, the historian of the Caesars, tells us that he inquired why Messalina, the Empress, did not come to the table, though she had been buried some days. He often ordered those whom he had condemned to death to dine with him the day after the execution, actually forgetting what had become of them and sending to reprimand them for their sluggishness in attending his banquets.

Thoughts often given expression to, come due like notes, or, like the planets in their orbits, reach perihelion on time. "By thy words thou art justified." Often we have people telling us that they nearly broke their neck trying to do certain things. They go away forgetting that such words are fishes spawn, and, though forgotten as the fishes forget their spawn, will some day throw them out of a carriage or down an embankment in a railway accident because their fruitage time has arrived.

Because you have forgotten your once familiar exclamations, do not be so silly as to suppose they will not arrive in your affairs at the proper moment. Violent expletives are making due haste to make violent conditions. All your adversaries are the legitimate offspring of such expressions as "I thought I should die;" "I was nearly killed;" "I am utterly distracted."

Life words come up for reviews like soldiers well drilled. The lessons of the past quarter now file past our mental vision. If they were understood they have already fruited, and new human environments now delight our once distraught hearts. For it is a point in pure Spiritual Science that every time a metaphysical proposition is clear to us we have a happy change of circumstances.

In our second lesson, we learned from the conversion of Saul by supernatural means that the scholastic world will either succumb to the Spiritual lightning now striking them with palsy, softened brain, or brittle bones, and will meekly recognize that it is spiritual lore they need, instead of so much Sanskrit and pneumatics, or they will drop like shadows into nowhere.

It brought up the doctrine of Seneca, born in the year 7 BC., that mankind must first get free from the bondage of death and then of poverty. It showed that if we set any limit to the action of the doctrine of Jesus we shall have some sort of ailment. For instance, if I do not believe that in the teaching that "My yoke is easy and My burden is light" I am to be set into delightful pathways where all care, all anxiety, all effort is to be taken from me. I shall have something equivalent to Saul's blindness to mark my limitation of Jesus Christ's teachings.

No one was ever known to put any limitation upon the absolute demonstration of all the extreme statements of Jesus Christ, who did not get hurt like Saul, who tried to limit the Christians, or did not finish up like Uzzah, who tried to stay with the ark. There is no miracle of interposition in your behalf out of the reach of your open acceptance of the extremest ideas of the transcendent doctrines of Jesus.

In the third lesson, the idea that we should never rehearse how well we used to do, nor tell how much we have turned off as skillful laborers in the past, was brought forward under the figure of Dorcas. It seems that talk of the past as superior to the present, is sure death to our ambition and courage. The past exploits are not superior to this day's abilities. Rise like the transfiguring Spirit you are in your native splendor, and tell of your powers and greatness this day. This is your Peter with his vigorous NOWNESS.

To be looking forward to great tasks that lie ahead of us is to be wearied in advance, like the pendulum in the fable, paralyzed like Aeneas, whom Peter cured by the idea of doing what belongs to us this moment, forgetting the past, ignoring the future. Evidently Peter had covenanted with the Spirit to take care of his reputation and he would do nothing for it. He had covenanted with the Spirit to do every good work this moment. It is delightful to the Spirit to have us make a solid agreement to let it do all things now. This keeps a continual renewal of strength, vigor, health, and life.

The fourth lesson taught that every sort of omen and prognostication is a prophecy of good. The world has always considered omens and signals to forebode death and disaster, but there was never one, which did not come expressly to foretell a great good. The way to meet an omen is to proclaim that it is a signal of new prosperity and renewed life. If evil came to a family after a strange phenomenon appeared, it was because the family twisted the promise from its beautiful purport.

Our fifth lesson teaches that we must take some line of high reasoning and stick to it. The descent from lofty descriptions of immaculate doctrines into small discussions of the foibles of people is accountable for many misfortunes, and what are called ups and downs of life. Keep a certain set of statements for each hour in the day. The mind and character will soon translate from adversities into a constant succession of happy awakenings.

By our sixth lesson, we were told that the usual missionary idea is totally wrong in that we go out to rescue men from the darkness of their ignorance, and the bondage of their sins. Going forth to seek lost souls is a subtle accusation against the creations of God. It taught that as all is mind, of course if we seek for ignorance we shall find it, but that law of seeking and finding does not make ignorance or sin reality. They will still remain imaginations of mind, not thinking as God thinks. Do you suppose God ever saw a heathen? No, He gave his own wisdom impartially to all mankind. Do you suppose God ever saw a sinner? No, He is too pure to behold iniquity. Then it is hunting ignis fatuus to be hunting out heathen and sinners. If we really love the South Sea Islanders we will praise them, not accuse them.

The next lesson taught how often it is the idea that we are not quite ready for carrying out projects, which puts off other events from transpiring. Whatever the externals may seem, the mind should insist upon NOW for its own readiness to do all things. Then the externals will train to promptness.

It explains that we have our healing powers with their infinite endurance and our defending powers, with everlasting strength. But, like Peter's angel of defense, they depart after one miracle, leaving us in seeming powerlessness for a long time. This is because we keep wishing and longing for more, more, like Oliver Twist, instead of giving cheerful thanks continually for what we do have now — like as the wonderful Kurozumi practiced so successfully.

The eighth lesson asked us to consider whether we would have all the people of the world fed, clothed, and sheltered, as the result of spiritual teachings, with their miracle-working efficiencies, or slay and labor and fight for our chances on the present material basis. By spiritual means, all these things are possible. Shall we throw our confidence upon the high seas of the Jesus Christ promises or hang back on the muddy bottoms of anguish with the striking world? Take the high winds of universal expectation. Narrow not your hopes down to your own lot alone.

If the woman left alone in widowhood and poverty cast herself upon God to take care of her, and those who had to work for their living sent of their treasures to support her, do you not see that they in their turn would receive easy assistance by the same principle, and still others would receive their bounties the same way, till only the hosts of heaven should be found ministering to a whole world? Was not Jesus fed and clothed by the angels? If the angels can feed one Man without killing some helpless animal, and clothe one Man without a single man's forced labor, can they not feed and clothe a world? Are the hosts of God few? Are the hosts of God unwilling?

Our ninth lesson tells us not to get tied to our opinions, but to go from mountain top to mountain top of Truth till the freedom of the untrammeled God is ours. It asks us to consider whether this idea is a reasonable description of the experience of the Omnipotent, viz., "God suffers for sinners even more than they suffer themselves." No. Omnipotence is the Principle of absolute goodness, which neither itself suffers nor permits suffering. All suffering is delusion. That lesson taught plainly that Paul did not need to agree with prophecies of evil, thinking they must be fulfilled. He might trace their origin to an error and erase their whole history, as a metaphysician would erase the whole history of sickness from its first blunder to its externalization.

He must have a powerful mind arise with enough of the absolute Truth in his heart's faith, to be perfectly well in his own body, renewed in youth by his doctrine, supported absolutely by his thoughts, so that the world may suddenly feel the almightiness of his doctrine by seeing his demonstrations. There shall not be one single breath in his speech or his writings about the power of a horde of opponents to darken his teachings. He shall not believe in any subtle region of his mind that he needs to protect himself from unjust or unkind thoughts. He shall not fear that he would come to want if he should give up his business or his goods. He shall not believe that an evil intention can possibly be carried out.

As Jesus came externalizing the hopes of ages, so the perfect doctrine shall bring forward its first perfect demonstration.

The tenth lesson explained that whoever will give the Spirit unresisted freedom, through him will find himself expressing twelve powers, corresponding to the twelve gates of the heavenly city opened by right doctrine. Gentiles, or those without a particle of religious feeling or tradition, are as likely to express the twelve Jesus Christ powers, as Jews, or those who represent religious feeling and creed. It showed that every young man, and young woman expects miracles to be wrought in his or her behalf, and if they would hold onto that expectation forever they would be forever young. They would be forever beautiful. It is not until they are tempted to be like the world by being pampered like Solomon or abused by experience with the way-wised of earth that they give utterly into not expecting time to fulfill their confidence. They get the first wrinkles with agreeing with the deceptions, which read like the beginning of Johnson's "Rasselas."

The next lesson explained by the history of Kurozumi that there is an elixir vitae, which we can breathe by learning how to do so. We set out with thoughts, which reason out a noble doctrine. We let nothing interfere with our confidence in the Truth of our principles. Soon we get beyond thoughts. We enter the realm of the unnamed Good. We breathe the electric elixirs of a realm undescribed. We find our unmixed principles have power over our life quite beyond our first announcement. Mary, the Mother of Jesus, brought Him forth by this high experience. Kurozumi brought forth healing skill by it. We shall bring the heavenly Jerusalem of the Apocalypse into sight by our great number of men and women, with their eyes set on things of God, expecting the God beyond Him we have described to work for us.

Our twelfth lesson shows how Washington's sincerity brought an angel to tell him of things to come. He was permitted to see the liberation of America from foreign yoke. He was permitted to see the liberation of the colored South from the yoke of belief in slavery. He was permitted to see the hosts of heaven come in these days to liberate us from the belief in our limitations as human beings.

We are now being taught that we are transcendent beings with transcendent powers. We have no need to be limited by Ignorance, poverty, or sickness. We must take off the yoke of our supposition that there is any difference between the Hottentot and the college president in Spirit and in Truth.

We rise to proclaim that all men are the direct handiwork of impartial, glorious God. Every idea of this kind takes form and speeds on and on. Washington saw the field of Armageddon. We are now on that field. We do not believe in fighting; we believe as people of God in letting the angels lift off the yokes. We do not believe in evil; we believe as a people in the angels of goodness working our cause easily, swiftly, and silently, by our unresisted confidence. If we experience hardships, it is because we have not taken refuge under the wings of our own doctrine.

December 18th, 1892

Made in the USA
Las Vegas, NV
25 January 2022

42344393R00210